AN UNCERTAIN TRADITION
American Secretaries of State in the Twentieth Century

McGRAW-HILL SERIES IN AMERICAN HISTORY

DAVID DONALD, *Consulting Editor*

AN UNCERTAIN TRADITION

American Secretaries of State

in the Twentieth Century

Edited by

Norman A. Graebner

PROFESSOR OF HISTORY
UNIVERSITY OF ILLINOIS

McGRAW-HILL BOOK COMPANY, INC. 1961

New York   Toronto   London

Preface

Together, the fourteen American Secretaries of State whose Secretarial careers comprise the subject matter of this book held the office for a span of sixty years. That the accession of John Hay to the Secretaryship in 1898 should introduce any volume on the Secretaries of the twentieth century appears logical enough: not only did he happen to occupy the office in 1900, but his years as head of the State Department mark the transition of American foreign policy from the old, realistic tradition of the nineteenth century to the new, more involved, and more confused tradition of the twentieth century. As a study of personalities, this volume does not purport to be a detailed history of American diplomacy since 1898. But since the Secretaries of State, by the obligations of their office, cannot escape some responsibility for national decisions in the realm of foreign affairs, there is little of major significance in the American diplomatic record itself which is not present in the successive essays of this book. Moreover, in their emphasis on men in action, these essays expose all the problems inherent in the American constitutional and political system for the formulation and maintenance of an adequate response to events abroad.

No one would deny the importance of the office of Secretary of State. Since the days of Thomas Jefferson's incumbency, the Secretary's essential role has remained unchanged: as the senior member of the Cabinet and the chief spokesman on external affairs, both to the President and to the world, he is charged with defining and carrying out the foreign policies of the United States. Yet that role has varied enormously from Secretary to Secretary, for every occupant of the office is essentially a unique personality whose importance depends upon his own qualities, upon the issues and the times, and upon the multitudinous domestic pressures which he cannot escape. Often the Secretary's previous mental preparation determines his entire conduct in office. In a sense his con-

v

victions regarding the nature of diplomacy decide to what extent his ideas can serve as the bases of viable policies, for it makes considerable difference whether he accepts as fundamental the traditional methods of diplomatic exchange or the more recent devices of moral disapprobation and the majority vote. Despite the complexity of world politics, the Secretaries of State since 1898 have seldom been trained in diplomacy but have come to the office from professional or political life. Most of them possessed only fragmentary knowledge of foreign affairs when they entered office.

It is questionable, however, whether the convictions of the Secretary of State are the key determinants in the creation of policy, for between his conception of what policy should be and the nation's actual behavior abroad are such modifying factors as the Secretary's relationship to the President, the attitude of Congress, the voices of the press, advisers inside and outside the State Department, and the various pressure groups that represent the public itself. It is seldom clear what elements in the American democratic process determine the character of specific foreign-policy decisions.

Every Secretary of State of this century, subjected as he is to all the political forces of the nation, has at times led a lonely existence. His detractors have generally centered in the Congress. Few Secretaries since 1900 would not have acknowledged some truth in the words of Henry Adams:

> The Secretary of State has always stood as much alone as the historian. Required to look far ahead and round him, he measures forces unknown to party managers, and has found Congress more or less hostile ever since Congress first sat. The Secretary of State exists only to recognize the existence of a world which Congress would rather ignore; of obligations which Congress repudiates whenever it can; of bargains which Congress distrusts and tries to turn to its advantage or to reject. Since the first day the Senate existed, it has always intrigued against the Secretary of State whenever the Secretary has been obliged to extend his functions beyond the appointment of Consuls in Senators' service.

Unfortunately, it has often been true that the greater have been the challenges abroad and the greater the need for national unity, the more bitter and demanding have been the congressional attacks on the Department of State. Perhaps the vulnerability of the Department rests in both the nature of the organization and its position in the American governmental structure. It is the only major department in the Federal government that does not command the allegiance of a significant group within the nation which identifies its specific welfare with that of the Department. Second, members of Congress have generally viewed the State Department as being snobbish, professional, undemocratic, and foreign, always engaged in the process of involving the country unnecessarily in affairs abroad. Throughout this century it has faced critics in Congress who have feared that its emphasis on excellence is a threat to the American concept of social equality and who have preferred an arrangement that "the least talented can operate, and the most intelligent cannot disturb." Third, since this important and semisecretive organization resides in the executive branch of government, it has served as the most defenseless of the executive departments to the jibes of congressmen who have found special delight in defending the prerogatives of Congress against executive usurpation. On those occasions when a Secretary has been repudiated even by the President, he has been reduced to a position of uncertainty in which his role becomes limited to trivialities.

To James F. Byrnes it was the function of a good Secretary of State to be unpopular and to carry the burden of defending the nation's interests abroad against the competing economic, regional, emotional, and religious pressures. Said Byrnes of an ideal Secretary:

> He must be strong enough to resist demands from factions within the country having at heart some particular or local grievance. It is proper that such particularized views and pressures should be expressed. That is the way our democracy works. There is no way of preventing this; nor should there be. But, at the same time, the secretary of state must be strong enough to say no. And this will make him unpopular.

Three Secretaries of State who held office within the years considered here have not been included in this volume: Robert Bacon, Bainbridge Colby, and Christian Herter. Robert Bacon served as Secretary for the month of February, 1909, at the conclusion of Theodore Roosevelt's second term. Bainbridge Colby was appointed Secretary of State to serve out the final year of Woodrow Wilson's Presidency, after Wilson demanded the resignation of Robert Lansing in February, 1920. Neither Bacon nor Colby was identified with any important decisions, policies, or reorganizations of the State Department. Colby served for almost a year, but the important postwar decisions of the Wilson administration had been made under Lansing. On the other hand, Edward R. Stettinius, Jr., who served only seven months, was involved not only in one of the major reorganizations of the Department but also in the important conferences at Yalta and San Francisco. Christian A. Herter had just assumed the burdens of office in the summer of 1959, when this volume was in the final stage of planning.

As editor of this volume, I wish to express my profound gratitude to all the contributors. In addition, special thanks are due to Richard D. Burns, Richard N. Current, and L. Ethan Ellis for their editorial assistance.

Norman A. Graebner

Contents

ix

1

The Year of Transition

1898

BY NORMAN A. GRAEBNER
University of Illinois

At the turn of the century a foreign ambassador in Washington observed that, although he had been at his post only a brief time, he had seen two different countries—the United States before the war with Spain and the United States after that war. In this picturesque remark, the diplomat recognized what some thoughtful Americans had already sensed—that 1898 was a turning point in the history of the Republic. What mattered was not that the United States had become a world power but that it had deserted, in the process of acquiring the Philippines, those principles of statecraft which had guided it through its first century of independence. This defiance of American diplomatic experience lay not in the mere absence of a precedent for expansion in the established policies of the United States, or even in the fact of expansion itself. It lay, instead, in the decision to anchor such unprecedented national behavior to abstract moral principles rather than to the political wisdom and common sense of the past. The newly acquired sense of moral obligation which propelled the nation on its twentieth-century course in world affairs was totally incompatible with the assumptions and methods which had permitted earlier generations of Americans to defend the perennial interests of the United States with style and distinction. After the events of 1898, the nation no longer possessed an unblurred diplomatic tradition which reached deeply into its own history or which alone could enlighten the thought and decisions of the future.

One essential element in the decline of political thought was the American diplomatic record itself. Even the most uninformed citizens were conscious of a stream of past diplomatic successes almost unparalleled in history. Throughout the preceding century the United States had gained what it wanted quickly and cheaply. It had freed the Mississippi Valley frontier of British and Spanish intrigue; taken the Mediterranean pirates off the backs of American seamen; driven the Spaniards out of Florida; the French out of Louisiana; the Mexicans out of Texas, New Mexico, and California; the British out of Oregon; the Russians out of Alaska; and, more recently, the Spaniards out of Cuba, Puerto Rico, and the Philippines. No nation in modern times had achieved its way more often, more completely, or at less expense.

Behind that catalogue of achievement lay all the ingredients of diplomatic success. That the United States in 1898 stood at the threshold of world power was not the result of continuing struggle against powerful neighbors which could be resisted only at great cost, if at all. For the American nation the advance to greatness had comprised the clearing of forests, the tilling of soil, the occupying of a vast, rich continental domain. Even when the United States ventured outside its private preserve to engage in war, it faced, after 1815, no nation more powerful than Spain. When its interests in the New World were challenged by England and France, its diplomacy benefited from the weakening effect of distance. But America's reliance on force, if less obvious than Europe's, was no less real. The strength of the United States in the late nineteenth century, relative to that of the major European powers, was the greatest that the nation had ever wielded. It took its precise form from the sheer size of the oceans, the dominance of the British navy, the magnificent functioning of the European balance-of-power system, the remoteness and backwardness of Asia, and the relative weakness of rivals in the New World. American diplomatic achievement, limited largely to the Western Hemisphere before 1898, was built on the solid foundation of ample power to match its essential requirements.

But this record of accomplishment had never been accidental. All official policy had been tied to the concept of national interest, with objectives abroad defined so precisely and in terms so limited that they could always be gained without the exhaustion of American energy. In the Western Hemisphere, the nation's fundamental interest, expressed by the Monroe Doctrine, was in preserving its unique position of predominant power. Only if the United States could prevent the acquisition of empire in this hemisphere by some European nation would that predominance remain unchallenged. To many European masters of *Realpolitik* the Monroe Doctrine appeared utopian, because it seemed to overreach American power. Yet the doctrine proved effective for the precise reason that it did not overextend the nation's commitments in the New World. So completely did American purpose conform to the realities of power in the

Atlantic world that the United States required neither war nor the threat of war to protect its interests. Not even when this nation was torn by civil war could France establish successfully a puppet monarchy in Mexico. Nor did President Lincoln feel any need to confront Napoleon III with a threat, for he knew that Mexico, despite its weakness and internal chaos, would generate enough opposition to drive the French forces out of that country. As he had predicted, the cost eventually became so high that Napoleon was happy to withdraw his army and permit the Emperor Maximilian to die before a Mexican firing squad. Never again was American purpose in this hemisphere seriously challenged by a European nation.

Late in the nineteenth century it became habitual for Americans to interpret the Monroe Doctrine as a statement of liberal purpose and to call upon it to maintain the *status quo* against European action. But in every crisis there were realists who restated the original concept of the doctrine as an expression of national interest in this hemisphere. "The true Monroe Doctrine," wrote Gustave Koerner in the *Nation* in the early eighties, "is the interest of our country.... Practically, we have always so acted, and so long as we have statesmen at the helm of state, and not mere 'doctrinairies,' ... we shall continue so to act, whether our action squares with the Monroe or any other doctrine or not. No doctrine will excuse us when we act unjustly, and none will prevent us from asserting our rights, at any cost, when our interest or honor is involved." Similarly, Lord Salisbury, the British Foreign Minister, challenged the relevance of the Monroe Doctrine to the Venezuelan controversy in 1895. "The United States," he wrote,

> have a right, like any other nation, to interpose in any controversy by which their own interests are affected; and they are the judge whether those interests are touched, and in what measure they should be sustained. But their rights are in no way strengthened or extended by the fact that the controversy affects some territory which is called American.... The Government of the United States is not entitled to affirm as a universal proposition, with reference to a number of independent states for whose conduct it assumes no responsibility, that its interests are necessarily concerned in whatever may befall those States simply because they are situated in the Western Hemisphere. It may well be that the interests of the United States are affected by something that happens to Chile or to Peru, and that that circumstance may give them the right of interference; but such a contingency may equally happen in the case of China or Japan, and the right of interference is not more extensive or more assured in the one case than in the other.

In regard to Europe, the only area with sufficient power to challenge the interests of the United States directly, isolationism was the underlying theory of American foreign policy. For the Founding Fathers, isolation was more than a geographical fact or the basis of a thoughtless preoccupation with inner-directed and self-sufficient pursuits. Indeed, the United States, with its expanding commercial empire, never pursued the solitude of such hermit nations as Japan and Korea. American isolationism was always political, not commercial or intellectual. The nation's refusal to enter alliances abroad was an effort to define its interests in terms of geography and to employ geography in the achievement of those interests. As President Washington reminded the country, "Why forego the advantages of so peculiar a situation?" Such convictions reflected, in addition, a realistic judgment of European power and the humble conclusion that the young Republic would only waste its energies if it engaged in struggles abroad which it could not control.

Above all, isolationism was the American version of the European preoccupation with diplomatic flexibility. Avoiding involvement abroad was a less important consideration than preserving the nation's freedom to carry out the decisions that best defended its interests. No nation can be completely free if it has bartered away its right to be neutral. If the United States maintained its independence of action better than did the powers of Europe, it was able to do so, not because of differences in intention, but because of geographical insulation. In the decades following 1815 the nation's record of involvement in European wars was still so recent that Americans could not regard the United States as invulnerable to pressures from abroad. The past had demonstrated the disturbing truth that any European war which ventured onto the Atlantic eventually involved the lands across the sea. What by the 1890s created the American illusion that the Atlantic was a genuine barrier against involvement was the fact that none of Europe's wars since 1815 had ventured onto the Atlantic.

This nation's positive interests in Europe were always identified with the balance of power. To thoughtful Americans it was not the mere abstention of the United States from European affairs but rather the precise political conditions of Europe that assured American security. The rise of any nation to an unchallengeable position on the European Continent would have threatened the United States with attack. American diplomatists could pursue a policy of isolationism throughout the years from 1815 to 1900 because they knew that the balance in Europe was adequate for the nation's needs. Unfortunately this favorable balance was ultimately taken for granted, and its relationship to American security was all but forgotten. By the nineties too many Americans no longer recognized the nation's vital stake in the health of Europe. The restoration of the Continent after the Napoleonic Wars had created conditions of such stability that the average citizen of the United States, enjoying perennial security at no cost, began to put his faith in the fact of isolation itself.

English power and diplomatic strategy were the keys to that balance of power which made American isolationism a wise and successful trans-Atlantic relationship. Many Americans still reserved their greatest antipathy for the British Empire, but offsetting this enmity was the knowledge that the United States and England shared a common historical heritage of language, literature, culture, law, politics, and even interests. Some writers, such as Brooks Adams, saw that England was the chief source of this nation's security and that the interests of the United States demanded nothing less than the continuance of British leadership in the affairs of the world. American diplomacy reflected this conviction. The settlement of the Venezuelan boundary dispute in the late nineties created the foundations for a new *rapprochement* between the two English-speaking nations.

Of Czarist Russia the American people knew little and cared less. Throughout the century the United States had enjoyed friendly relations with this remote empire, for the interests of the two nations converged in their mutual desire to limit the ambitions of Western Europe. Russia was never regarded as a threat to the European balance of power. To American diplomats it was the new German Empire that was upsetting the balance, although few regarded that nation as a danger to the peace. The United States Ambassador lauded the creation of German unity as a source of stability in Central Europe. Of the German people he wrote in February, 1871: "Indeed, people of every degree long for peace, and long for its continuance. I am, therefore, of the opinion that Germany in the coming years will devote its immense energies to the improvement of its laws, the establishment of its liberties, and the development of its great resources." The new German army, the Ambassador assured officials in Washington, was a force for peace and stability in Europe. Germany, after all, was surrounded by enemies.

By the end of the century Alfred Thayer Mahan was challenging the continuing concept of isolation. American interests were becoming too widespread, too enmeshed in the affairs of Europe, he wrote, to be entrusted to the oceans alone. The balance of power, he warned, was no longer stable. Germany, whatever the legitimacy of its drive for colonies and its naval ambitions, required watching, for German policy would eventually threaten the interests of other nations and thus endanger the peace of the world. Mahan, like Brooks Adams, suggested closer ties with England, for he also recognized the close affinity between British naval power and American security. It was time, concluded Mahan, that the United States enter the arena of world politics with an active policy designed to perpetuate the European balance of the past.

In Asia the national interest of the United States was less clearly defined. An American commercial empire stretched across the western Pacific, but to the extent that it was a recognizable commitment in American policy it was not challenged by changing conditions in the Orient. American interests, it appeared, could best be promoted through the preservation of order in China, not only because the Chinese market seemed to offer untold, if reluctant, possibilities for American business but also because American missionary activity there had created in the American mind an attitude of paternalism toward that amorphic empire. Chinese political and territorial integrity became the keystone of the American concept of a stable and profitable Far East.

China was preserved from partition in 1898 by both European rivalry and American patience, and the Open Door policy which followed anchored American interests in the Far East directly to the territorial integrity of China. Behind such a broad commitment was the conviction that any conquest of China by another nation would create such a vast accumulation of power that it would threaten the entire American position in the Far East. The Westernization of Japan was viewed as no threat to China. But the sudden rise of Japanese ambition and power, demonstrated by Japan's aggression and easy victory in the Sino-Japanese War of 1894, led Mahan to observe: "It has thus become evident that the weight of Japan in the international balance depends not only upon the quality of her achievement, which has been shown to be excellent, but upon the gross amount of her power." The American purpose in Asia, though vaguely stated, was the maintenance of a balance of power among the three dominant forces of China, Japan, and Russia.

II

American diplomacy in the nineteenth century was rooted firmly in the realistic tradition of the modern world. President Washington and his Secretary of the Treasury, Alexander Hamilton, established the pattern of American behavior. "In every act of my administration," Washington wrote in 1795, "I have sought the happiness of my fellow citizens. My system for the attainment of this object has uniformly been to overlook all personal, local, and partial consideration; to contemplate the United States as one great whole, . . . and to consult only the substantial and permanent interest of our country." In his Farewell Address he warned the nation to expect no more of others, declaring that "it is a maxim, founded on the universal experience of mankind, that no nation is to be trusted further than it is bound by its interest; and no prudent statesman or politician will venture to depart from it."

But this realistic, if limited, concept of American foreign policy was challenged from the beginning by those who believed that American action abroad should seek the fulfillment of the nation's democratic mission. Opposing Washington's proclamation of neutrality in 1793, Thomas Jefferson urged a pro-French policy on the basis of three moral principles:

the United States, he wrote, should be faithful to its treaty obligations, reveal its gratitude to a nation whose aid alone made independence possible, and declare its affinity for republican institutions. James Monroe, Jefferson's disciple, declared before the French Convention in 1794 that "republics should approach near to each other." Yet the continuing effort to identify American interests with revolutionary movements abroad never challenged in practice the fundamental concepts of Washington and Hamilton. Prior to the 1890s, the demand that the United States underwrite liberal revolutions always emanated from men who carried no direct responsibility for American decisions. For this reason the perennial appeals to idealism generally had less diplomatic purpose abroad than political purpose at home. The vigor with which every presidential administration during the Republic's first century countered these idealistic pressures measures the true depth of the nation's tradition of realism.

It is significant that Jefferson, as President, followed the dictum of Washington closely and employed his diplomatic authority to maintain the balance of power in Europe. James Monroe, as President, chided Henry Clay, the popular Kentuckian, for his support of the independence movement in Latin America. To Andrew Jackson he wrote that he would recognize Latin-American independence when the aspiring nations to the south had demonstrated their ability to cast off Spanish rule. Before that, Monroe concluded, they would not merit the recognition of the United States.

To many Americans the world of the early 1820s appeared particularly oppressive. The Greeks had staged an independence movement only to be suppressed by Turkish barbarities. Editors Hezekiah Niles of *Niles' Register* and Edward Everett of the *North American Review*, joined by Daniel Webster in Congress, rebuked the Monroe administration for its apparent indifference toward human suffering in other parts of the world. Secretary of State John Quincy Adams, in his famous address of July 4, 1821, read a lecture to those who demanded that the nation support a policy of liberation abroad:

> America ... has abstained from interference in the concerns of others, even when the conflict has been for principles to which she clings, as to the last vital drop that visits the heart. She has seen that probably for centuries to come, all the contests of that Aceldama, the European world, will be contests of inveterate power and emerging right. Wherever the standard of freedom and independence has been or shall be unfurled, there will her heart, her benedictions, and her prayers be. But she goes not abroad in search of monsters to destroy. She is the well-wisher to the freedom and independence of all. She is the champion and vindicator only of her own. ... She well knows that by once enlisting under other banners than her own, were they even the banners

of foreign independence, she would involve herself beyond the power of extrication, in all the wars of interest and intrigue, of individual avarice, envy, and ambition, which assume the colors and usurp the standard of freedom.

But philhellenic enthusiasm in the United States would not permit the Monroe administration to ignore the Greek situation. During the Cabinet conference that led to the Presidential message of December, 1823, the President announced his intention of acknowledging Greek independence and recommending that Congress authorize an appropriation to send a mission to Greece. But again Adams warned that any support of the Greek cause would involve the United States in the unstable Eastern question. When Adams discovered the famed Albert Gallatin in the President's office, urging Monroe to aid the Greeks with a naval force and a loan, the Secretary confided to his diary, "Mr. Gallatin still builds castles in the air of popularity, and, being under no responsibility for consequences, patronizes the Greek cause for the sake of raising his own reputation. His measure will not succeed, and even if it should, all the burden and danger of it will not bear upon him, but upon the Administration, and he will be the great champion of Grecian liberty." Adams favored the independence of Greece, but he would assume no responsibility for bringing it about. He helped to formulate the principles of hands-off and non-colonization for the Western Hemisphere, but he opposed commitments in Europe which might exceed the nation's power to achieve.

In his famous message of December, 1823, Monroe repeated forcefully Adams's principle of abstention from European wars and revolutions: "It is only when our rights are invaded, or seriously menaced, that we resent injuries, or make preparations for our defense." He disposed of the Greek issue with a general note of sympathy, spelling out the historic attitude of the United States toward the internal affairs of European countries. "Our policy in regard to Europe," he wrote, "which was adopted at an early stage of the wars which have so long agitated those quarters of the globe, nevertheless remains the same, which is, not to interfere in the internal concerns of any of its powers; to consider the government *de facto* as the legitimate government for us; to cultivate friendly relations with it, and to preserve those relations by a frank, firm and manly policy, meeting in all instances, the just claims of every power, submitting to injuries from none." Monroe's message reiterated the fundamental realistic traditions of American foreign policy. He again identified this nation's interests with the balance of power in Europe, not with revolutionary causes, which must succeed or fail on their own.

When revolution swept across Europe in 1848, American idealism again burned brightly. The United States Minister at Paris recognized the provisional government of France, adding hopefully that "if the Union gives to others the choice of government without interference, it naturally feels gratified at seeing another nation, under similar institutions, assuring to themselves the benefits of social order and public liberty." The United States Senate passed a congratulatory resolution and dispatched it to France. "We know what is going on in the world," admitted the Senate, "and we cannot avoid taking sides with the people of Europe without betraying the great cause of human liberty." In New York an enthusiastic throng at Lafayette Hall adopted a resolution which declared that the establishment of a republic in France "constituted a new and bright era in the world's history ... and imparts hope and light to the oppressed and toiling nations of Europe." But Edward Bates of Missouri reminded the nation that moral sentiment was not synonymous with policy.

By 1849 the country's attention was focused on Hungary's heroic struggle against Austrian rule. That summer, while the nation applauded, Secretary of State John Clayton dispatched Ambrose Dudley Mann as a special agent to enter Hungary and offer American encouragement. After winning momentary success under their eloquent leader, Louis Kossuth, the Hungarians were overwhelmed by Russian troops brought to the aid of Austria. Early in January, 1850, Senator Lewis Cass, the Michigan Democrat, proposed a resolution demanding that the national administration break off diplomatic relations with Austria. Henry Clay, leader of the Whig forces in the Senate, took strong exception to the proposal. The *New York Atlas* commented editorially: "We do not think it is the duty or the province of the United States to undertake to say that Austria is beyond the pale of civilized life, and unentitled to the rights of diplomacy and humanity. ... The United States cannot afford to make the cause of every broil in which the States of Europe become involved, an affair of their own." In his message of December, 1850, President Millard Fillmore explained his determination to avoid being drawn into the revolutionary affairs of Europe:

> Among the acknowledged rights of nations is that which each professes of establishing that form of government which it may deem most conducive to the happiness and prosperity of its own citizens. ... The People of the United States claim this right for themselves and readily concede it to others. Hence it becomes an imperative duty not to interfere in the government or internal policy of other nations and although we may sympathize with the unfortunate or the oppressed everywhere in their fight for freedom, our principles forbid us from taking any part in such foreign contests.

Secretary of State Daniel Webster followed the President's message with his famous note to Chevalier J. G. Hülsemann, the chargé d'affaires at the Austrian legation. In answering the Austrian protest that the United States had revealed too much interest in Hungarian liberation, Webster made it clear that the nation would continue to cheer the forces of liberation in Europe but would engage in no action which might give weight to its words. The United States had always abstained from interference in the political changes of Europe, but the American people, Webster added, "cannot fail to cherish always a lively interest in the fortunes of nations struggling for institutions like their own. But this sympathy, so far from being necessarily a hostile feeling toward any of the parties to these great national struggles, is quite consistent with amiable relations with them all." Even Webster admitted that this patriotic outburst was aimed more at a dividing America than a revolutionary Hungary.

American enthusiasm for the cause of the oppressed was boundless at the announcement, late in 1851, that the picturesque Kossuth was about to visit the United States. The booming of cannon in New York Harbor on December 15 announced his arrival. His triumphal tour of the nation set off a Kossuth craze. Congress proceeded to debate a resolution that welcomed the Hungarian leader to these shores and extended "the sympathy of Congress and the people of the United States to the victims of oppression everywhere." The voices of American orators throbbed with concern for the Hungarians. "We shall rejoice," declared Webster, "to see our American model upon the Lower Danube and on the mountains of Hungary." Articles on Hungary filled the press; Hungarian menus and Hungarian wine became the specialties at good restaurants throughout the North.

At Springfield, Illinois, a meeting adopted resolutions which praised Kossuth as "the most worthy and distinguished representative of the cause of civil and religious liberty on the continent of Europe," demanded that the nation's sympathy "be exerted in favor of the people of every nation struggling to be free," condemned the Russians for their unwarranted suppression of the Hungarian revolt, and admitted reluctantly that it was not the obligation of the United States to foment or assist revolutions in other countries. Cass, warming to the presidential campaign of 1852 as a leading spokesman of the "Young America" movement in the Democratic party, told a New York audience: "I do not advocate going to war ... but the time is coming when the voice of this nation will be potential throughout the world. I trust the time will soon come when not a hostile drum shall roll, and not a hostile cannon be fired, throughout the world, if we say, 'Your cause is not a just and right one.' "

More realistic Americans again reminded the enthusiasts that the effort to create policy out of sympathy was dangerous to the United States and worthless to Hungary. William H. Seward of New York attacked the Kossuth resolution in the Senate as a move which might commit the Congress "to some act of intervention in the affairs of Europe, by which the Government of the U.S. may be embarrassed in its foreign relations."

Clay reminded Kossuth privately that, even if the United States did declare war on Russia, it could not transport men and arms across the ocean. The Hungarian leader soon discovered that he had been victimized by the very enthusiasms which he had unleashed. Politicians toasted him warmly but refused to vote a dollar for his cause. Eventually he returned to England with the disillusionment that comes to those who expect too much of sentiment.

Even when the nation grew stronger, the American policy of nonintervention remained absolute. To President James Buchanan, in 1857, this traditional American principle meant that the nation "ought to cherish a sacred regard for the independence of all nations, and never attempt to interfere in the domestic concerns of any unless this shall be imperatively required by the great law of self-preservation." Circumstances might arise in which the interests and the security of the United States would demand foreign involvement. What mattered was that the nation be free to act as the defense of the national interest abroad might dictate.

Abraham Lincoln, like his predecessors, avoided moral commitments in Europe which he knew American power could not fulfill. Rather than expose himself and his administration to the psychological and political pressures that always come to bear on leaders when something specific is expected of them, Lincoln refused to involve the United States in the effort of Polish revolutionaries, early in 1863, to throw off the tyranny of the Russian Czar. The French government sent an appeal to the United States for support in exerting "a moral influence on the Emperor of Russia." Secretary of State Seward responded for the Lincoln administration. In a letter to the French government of May 11, 1863, he acknowledged the American interest in public order and humanity. But he added positively: "Notwithstanding ... the favor with which we thus regard the suggestion of the Emperor of the French, this government finds an insurmountable difficulty in the way of any active cooperation with the governments of France, Austria, and Great Britain. ..."

Revolutionists in every country, Seward admitted, had been attracted to American democratic idealism in their search for sympathy and active support. But the United States, he continued, had never defied the counsels of President Washington that "the American people must be content to recommend the course of human progress by the wisdom with which they should exercise the powers of self-government, forbearing at all times, and in every way, from foreign alliances, intervention, and interference." There had been many "seductions" to involve the United States in events abroad, such as the Hungarian revolution, but each appeal had been disallowed by the American government. He added: "Our policy of nonintervention, straight, absolute, and peculiar as it may seem to other nations, has become the traditional one, which could not be abandoned without the most urgent occasion, amounting to a manifest necessity. . . ." The nation's policy of nonintervention, moreover, was not without advantage to the interests of mankind, for it meant that this country would not interfere with a people's right to choose its own form of government. Seward made it clear that, if the United States had good wishes for the progress of humanity in Europe, it would not defy its own principle of self-determination.

Throughout the first century of its history, the government of the United States consistently repulsed the pressures of idealism in the conduct of its foreign relations. It refused to employ either diplomacy or force in the cause of the oppressed or to withhold recognition of *de facto* regimes because their concepts of politics and morality did not conform with those of this nation. American leaders persistently chided those not responsible for national policy who would raise false hopes abroad through appeals to sentiment at home. Fundamental American practice followed that of the great European diplomats from Castlereagh to Bismarck.

The policy of nonintervention was no denial of America's democratic mission; it meant only that the nation's liberalizing influence was limited to example. By keeping its democratic institutions inviolate, the United States would not only prosper but also stimulate the evolution of democracy everywhere. It would help the oppressed of Europe, said Horace Greeley's *New York Tribune* in September, 1848, not by employing physical force, but by exhibiting to Europe "the spectacle of a nation lightly and gently governed, yet scrupulously respecting and maintaining personal rights . . . of a press without shackles, yet never an object of official apprehension or alarm. Such, in our view, are the sentiments, the policy, which patiently, unfalteringly pursued by this country, will most powerfully contribute to hasten and secure the resurrection of liberty in Europe and its final triumph throughout the world." The world knew what Americans desired, one Kentuckian reminded the Senate in 1852; what mattered was that this nation "present to all mankind a continued example of a people capable of governing themselves with economy, so as to secure every human right . . . well worthy of their admiration and imitation." It was far better, warned Clay, to "keep our light burning on this western shore, as a light to all nations, than to hazard its utter extinction amid the ruins of fallen or falling republics in Europe."

III

American diplomacy in the nineteenth century demonstrated that a democratic structure of government is no barrier to the creation of a perennially sound response to the challenges of external affairs. The century had its doubters who had to be convinced. Alexis de Tocqueville, the brilliant French critic of American democracy, wrote in the 1830s: "Foreign politics demand scarcely any of those qualities which a democracy possesses; and they require, on the contrary, the perfect use of almost all those faculties in which it is deficient." Only with difficulty, he noted, could a democracy "regulate the details of an important undertaking, persevere in a fixed design, and work out its execution in spite of serious obstacles." Actually, American diplomacy, functioning through the nation's political and constitutional system, was conducted with the skill and precision that the world had come to expect of the British and French Foreign Offices. The United States would perform in its foreign relations, it appeared from the record, as well as the American mind and American political responsibility would permit.

To meet the demands of foreign affairs, Congress established the State Department in June, 1789, and from Washington's administration on, the Secretary of State has been the most carefully selected official in the government. During the first forty years of the Republic the office of Secretary remained predominant by the sheer importance of events abroad. So important were the affairs of Europe to the nation's well-being that all the predecessors of Andrew Jackson in the Presidency had built much of their reputations in the areas of diplomacy or war. Most of the early Secretaries were men of broad experience in foreign capitals. Several of them, particularly Thomas Jefferson, James Monroe, and John Quincy Adams, were exceptionally well versed in international affairs. During the following decades only James Buchanan (1845–1849), Edward Everett (1852–1853), Lewis Cass (1857–1860), and John W. Foster (1892–1893) preceded their years in the Cabinet with diplomatic service abroad. Yet such a background was no sure measure of success, and such outstanding diplomatists as William H. Seward (1861–1869), Hamilton Fish (1869–1877), and James G. Blaine (1881, 1889–1892) had had no experience in foreign affairs when they assumed their duties.

Throughout the nineteenth century the United States maintained no regular diplomatic service abroad. Most diplomats earned their appointments through party affiliation, personal wealth, or social position, seldom through training. Many lacked knowledge; some lacked dignity, although few were as tactless as John Randolph, who allegedly commented, when presented to the Czar in 1830, "Howaya, Emperor? And how's the madam?" Those who achieved distinction abroad did so largely by the accident of being able men. Some, whatever their personal qualifications, served the nation intelligently and resourcefully. Among those who represented the United States well in the courts of Europe were Albert Gallatin, James Monroe, John Quincy Adams, Washington Irving, George Bancroft, Henry Wheaton, Edward Everett, and Charles Francis Adams. In the Far East it was Townsend Harris whose patient negotiations achieved the commercial treaty with Japan in 1858. Anson Burlingame was responsible, in large measure, for the success of American diplomacy in China in the late nineteenth century, and the Chinese government employed him as its representative on a special mission to the great nations of the West.

Perhaps the rather haphazard diplomatic service reflected the American sense of security and the gradual withdrawal of the United States from the affairs of the Eastern Hemisphere after 1823. By English and French standards, American representatives were poorly paid. In many important capitals of Europe the United States did not even maintain an embassy, but expected the minister to rent suitable quarters. Henry Wheaton, one of the most illustrious of American representatives abroad, recorded privately, in May, 1836, his judgment of the American diplomatic service:

> The Austrian cabinet is on the point of forming a new commercial union with the states of Northern and Central Italy, and it should be the duty of our minister at Vienna to keep watch of this movement and turn it to our advantage. If Mr. Calhoun could have seen with his own eyes how badly our affairs have been managed for years in the different European courts, from ignorance of official forms and of that language which is the universal tongue of diplomacy, without which a diplomatist might as well be deaf and dumb, as well as from the lack of experience which, in our profession as in every other, gives a decided advantage to those who possess it, he would be convinced of the importance of having the *principal missions*, at least, occupied by men who possess these qualities. At least those who unite the desired qualities ought to be employed where they can do most service, while incapable men should be turned out without favor or partiality. Those who have served the country faithfully and skilfully ought to be encouraged and transferred from one court to another, which is the only advancement that our system admits of. The only way of making up for the insufficient salaries given under our system would be to vote new outfits, for those who have deserved them, whenever the interest of the country would justify and demand their transfer to another post. Such is my way of looking at things; it is the result of much observation and reflection.
>
> I believe that there is still much to do to advance our political and commercial interests in Europe, and nothing vexes me more than to hear an American minister say, whatever the court may be to which he is accredited, "There is nothing to do *here*," or "Nothing *can* be done." I do not know a post, whether important or not, which could not offer a zealous, active, and skilful agent the opportunity of doing something for the interests of his country.

If the American Constitution was no barrier to successful diplomacy, it presented special problems to those charged with the conduct of the nation's foreign relations. The Founding Fathers, in creating the Constitution, were close enough to the problems of war and diplomacy to design a strong structure of government. But in guaranteeing democratic control of the management of foreign affairs through the device of separation of powers, they aggravated the task of defining and maintaining a consistent foreign policy. The vagueness of the Constitution in diplomatic matters not only invited the Congress to struggle for the privilege of directing the nation's affairs abroad but also subjected diplomatic questions to the vicissitudes of American politics. Through debate, occasional demands for diplomatic correspondence, or the threatened use of the purse, congressmen could exert persistent pressure on the executive branch to modify its policies or could reap partisan advantage from their attack even when they had no intention of altering the decisions of the government. Seldom were the sustained congressional attacks on established policy in the nineteenth century meant to achieve more than political rewards at home, and those who resorted to such partisanship did not ease the task of the government in disposing of its responsibilities abroad with wisdom, tranquility, and compromise. Fortunately, most important negotiations were conducted in secrecy. This permitted responsible officials to escape much of the public pressure.

American leadership in the nineteenth century triumphed over its domestic detractors simply because it remained politically and intellectually sound. It followed the dictum of Hamilton that the executive had the double obligation to pursue the territorial, commercial, and security interests of the United States and to defend its policies with energy. Until the 1890s, American diplomatists guarded carefully the concept of limited objectives and limited power. In 1894, when the United States ventured into an imperialistic quarrel with the British and Germans over Samoa, Secretary of State Walter Q. Gresham complained to President Grover Cleveland:

> It is in our relations to Samoa that we have made the first departure from our traditional and well-established policy of avoiding entangling alliances with foreign powers in relation to objects remote from this hemisphere. . . . If the departure was justified, there must be some evidence of detriment suffered before its adoption, or of advantage since gained, to demonstrate the fact. . . . Every nation, and especially every strong nation, must sometimes be conscious of an impulse to rush into difficulties that do not concern it, except in a highly imaginary way. To restrain the indulgence of such a propensity is not only the part of wisdom, but a duty we owe to the world as an example of the strength, the moderation, and the beneficence of popular government.

During the following year President Cleveland explained to the American people why he would not formulate policy toward Cuba and Spain on the basis of liberal sentiment. In his message of December, 1895, he said:

"Whatever may be the traditional sympathy of our countrymen as individuals with a people who seem to be struggling for larger autonomy and greater freedom, deepened, as such sympathy naturally must be, in behalf of our neighbors, yet the plain duty of their Government is to observe in good faith the recognized obligations of international friendship." Such views, he added, must prevail over "any shock our human sensibilities may have received from the cruelties which appear to especially characterize this sanguinary and fiercely conducted war." But the day was approaching when such realistic definitions of national interest would no longer determine the fundamental foreign policies of the United States.

IV

The war with Spain in 1898 shattered finally much of the nineteenth-century tradition in diplomacy. Idealism had played a powerful, if negative, role in American thought. In Europe its aim was the establishment of liberal governments against the forces of repression, rather than the more limited goal of maintaining the balance of power. To that extent it was no guide for action. But with the Spanish-American War moral abstraction as a mass phenomenon was substituted for the political realism which had circumscribed all previous American diplomacy. The war of 1898 was not the result of any deliberate weighing of interests and responsibilities. It was a people's war, rationalized almost entirely in humanitarian terms.

Historians agree generally that the United States had no legitimate cause for declaring war on Spain. The Spanish government recognized its failure in Cuba and by 1898 had done much to alleviate conditions on the island. It sought to avoid war with the United States and moved forward as rapidly as Spanish opinion would permit in meeting the demands of American leadership. But the yellow press in the United States, after the destruction of the *Maine* in Havana Harbor, demanded war. The conviction of Republican editors and politicians that the cause of Cuba was both popular and just mobilized both the Republican majority in Congress and the McKinley administration behind the clamor for action. Two days after the President learned of the Spanish capitulation to his demands, he sent his war message to Congress.

Few Americans attempted to justify the war in terms of American national interest. "Our own direct interests [in Cuba] were great...," observed Theodore Roosevelt in his *Autobiography*. "But even greater were our interests from the standpoint of humanity. Cuba was at our very doors. It was a dreadful thing for us to sit supinely and watch her death agony." Walter Hines Page termed the war "a necessary act of surgery for the health of civilization." To Senator John T. Morgan, writing in the *North*

American Review, the United States had been drawn into the war by a sense of humanity and "duty we owe to Christian civilization." The fact that the United States achieved its initial goal of freeing Cuba and thus fulfilling a great moral purpose at little expense to itself merely strengthened the new American conviction that policy anchored primarily to national interest was no longer legitimate for a nation so fortunate in its institutions and so powerful in its military and economic potential to render good.

Traditional political considerations played no greater role in the acquisition of the Philippines than they did in the declaration of war. The new venture in imperialism in the Far East was so sudden and unpremeditated that the nation was never permitted to judge its consequences. The islands were acquired so painlessly that the new commitments did not even disturb the nation's isolationist habits of thought. From the beginning, the Philippines were a strategic liability, for they lay across the Pacific in a vast area where other nations deployed greater power than did the United States. It was only the temporary absence of any challenge to this distant outpost that permitted the nation to escape the normal penalty for creating ends of policy without any consideration of means.

In its declaration of war on Spain, the United States claimed no objective other than that of liberating Cuba. Even this limited purpose required some degree of military victory over Spain. To destroy Spanish sea power in the Pacific and thus protect American commerce, the administration ordered Commodore Dewey to Manila Bay, where he destroyed the Spanish fleet at anchor without any loss of American life. The President next dispatched an expeditionary force to reduce Spanish power and guarantee order and security in the islands.

Suddenly the nation faced an unanticipated dilemma. What was to be the disposition of the Philippines now in American hands? For weeks the *New York Times* revealed the general uncertainty. On May 1, it declared simply: "Whether the station will be retained after the war by the United States will not now be determined." The islands, it added, might afford a good naval base and protection for American commerce, but any seizure of the islands, the editorial warned, would require some explanation to Europe. Two days later the *Times* opposed the return of the islands to Spain but could propose no clear alternative. The Philippines apparently were not fit for self-government, but all the arguments against Hawaiian annexation applied even more strongly to the Spanish possessions. Perhaps the nation had no choice but to auction them off to the highest European bidder. On May 4, the *Times* editorial agreed to the return of the Philippines to Spain in exchange for the independence of Cuba and a cession of Puerto Rico to the United States. "But the actual annexation of the Philippines," continued the *Times,* "would be as inadmissable as the actual annexation of Cuba, the desire for which we have disclaimed." Yet the same editorial concluded that it might be better to keep the islands than to turn them over to England, France, or Germany.

Such confusion continued. On May 6, the *Times* answered Lord Bryce's prediction that the war against Spain would feed American ambition with the retort that a strong Christian does not become a brawler. Three days later, the *Times* concluded that the only choice open to the United States was to accede to its new position among nations and to govern the islands, accepting the advantages on the one hand and the burdens on the other. But the doubts and confusion appeared equally profound within the administration, for the *Times* reported, on May 16, that "neither in the White House nor the State Department is there any definite conviction or determination concerning the future direction of the national policy with regard to the disposal of those over-sea possessions, over which the American flag will be flying when the war is over."

Slowly a national policy emerged. At the end of July, 1898, the President announced that any truce with Spain must include the condition that the United States continue to occupy Manila until the conclusion of a treaty. Finally, on September 16, the administration clarified its intentions in the instructions to its peace commissioners. The President wrote:

> Without any original thought of complete or even partial acquisition, the presence and success of our arms at Manila imposes upon us obligations which we cannot disregard. The march of events rules and over-rules human action.... We cannot be unmindful that without any desire or design on our part the war has brought us new duties and responsibilities which we must meet and discharge as becomes a great nation on whose growth and career from the beginning the Ruler of Nations has plainly written the high command and pledge of civilization.

That the United States acquired the Philippines reluctantly does not mean that it had no freedom of choice. But that freedom had been almost destroyed by the initial decision to conquer the islands. For once they had been liberated, they had to be either restored to Spain or brought under the protection of the United States. The islands lacked the power to maintain their own independence, and thus to cast them adrift after freeing them appeared to constitute total irresponsibility. The order to destroy Spanish authority at Manila was crucial. Thereafter all avenues of escape from a self-imposed dilemma seemed to be closed. The final decision to annex the islands was rationalized, like the war itself, with appeals to sentiment. There was nothing left to do, William B. McKinley explained to the country, "but to take them all, and to educate the Filipinos, and uplift and civilize and Christianize them, and by God's grace do the very best we could by them, as our fellowmen for whom Christ also died...."

So remote were the burdens of empire that many Americans assumed that the acquisition of the Philippines strengthened the nation. Unfortunately, this would have been true only if the cost of maintaining an adequate defense of the islands were offset by sources of power in the new territories which equaled or exceeded the power required for their defense. Actually the Philippines were so distant and defenseless that they constituted a hostage which other nations could use in bargaining with the United States. So extensive were American commitments in the Far East that the nation's reliance on British navy became even greater than before. The English *Saturday Review*, in December, 1898, observed that the American peace negotiators involved in acquiring the Philippines were

> making their bargain ... under the protecting naval strength of England. And we shall expect, to be quite frank, a material *quid pro quo* for this assistance. We shall expect the States to deal generously with Canada in the matter of tariffs; we shall expect to be remembered when she comes into her kingdom in the Philippines; above all, we shall expect her assistance on the day, quickly approaching, when the future of China shall come up for settlement. For the young imperialist has entered upon a path where she will require a stout friend. ...

American policy in 1898 had destroyed the nation's basic isolation from the Eastern Hemisphere by extending the Monroe Doctrine to the western Pacific. Only the splendid victory over the Spanish squadron at Manila obscured the magnitude of the nation's new obligations. As Thucydides, the Greek historian, wrote many centuries ago, "You cannot decline the burdens of empire and still expect to share its honours." For this challenge of empire there was no precedent in the American experience. The wisdom of the past which might have established guidelines of action had been forgotten. Those occasional warnings that the United States possessed neither the naval forces adequate for the defense of its far-flung commitments nor the interest in building them passed almost unnoticed. The suddenness and completeness of the changes wrought by expansion measured the extent to which illusions emanating from the habit of easy success had supplanted analysis in the conduct of the nation's foreign affairs.

V

Unfortunately, American diplomatic achievements carried a deferred penalty. Confident in the knowledge that victory had always seemed to reward its efforts abroad, the nation no longer accepted the necessity either of abiding by the principle that ends be limited by means or of defining its long-term interests in any cohesive fashion. If the United States had experienced success in the past without huge cost to itself, it could do so in the future. No foreign enemy could challenge its security.

Abraham Lincoln had said as early as 1838 that danger, "if it ever reach us, . . . must spring up amongst us. It cannot come from abroad. If destruction be our lot, we must ourselves be its author and finisher. As a nation of freemen, we must live through all time, or die by suicide."

What characterized the American outlook on the world in the years after 1898 was not merely the assumption of omnipotence but the identification of that omnipotence less with physical power than with the peculiar qualities of American civilization itself. Unmindful of the role which its industrial capacity or the balance of power had played in its previous triumphs, the nation found its strength rather in its low taxes, its free-enterprise system, and the moral promise of its democratic structure. David Starr Jordan summarized cogently, in February, 1899, the reasons for American progress when he said, "Our farmer carried no soldier on his back." Admitting that the United States had interests that blanketed the globe, he denied that they required the protection of armies. "Force of brains is greater than force of arms," he declared, "more worthy and more lasting." As long as the nation guarded its great domestic traditions of freedom and *laissez faire*, it would be secure.

This rejection of the element of force as the basis of national or international politics conformed completely to the prevailing optimism of the age. Nineteenth-century rationalism had denied the essentially evil nature of society and had anticipated a rational world, free of conflict, oppression, tyranny, and other irrational uses of power. American progress during that century, gained amid limitless opportunities and with a minimum of conflict and coercion, substantiated the illusion that force was giving way to consensus in the resolving of human problems. World opinion, the expression of that consensus on the international scene, would soon replace power politics completely as the great force in affairs among nations. Supported by that opinion, a virtuous country could terminate its conflicts abroad without concession or war, political or military commitments, involvement in power politics or the balance of power, or the expending of its wealth and resources beyond its continental limits. Aggressive powers might still resort to the sword, but they would not have their way against the combined sentiment of an innocent world.

Increasingly, after 1898, the United States came to view itself as an innocent nation. Satiated with the territorial gains of the Spanish-American War, it could enter each crisis thereafter without asking anything for itself. This encouraged its spokesmen to rebuke those nations which insisted that the present held too little for them and that their security and well-being required alterations in the *status quo* which necessitated the defiance of treaty arrangements. From its favored position among nations, the United States gradually identified its interests in the world with peace, order, and stability, for the perpetuation of such enemies of change would assure the nation its continued predominance at relatively little cost to itself. Not even the American democratic mission was any genuine challenge to the world order as it existed in 1898, for the countries of Europe and Asia which thereafter seemed to be guilty of repressing freedom were always those which sought to upset the *status quo*. Thus the American crusade of liberation was usually reduced to a moralistic device to undo aggression and prevent change which would threaten this nation's interests.

Within this new conceptual framework there was no possibility of maintaining the traditional balance between ends and means. The past reliance on physical power, always a limited entity, had confined rather than expanded American ambition. But moral purpose, operating in a supposedly rational world, created limitless expectations among those who claimed the selfless obligation to serve mankind. Such ends eliminated completely the primary question of means, for if national intent, at least in theory, was directed at the achievement of universal freedom, the assurance of success lay in the simple desire of men to be free. Herein lay the ultimate promise of victory in repulsing any serious assault on the *status quo*, for conquest cannot exist without repression. That human quality which assured the lifting of new oppression always assured thereby the eventual failure of aggression. What remained of policy was the futile but innocuous determination to remind the world of the benefits of democracy and to chide those enemies of the moment who always seemed to stand in the path of its triumph. Confronted after the turn of the century, both in Europe and Asia, by powers which identified their interests with change and accepted the legitimacy of force in achieving it, American leadership could escape its dilemmas only by hasty improvisation which succeeded often in protecting the nation's interests but seldom in establishing its precepts.

2

John Hay

1898-1905

BY FOSTER RHEA DULLES
The Ohio State University

In late September, 1898, two ships passed each other in mid-Atlantic. The eastbound was taking William R. Day, the outgoing Secretary of State, to the Paris conference that would conclude a peace treaty between the United States and Spain; aboard the westbound vessel was John Hay, returning from his ambassadorial post in London to take Day's place at the head of the State Department. There was something symbolic about this coincidence, for it reflected the critical changes of that year in the history of American foreign policy. In the long past the United States had generally stood aloof from the complex interplay of international politics, rigidly maintaining its complete independence of action through the careful avoidance of any political commitments; the future was to find it increasingly involved in world affairs and destined ultimately to abandon its onetime isolationism altogether.

John Hay was the first Secretary of State in this new era. He was not himself primarily responsible for the important new developments in foreign policy that lay over the horizon of the twentieth century. He was often swept along, sometimes almost in spite of himself, by the tide of great events. "No man, no party," as he himself wrote on one occasion, "can fight with any chance of success against a cosmic tendency." But with his abiding faith in the beckoning destiny of America and his strong sense of the importance of sustaining his country's influence in international affairs, he played no small part in helping to adjust national policy to the new circumstances marking the nation's emergence upon the world scene as a great power.

Theodore Roosevelt once stated that Hay was not only "a great figure but a unique figure." Another time, after the latter's death, the President wrote rather pettishly that Hay's usefulness had been no more than that of "a fine figure head." A sounder evaluation of John Hay as the nation's first Secretary of State in the twentieth century should lie somewhere between these two contrasting statements by the volatile Roosevelt.

II

Hay assumed the duties of Secretary of State with a broader background of diplomatic experience and greater familiarity with international politics than had any of his predecessors since the opening years of the nineteenth century. He was indeed admirably equipped for his high post. Just sixty years old at the time of his appointment, he even looked very much the diplomat—his trim figure, finely chiseled features, and closely cut Vandyke beard giving him an air of quiet distinction. His rather aristocratic manner was above all suave and polished. Modest and unassuming, he was also a witty conversationalist. Although his moods easily alternated between gaiety and quiet melancholy, his friends all attested to his social charm. He was something of the dilettante, decidedly ease-loving (Henry Adams once wrote sardonically that his ambition "was to escape annoyance"), highly adaptable, and so constituted as to bring to diplomacy an instinctive tact and spirit of accommodation.

Hay was a native of the Middle West, born in Salem, Indiana, on October 8, 1838, but his marriage and his career led him to an ever-closer identification with the more sophisticated society of the East. The range of his activities, after he left home to study at Brown University, was amazing. He acted as wartime secretary and military aide to Lincoln, served as a member of the American legations in Paris, Vienna, and Madrid, worked for a time as an editor on the staff of the *New York Tribune,* engaged in business in Cleveland for several years, acted as Assistant Secretary of State in the Hayes administration, and became widely known as a writer—a poet, novelist, travel diarist, and biographer. His most significant literary work was the great biography of Lincoln, written in collaboration with John Nicolay; but a broader public knew him as the author of *Pike County Ballads,* and his "Jim Bludsoe"—the tale of the heroic steamboat captain who died to save his passengers' lives—was among the most popular poems of his day:

> Christ ain't going to be too hard
> On a man that died for men.

Hay had lived in Washington, though making frequent trips abroad, for some eleven years before President McKinley made him American Ambassador to the Court of St. James's. A man of independent wealth, a stanch Republican anxious for public service, an intimate associate of such prominent, political-minded men as Henry Adams, Henry Cabot Lodge, and Theodore Roosevelt, he had long hoped for the sort of foreign post that he finally attained in reward for his political support of McKinley in 1896. And in London he was eminently successful. No one could have worked more skillfully to cement the growing Anglo-American *rapprochement* that characterized the late 1890s. Hay thoroughly enjoyed English society, made countless friends, and was completely at home in the great country houses where he was always a welcome visitor. It was an existence that appealed immensely to his aristocratic prejudices; Henry Adams was later to write that these were undoubtedly "the happiest months" in Hay's entire life.

In such circumstances Hay hesitated for a time before accepting his appointment as Secretary of State. He did not relish the thought of the arduous duties the new post would entail, he was concerned over his health, and he at least professed to feel a sense of inadequacy in taking over such important responsibilities. These hesitations reflected his desire for quiet and comfort, a lifelong preoccupation with his physical well-being, and a less easily defined lack of confidence in himself, which sometimes seemed to be a literary pose. After drafting one letter refusing the appointment, he nevertheless set aside his doubts and hesitations and accepted it. His biographer, Tyler Dennett, attributes his decision to a sense of duty, but the ambition which always warred with his love of ease surely had a part in it.

In spite of the expansionist proclivities of many of his intimate friends in Washington, Hay was not himself originally an imperialist, and he was never a jingoist. But he had accepted the war with Spain—"as necessary as it is righteous"—and he was to grow increasingly responsive to the opportunities that it opened up for the expansion of American power, American influence, and American trade. His point of view was distinctly internationalist rather than isolationist, in the later sense of these somewhat ambiguous terms, and he would allude confidently on one occasion to what he called "our Pacific work." Hay was fully prepared, that is, to accept all the ambitious consequences of the nation's emergence upon the world stage.

His deepest convictions on foreign policy, however, centered about what he considered the imperative necessity of maintaining close and cordial relations with Great Britain. His strong sympathy for England was repeatedly demonstrated during his days as Ambassador, and he had taken the occasion of his one political address to summon the peoples of Great Britain and America to increasing cooperation in world affairs. They were knitted by a thousand ties of origin, language, and kindred interests, Hay declared, and it was evident "that there is a sanction like that of religion which binds us to a sort of partnership in the beneficent work of the world." Hay never wavered in support of this position. His friendly and sympathetic attitude toward Great Britain, especially during the Boer War, when so many of his countrymen were highly critical of British policy, repeatedly led to charges of "a blind devotion," but this was an issue on which he felt completely sure of himself. "As long as I am here," he wrote Henry White in August, 1899, "no action shall be taken contrary to my conviction that the indispensable feature of our foreign policy should be a firm understanding with England."

Hay was not the man to become the aggressive architect of a long-range foreign policy. Under both McKinley and Roosevelt, he served rather as a highly skillful instrument for implementing policies which were often little more than an expedient answer to immediate events. Here again, his forte was compromise and accommodation. Hay never experienced any difficulties under McKinley. He had the greatest respect for the President, and the two men worked well together. McKinley often exercised more influence on policy than has been generally realized, but he was usually content to stand in the shadows. Hay's name, rather than McKinley's, is consequently identified with almost every diplomatic move that the administration made after the Treaty of Paris of 1899. Upon Roosevelt's accession to the Presidency in 1901, Hay's status gradually changed. The Secretary's role was to become an increasingly subordinate one, and even when he made important contributions to policy, it was now the President who sought and obtained the limelight. But although there were to be occasions of real friction, with Hay seeking to restrain his impetuous chief, the two men remained good personal friends.

After the election of 1904, the vigorous proponent of "speaking softly but carrying a big stick" monopolized the scene more and more. This was due primarily to Roosevelt's desire to direct foreign policy himself, but an important contributing factor to the eclipse of his Secretary of State was the latter's increasing ill-health. For many months before his death on July 1, 1905, Hay actually had little part in the handling of state affairs.

Hay had not looked forward to conducting the business of the State Department. It did not involve anything like the tasks a Secretary of State would face in later years, but routine of any kind was always an onerous burden for him. The entire staff in Washington numbered no more than some sixty persons in 1898, and there was a leisurely, old-fashioned atmosphere about the State Department offices, where, as Tyler Dennett has written, "the typewriter was viewed as a necessary evil and the telephone was an instrument of last resort." Hay once complained, with the literary exaggeration he often affected, that his chief duties were fighting claims made against the United States by the citizens of foreign countries, pressing the often fraudulent claims of American citizens against other governments, and finding diplomatic offices for the friends of senators. There was, however, an increasing amount of official correspondence as time went on, and here Hay had the exceedingly able help of the Second Assistant Secretary of State. Alvey A. Adee had held this post since 1886 and was, in his own person, a sort of permanent civil service. Not only did he write most of the diplomatic messages that went out over the Secretary's signature, but he generally handled the formal and routine business of the State Department. Still, Hay was often unhappy over the want of leisure in his office job, and he once described his Secretarial existence as "this life of dreary drudgery." Unburdening his soul to Henry Adams, Hay commented: "The worst of my present job is that I can delegate so little of it. It is a grim grey world you have left me to, with nobody to talk to, or to walk with, to keep me in the straight path by showing me the crooked. . . . I grow wanner and wanner, day by day."

Hay got along well with nearly everyone. The friendliness that marked his relations with McKinley and Roosevelt also characterized his associations with the men in both their Cabinets. He had a close personal relationship with many members of the diplomatic staff, especially Henry White, and he won the friendship and esteem of the foreign envoys in Washington. There was only one exception, and a highly important one, to Hay's ability to work in harmonious accord with other members of government. He could not get along with the Senate. He resented its role in the approval of treaties, rarely consulted the members of its Committee on Foreign Relations, and in private letters, if not in public statements, outspokenly condemned what he considered its ignorant, partisan, inherently obstructive attitude. His difficulties grew primarily out of the Senate's disapproval of treaties which it considered too favorable to Great Britain, and Hay was repeatedly exasperated by what he believed to be its wholly unjustified prejudices.

Hay often complained that the normal give-and-take of diplomacy was rendered impossible for the United States by the attitudes of the Senate. "No fair arrangement between us and another power will ever be accepted by the Senate," he wrote to Nicolay in 1900. "We must get everything and give nothing,—and even then some malignant Senator or newspaper will attack the deal, and say we have surrendered everything,—and that scares our cowardly friends out of their wits." In another letter to Nicolay, Hay illustrated the precise manner in which the Senate, in his judgment, strangled the nation's diplomacy:

> The worst of all is the uncertainty about what the Senate may do in any given case. You may work for months over a treaty, and at last get everything satisfactorily arranged, and send it into the Senate, when it is met by every man who wants to get a political advantage or

to satisfy a personal grudge, everyone who has asked for an office and not got it, everyone whose wife may think mine has not been attentive enough—and if they can muster one third of their Senate and one, your treaty is lost without any reference to its merits. That is our predicament now in our Canadian controversy. I could draw up in twenty-four hours a settlement which would be perfectly satisfactory to Lord Salisbury and me. But the odds are two to one that Canada would not accept it or that our Senate would throw it out. It is a well nigh hopeless case. ...I must feel [sure] of my ground somewhat, before risking a defeat in the Senate, which ought to involve my continuance in the Government. I would gladly go out on such an issue, if it were not to damage the President next year.

III

The first task confronting Hay upon his return to Washington in September, 1898, was the conduct of the peace negotiations with Spain. His part, however, consisted of little more than dispatching to the American delegation in Paris the instructions drawn up by President McKinley. The issue of whether the United States should take over the Philippine Islands—the only real question that arose after the conclusion of hostilities —had really been decided before Hay entered office. The favorable reaction to the imperialistic speeches McKinley made on his swing through the country in October further convinced the President that "duty requires we should take the archipelago." Spain was to protest bitterly, but although he was willing to approve a payment of 20 million dollars for the islands, McKinley stood firmly by the decision he had reached. On October 26, Hay cabled the final instructions to the peace delegation in Paris. The President felt that the United States had to acquire either all the islands or none of the islands and that, since the latter course was wholly inadmissible, "the former must therefore be required."

There is no evidence that Hay played any significant part in this decision, but neither is there any sign that he disapproved of it. He had raised no objections when the first indications of what the President had in mind were relayed to him in London. He had reported at the time—and this must certainly have influenced his own views—that Great Britain would wholly approve such a solution to the dilemma created by the victory of Manila Bay. Hay was a passive, but willing, agent in helping to carry out one of the most momentous decisions in the history of American foreign policy.

But if he had no major influence on the first important development during his years as Secretary of State, Hay promptly found himself deeply involved in a number of other issues that foreshadowed the role that the United States was to play in world affairs during the coming years: the determination of policy in eastern Asia in the face of a threatened division of China among the European powers; the consolidation of America's position in the Caribbean and the possible construction of an Isthmian canal; the settlement of the status of the Samoan Islands consequent upon the breakdown of the tripartite agreement under which the United States, Great Britain, and Germany shared their control; and, in a somewhat different category, a dispute with Great Britain over the boundaries between Alaska and Canada that had been greatly acerbated by the discovery of gold in the Klondike. Though widely different in many ways, these issues had a common denominator: they all had an important effect on Anglo-American relations.

Hay approached these problems determined to uphold the national interest in the light of the United States's new world position, but he was equally committed to seek solutions that would in no way damage the existing Anglo-American accord. Actually he would have liked to cooperate ever more closely with Great Britain—whether in the Pacific or in the Caribbean—but he realized that neither the country nor the Senate would support anything in the nature of an alliance. There was no combating what he considered the "senseless prejudices" of his countrymen in the field of Anglo-American relations.

These problems were resolved at the turn of the century in what appeared to be the nation's best interest and without prejudice to Anglo-American understanding. The Open Door policy in China, the successful assertion of the right of the United States to build and fortify what became the Panama Canal, the annexation of American Samoa, and a satisfactory solution to the Alaskan boundary dispute were not only victories for American diplomacy but sign and symbol of the nation's new position in world affairs. John Hay conducted the formal negotiations that led to the immediate resolution of these problems. His diplomacy was widely hailed, and he gained immense stature at home and abroad. His contemporaries were prepared to recognize him not only as an extremely able diplomat but as a great statesman. It is necessary, however, to examine these major negotiations with somewhat more care to determine the extent to which Hay was entitled to the credit so enthusiastically accorded him.

IV

Hay's name is most closely associated with the policy of the Open Door in China. Although it was, from one point of view, no more than the projection of a policy that the United States had pursued persistently since the opening of its relations with China in the 1840s, it took on new dimensions under Hay's direction and was to acquire an importance that deeply affected the entire American position in eastern Asia. It is not an exaggeration to state that the Open Door policy led ultimately to the war with Japan, forty-odd years later.

Hay's interest in the Open Door would appear to have been first aroused not so much by concern with conditions in China as by the original British proposal, made while Hay was still in England, that the United States take joint action with Great Britain in opposing any move by the European powers that might restrict "the opening of China to the commerce of all nations." He was disappointed when President McKinley rejected this overture, but upon becoming Secretary of State, he was forced to recognize that public opinion made any such collaboration politically impossible. He consequently dropped the idea altogether.

During the winter of 1898–1899, however, pressure began to mount within the United States for some sort of action which would safeguard American commercial interests in China in the face of the continued foreign encroachments upon that hapless empire. An important argument for retention of the Philippines had been the opportunities that such a foothold in eastern Asia would afford for the expansion of American trade, and it now appeared that the powers might seek to shut the United States out altogether from their respective spheres of influence in China. The State Department was deluged with petitions and memorials from trade associations urging that something be done, and newspaper editorials became increasingly critical of what was said to be the failure of the McKinley administration to protect American interests.

Despite these pressing circumstances, it was not Hay who took the initiative in what was to become an American pronouncement on the Open Door. The proposal for such a move came from his Adviser on Far Eastern Affairs, William W. Rockhill, who had in turn been aroused to action by his close friend Alfred B. Hippisley, an Englishman in the employ of the Chinese Imperial Maritime Custom Service who was visiting Washington during the summer of 1899. These two men persuaded Hay to dispatch what were to become the famous Open Door notes, and there is indeed a delightfully casual air about the final stage in their preparation. "If you have time between now and next Wednesday," Hay wrote Rockhill from his summer home in New Hampshire on August 24, 1899, "to set down your views on this question—in the form of draft instructions to Mr. Choate, Mr. White, Mr. Tower, and Gen. Porter—I would be greatly obliged.... I am taking a good deal for granted—your presence in Washington, your leisure, and your inclination to give us a *coup d'épaule*. But if it should not be convenient, all right."

It was convenient. The instructions were duly written and were approved virtually without change by both Hay and McKinley. The first notes were dispatched on September 6 to the American envoys in Great

Britain, Germany, and Russia, and similar messages were later sent to the nation's representatives in Japan, France, and Italy.

The Open Door notes sought no more than assurance by the powers that there would be equality of trade within their respective spheres of influence in China. Rockhill would have favored taking a stronger position —a declaration that would constitute an American pledge to assist China in maintaining the integrity of the empire—but both he and Hippisley recognized the need to keep their proposals down to an absolute minimum if they hoped to win Hay's approval. Even more important, what they were suggesting was an entirely unilateral statement of policy that was directed as much against Great Britain as against any other power. Although an Englishman, Hippisley was in no way acting as a spokesman of British interests, whereas Rockhill flatly stated at this time that "England is as great an offender in China as Russia itself."

Secretary Hay's tour de force, his significant contribution in the evolution of the Open Door policy, was his bold acceptance of the extremely equivocal replies the powers made to his notes as constituting a complete endorsement of the proposed American policy. He suavely announced, on March 20, 1900, that these replies were "final and definitive." He astutely put the powers on record as approving the Open Door, thereby seeking to build up the moral pressure which would compel them to adhere to it. The American press, in spite of a more skeptical attitude in other countries, at once hailed the declaration of the Open Door policy as one of the most brilliant and important achievements in the whole history of American diplomacy.

It was also good politics—a consideration of which John Hay was always acutely aware—for it provided President McKinley with a diplomatic triumph in an election year. His administration was under attack for its aggressive policies in subduing revolt in the Philippines, but this move in China appeared not only to satisfy the demand for protection of American trade interests but also to uphold the rights of the Chinese against all foreign encroachments. It was directed against imperialism. Hay had coupled the claims of economic expansion with idealistic support for America's historic mission in supporting the cause of freedom. The United States had made an impressive entry upon the international stage. Little wonder that the American people so generally ignored the realities of the power politics of eastern Asia in applauding Hay's noble gesture.

A first test of his policy came within the year, as the Boxer Rebellion convulsed China and impelled the powers to join forces in a military expedition for the relief of the besieged foreign legations in Peking. The United States could not stand aside. It was prepared to take part in the expedition. But Hay was concerned with saving his policy, now more than ever in danger, and in seeking to do so he carried it to a logical conclusion. In a circular note to the powers on July 3, 1900, he declared that it would be the policy of the United States to seek a solution of the new crisis in China that would not only safeguard the principle of equal and impartial trade with all parts of the Chinese Empire but also preserve China's territorial and administrative entity. He did not formally ask the powers to concur in this policy, but he hoped to place them in a position where they would have to do so.

The problems created by the relief of the legations, by the powers' demands for indemnities, and by the maneuvering for diplomatic advantage in Peking were to become immensely complicated. Hay repeatedly despaired of any agreement's being reached that would safeguard China's interests, and he was forced to recognize that, although the powers continued to pay lip service to the Open Door, they had little real interest in maintaining this principle except when it was to their individual benefit to do so. At one time, in November, 1900, Hay himself seemed ready to give up altogether and to seek a naval base for the United States at Samsah Bay, in Fukien, as an American equivalent for the leased territories and spheres of influence of the other powers. This project was not publicly known at the time, was perhaps never taken very seriously, and was quickly dropped upon the objections of Japan, which felt that such an American base would intrude upon its own sphere of interest in Fukien. Nevertheless, it was indicative of the confused international crosscurrents complicating the situation in Peking.

In spite of this momentary aberration, however, Hay succeeded in exercising a moderating influence upon the demands being made by the other powers in concluding the so-called Boxer Protocol. The Chinese Empire was not dismembered. It was not true, of course, that Hay "saved" China. The further partition of her territories was prevented by the rivalries of the European nations and by their jockeying for political strength in eastern Asia. But the American assertion that the principle of Chinese territorial integrity was a natural corollary of the Open Door provided a moral basis for continued opposition to any moves to bring the tottering Manchu empire under foreign control. Here Hay's diplomacy was highly successful.

The real difficulty for the United States, as its Secretary of State soon realized, was that it had taken a position in regard to China that it was not prepared to sustain by any sort of forcible action. The national interest was not sufficiently engaged to justify any further intervention in upholding the Open Door. The American people might enthusiastically applaud Hay's generous diplomacy, but they never had the slightest intention of backing it up by arms should it be seriously challenged by any other power. Therefore, when Russia continued to press its claims for special privileges in Manchuria in complete disregard of the Open Door, Hay found himself in an equivocal position which revealed the fundamental weakness of what he was trying to do in Asia. The press might still feel that it was necessary only to reassert a high-minded principle to win its universal acceptance, but a frustrated and exasperated John Hay knew better. "The talk of the papers about our 'pre-eminent moral position giving us the authority to dictate to the world,' " he commented testily, "is mere flap-doodle."

All his diplomatic protests against Russia's subsequent maneuvers in Manchuria were unavailing. He exclaimed bitterly against the hopelessness of trying to deal with a government "with whom mendacity is a science," but the basic difficulty, he realized, was Russia's knowledge that the United States could not take a really firm stand in Manchuria. He admitted the impasse very frankly in his correspondence with a greatly disturbed Japanese government, which considered the Russian advance in Manchuria a threat to Japan's national security. The United States, Hay wrote early in 1901, was not prepared either singly or in concert with any other powers to enforce its views on the Open Door and China's political integrity "by any demonstration which could present a character of hostility to any other power."

When Japan later accepted the challenge of Russian aggression in Manchuria and the two nations found themselves at war, Hay was again to strive valiantly to sustain the principle of the Open Door by diplomatic pressure. He proposed, in February, 1904, that the belligerents respect China's neutrality and administrative entity. It then became the interest of the United States to seek a balance of the opposing forces in eastern Asia as the best means of preserving China's full independence. By the time of the Russo-Japanese conflict, however, Theodore Roosevelt was moving in to direct foreign policy in a part of the world which he had heretofore left largely to Hay. The concept of "balanced antagonisms" in eastern Asia must be attributed to the President rather than to his Secretary of State.

Hay's Far Eastern policy has been strongly criticized on various and sometimes conflicting grounds. He is said to have been completely unrealistic, accepting the idea of the Open Door largely because it had a high-minded and idealistic ring; he is said to have acted on wholly pragmatic grounds, introducing an ambitious program of "open door imperialism" in continuing support of American trade and business. Much that has been written about Hay's diplomacy interprets it in terms of later developments over which Hay, of course, had no control whatsoever and concerning which he might himself have acted quite differently from his successors in the State Department.

His motives and ideas in 1899–1900 were certainly mixed. They were compounded of concern for the development of American trade and commerce, an idealistic conception of the part the United States might

play in helping China, and the desire to make a gesture that would dramatize the nation's new role in world affairs. But when he developed the
proposals first made by Rockhill and Hippisley so as to place the United
States in the position of championing not only the Open Door but Chinese
independence, he went beyond the practical limits of American foreign
policy.

He was soon to realize that this position was untenable, and he was then
ready to retreat. But even while he was backing away from any positive
support of the Open Door, his diplomatic espousal of the doctrine helped
to fasten upon the American mind a conviction that the United States
was committed to the defense of China's territorial integrity. The subsequent history of the Open Door policy, in its broadest sense, was consequently a series of alternating advances and retreats until a final challenge
by Japan appeared to leave the United States no alternative other than
to accept war in the doctrine's defense.

V

While Hay was setting forth American policy in eastern Asia,
he was also involved in the events that were to establish American hegemony in the Caribbean as an equally important consequence of the war
with Spain. His role in this area of diplomatic activity, however, was never
so important as his role in eastern Asia. As Roosevelt increasingly assumed
direction of foreign affairs—the Venezuela incident, the Panama Canal
issue, the Santo Domingo episode, and the enunciation of the Roosevelt
Corollary to the Monroe Doctrine—Hay did little more than acquiesce
in the President's decisions and carry on the diplomatic negotiations that
put them into effect.

Hay's first task in Latin-American affairs—and this was before Roosevelt became President—was to secure a modification of the old Clayton-
Bulwer Treaty between the United States and Great Britain that would
enable the United States to build an Isthmian canal. Hay succeeded in
doing so to his own entire satisfaction in the first Hay-Pauncefote Treaty,
which was signed on February 5, 1900. But in what his critics were to call
an unwarranted surrender to Great Britain, he had not obtained recognition of the right of the United States to fortify as well as build the pro-
spective canal. An outraged Senate, doubly incensed because Hay had not
conferred with its Committee on Foreign Relations, proceeded to amend
the treaty so drastically that Great Britain refused to ratify it.

This was the occasion of Hay's most virulent outbursts against the
Senate. He attributed its attitude wholly to anti-English prejudice and
wrote angrily to one correspondent that he had "underrated the power
of ignorance and spite, acting upon cowardice." Only wiser counsels

persuaded him not to resign in protest. But the inconclusiveness of the first Hay-Pauncefote Treaty provided substantial justification for the Senate's position, if not for its actual tactics in amending the treaty. Once Hay had recovered from the shock of having his policy rejected, he proceeded to the negotiation of a new agreement. The second Hay-Pauncefote Treaty, signed November 18, 1901, in effect gave the United States everything the Senate had wanted, with tacit acknowledgement of this country's right to fortify any canal it might construct. Hay had redeemed himself, but in this instance the Senate, rather than the Secretary of State, was formulating policy.

Hay's contribution to the final settlement of the problem was nevertheless not without significance. He had conducted the difficult British negotiations with tact and skill; the English fully realized that they had a good friend at court. Great Britain's ready surrender of its interests in the Caribbean was a result of its awkward world position in the midst of the Boer War and its consequent willingness to accept the extension of the power of a friendly United States, but Hay's deft diplomacy made such a retreat far easier for the British leaders.

Before the next step was taken in the train of events that led to the actual construction of the Panama Canal, the Venezuela dispute of 1902, involving the joint blockade of that country by Great Britain and Germany to enforce the collection of debts, created for a time considerable popular excitement. Hay, who Roosevelt once said was "foolishly distrustful of the Germans," was deeply concerned over this situation and the possible threat to the Monroe Doctrine, but it was the President who formulated American policy and exerted the influence that finally led to the dispute's arbitration. The one contribution Hay would appear to have made was in persuading Roosevelt that he should not himself serve as arbitrator.

This incident involved the still highly controversial question of whether Roosevelt actually issued an ultimatum which caused Germany to accept the arbitration proposals. Although the most recent scholarship suggests that the President did indeed exert decisive pressure to force German compliance with American policy, there is no suggestion that Hay even knew of this phase of the President's personal diplomacy. "I did not consult Hay or anyone else," Roosevelt was later to state in his story of the negotiations, ". . . any more than I consulted him about the Panama business until I had acted, for councils of war don't fight."

This rather cavalier dismissal of the Secretary of State was perhaps typically Rooseveltian, but it remains true that, in both the Venezuela and the Panama affairs, Hay did little more than carry out the formal aspects of the President's policy. In respect to the negotiations and actions that finally led to the acquisition of the Panama Canal Zone in 1903, Hay drew up the treaty with Colombia, which that country then refused to ratify; dispatched the note that so promptly recognized the new republic of Panama after the extremely convenient revolt in that little country; and then concluded with efficient speed the new treaty wherein Panama granted the United States the rights for a canal zone that Colombia had refused.

This precipitate course of action, which was to bring such harsh criticism upon the unbowed head of Roosevelt, would appear to be out of character for his more diplomatic and conciliatory Secretary of State. But Hay, it appears, had much the same opinion of Colombia's obstructive tactics as did his chief. "Talking with those fellows down there," he once wrote, ". . . is like holding a squirrel in your lap and trying to keep up the conversation." He was incensed by Colombia's stand, and although he certainly had no part in instigating the revolt in Panama, he had no hesitation about acting quickly when Panamanian action opened up opportunities for an easy solution of the whole problem.

If Hay ever had any misgivings about the policy which Roosevelt was later to summarize dramatically in the statement "I took Panama," he did not express them in either his public papers or his available private correspondence. He was again a willing instrument. "I had no hesitation," Hay admitted in December, 1903, "as to the proper course to take, and have had no doubt of the propriety of it since."

The problems that next arose in the Caribbean centered on Santo Domingo and the President's efforts to forestall any recurrence of the Venezuela imbroglio. This episode did not really involve Hay; not only was Roosevelt now making policy completely on his own, but the Secretary of State's health was rapidly failing. Hay took part in the campaign of 1904 that led to Roosevelt's successful re-election and was to remain in the Cabinet, but he no longer had the strength to perform fully the duties of his office.

VI

In the meantime, the dispute over the Alaskan boundary, with which Hay had been confronted when he first assumed office, was finally reaching a settlement. There had been other issues—participation in the First International Peace Conference at The Hague, the attempt to negotiate a series of arbitration treaties, the final conclusion of the agreements establishing control over American Samoa—but they did not present any important problems of policy. On the Alaskan boundary, Hay was caught in the dilemma of trying both to uphold an American position of whose soundness he had no doubt and to maintain, at the same time, the close accord with Great Britain that he continued to consider the very foundation of American policy.

He had originally proposed, in 1899, the appointment of a six-man commission—three Americans and three Britishers—to settle the dispute. Upon Canada's rejection of this plan, a temporary *modus vivendi* had been reached and the issue remained dormant for three years. It was always in the background—during the Boer War, during the negotiations over the Open Door, during the controversy over the Hay-Pauncefote Treaties —and Hay's constant preoccupation was to prevent the Alaskan boundary question or anything else—from weakening the bonds of Anglo-American friendship. Whenever the Secretary of State was forced to act along lines that he felt endangered this accord, he exercised all his tact and all his diplomacy in easing Great Britain's path and making as acceptable as possible the concessions that circumstances might compel that country to make.

When Canada finally indicated in 1902 that it might be willing to accept the proposal that Hay had made three years earlier, the Secretary of State urged Roosevelt to authorize the negotiation of a treaty to carry this plan into effect. The President was at first highly reluctant. He was fully persuaded that Canada's claims were completely without merit, and he was consequently unwilling to submit the issue to any sort of arbitration, since this would tend to split the difference between the two contending parties. Hay argued that his plan was not arbitration: with three American members on a six-man commission, the United States could not lose, and a single pro-American vote on the part of the British would mean recognition of American rights. Still somewhat suspicious of Hay's approach, Roosevelt finally agreed in the interests of Anglo-American understanding and allowed Hay to proceed with his negotiations. In January, 1903, the Secretary succeeded in concluding the Hay-Herbert Treaty, embodying his plan for a six-man commission of impartial jurists.

But Hay still had to deal with a chief who seemed intent on upsetting his careful diplomacy. Roosevelt appointed to the commission three Americans (including Henry Cabot Lodge) whose known views hardly entitled them to be considered "impartial jurists," and he then proceeded to intimate, taking pains that his views should be informally transmitted to the British government, that unless the commission rendered a decision in favor of the United States, he would ask Congress for the necessary authority to run the boundary line as "we" thought best. Hay did everything possible to restrain Roosevelt, reminding him that, with the dispute under adjudication, the President had no warrant for expressing his own opinion, and he sought through conciliatory messages to his own friends in England to counteract Roosevelt's interference.

When the commission finally decided in this nation's favor (Lord Chief Justice Alverstone of Great Britain voting with its American members), Hay joyfully declared that "we have got everything we claimed." The question remains, however, whether it was Hay's conciliatory approach or Roosevelt's tacit threats that enabled the United States to win this diplomatic victory. Hay, in any event, saw a further vindication of his policy of friendship toward Great Britain. He believed that the cooperation he had fostered constantly in meeting the issues of both eastern Asia and the Caribbean had encouraged the peaceful settlement of the boundary dispute and that this, in turn, had strengthened still further the Anglo-American entente. If Great Britain's political isolation in Europe and its fears of the rising power of Germany were forcing the country into American arms, it was Hay who continually kept American arms open. He helped to lay the basis for that alliance among the English-speaking peoples which was for him an unattainable dream but which time would ultimately see realized.

VII

"In his eight years of office," Henry Adams wrote of John Hay, "he had solved nearly every old problem of American statesmanship, and had left little or nothing to annoy his successor. He had brought the great Atlantic powers into a working system.... For the first time in fifteen hundred years a true Roman *pax* was in sight, and would, if it succeeded, owe its virtues to him."

In the period immediately following Hay's death, there appeared to be some justification for this striking statement. The United States stood before the world as a nation that had made good its rise to power and was exercising its great influence in support of peace and international stability. It was putting its own colonial house in order, with the grant of increasing self-government to the subject peoples it had brought under its control. It was seeking a peace in eastern Asia that would safeguard the independence of China and commercial equality for the Western powers. It had built up its strength in the Caribbean and was prepared to construct a great Isthmian canal that would benefit all the world. It had resolved the issues that had been in dispute with Great Britain and had re-enforced Anglo-American friendship as the bedrock of its national policy in the new world of the twentieth century.

In many instances, however, the high promise of these developments marking American emergence on the stage of world politics was not to be fulfilled. Certainly there were still problems facing the United States that might, to put it very mildly, annoy Hay's successors in the State Department. Moreover, for all their pride in the nation's achievements, the American people were not yet fully prepared to accept the responsibilities that their new world power imposed upon them.

But, again, what part did John Hay actually play in these developments, and what view did he have of America's destiny? There is sometimes a note of frustration and even of melancholy in his private correspondence. He seemed to feel that his hands were tied and that he was being held back by a public indifferent to what he was trying to accomplish. Such complaints, however, often reflected his own indecisions and uncertainties. Hay was an internationalist in his broad conception of his country's responsibilities and opportunities, but for all his rather vague thoughts about extending to the world what Henry Adams called "McKinleyism"—the system of trusts and combinations that appeared to promise industrial peace on the domestic front—he did not importantly pursue any such ambitious program. Although he remained resolutely faithful to his sense of the importance of preserving Anglo-American friendship, his policies more generally were either dictated by events or determined by the views of stronger personalities.

Hay never fully understood—as did Theodore Roosevelt—the realities of the international politics of his day or the complex of rivalries that bedeviled his attempt to maintain the Open Door in China. He knew, however, that the United States could not retreat to the nineteenth century. Maintaining that "we must go forward," he sought to exercise a moral leadership reflecting the inherent idealism of the American people. But as a conservative who still had a somewhat nineteenth-century outlook, he was not always certain how such aims and aspirations for a peaceful world could be most effectively pursued.

Under the compulsion of an irresistible "cosmic tendency," he accepted the implications of an imperialism that he had originally opposed, and he worked willingly with McKinley for its effective implementation. Feeling driven to do something about China, he accepted the proposals of his State Department advisers for the Open Door, embarked upon a policy that he himself almost at once began to question, and involved the United States in a contradictory situation whose ultimate consequences were to be war with Japan. Seeking a free hand for the United States in the Caribbean, he at first bungled the negotiations with Great Britain and thereafter did little more in that diplomatic area than follow Roosevelt's impetuous leadership. He provided a formula for settlement of the Alaskan boundary dispute, but it was the President who exercised the pressure that was perhaps most responsible for the decision recognizing American claims.

Yet such considerations do not give the whole story of John Hay as Secretary of State, any more than do Henry Adams's fulsome encomiums or the extravagant praise of so many other of his contemporaries. Hay made a great contribution to his country through his exceedingly able, dignified, and restrained representation of its interests during the first years of its coming of international age. Even though he did not always initiate policy, no one could have conducted the diplomacy it entailed more skillfully. With a fine gift for the proper phrase and a keen sense of what a later generation would call public relations, he was always an excellent spokesman for American interests. At a time when the other major nations were inclined to look very much askance upon this newcomer among the great powers, Hay won both for himself and for the United States a high degree of international respect.

John Hay was more a diplomat than a statesman. The distinction with which he filled the former role nevertheless entitles him to an honored position among the Secretaries of State of the twentieth century.

3

Elihu Root

1905-1909

BY CHARLES W. TOTH
University of Puerto Rico

On February 1, 1904, the day that Elihu Root resigned as Secretary of War, President Roosevelt wrote to Mrs. Root: "I shall never have, and can never have, a more loyal friend, a more faithful and wiser adviser, nor will the government ever be served by any man with greater zeal, efficiency and success." Root's years as Secretary of War in the McKinley and Roosevelt administrations had been successful indeed, and among the most satisfying in his long career as public servant and elder statesman. His appointment to this post, during the tumultuous months following the Spanish-American War, was due primarily to his reputation both for administrative efficiency and for legal talent and learning. Hesitating to accept an office about which he knew nothing, Root was told over the phone that "President McKinley . . . is not looking for anyone who knows anything about war or for anyone who knows anything about the army; he has got to have a lawyer to direct the government of these Spanish islands and you are the lawyer he wants."

Root's record as Secretary of War is beyond the scope of this study. Suffice it to say that he contributed all that McKinley desired, serving with a kind of quiet detachment which made it possible for him to maintain his administrative efficiency even in the face of hostility and attack. By 1902 Root had organized America's new little empire in the Caribbean and western Pacific, much to the relief of the Republican leadership. Whether he had secured peace, especially in the Philippines, was questionable, but he did bring order. Fortunately, Secretary Root's approach was humanitarian and paternalistic, not despotic. Speaking before the Union League

40

Club in 1925 at a dinner given in honor of his eightieth birthday, Root looked back upon his work with the remark that "Cuba and Puerto Rico and the Philippines set off against the treatment of Mexico and the Indians show how our people have changed and grown in grace."

Although President McKinley was not looking for anyone who knew anything about the Army or war, Root did not hesitate to explore these matters, and he initiated basic reforms in the organization of the Army which were to prove valuable for the future. He introduced the General Staff system, reorganized the National Guard, and established an Army War College. In retrospect, these efforts were recognized as vital to America's successful participation in World War I, and at one time Newton D. Baker went so far as to remark that "without that contribution from him, the participation of the United States in the World War would necessarily have been a confused, ineffective and discreditable episode."

Root became Secretary of State on July 7, 1905, following the death of John Hay, with whom he had worked on terms of close friendship. Ever the lawyer, Root frequently remarked that his only client was his country. But more often than not his client was Theodore Roosevelt, and, indeed, Root knew his client well. As a "strong" President, Roosevelt was often his own Department of State, and Root, as Secretary, made no attempt to overshadow his chief, concerning himself primarily with the unenviable task of carrying out the details of actions initiated in the White House. This is not to imply, however, that Root was merely a meek servant. On the contrary, the record shows clearly that Roosevelt relied considerably on the advice of his Secretary and that Root never hesitated to give his opinion on the problems which confronted the administration. But he always remained the "faithful adviser" to the President, whom he once referred to as "the most advisable of men."

Root was of considerable value to President Roosevelt on the political scene. His association with well-to-do elements in American society during his years as a corporation lawyer helped to forge a closer link between Roosevelt and the more conservative membership of the party. Speaking frequently before business and professional groups on behalf of the President, Root tried to allay some of the fears which he knew existed. In one of his many preconvention speeches in 1904, he told the Union League Club that "President Roosevelt was the greatest conservative force for the protection of property and capital . . . during the years that have elapsed since President McKinley's death." Interestingly enough, Root not only believed what he said but apparently never changed his mind. A decade later he would lament before the same group that "when we elected McKinley . . . it was the business man of the United States who controlled the election. . . . I say the scepter has passed. The control has changed, and . . . there lies the reason for the stagnation, the hesitation, the timidity, the unwillingness of American enterprise today." However, Root was not thinking of Roosevelt's "Square Deal," but of Wilson's "New Freedom." He was always an orthodox Republican.

President Roosevelt, perhaps instinctively, regarded Root as a healthy counterforce to his own enthusiastic, and sometimes impulsive, manner; and Root did exercise a valuable check on Roosevelt's easily excitable nature. But aside from these considerations, one of the basic reasons for Root's appointment as Secretary of State was his proven ability to work with Congress. Root's predecessor, John Hay, was unable, or unwilling, to work with Senate leaders, and he evidently considered it beneath the dignity of his office to appear before congressional committees. Not so with Root, who felt that frequent discussions between executive and congressional leaders on diplomatic problems were essential to the eventual success of the nation's foreign policy. Secretary Root once declared that "the committees are anxious to do what is best for the country, and when you have created such a belief in their minds, you can carry on a campaign." But Root was ever conscious of the problem of formulating foreign policy for a democracy that was accustomed to achieving success without costly wars or serious diplomatic concessions. "It appears that diplomacy as viewed from the opposition American standpoint has but two phases," he once wrote to Hay. "If we agree with any other power on any subject there is a secret alliance; if we disagree there is a conspiracy to get up a war and foster a soldier on the back of every American laborer." With Root as Secretary of State, Roosevelt enjoyed somewhat smoother going with Congress than he had during Hay's incumbency. Root was always realistic enough to know how far Congress would go on a particular issue. Moreover, Root, as well as Roosevelt, enjoyed the friendship and support of such Senate leaders as Henry Cabot Lodge and Shelby M. Cullom.

Historians generally agree that Root did not inaugurate any significant changes in the character of American foreign policy. By 1905, the interests of the United States had become world-wide, and there was an increasing demand for American participation in world affairs. As President Roosevelt admitted to André Tardieu in 1908: "I wish that all Americans would realize . . . that we are and that we shall be involved in all great questions . . . the whole American people must become accustomed to this idea. They must be made to feel and understand these international interests." This feeling was basic to Roosevelt's thinking on foreign-policy matters, and as Germany and Japan emerged on the international scene as militant forces, he gave increasing attention to the question of the balance of power. Germany concerned him especially, and as American interests became more and more linked with the Atlantic powers, it also became increasingly imperative, as Roosevelt stated, that the United States help "keep matters on an even keel in Europe."

II

To help keep matters on "an even keel," Roosevelt made available the good offices of the United States in establishing peace between Russia and Japan and brought about American participation in the Algeciras Conference in 1906. Actually it was the German Kaiser who prepared the way for this nation's participation at Algeciras, with his appeal to Roosevelt to help settle the conflicting claims of Germany and France in Morocco. The President moved warily at first, in part because the recent death of John Hay had deprived him of a close personal adviser. But his success in terminating the Russo-Japanese War in 1905 with the Treaty of Portsmouth had given him enormous encouragement and prestige. One American ambassador confided to Root that Roosevelt's work at Portsmouth "singles him out as the arbitrator to whom all can turn when dissentions threaten to bring on war in any part of the globe." However, the opportunity to assert his power and add to his prestige was not the primary factor which determined Roosevelt's willingness to involve himself in the affairs of the world. The President was concerned with any problem that might ultimately affect the interests and security of the United States, and the crisis in Morocco was just such a problem. President Roosevelt was quick to understand that the crisis, although European in origin, was more than European in scope. The resignation of Delcassé, the French premier who sought a unilateral disposition of Moroccan sovereignty, had eased somewhat the fear of war. But Germany had thus scored a diplomatic victory, and the situation was made more tense by the fact that the German government insisted upon a settlement of the Moroccan question by a conference of powers. It was upon this meeting that the honor of Germany appeared to hinge.

Roosevelt finally persuaded the French government to accept the idea of a conference, but not until he had committed the United States to the support of French claims and ultimate French hegemony in Morocco. Although Roosevelt declared that he would "treat both sides with absolute justice," he did not hesitate to instruct Ambassador Henry White to "keep friendly with all but help France get what she ought." Henry Cabot Lodge, just returning from Europe, expressed the similar conviction that the American delegate "must keep on the best terms with the German delegate, and yet when it comes to action support France to the extent of his power." The Moroccan crisis brought to the surface the pro-British, anti-German feelings and sentiments of an influential segment of

American leadership. Roosevelt had already clearly indicated that he shared this attitude when, following the Alaskan boundary settlement, he concluded happily that "I feel very differently towards England from the way I feel towards Germany." As the years rolled on toward World War I, there really was no doubt where American sentiment lay. As Foster Rhea Dulles has written, "The old balance of power was threatened ... and in the new interplay of power politics, [the United States] moved steadily toward a closer *rapprochement* with Great Britain as that nation whose interests most nearly coincided with her own."

Root took up his duties as Secretary of State in the midst of the crisis in Morocco. It was his initial reaction that "our interests are not sufficient to justify us in taking a leading part." At the same time, however, he could see an opportunity for America to exercise "moral influence." Even when the conference at Algeciras was under way, in February, 1906, Root could not share the enthusiasm of the President. Root wrote to Whitelaw Reid in London that "we have not yet considered that there was a situation in which any move by us would be practically useful." And a few months later, while on his tour of South America, the Secretary presumed that Brazil and the United States were "alike in that we have no concern in the primary objects of European diplomacy; we are free from the traditions, from the controversies." Yet when Root sent the instructions for the American delegation at Algeciras, it was the President's view which prevailed. Henry White was told, among other things, "to keep the peace and make it as difficult as possible for any one to pick a quarrel."

The conference at Algeciras was frightening to many Americans, for it appeared to threaten the tradition of isolation which pledged honest friendship with all nations but entangling alliances with none. And this tradition was hallowed, since the isolationists went straight back to the Founding Fathers in defense of their position. The words of Washington, Jefferson, and Adams, quoted largely out of context, were uncritically accepted as final.

Root understood clearly the depth of this isolationist sentiment and managed to steer a middle course between the traditional reliance on the Atlantic and Roosevelt's intention to have the United States play a more active part in world affairs. Thus to a considerable extent he personified the confusion in American thinking about the role which the United States should play as a nation of expanding interests. Although basically distrustful of the balance-of-power concept and doubtful about the value of American participation in the Algeciras Conference, which he considered to be based upon a "tenuous thread of interest," Root's legal mind produced the required mental gymnastics. Eventually he found what appeared to him a satisfactory solution: the United States had been able to preserve peace during the crisis, not by the power of its involvement, but rather by its "power of detachment." A neat semantic trick, indeed, but such verbal juggling was increasingly resorted to as the United States faced the growing demand for participation and leadership in world affairs but remained unwilling to pay the price of power. The classic example was the insistence upon the use of the term "associated power" instead of "allied power" during World War I. As Julius Pratt has remarked of this hairsplitting, "The distinction was not important—a mere gesture out of respect to the American tradition against 'entangling alliances.' " But it was of great importance to the isolationists.

In order to satisfy the Senate, Root disavowed any political interest in Morocco as well as any responsibility for the enforcement of the agreements made. He informed Senator Cullom of Illinois, Chairman of the Committee on Foreign Relations, that "the reservation under which we signed [the treaty] was made as broad as possible.... The Committee will see that we have carefully avoided any entanglement in European affairs." The Senate consented and ratified the treaty, but not without appending the reservation that American participation at Algeciras was "without purpose to depart from the traditional foreign policy which forbids participation by the United States in the settlement of political questions which are entirely European in their scope." For most Americans the Senate's reservation made it clear that Algeciras did not inaugurate a new era in American foreign relations.

III

Root undertook the task of becoming his own State Department with his proposed trip to Latin America during the summer of 1906, and the President allowed him to have full rein. As Roosevelt later remarked, "We have done more as regards these states than ever before in the history of the State Department. This work has been entirely Root's. My part in it has been little more than cordially backing him up." Actually, the success of the proposed visit to South America (which finally included Brazil, Uruguay, Argentina, Chile, Peru, Panama, and even Colombia) depended largely upon the absence of the Roosevelt personality. The tour followed hard on the heels of the Roosevelt Corollary to the Monroe Doctrine, the announcement of which had added greatly to Latin America's already existing suspicion, distrust, and hostility toward the United States. It was thought that only Secretary Root, acting alone, could bring any substantial success to the purpose of spreading what one scholar has referred to as the "Root Doctrine" of friendly interest and kindly consideration.

This is not to say that Root proposed to disavow the Roosevelt Corollary, which provided a formula for "preventive intervention" on the part of the

United States by which all excuse for European political involvement in the Latin-American states, especially in the region of the Caribbean, would be removed. As Roosevelt had put it to Congress in December, 1904, "Chronic wrongdoing or ... impotence ... may force the United States to the exercise of an international police power." In the following year the Dominican Republic, under the first application of this principle, virtually became an American protectorate. Root had recognized the opportunity to expand American achievements abroad by promoting efficiency and order on beleaguered islands, and he often looked back on such national efforts with great satisfaction. "Puerto Rico now is a prosperous and happy community," he wrote in 1904, "and in the Philippines, where they knew not law ... where the poor, little brown men had never heard of aught but arbitrary power, they are beginning to learn what liberty means ... we shall teach the people of Central and South America the same lesson." Then, in a burst of Anglo-Saxon pride, and perhaps with the Dominican Republic already in his thoughts, Root declared finally that "our army officers have become ... commissioners of charity ... teachers of the art of self-government."

Root was the author of the Platt amendment, which gave the United States the right to intervene in Cuba, and he took occasion to remark that this amendment supplied a basis in international law for intervention under the Monroe Doctrine. On one occasion he referred to the Platt amendment as "the Monroe Doctrine, but with international force," thereby anticipating by several years the corollary which President Roosevelt later supplied. Yet on his tour through South America Root tried hard to relegate the question of the Monroe Doctrine to the background, although he could not succeed entirely. In his major address to the Third Conference of the American Republics at Rio de Janeiro, which was the immediate reason for his visit, Root felt that at least a passing remark was necessary to ease Latin-American concern. On this occasion he asserted that the Monroe Doctrine was nothing more than an abiding faith among the people of the United States in the ability of the Latin-American states to govern themselves. It was ironic that Secretary Root gave the speech in a building which the Brazilians had constructed especially for the occasion and which they had christened the Palacio de Monroe.

Whatever his earlier remarks concerning Latin America, Root harbored the contempt toward the republics to the south which was held by some of his contemporaries, including President Roosevelt himself. Root had that sense of superiority which resulted from a deep-founded belief in the great civilizing force of Anglo-Saxon institutions, together with a faith in the messianic role of American democratic ideals. As he had remarked on the eve of his Secretaryship, "How noble and elevating are the possibilities of the future. Going through our period of isolation, passing beyond the time of selfishness where we were . . . thinking only of our own interests, there is opening before us the vista of missionary life." Root gave expression to a vision of American influence in the world which was as old as the Declaration of Independence and which had been a recurring theme in American thought during the generations following the establishment of the Republic.

Shortly after Root's return from South America, President Roosevelt wrote at some length to Congress (December, 1906) on the subject of the Secretary's tour. "An idea had become prevalent," declared Roosevelt, "that our assertion of the Monroe Doctrine implied an assumption of superiority, and of a kind of right to exercise some kind of protectorate. . . . It was part of Secretary Root's mission to dispel this unfounded impression." Root, of course, could hardly dispel this impression when the events in Cuba, Panama, and the Dominican Republic revealed that it was hardly unfounded. Yet Secretary Root's visit to South America was not unsuccessful. He had worked hard during the months prior to his departure to develop the most cordial relations with the Latin-American Ministries in Washington, and his intimate friendship with Ambassador Joaquin Nabuco of Brazil helped greatly to produce that initial success in Rio de Janeiro upon which the rest of the trip depended. The leaders of South America were indeed flattered by the historic visit of an American Secretary of State, a visit which was in itself symbolic of things to come in the history of American diplomacy in the twentieth century.

Although the Rio Conference did not produce any concrete settlements in regard to the major issues before it (it referred the questions of intervention and arbitration to the coming conference at The Hague), Root's doctrine of "friendly interest and kindly consideration" was not without its rewards. His intellectual vigor and personal charm did much to foster more cordial relations between the United States and the great continent to the south, and during the remainder of his term Root worked incessantly to further those relations. During the Hague Conference in 1907, he sought successfully to obtain proper representation for Latin America. Root promoted the organization of the Central American Peace Conference, which created the first arbitral system for that region. It was his influence that prompted Andrew Carnegie to provide the funds for the erection of the Pan American Union Building at Washington in 1908. Above all, and much to his credit, Root sought steadily over a period of more than two years to lessen the hostility of Colombia which had resulted from Roosevelt's successful, though questionable, action in securing the Isthmus of Panama. Quite dramatically, a few hours before he left office in January, 1909, Root managed to negotiate a series of accords with the Colombian authorities. Considering the condescending atmosphere in which he performed this work, marked above all by the negative attitude of the President himself, this negotiation can be considered a remarkable achievement. However, even this effort proved fruitless when a sudden change of government occurred in Colombia shortly after Root's retirement.

It seems apparent that Root's special concern for the republics to the south brought a more moderate approach on the part of the Roosevelt administration in its later dealings with the republics of the Caribbean. In 1904, for example, President Roosevelt was impatient with the situation in Venezuela, stating to Secretary Hay that only intervention would ultimately teach "those Dagos" a sense of decency. To Root the crisis in Venezuela was a direct threat to his policy of building friendship in Latin America, and he urged patience toward the Castro regime. On the eve of his departure for South America, Root wrote to President Roosevelt that "Venezuelan affairs should be allowed to rest until the Conference is over." After his return to the United States, Root wished to preserve the fruits of his trip, and although on occasion he admitted sadly that the Venezuelans were governed by an irresponsible tyrant, he wrote to Carnegie that "to use force with Castro would only help him and would be an abandonment of principles, while if let alone Castro by following his methods would destroy himself." In the meantime the Secretary's influence helped to bring about a suspension of the Roosevelt Corollary, if not its modification, when the French Ambassador in Washington was told that France could adopt a policy of intervention in Venezuela on the promise that there would be no permanent occupation of territory. The fact that the Ambassador enjoyed a privileged position in Washington and was on very intimate terms of friendship with Root accounts in part for the modification. Besides, a closer relationship between the United States and France had developed as a result of the Moroccan crisis.

IV

On October 11, 1906, the San Francisco Board of Education issued an order stating that "the Trustees shall have the power to exclude children of filthy or vicious habits ... [or suffering] from contagious or infectious diseases, and also to establish separate schools for Indian children and for children of Mongolian or Chinese descent." With a steady flow of Japanese coming through the Hawaiian Islands into Mexico and Canada, and eventually into California, there was no doubt at what group this proposed legislation was being directed. The Japanese government did not hesitate in issuing its protest. Considerable diplomatic activity ensued, finally culminating in the now-famous "Gentlemen's Agreement" of 1907, in which the United States agreed that Japan might issue passports "to former residents, to parents, wives or children of residents, and those already having agricultural interests," and both Washington and Tokyo pledged themselves to check the illegal flow of Japanese immigrants into the United States.

The importance of the Gentlemen's Agreement to American diplomatic history is twofold. First, it illustrates the thinking of the Roosevelt administration in connection with the rise of Japanese power in the Pacific. Second, it led to the Root-Takahira Agreement of 1908, which brought a new orientation in American foreign policy with respect to the Far East, although this was not admitted at the time. The dominant theme in American Far Eastern policy since the turn of the century had centered about the so-called Open Door for China, which had been proclaimed by Root's predecessor, John Hay. This policy, which sought to restrain the imperialist activities of the great powers with regard to the amorphous Chinese empire, finally produced a series of somewhat reluctant agreements to respect Chinese territorial and administrative integrity and to adhere to the principle of equal trading in the respective spheres of influence. Heralded by the McKinley administration as a great diplomatic achievement, it was in reality a serious overcommitment on the part of the United States, a fact which became increasingly obvious as Russia and Japan began to extend their influence at the expense of China. This nation's unwillingness to stand behind Hay's celebrated diplomatic victory confronted the Roosevelt administration with a serious challenge as early as 1901, when the Japanese demanded to know what position the United States would take as a result of Russian encroachment in Manchuria. Secretary Hay was forced to acknowledge "that the United States was not prepared . . . to enforce [the Open Door] . . . by any demonstration which would present a character of hostility to any other power." The obvious disinclination of the United States to back up its commitments in the Far East became even more evident after Japan defeated Russia in 1905.

During the summer of 1907, when Secretary Root was absent from Washington because of illness, President Roosevelt approached a stage of panic in his fear of possible war with Japan, a fear which was accentuated by the fact that the President had not been so successful as he had hoped in obtaining congressional approval of further naval construction. "I am more concerned over this Japanese situation than almost any other," Roosevelt confided to Root, and the President's anxiety reached such a pitch that he brought the entire Board of Education from San Francisco to the White House, together with the city's mayor, who was under indictment at the time for bribery and embezzlement, in order to impress them with the fact that the problem in California involved the whole country, with peace or war with Japan hanging in the balance. "Thank heaven we have the navy in shape," the President wrote to his Secretary; but the shape of the Navy apparently did not give Roosevelt full peace of mind, for at one of the Cabinet meetings he discussed the shipment of mortars to the Philippines for defense against possible invasion. Secretary of War William Howard Taft submitted a detailed report to Roosevelt, outlining the proper steps for defending the Pacific islands and the West Coast. Postmaster General George Meyer wrote that Roosevelt on one occasion during the summer of 1907 really considered a Japanese attack "imminent or liable."

The mounting tension was eased somewhat in September by the cordial reception that Secretary Taft received in Tokyo. In his famous telegram, Taft stated that "the Japanese government is most anxious to avoid war; they are in no financial condition to undertake it." Root held the same opinion and, in fact, had never really shared Roosevelt's fear of imminent attack, although he was not unconcerned over the growth of ill feeling. At one point Root warned the President that "nothing will disturb the smug satisfaction with which the San Francisco officials pursue a policy of insult and irritation sure to land us in war."

This growing concern over the possibility of war with Japan in large part helps to explain the Root-Takahira Agreement, an agreement which was greeted, by national habit, as a significant victory for American diplomacy. True, the Open Door policy was proclaimed again, with both nations promising "to preserve the common interest of all powers in China by supporting by all pacific means at their disposal the independence and integrity of China and the principle of equal opportunity... of all nations in the Empire." However, both countries also firmly resolved "to reciprocally respect the territorial possessions belonging to each other." One important clause declared that "the policy of both governments [be] directed to the maintenance of the existing *status quo* in the region above mentioned."

Professor Richard Leopold, a recent biographer of Root, has accused scholars of having pored over the clauses of the Root-Takahira Agreement "as if they were a Biblical text." But the truth of the matter is that this agreement represented a significant diplomatic victory for the Japanese. The American policy of protecting the common interest in China was predicated upon the use of "all pacific means," and the growth of Japanese power challenged both the method and the objectives of that policy, as had the extension of Russian influence earlier. Faced with what he thought was the possibility of war, Roosevelt sought the preservation of good relations at the expense of the principles of John Hay. Writing to President Taft in 1910, Roosevelt touched upon the heart of the matter when he remarked that "it was peculiarly our interest not to take any steps as regards Manchuria which will give the Japanese cause to feel, with or without reason, that we are hostile to them, or a menace—in however slight a degree—to their interests." It might be added that President

Roosevelt, basically a realist, was not unaware that the Open Door was a policy that the United States could not enforce. "I do not believe," Roosevelt wrote, "in our taking any position anywhere unless we can make good...if the Japanese choose to follow a course of conduct to which we are adverse, we cannot stop it unless we are prepared to go to war."

Actually, neither the Roosevelt administration nor the American public was hostile toward Japan (although suspicion and fear were present), and the world cruise of the American fleet in 1908 was nothing more than a precautionary move at a trying moment in diplomatic relations. Perhaps the President spoke for American opinion when he wrote to the chairman of the House Committee on Military Affairs that "Russia's triumph [in 1905] would have been a blow to civilization." Japan, then, stood for progress and civilization—Russia for tyranny and barbarism. For both Roosevelt and Root the events of 1904–1905 in the western Pacific represented a re-enactment of the story of David and Goliath. A few days after the surprise attack upon the Russian fleet by the Japanese at Port Arthur, Root had spoken glowingly of Japan's success, asserting that "the reason why the little Japanese torpedo boats were able to destroy the power of great Russia...was that the Japanese hold the love of country...to a degree that has never been equalled since the days when Rome conquered the world." And on the eve of the Gentlemen's Agreement, speaking before the American Society for International Law, Root declared that "we have always been proud of [Japan's]...wonderful development—proud of the genius of the race that in a single generation adapted an ancient feudal system...to the most advanced standards of modern Europe and America."

What, then, was the significance of this sympathy for Japan? Perhaps Roosevelt summed it up well in his later remark to Taft that the Open Door was an excellent principle in so far as it could be maintained by diplomatic agreement. In other words, if the United States would not actively maintain this principle beyond the use of moral force, what could be better than to hand this task over to a "friendly civilized nation" which would undertake to fight America's battle in defense of the Open Door? Though this would admittedly involve some risk, it was an attractive idea. At the same time, Japan would act as a check upon Russian attempts to expand in Manchuria. Interestingly enough, Roosevelt never lost sight of the value to the United States of the balance of power in the Pacific, so that even though he felt that a Russian triumph in 1905 would have been "a blow to civilization," he also believed, as he declared to Senator Lodge, that Russia's "destruction as an Eastern Asiatic Power would also...be unfortunate. It is best that she should be left face to face with Japan so that each may have a moderating action on the other."

Root had the task of dealing with the Chinese reaction to the agreement of 1908. Chinese officials, wisely fearful of Japanese ambition in the Far East, felt that the new agreement assured them nothing more than the privilege of not being further dissected unless all had equal slices. Root was impatient with Chinese criticism and hostility, and his attitude toward China represents the one exception to the consistent application of his doctrine of "friendly interest and kindly consideration." This impatience had already manifested itself earlier, in connection with the Chinese attempt to get the United States to amend its exclusion laws. Root was not unopposed to amendment, but he was angered at the Chinese boycott of American goods. At one time he considered a policy of holding the Chinese government responsible for the damage to American commerce. When the able Chinese Minister in Washington, Chentung Liang Cheng, told Secretary Root that he failed to see how his government could compel Chinese merchants to purchase American products if they preferred the products of other nations, Root replied that the boycott was being sponsored by the Chinese government and that the latter had no legal right over the economic affairs of the nation. On top of this surprising remark, Root admonished the Chinese Minister to use his influence to bring the boycott to an end, reminding him that the American remission of indemnity for the Boxer Rebellion could be discontinued at any time. Root was then satisfied that the United States had shown "quiet, firm maintenance of our position" with respect to Asia.

V

In the midst of this anxious diplomatic activity, Secretary Root became involved in a project which turned out to be a lifelong endeavor —the establishment of a permanent international court of justice, a kind of supreme court to which the grievances of nations could be brought for impartial adjudication. The immediate event that stimulated Root was the Second Hague Conference, held at last in 1907. Although Root was not successful in obtaining anything more than a system of voluntary arbitration, he continued to devote his remaining years as elder statesman to the pursuit of a permanent court.

Several years of negotiation preceded the meeting of the Second Hague Conference. President Roosevelt had taken the initiative in 1904, but the Russo-Japanese War prevented any progress. When, in 1905, the Russian Minister suggested that the Czar be allowed to call the conference, Roosevelt wrote to Root that he did not mind at all, since he did not particularly want "to appear as a professional peace advocate—a kind of sublimated being of the Godkin or Schurz variety." When the Czar finally arranged the meeting for the summer of 1906, Root sought successfully to postpone it until the following year, with the argument that it would conflict with the scheduled meeting of the Third Pan-American Conference. The Latin-American republics had requested a general invitation in 1901, and it was Root's intention to champion this invitation in the interest of hemispheric unity and good will.

The invitation from St. Petersburg stressed the idea of promoting international peace but, unlike the invitation of 1899, avoided mention of disarmament. The American delegation was instructed not to press for disarmament if the European powers were opposed. As Root wrote to Henry White, "If ... Europe appears unwilling, we should hardly feel called upon to try to force disarmament upon her." Actually there were many, including President Roosevelt, who had mixed feelings about the disarmament issue, especially since it appeared to revolve primarily around the question of naval construction. Roosevelt was an advocate of a larger navy and, during 1906 and 1907, was actually trying to obtain the necessary funds from Congress. Yet the Roosevelt administration did not want to convey the impression that the United States opposed disarmament, and Root instructed the Hague delegation that, if the subject was brought up, "we should let it be known that we favored it." Roosevelt's solution to this apparent conflict was the suggestion that the United States should stress reduction in the size of battleships rather than reduction in quantity. The President feared the impractical approach of the visionaries in a world which was rapidly growing more complex, and he wrote to Reid in London that "we must not grow sentimental and commit some Jefferson-Bryan-like piece of idiotic folly such as would be entailed if the free people that have free governments put themselves at the hopeless disadvantage compared with the military despotisms." Continuing this theme in a letter to Carnegie, Roosevelt remarked that he was truly interested in disarmament and that "it would be safe ... if there were some system of international police; but there is now no such system."

Root's primary interest in the Hague Conference lay not in disarmament but rather in something which he considered much more fundamental—the creation of an arbitral system which would strike at the very roots of war. In this sense he, too, was something of a visionary and an idealist. Root's approach to the complicated subject of war and peace in the twentieth century was strictly that of a legalist. He viewed the crises of his time, not as expressions of great social and political movements, but as international disputes "ultimately based upon conflicts as to rights, which are based on facts and therefore justiciable." As for the more complicated matter of conflicting policies and feelings, Root suggested that these be disposed of by "reason and kindly consideration." For Root, to whom life had been kind, the world was essentially a reasonable place, with a substantial amount of international law and a universal desire for justice and order already in existence. The solution, then, was a simple one,

if only men could be made to understand. It consisted essentially of selecting competent jurists from all parts of the world who could judge the
conflicts over rights. The possibility of war would thus be disposed of
through "the sense of honorable obligation which characterizes the judicial departments of civilized nations." Year after year Root hammered
out this theme before the American Society of International Law (of
which he became president in 1906), stating that it should be the policy
of the United States to establish and extend the rules of right conduct
accepted by "the common judgment of the millions of sane and honest
people." "All over the world," continued Root, "the great need of civilization now is the renaissance of respect for the law."

Although Root had to be satisfied merely with the suggestion for voluntary arbitration at the Hague Conference (the principle of obligatory
arbitration was accepted in the abstract only), what he actually worked for
was the establishment of a truly permanent court based upon obligatory
arbitration. As Root told the meeting of the National Peace Congress in
1907, "It seems natural to us that nations, however great, and rulers, however powerful, should go before a court and submit the question whether
their actions and their views accord with the principles of justice." In
stressing the need for an international court, Root remarked that "arbi-
trators too often act diplomatically rather than judicially; they measure
their responsibility and their duty by the traditions, the sentiments, and
the sense of honorable obligation." Root, then, preferred the lawyer's
"sense of honorable obligation" and had little confidence in the ultimate
value of diplomacy. "Instead of a sense of responsibility for impartial
judgment which weighs upon the judicial officers," declared Root on
numerous occasions, "an international arbitration is often regarded as an
occasion for diplomatic adjustment." Thus for Root the technique of
"diplomatic adjustment" was fraught with all kinds of danger. Always
the lawyer, with the lawyer's worship of the sanctity of contract, he
sought to reduce international affairs to a justiciable level and to bring
all mankind before the bench of human reason. However, there would
still be room for diplomacy, since policies and feelings would have to be
dealt with by "kindly consideration."

Root, like many of his contemporaries, retained his basic distrust of
diplomacy, a distrust which was later intensified by the shock of World
War I which, he complained, "began by a denial on the part of a very
great power that treaties are obligatory." Root was then to feel even
more strongly that "concerts of Europe and alliances and ententes and
skillful balances of power all lead ultimately to war.... Only the possibility of establishing real restraint by law seems to remain."

Root's plan for a court of arbitral justice failed of adoption at the Second
Hague Conference when the representatives deadlocked on the question

of how the judges should be selected. This question remained unsettled until Root's suggestions were incorporated into the World Court plan after World War I. A resolution was finally adopted at The Hague in 1907, however, pledging the pacific settlement of international disputes by voluntary arbitration. At the time, it was generally understood that the principle of the Anglo-French Arbitration Treaty of 1903 would prevail, which declared that questions would be submitted "provided that they do not affect the vital interests, the independence, or the honor of the countries involved." And it was with this understanding that the Senate accepted the Hague Convention of 1907. But the Senate added the limitation that nothing contained in the convention "shall be so construed as to require the United States to depart from its traditional policy of not intruding upon, interfering with, or entangling itself in the political questions of policy ... of any foreign state."

The Hague meeting made no progress on the question of disarmament other than the formal acknowledgement of the serious increase in armaments and the suggestion that "the governments should undertake again the serious study of this question." Although the results of the conference received considerable criticism in the United States, Root refused to be pessimistic and appeared satisfied that the Hague meeting "was another major step toward the reasonable and peaceful regulation of international conduct." Speaking before the National Peace Congress, he remarked that the world had now entered upon an orderly process through which, step by step, "there may be continued progress toward making the practice of civilized nations conform to their peaceful professions." In other words, Root was satisfied with small gains in the hope that time would remove major obstacles. Perhaps future conferences would adopt the means toward a more effective system of guaranteeing a reasonable and peaceful regulation of international conduct. Root never lost his confidence in the ultimate value of the conference system for dispelling misunderstandings and allaying fears. Following World War I, he continued to insist that, if Sir Edward Grey had secured the conference he sought in July, 1914, the great war would have been averted. However, Root never developed much interest in any sort of league of nations, although he was later to accept the idea with reservations. In the speech he prepared for the acceptance of the Nobel Prize in 1913, Root declared that the world was not ready for a parliament of nations to police against war and that "there is no nation in the world which would seriously consider a proposal so shocking to the national pride and patriotism of its people."

For Root there were other accomplishments at The Hague which were significant. In the first place, he was pleased by the presence of the Latin-American republics, believing strongly that this signalized the recognition of South America as an active force in the affairs of the world. Yet all was not smooth-going, for although the United States sponsored the Porter resolution, which forbade the use of force by any nation to collect debts, the Latin delegates objected to the fact that it provided exceptions. The employment of force was allowed if the debtor refused to arbitrate or, having arbitrated, refused to abide by the decision. The Latin-American representatives effectively opposed the Porter resolution, but they failed to gain general acceptance of the Drago Doctrine, which forbade the use of force under any condition.

Root was also gratified by his successful effort, at The Hague, to continue the work of Olney and Hay in securing bilateral treaties of arbitration. The treaties arranged by Hay had been withdrawn by Roosevelt in 1905, when the Senate rejected the idea of a general treaty and insisted that a separate treaty be made concerning each matter to come before a board of arbitration. It required much diligence on the part of the Secretary to persuade the President to change his mind. But Root eventually succeeded, and by the eve of his retirement he had managed to negotiate twenty-four bilateral arbitration treaties. The consent of the Senate was required for each decision, and no treaty was to touch upon the "vital interests, the independence, or the honor of the countries involved." But here again Root was satisfied with small gains. And to his great satisfaction, on his very last day in office he signed, together with James Bryce, an arbitration treaty between the United States and Great Britain which finally led to a solution of the Newfoundland fisheries dispute that had plagued both countries since 1783. The Senate quickly consented, and President Taft wisely selected the former Secretary of State to represent the United States at The Hague, thereby helping Root crown his "greatest diplomatic achievement" with the success it deserved.

VI

One of Root's most substantial contributions was the strengthening of the diplomatic corps through much-needed reform. This reform was brought about by the extension of the merit system to the Consular Service through an Executive order of July 27, 1906. There was considerable opposition to Root's efforts, but he had the necessary backing of the President. The State Department itself (which was a completely separate division until 1924) needed reorganization rather than reform, but Root's efforts in this direction amounted to very little, because of the pressure of other business. He did allow finally for the system of divisions within the Department by authorizing the creation of the Division of Far Eastern Affairs in 1908. Philip C. Jessup, his biographer, suggests that whatever reluctance Root had in this matter was largely the result of his personal dislike of Huntington Wilson, the Assistant Secretary who had devised the reorganization scheme. Root also suggested the plan, adopted later, which provided for members of the home service to go into the field for experience.

On the eve of Secretary Root's resignation in January, 1909, President Roosevelt wrote to him that "in my judgment you will be regarded as the greatest and ablest man who has ever filled the position of Secretary of State." Although such letters of commendation are legion in American documentary history, this was not merely a perfunctory note to help close out a career. During the previous year, when Roosevelt had considered the subject of his own successor, he had written to Oscar King Davis that "Root is really for the public programme that the boys call the 'Roosevelt policies.' If he were to succeed me there would be no question about their being carried out." But the President weighed all the factors carefully, including his knowledge that Root would not campaign for himself, and finally concluded that "Root would make the best president, but Taft the best candidate."

Elihu Root was not a politician. He was essentially an administrator who also possessed certain qualities of statesmanship. He had no taste for speaking before political crowds and felt more at home addressing business, civic, and professional organizations, such as the Union League Club and the American Society for International Law. Root was an orthodox Republican and a dyed-in-the-wool conservative in a period when the nation was demanding a "Square Deal" and a "New Freedom." Therefore it is questionable whether Root would have made the "best president," as Roosevelt thought, although he might have attempted to carry out the Roosevelt policies out of sheer loyalty. What troubled Root was the fact that the scepter was passing from the businessman and that government was rapidly falling into the hands of men "who distrust the man of business, who suspect the man of business." As Secretary of War, as Secretary of State, and later as Senator and elder statesman, Root was frequently called upon to make eulogies. His most emotional effort was the speech he delivered upon the death of J. P. Morgan, who was, for him, "a simple minded modest benefactor who has done good in secret." Root felt strongly that the division between rich and poor was only the result of increased prosperity, and although he did not declare himself against unions, he was outspoken in his conviction that they "sought to hold down industry, activity, and ambition to the level of sloth, of incompetency, of stupidity."

But Root's conservatism and orthodoxy are not in question here. Root was thoughtful and highly intelligent. He brought great talent and ability to the office of Secretary of State, and he contributed greatly to the statesmanship which is a first requirement of that office. In addition, he had the ability and the humility to work with a "strong" President who was often determined to have his own way. Root had, if not an aristocratic, at least a noble, manner about him. He possessed all the intelligent conservatism of the professional background in which he was reared, together with the caution which naturally comes from the lawyer's training. Root was not a warm personality, but he had many close friends and devoted followers who appreciated his basic kindness. He was generally firm, but almost always gentle. The *Washington Evening Star*, in reviewing Elihu Root's career at the time of his death in 1937, perhaps summed up the character and personality of Root best with the observation that "his position was Olympian."

4

Philander C. Knox

1909-1913

BY WALTER SCHOLES
University of Missouri

When William Howard Taft was elected to the Presidency in November, 1908, the jingoism of the late nineteenth and the early twentieth centuries was almost spent. The nation was recovering from the panic of 1907, but the experience had been sobering. If the foreign policies of the new administration were to match the country's mood, they would of necessity be practical and restricted to what were clearly American interests. A Secretary of State of the type that Taft had in mind would almost assure harmony between mood and policy, for above all he sought a man who was a conservative and who had achieved success. After both Henry Cabot Lodge and Elihu Root had refused the post, Taft, on Root's suggestion, offered it to Senator Philander C. Knox. Knox accepted in mid-December, 1908.

Knox was born on May 6, 1853, in Brownsville, Pennsylvania, where his father was a banker. After his graduation from Mount Union College in Ohio, Knox read law for three years and, in 1875, was admitted to the Pennsylvania bar. During the twenty-five years that he practiced law in Pittsburgh before entering public service, he became a successful corporation lawyer and a wealthy man. In 1899, President McKinley invited him to join the Cabinet as Attorney General, but Knox was so engrossed in the formation of the Carnegie Steel Corporation that he refused. Two years later the President repeated his invitation, and this time Knox accepted. He continued as Attorney General when Theodore Roosevelt succeeded McKinley, and it seems ironic, in view of his background, that he should have been the executor of Roosevelt's plans for curbing the

59

trusts. Roosevelt thought so well of his Attorney General that he offered him a seat on the Supreme Court, but Knox declined, as he would do again during the Taft administration. When Senator Matthew S. Quay died in 1904, Governor Samuel W. Pennypacker named Knox to the vacant seat. In the credentials which he forwarded to the Senate, the Governor stated that Knox could hold the office "as long as he behaved himself," a typical Pennypackerism which almost convulsed the august upper chamber. Upon the expiration of Quay's term, the Pennsylvania Legislature elected Knox for the full term of six years.

The new Secretary of State, whom Roosevelt referred to as "little Phil," was a small, stocky man with a boyish face that belied his years. Although he was not much inclined to participate in the social life of the Capital, Knox was well known in club circles. Indeed, his hobbies were golf and horses. In Washington he lived in a handsome rented house on K Street. Here, in the small library next to his bedroom, he would sit through the early morning hours, sipping coffee and doing his homework. Usually he reached his office about ten or ten-thirty and worked until lunchtime. He seldom returned in the afternoon, except on Thursdays, the regular calling day for foreign representatives, and on days when he had special appointments. The well-dressed, well-groomed Secretary was a familiar figure at the Shoreham and the Metropolitan Club, where he often had lunch. He was frequently accompanied by his First Assistant Secretary and chief adviser, Francis M. Huntington Wilson, and the two men would discuss Departmental affairs over cocktails and a leisurely meal. Afterward, Knox would stroll home for a little nap, and later, if the weather was pleasant, would drive out to Chevy Chase for golf. To avoid the Washington summers, he spent much of his time at Valley Forge Farms, his estate near Philadelphia, where he kept a fine stable of fast trotters. During the winters he took his vacations in Florida.

Knox's predecessor in office, Elihu Root, had been reluctant to pass much of the work on to his subordinates, and he had consequently found the Secretaryship exceedingly burdensome. Taft had urged Root to undertake a general reorganization of the Department, but although he did take some steps in this direction, the Department was still in need of a thorough overhauling when Taft became President. Taft and Knox agreed immediately on the importance of devising a more efficient system; Knox believed in delegating most of the work to his subordinates so that he might keep his mind clear for top-level planning, and, even before taking office, he had requested Huntington Wilson to work out a reorganization scheme. It was their goal both to bring about greater efficiency in the working of the Department itself and to make it a better instrument for giving assistance to Americans interested in foreign trade and investment.

Wilson had given considerable thought to the problem of Departmental organization and, even while serving under Root, had recommended splitting the Department into various geographical divisions. Root was unenthusiastic, although he did consent to the establishment of a Division of Far Eastern Affairs. Now Wilson had the opportunity to put his ideas into effect, and he deserves much credit for the reforms which he recommended. Probably the most important innovation under his scheme was the creation of additional politico-geographical desks, which would include, besides the already functioning Division of Far Eastern Affairs, divisions for Western Europe, the Near East, and Latin America.

Despite the great improvement brought about through this reorganization, there was still criticism that the Department was inefficient. At least two foreign representatives, German Ambassador Count von Bernstorff and British Ambassador Lord Bryce, were of this opinion. Bryce said that there was a complete want of organization in the American State Department and that the administrative arrangements were far behind those of England and Germany. In fact, Bryce went so far as to say that the ways of the Department reminded him of Constantinople. Since a number of newspapermen, as well as leading politicians, also commented on the poor organization of the Department, it can be assumed that, if a good beginning had been made, much still remained to be done. Bryce also complained that the Department allowed matters to drift, a fault which he believed stemmed at least partly from the dilatoriness of the Secretary of State. Bryce was not alone in his charge; others said bluntly that Knox was lazy. As early as December, 1909, George Hill of the *New York Tribune* commented privately that there was much public criticism of Knox's administration of the Department of State. In Hill's opinion the criticism was due chiefly to the fact that the Secretary was determined not to ruin his health by working as hard as some of his predecessors had done. It is true that Knox made the major policy decisions and would allow no interference from within the Department, but once he had set the broad outlines, he paid little attention to how his subordinates carried on the day-to-day relations.

Knox, in his thinking on foreign policy, accepted the tradition which barred all political agreements that might entangle the United States in the quarrels of Europe. Neither he nor Taft believed in the annexation of territory, for that would mean permanent political ties and greater expense for the American taxpayer. This did not, however, rule out temporary intervention through military force if the Secretary considered such action necessary to maintain political stability or to protect American citizens and their property. It was only natural for Knox to apply to foreign policy the same basic objectives which governed his views on domestic issues. His goals of progress, efficiency, law, and peace had their roots in Anglo-Saxon political institutions, in the capitalistic system, and in the sanctity of contract. Progress to Knox meant economic and political stability at home and abroad, and the Secretary was determined to use American trade and investment abroad as a lever to help backward areas contribute to this goal. Both Knox and the President stressed "dollars not bullets" as the basic concept of their foreign policy. Where the United States had interests, or hoped to develop them, it had an obligation to help nations in trouble, and the best way to do so was through the stabilizing agency of loans. Money tended to have a quieting effect of itself; in addition, the Secretary believed, "the borrower is the servant of the lender," so that any country under financial obligation to the United States could not escape accepting some measure of tutelage along with the loan. The instruction and supervision would, of course, benefit greatly not only the country being instructed and supervised but also the rest of the world, especially the United States.

II

In the case of the Latin-American countries, the United States appeared to be under a special obligation, for Knox and Taft felt that it was unfair to use the Monroe Doctrine as a device to prevent European nations from interfering in Latin-American affairs and then to deny American responsibility when one of these republics got into financial trouble. In the Caribbean and Central America, the United States had both political and strategic interests, which American investment and trade were designed merely to protect and expand. Knox's Latin-American policy, with which Taft agreed, might be called the ultimate in dollar diplomacy, for here the United States faced little opposition from European countries. This area, moreover, was of increasing importance to the United States because the Panama Canal was under construction and Great Britain was withdrawing from the Caribbean. Sir Edward Grey, the British Foreign Minister, made it perfectly clear to Lord Bryce that England would make no political move in this area so long as the United States kept an open-door policy. It is true that the British, on occasion, did intimate that the United States was not playing fair in the matter of equal economic opportunity for British subjects, but such objections were never strong enough to cause Knox any real concern.

After considerable fumbling, Knox worked out a policy for Latin America grounded in three basic ideas. First, it was the primary concern of the United States that these countries have politically stable governments whose power was based on free elections. At times the administration might use pressure to bring about the nomination of a man it could trust, so that he could be "freely elected." Second, American financial interests were to be encouraged to cooperate by making loans to help those governments of which the Department approved or at least found tolerable. Here it must be pointed out that the bankers seldom forced their plans on the Department. Rather, the Department had to work very hard to get bankers to interest themselves in the political and economic affairs of Latin America. To be certain that both parties were protected, the Department examined all contracts carefully. It insisted also that the Latin-American governments involved agree to some sort of control over customs collection as a guarantee of repayment. Third, should both political pressure and financial aid fail to maintain peace, the United States would be justified in either threatening intervention or actually intervening with troops. But the object of intervention, in theory, would be only to restore order and not to protect American business. Knox and his subordinates often pointed to the political and economic stability of the Dominican Republic as a good example of what could be accomplished through a thoughtful government policy.

In 1909, when Knox took over the Department of State, revolutions were a constant factor in all but two of the Central American states. The two stable countries were not happy exceptions, however, for José Santos Zelaya in Nicaragua and Estrada Cabrera in Guatemala held their nations in a firm dictatorial grip. Economic stagnation, political corruption, oppression and suppression—these were the hallmarks of the "republican" governments of Central America. From the moment that Knox assumed direction of American foreign policy, it was clear that he had some new ideas for stabilizing the area and making it more accessible to American investment and that he was prepared to take more forceful steps to make his ideas work than had any previous administration. One of the big stumbling blocks to peace in Central America was the constant threat to Honduran sovereignty from her neighbors. The biggest offender in this respect was Zelaya of Nicaragua. Knox wanted to neutralize Honduras and to control Zelaya, and in his judgment the most effective way to achieve this twin goal was to secure Mexican cooperation in enforcing the Convention of 1907. In that pact, at the urging of the United States, the Central American countries had pledged themselves to respect the neutrality of Honduras and to settle their disputes through a permanent Central American court. The Mexican government had helped the United States in these negotiations, but neither of the two major powers had actually signed the agreement. They were at most morally responsible. When Mexico realized that cooperation with the United States might mean joint intervention, it backed away and even went so far as to say that it had no interests south of Guatemala.

Undeterred by the prospect of unilateral action, Knox had the Department draft plans for control of Honduran customs collections. His subordinates worked hard to find an American banking firm interested in making a loan which would provide for the debts of Honduras and the establishment of the collectorship. Finally, in the summer of 1909, J. P. Morgan & Company agreed to involve itself in the Honduran affair. Working closely with the Department, its officers made an arrangement with British bondholders in Honduras and then signed a loan contract with that country. But it was not until January, 1911, that the United States signed a treaty which placed the collection of customs in the hands of an official nominated by the bankers and approved by the President of the United States. In the end, however, Knox's hope of stabilizing Honduras failed, for the Senate refused to approve the treaty.

Dealing with Zelaya was an even thornier problem. But in October, 1909, a conservative revolt led by Juan E. Estrada broke out in Bluefields, Nicaragua, against the dictator-president; and although the Department officially remained neutral, the American Consul on the spot showed marked favoritism to the rebels. Zelaya helped Knox by ordering the execution of two American soldiers of fortune captured while fighting for Estrada. When the news reached Washington, Knox held a conference with high officials of the Navy and State Departments, after which he broke off diplomatic relations with Zelaya. As a result, Zelaya was forced to resign in mid-December, but one of his supporters, José Madriz, assumed the Presidency. Showing little consideration for American policy, Mexico recognized the new regime, and Great Britain was willing to do the same; but Knox was determined not to have anything to do with Madriz. Madriz seemed to be winning, however, and probably would have defeated the conservatives if the commander of the U.S.S. *Paducah* had not prevented him from closing in on the rebel forces at Bluefields. Although it was not unusual for a powerful nation to intervene when the lives and property of its citizens appeared to be endangered, Knox was criticized for instructing the Navy to interfere. He maintained that he had acted according to international law. Despite the administration's efforts to help Estrada, it could hardly have expected his side to win, for Madriz still controlled most of Nicaragua. Knox at this stage seemed to have no real policy, but fortunately for him the Estrada forces finally triumphed and, in late August, 1910, entered Managua, the capital.

This time Knox was ready. He immediately demanded that Estrada give complete assurances about the policy he would follow and that he agree to contract a loan in the United States secured by a customs collectorship. Estrada was forced to assent, for his position was too weak to permit any alternative. Shortly thereafter, Knox sent a Latin-American expert to Nicaragua to obtain a written commitment from Estrada. In what became known as the Dawson Pacts, Estrada agreed to provide a new constitution which would abolish monopolies, to adjust United States–

Nicaraguan claims, to ask the United States government's help in obtaining a customs-guaranteed loan, and to punish the murderers of the two Americans.

The Dawson Pacts, although designed specifically for Nicaragua, could have served as Knox's blueprint for stability in the entire Caribbean and Central American region. The loan would put the Nicaraguan government on its financial feet, and American management of revenue from customs' payments would keep it there. These two operations would in turn reduce political turmoil to a minimum. But no one seemed prepared to cooperate with the Secretary. In Nicaragua the "good" men proved unable to maintain themselves in power without the aid of American marines; in the United States the Senate rejected the treaty which embodied the pacts. American policy had indeed been a factor in Zelaya's fall from power, but in the end the United States had been committed to military intervention. Knox's attempt to win Mexican cooperation failed, and so did his efforts to neutralize Honduras. The results of the Secretary's policies in Central America could hardly be termed successful.

III

Knox believed that the Department should be active in promoting opportunities for American business, and his efforts on behalf of firms seeking naval contracts from the Argentine government illustrate clearly how the Department worked to expand American markets. In 1908, Argentina approved the expenditure of funds to increase its navy, although at the time it lacked money for immediate construction. The Roosevelt administration showed little interest in Argentina's naval plans, but the advent of Taft and Knox signaled a complete change of attitude. At Knox's behest, American bankers subscribed a loan to Argentina, which made it possible for that government to ask for bids on the new ships, and the Navy cooperated by giving the Argentine Minister of Marine the specifications of the latest American dreadnought, with a request that he treat the matter as confidential. Charles H. Sherrill, the new Minister sent by the State Department to Buenos Aires to help the American shipbuilders, used his own kind of pressure. In a conversation with the Argentine Foreign Minister, he stressed the isolated position of Argentina— surrounded as that nation was by the hostile coalition of Brazil, Uruguay, Bolivia, and Chile—and intimated that in the circumstances it might be well for Argentina to cultivate the friendship of the United States. This was too good an opportunity for the Argentine Minister to pass up; he bluntly asked Sherrill whether the United States would support his country in a war with its neighbors. Sherrill actually referred the inquiry to the Department, which advised him to proceed cautiously in the matter of committing the United States to a political connection of any nature.

The outlook seemed favorable for American bidders, and telegrams and letters flashed back and forth among the Department, the bankers, and the shipyards. But, in the fall of 1909, Knox moved on another front, without realizing, apparently, how his action might affect the Argentine contracts. Relations between Chile and the United States had been clouded for years by an old American claim against Chile, known as the Alsop Claim. The Secretary decided that Chile had evaded its obligations long enough and demanded prompt settlement. When this ultimatum aroused great resentment all over Latin America, and especially in South America, he quickly retreated and said that he had made arrangements for arbitration.

Shortly after the ultimatum to Chile, Argentina opened the bids for the new vessels. Two American firms quoted the lowest construction price, but the British, exploiting the emotions raised by America's recent demands on Chile, persuaded the Argentine naval commission to allow a British firm to lower its bid in order to bring it under that of the Americans. Sherrill appealed to the Secretary, who responded admirably. Knox proclaimed that it had really been the Argentine Minister in Washington who had suggested arbitration on the Alsop case. Moreover, the Department announced that a squadron of American warships would be sent to the Argentine Centennial Celebration in May, 1910, and that the United States would make a substantial appropriation for the Pan-American Conference to be held at Buenos Aires two months later. With these promises in hand, Sherrill was able, in January, 1910, to swing the award of the two ships to an American firm. Knox and Taft were elated. The existence of the Department of State now seemed to be justified, for it had used diplomacy to help American businessmen. The President even stressed this diplomatic success in his message to Congress. Both Taft and Knox were men of peace, but they were not opposed to supplying dreadnoughts to other nations in the interests of American prosperity.

Yet the aggressive policies pursued by Knox in Latin America were largely unsuccessful. With his habit of leaving things to his subordinates, the Secretary tended to wait until a real crisis arose before he assumed command. Furthermore, the Latin Americans found the policies of the United States offensive, and the damage to inter-American relations was compounded both by the often tactless and inconsiderate method in which they were carried out and by the obvious fact that Knox did not regard the Latin Americans as his equals. In Root's opinion, Knox did not have the temperament to work with the Latin Americans, but Knox and Taft, on the other hand, believed that Root had spent too much time on his "precious Latin Americans" without getting anything accomplished. A study of Latin-American reaction reveals that Root was correct in his estimate of the situation. The whole effect of Knox's policies was to create a great reservoir of ill will in Latin America, which contrasted strikingly with the kindly feeling that Root had cultivated so assiduously and had bequeathed to his successor.

IV

Another area which bore the brunt of the Taft-Knox diplomacy was the Far East. The new administration made it clear as early as 1909 that it considered China one of the most important fields for American diplomacy. There was to be "a new phase of the traditional policy in China and with special reference to Manchuria." One reason for the new orientation was the President's background. He was familiar with the Far East, for he had served almost three years in the Philippines and, as Secretary of War, had on two occasions conferred in Tokyo with Japanese leaders. In the fall of 1907, he gave a speech in Shanghai which provided a good preview of the policy that his administration would adopt. After reaffirming Hay's Open Door policy, Taft went on to remark that the China trade was large enough "to require the Government of the United States to take every legitimate means to protect it against diminution or injury by the political preference of any of its competitors." The United States had been slow to realize the importance of this trade, which had grown without any encouragement from the government, but Taft was convinced that in the future there would be no reason to complain of apparent government indifference. He advocated administrative and governmental reforms in China and the development of its natural resources; these measures, he believed, would ultimately enable China to enforce the Open Door policy without foreign assistance.

Two high-ranking officials of the State Department had also served in the Far East, Huntington Wilson in Japan and Willard Straight in Manchuria. Although Straight left government service in June, 1909, to become the representative of the American financial group in China, he continued to send information and advice to the Department. Both of these men were ardent advocates of a forward policy, and they shared a deep suspicion of Japanese designs on China, especially on Manchuria.

Both Taft and Knox accepted the view that China offered an excellent opportunity for American enterprise. This was a long-held American belief, and the *Brooklyn Standard Union* was only voicing the general opinion when it declared that China was the "greatest uncut commercial melon in the world." The administration intended to secure a share of this melon for the United States, and when Chinese concessions, particularly to Japan, threatened to narrow the scope of American participation, it adopted an aggressive policy to protect the American interest. Taft and

Knox, being lawyers, took a legalistic view of the China problem. As Taft put it, all the great powers interested in the China trade had subscribed in writing to the wisdom of Hay's Open Door policy and had declared their adherence to it. Taft and Knox maintained that, consequently, the United States had every right to expect and insist that this commitment be honored.

Both the President and the Secretary of State believed that a change must be made in the Peking legation if their policy was to achieve any degree of success. The incumbent, Minister William W. Rockhill, was a respected Sinologist and diplomat, but Taft regarded him as a mere dilettante, and Knox considered him not only too hesitant about pushing American demands before the Chinese government but also not sufficiently alert in detecting openings for American trade. To them the solution consisted in sending a businessman to fill the post and transferring Rockhill to St. Petersburg. This was done promptly.

In the spring of 1909, Knox faced a situation which to him had serious implications for the economic and political position of the United States in China. Backed by their respective governments, a tripartite group consisting of French, English, and German bankers negotiated an agreement to lend money for the construction of two important railroad systems, one from Hankow to Szechuan and the other from Hankow to Canton. Economically, American nonparticipation in what was known as the Hukuang Loan meant loss of investment outlets and also of markets, for United States firms would not be entitled to supply any of the materials needed for construction. Even more important from the long-range point of view, the terms of the loan departed from the usual practice by pledging internal (provincial) revenues as security. Knox felt that this procedure involved important political considerations and that participation was essential if the United States was to exercise an influence equal to that of the other powers. In Knox's words, the "United States is concerned in the development of China, in the maintenance of its political integrity and primarily therefore in its financial affairs."

Negotiations had been in progress for months, but not until the agreement was drawn up, early in May, 1909, did the Department swing into action. It organized five New York banking houses to serve as its instrument in handling the American share of the loan. Apparently through Knox's direct initiative, the Department began looking for some basis on which the United States could demand entry into the deal. Ultimately the United States based its claim on the written assurance given by China to Minister E. H. Conger in 1904 that, if China was unable to raise money for construction of a railroad from Hankow to Szechuan, it would give American and English capitalists the first chance to finance the line. Late in May, Knox instructed Rockhill to protest American exclusion, but the Chinese, though insisting that they would have been happy if the Americans had been among the original negotiators, pleaded that it was now too late for them to join.

Knox then appealed to the European nations, particularly England, but received no encouragement. Grey pointed out that in 1905 England had twice invited American participation in railroad loans covered by the Conger agreement and that, since the United States had not responded to these inquiries, the English regarded American rights as having lapsed. Grey thought the delay entailed in arranging for American participation would endanger the whole project. He complained that this was the first indication he had had of American interest, although the negotiations had been common knowledge for months. The Foreign Offices of Germany and France shared Grey's resentment at American procrastination in making clear its position. But after being subjected to constant pressure, Great Britain, at the end of June, 1909, reluctantly conceded to American participation, on condition that such action would not endanger the loan, that the United States would waive its protest, and that the American financial group would come to a satisfactory arrangement with the European bankers. France and Germany followed the English lead.

Eager to have the final arrangements for the loan completed, Chinese officials continued to insist that the time was inopportune to reopen the Hukuang negotiations, though they repeated that they would welcome American participation in future loans. But Knox did not consider the bait of future loans as a sufficient *quid pro quo* for waiving this nation's "present undoubted rights." The importance he attached to these rights was revealed by the fact that he instructed Chargé Henry Fletcher to warn the Chinese government that, if it refused to do its duty toward the United States, the President might feel justified in discontinuing the remission of the indemnity of the Boxer Rebellion. When the Chinese continued to evade and delay, Knox enlisted the aid of President Taft. In July, the President's personal appeal resulted in China's capitulation. With the State Department keeping a careful check on every diplomatic and financial maneuver, the tedious negotiations continued until final agreement was reached in May, 1911. Knox had won his victory, but at the expense of antagonizing three European governments.

While the State Department was forcing its way into the Hukuang Loan, it was keeping a watchful eye on developments in south Manchuria which it feared might violate the Open Door principle. Since January, 1909, Japan had been negotiating with China for the settlement of various Japanese claims dealing with, among other things, mining and railroad concessions. By the middle of August, Knox had reason to believe that the final outcome would violate Chinese political and economic integrity and consequently the rights of other nations. When China surrendered to Japanese demands in the so-called September agreements, signed on the fourth of that month, Knox directed E. Carleton Baker of the Far Eastern Division to investigate whether, in view of the large and indefinite mining rights given Japan, the time was now approaching, or had perhaps arrived, to protest in the name of the Open Door. In his report, submitted early in October, Baker informed the Secretary that he believed the mining concession offered sufficient grounds for a protest. But he advised that it be made, if possible, in conjunction with other powers. Baker concluded that Japan's probable goal was "to secure such control of the mineral resources and transportation facilities of Manchuria, and possibly Manchuria itself, as will enable her to exploit that country." There is no indication that an attempt was made, even informally, to sound out any of the European powers, and the protest, to which so much consideration had been given, was never made. Instead, on November 15, the Department issued a statement declaring that the United States accepted the agreement of September 4 as it related to mining rights in Manchuria, but no reference was made to railroad concessions.

Knox was so preoccupied with the political situation in Manchuria that he retired to his library at Valley Forge to brief himself by studying John Bassett Moore's *Digest*. On October 8, he wrote a personal letter to Henry M. Hoyt, the Department Solicitor, telling Hoyt that he did not want the letter filed because "it only represents impressions made during the process of trying to come to some clear understanding as to what our immediate duty is in regard to conditions in China." The precise conditions with which Knox was concerned were the Manchurian mining and railroad concessions recently granted to Japan. Citing Moore, Knox sketched the background of the Open Door policy of the United States, adding that the "development of China had not progressed to such an extent, at the time the doctrine of the 'open door' was promulgated, as to make it much more than a theory for harmonious action. This theory has not been really tested in a concrete way and in its application to matters of great importance as it seems likely now to be." He then singled out Hay's statement that, when China ceded to any corporation or company the exclusive rights and privileges of opening mines, establishing railroads, or in any other way developing Manchuria industrially, such action could only be viewed with the gravest concern by the United States. Knox stated that he had formulated three propositions for Hoyt's consideration, adding that Hoyt could discuss them with whomever he pleased as long as he remembered that they were tentative. For Knox, however, these notions comprised a possible starting point for setting down "in some concrete and simple form the rules by which we are willing to be guided and to which we would desire the other Powers to adhere."

Although Knox regarded mining concessions as sufficiently important to offer the technical basis for a protest on the Sino-Japanese agreement, the Secretary's real concern was railroad concessions. In brief, his first two propositions stated the principles on which all future arrangements for railroad construction in China were to be based: (1) all powers interested in equality of trade had the right to participate in railroad loans, whether or not the right in any specific case was given them by treaty, and (2) a railroad concession was no title to a monopoly. The third proposition disavowed any desire on the part of the United States to acquire Chinese territory or to interfere with the Open Door. Certainly the neutralization scheme that Knox ultimately proposed was based in part on these general principles, but it also reflected the views of Willard Straight, who had clarified and influenced the Secretary's ideas on this subject.

Straight had arrived in Peking in August, 1909, when persistent Japanese pressure was encouraging China to seek concrete American and other non-Japanese investments in Manchuria as a counterweight to Japanese influence. The Chinese, approaching Straight directly, opened negotiations for a concession to finance and construct a railroad from Chinchow in south Manchuria to Aigun on the Amur. Straight kept the Department informed not only of his progress but also of his hopes for the future. Once the Chinchow-Aigun construction was under way, he envisioned negotiations with Russia to bring about its withdrawal from the area. With this accomplished, the United States could force Japan to relinquish its political hold and thus restore Manchuria to China by "virtually neutralizing the country." On October 2, China signed a preliminary agreement for the concession.

Knox now had a substantial American claim to protect, and he promised to give the project his diplomatic support, on the condition that Britain would do the same. In reply to American inquiries, Grey declared that the Japanese were afraid of the competition the proposed railroad would offer their south Manchurian line and had requested, as compensation, the right to participate in the new construction. Grey wanted to know simply what Knox thought would be fair to Japan.

Knox's reply, telegraphed to London on November 6, stated that the United States would favor ultimate participation by all interested powers in the Chinchow-Aigun railroad. But before he embarked on the project, he asked the English to consider two other more comprehensive proposals. The first he described as "perhaps the most effective way to preserve the undisturbed enjoyment by China of all political rights in Manchuria and to promote the development of those Provinces under a practical application of the policy of the open door and equal commercial opportunity." To achieve this end, he suggested that an international syndicate lend money for the purchase of all the Manchurian railways on China's behalf and exercise supervision over them during the term of the loan. Should this solution prove to be barren, Knox suggested as an alternative an

invitation by the United States and Great Britain to all interested powers
to participate in the Chinchow-Aigun railroad and in whatever additional
lines future commercial development in Manchuria might demand. At the
same time, these nations would supply funds to China for the purchase
of any rail lines which might be offered for inclusion in this system.

This neutralization scheme was a magnificent concept, for it appeared
to be aimed at ultimate control by China of her own economic and political
affairs. There was only one drawback: it never had a chance of success.
It was doomed to failure both in conception and execution, and it seems
strange that Knox, who saw clearly the obstacles to American policy in
the Far East, should have entertained any hopes for it. Before becoming
Secretary of State, he had worked diligently at Valley Forge to prepare
himself for the post. In his background study, he had emphasized Far
Eastern affairs. He obviously emerged with some understanding of the
situation, for he wrote Taft that as long as the United States was content
to confine itself to diplomatic generalities, no one would take it seriously,
but that once it attempted to carry out its policy to some logical end, its
course would encounter more opposition. On another occasion he warned
the President that he could not commit the United States to any pro-China
policy in opposition to the aims and acts of the other powers, notably Japan
and Russia. In proposing the neutralization scheme, Knox admitted to Grey
that it "would naturally require the cooperation of China and of Japan and
Russia."

But Knox made no effort to secure Russian and Japanese concurrence
in his initial proposals—which the London *Times* rightly characterized as
"precipitous diplomacy." His claim that the advantages of such a plan
should be obvious to Japan and Russia was naïve, for the scheme was clearly
an attempt to establish American dominance in Manchuria. To imagine
that Japan would willingly surrender its favorable position, won by war
and long negotiations with China, was no more than wishful thinking.
Nor was Russia in any mood to add to the losses which it had suffered
in the Russo-Japanese War. The Russians, in fact, were more violent in
their denunciations than the Japanese. After Rockhill had presented the
plan to Alexander Iswolsky, the Russian Foreign Minister, the latter observed that American policy in Manchuria was driving his country into
the arms of Japan.

In the spring of 1910, Sir William Tyrrell, a key official in the British
Foreign Office, wrote to Bryce that he was sorry that Knox had taken up
the question of the Manchurian railroads, adding that "it seems a pity that
he had no one to advise him of the risks and dangers attendant on such a
policy. He has done himself no good." Within the Department of State,
evaluation of Knox's China policy was even more severe. A memorandum
drawn up by the Far Eastern Division and read to the Secretary in August,

1910, declared bluntly that the American policy in Manchuria had failed. It had won the ill will of Russia, irritated Japan, and failed of support in France and England.

Not only did Knox ignore the facts of life in the Far East, but he did not even grasp the ramifications which the European alliance system had for American foreign policy. By 1909, England had become acutely aware of the acceleration in the German naval program and thus was no longer in any position to irritate its Japanese ally. Furthermore, Bryce made it plain to Knox that, because of the agreements reached with Russia over Persia in 1907, Great Britain would not support the United States at Peking over Russian protests. Yet the Secretary sought and expected British support for a China policy aimed at two of Britain's allies. By his Far Eastern misadventure, Knox himself affected the European alliance system, for the fear of American penetration into Manchuria contributed to the Russo-Japanese *rapprochement* of which Iswolsky had warned.

V

The freedom that any Cabinet member has in initiating and executing policy is largely determined by his relationship with the President. The ties between Taft and Knox were close, for Taft consulted his Secretary of State at length even before Inauguration Day, and after March 4, 1909, it was evident that the President relied heavily on his advice. This was due not only to Knox's known executive ability and his knack of getting down immediately to the important things but also to the fact that the two men held similar views on many matters. Foreign policy came within the area of their agreement, and for that reason it is difficult to determine which of them was responsible for any specific course of action. A reasonable assumption seems to be that they discussed the broad outlines of policy and that the Department of State, with Taft's cooperation, then became responsible for carrying through the required diplomatic negotiations. Knox saw to it that the President was kept well informed of the Department's activities, and Taft, for his part, passed on all pertinent information to the Department. There was, however, one notable exception to this pattern. Taft, without consulting either Knox or the Department, ordered American troops to the Mexican border in the spring of 1911.

During most of the nineteenth century Americans had been reluctant to invest in Mexico because of its frequent revolutions and political turmoil. But when the dictatorship of Porfirio Díaz brought peace and stability, plus very favorable terms of investment, Americans became more and more inclined to send their capital south of the border. By 1910 they owned about a billion dollars' worth of railroads, mines, and other property, and over forty thousand American citizens lived in Mexico. In that year, however, the outbreak of a number of revolts signalized a new period of Mexican unrest, and by March, 1911, a real threat to the friendly Díaz regime seemed to be developing. The question arose whether the Mexican government could adequately protect Americans and their property. The situation was further complicated by the activities of rebel sympathizers, both American and Mexican, living in Texas and Arizona. Some of the aid which they gave the revolutionists was entirely legal under the terms of the neutrality legislation of the United States, but there was, in addition, extensive smuggling of arms and ammunition. The situation was deemed sufficiently serious for the Department to send copies of all reports from Mexico to the President, a procedure which usually indicated that a crisis was approaching. But conditions did not seem grave enough for the Secretary to postpone his vacation at Palm Beach.

Shortly after Knox left Washington, Ambassador Henry Lane Wilson arrived from Mexico and had a long interview with Taft. Later the Ambassador said that he had simply repeated to the President what he had been reporting in his dispatches. No doubt this was true, but the oral presentation had a much greater impact on the President. Wilson informed Taft that all Mexico was boiling and that the disturbances were merely symptomatic of the general condition of the body politic; the situation, he warned, could explode at any moment and would do so, in fact, as soon as a leader appeared. The Ambassador added that the Americans in Mexico were alarmed by the strong anti-American feeling among the Mexicans and were looking to the United States government for protection.

Taft considered briefly what Wilson had told him and then summoned Secretary of War Jacob M. Dickinson, Secretary of the Navy George von L. Meyer, and General Leonard Wood, Chief of Staff. At this conference, which included no representative of the Department of State, Taft described the Mexican situation and asked what could be done about getting troops to the border. Meyer reported that the Navy had been working on plans for naval exercises in the Gulf of Mexico; Wood said that the Army could send sixteen thousand men to the border without great effort. Such a troop movement would, in fact, be an excellent training opportunity, since spring was the best season for maneuvers in Texas. Taft concluded that sending the troops would strengthen the forces for law and order in Mexico, would prevent filibustering expeditions, and would put both Mexican parties on notice that the United States was ready to defend its rights if the occasion arose. On March 7, the necessary orders were issued.

It was only then that Taft informed Huntington Wilson of the steps he had taken, and not until March 11 did he write to Knox, who was still in Florida. Taft, in turn, attempted to convince the press that the troops were in Texas for the usual spring maneuvers, but this was so obviously false that all sorts of wild rumors developed. The President, consequently, had to assure the Mexican government that he had no intention of intervening and to appease Congress by promising that there would be no intervention without prior congressional approval.

Taft's venture into diplomacy, unadvised by the State Department, had proved him an amateur. In the early part of 1913, when he was again considering a concentration of troops on the Mexican border, the President consulted Knox.

VI

When the successful conclusion of any matter involving foreign policy depended upon the cooperation of Congress, Taft and Knox were most likely to suffer a defeat. There were three chief reasons for the administration's unhappy relationship with the legislative branch, two of which stemmed from the domestic political situation itself. Not only was Congress asserting itself in an effort to regain the power that it felt Roosevelt had unlawfully concentrated in the hands of the executive, but the Progressives were in revolt against the Taft administration. Knox aggravated an already unfavorable situation by displaying little skill in his dealings with the Senate—a remarkable deficiency in view of his own service in that body. His handling of the arbitration treaty with Great Britain is a good example of his lack of finesse.

Although Taft probably had greater faith than Knox in the efficacy of courts and judicial procedures for eliminating war, both men sincerely believed that chances for world peace would be greatly advanced if all nations would agree to settle their disputes through arbitration. At Taft's direction, Knox began negotiations for an arbitration treaty with Britain, and by mid-March, 1911, the Department had completed a draft copy. After Bryce had given it his general approval, it was sent to Root for his personal opinion. The heart of the treaty was the provision calling upon the contracting nations to arbitrate all differences between them that were "justiciable in their nature by reason of being susceptible of decision by the application of the principles of law or equity."

Both Taft and Knox made speeches in support of the treaty, the President being especially active in this regard. Most of the press came out in favor of it, and as far as the American people were concerned, this was probably the most popular measure the administration had attempted. Nevertheless, the Senate refused to accept the administration's version of the treaty. Most of the blame for the rejection must fall on Knox. He did not consult the Senate Foreign Relations Committee on the proposed draft, nor did he keep Senator Lodge informed about the negotiations. Lodge went to confer with Knox on the subject of the treaty as early as

mid-June. When he did not find the Secretary in his office, he called on
the President. Taft told the Senator that the treaty had been drafted and
that the English Foreign Office was studying it. Whether greater concern
for the prerogatives of the Senate would have made much difference is
unknown, but former Secretary Root was certainly correct in telling a
friend that the Senate felt that it had been slighted.

Once the treaty came before the Senate, Knox kept in close touch with
Shelby M. Cullom, ranking Republican member of the Foreign Relations
Committee. But by then it was too late. For one thing, many Southern
Senators were afraid that their states would be forced to arbitrate claims
arising from unpaid bonds. An even more important factor was the Senate's
belief that the treaty impaired its authority over the treaty-making process.
The outcome was a document amended almost beyond recognition and an
administration so discouraged that it never again made an effort in the
direction of arbitration treaties. In Lord Bryce's opinion, Knox was responsible for the inept handling of the treaty. Andrew Carnegie, one of its most
ardent supporters, thought it had been "bungled beyond belief."

The Secretary had no better luck with three financial treaties that were
fundamental to the achievement of his purposes. His arguments in urging
ratification of those with Nicaragua and Honduras, referred to earlier,
summarized well his goals in the Caribbean and Central America. He
believed that the practical measures embodied in the treaties would lay
the foundations for peace in the vicinity of the Panama Canal. Denying
that the treaties would involve political entanglements, Knox contended
that they would actually reduce the need for interference in Central American affairs, because thereafter both American diplomacy and American
capital would help the neighboring republics keep their own houses in
order. At the same time, the treaties would give a vast commercial advantage to the United States. Knox tried a variety of approaches in his effort
to win Senate approval. He worked closely with Senator Cullom, and he
prevailed upon the President to write letters to all the senators asking them
to support the treaties. He even sought the support of the chambers of
commerce. But there was too much senatorial opposition to the treaties,
especially from Democrats and Republican Progressives.

Knox also worked hard for the third treaty dealing with financial arrangements—the treaty with Liberia. He testified before the Senate Foreign Relations Committee and entertained the committee members at a
dinner at his home. But the committee assured Knox that the Senate would
not tolerate a financial treaty that might lead to political commitments. It
was not clear that the Liberian treaty would permit the United States to
avoid involvement with Great Britain, France, and Germany. Again the
Secretary saw his efforts fail.

Yet Knox was not completely inept in his dealings with the Senate. Early

in 1911 he showed that he had the ability not only to carry through difficult treaty negotiations successfully but also to calm senatorial fears on
the very delicate subject of Japanese immigration. The Treaty of Commerce and Navigation, signed by the United States and Japan in 1894
and due to expire in 1911, contained a clause prohibiting the entry of Japanese laborers into the United States. To please the Japanese, Knox eliminated all reference to this subject in the new instrument. He did not inform the Western Senators of this omission, for this would have given
them time to stir up opposition against the treaty. But he did take the Senate
Foreign Relations Committee into his confidence. The *New York Tribune*
later noted with approval this change of tactics and predicted, incorrectly,
that Knox would continue to follow this practice in the future. When
the new treaty was made public, the Western Senators immediately voiced
strong disapproval, but Knox was able to soften their stand when he appeared before the Senate Foreign Relations Committee on February 22 and
submitted the diplomatic notes exchanged by Japan and the United States.
These notes made it perfectly clear that Japan understood fully the right
of the United States to impose any legislative restriction it thought proper
on the immigration of laborers from Japan or any other country. To disarm the opposition still further, the committee adopted a resolution to
the effect that the failure of the treaty to mention immigration could not
be construed as indicating any change of view on the part of the United
States. Whereas this addition eliminated any possibility that the Japanese
might misunderstand the American position, it permitted the treaty itself
to avoid reference to a restriction which the Japanese people regarded as
humiliating. The committee then approved the treaty unanimously, and on
February 24, after a brief fight on the Senate floor, the treaty was ratified.
Thus, by cooperating with the Committee on Foreign Relations, Knox
had been able not only to win support for his position but also to satisfy
both the American and the Japanese demands on the subject of immigration.

Throughout his term of office, Knox's relations with the press were not
particularly cordial. This is not surprising in view of his opinion of the
organs of public information. He accused the press of ignorance. The
newspapers, in retaliation, assailed his foreign policies frequently and vio-
lently, singling out for special attack whatever they did not understand.
The violence of the assault, it seemed to Knox, varied directly with the
depth of the ignorance. But instead of assuring himself that the press had
the correct information from which to publicize and analyze the Department's activities, Knox was extremely reticent. Although he was disposed
to be intolerant of mistakes made by the press, neither he nor his assistants
made any effort to sift truth from error in the recurring rumors. After the
stories appeared in print, the Department usually denied them with some

acerbity. Hay and Root had made a practice of holding informal talks with the four or five reporters assigned to the Department of State, but Knox discontinued the custom. On occasion he received members of the press individually in the evening at his home, but he never faced them as a group.

VII

To Knox, the chief duty of the Secretary of State was to promote and protect American economic interests abroad and to work for stable and legal governments in what today are called underdeveloped areas. As a result, the Department of State under his leadership paid little attention to the crucial diplomatic maneuvers of Europe that were then leading to war. Instructions and dispatches relating to the major countries of Europe reflected little interest in European affairs; they were concerned largely with peripheral economic matters in other areas of the world. The amount of correspondence dealing directly with Germany or France, for example, was small in volume compared to that concerned with Liberia, Nicaragua, or China. Both Taft and Knox were proud to call their policy "dollar diplomacy." The administration's intentions may have been praiseworthy, but seasoned American diplomats criticized its methods as unrealistic, and American liberals condemned its objectives as overly favorable to business interests.

In any assessment of a Secretary of State the question to be answered is, Did he add luster and dignity to the office and serve the best interests of the nation? Certainly Knox should be credited with some accomplishments, but in general he added little to American prestige. Both his ends and his means reveal that Knox regarded diplomacy less as an instrument for regulating political intercourse between nations than as a means of promoting American economic interests. His actions contained little that was "moral" by American standards; at times they were naïve. He failed because he lacked the depth of knowledge and the stature needed to be a great Secretary of State. Hucksterng and diplomacy are not synonymous.

5

William Jennings Bryan

1913-1915

BY RICHARD CHALLENER
Princeton University

The passage of time has been unkind to the reputation of William
Jennings Bryan. Few can call to mind the image of the young crusader
who voiced the protest of the prairie farmer and who thrilled huge audiences with his impassioned demands for social justice; instead, there has
emerged the picture of a stubborn, often obtuse defender of outmoded
ideas, a man who failed to keep abreast of his times and who, characteris-
tically, passed from the American scene while trying to prevent the teaching of the principles of evolution. Indeed, even at the time he was serving
in the Cabinet of Woodrow Wilson, Bryan represented, not the wave of
the Wilsonian future, but the legacy of the Populist past; he was a man to
whom many Democrats owed deep political obligations but for whom the
more sophisticated Progressives already had an abiding distrust. And, in
mid-century America, even the values of the agrarian tradition which
Bryan represented have become suspect; the contemporary historian often
interprets Bryan as the foremost exponent of an unfortunate "agrarian
myth" which no longer has a place in an urbanized, industrialized society.

Bryan's record in the Department of State produced little admiring
comment from either contemporaries or later historians. His appointment
as Secretary of State was the signal for all but a few loyal Democratic
newspapers to launch scathing criticisms and to continue the barrage as
long as he remained in office—whether the subject was his aversion to
alcohol, his handling of appointments in the diplomatic service, or his
reaction to the German submarine. His resignation in 1915, an act which
Bryan hoped would rally the country to the cause of peace, merely added

79

to the tumult and provoked at least one influential daily to write of his "unspeakable treachery." There was, to be sure, a brief period in the 1930s when Bryan was held in higher regard. In a decade when Americans rejected all world responsibility and regarded their participation in World War I as the greatest aberration in the nation's history, writers were at least willing to credit Bryan with good intentions. He, after all, had realized that money was the greatest of all contrabands and that defense of the right of Americans to travel on belligerent passenger vessels would lead to conflict with Germany. But even in revisionist historiography Bryan does not emerge as a compelling figure. If his pacifistic instincts were sound, he could not develop a policy which would halt the drift toward war. If he did foresee the future with clairvoyance, he was still powerless to win Woodrow Wilson to his point of view. For, as many have pointed out, Wilson was his own Secretary of State whenever the great issues were under debate, and Bryan was necessarily cast in the role of subordinate whenever the President chose to tap out messages to foreign governments on his famous portable typewriter.

Indeed, whether one examines the contemporary or the historical record, it is almost ridiculously easy to file a long bill of particulars against the "Great Commoner." There is virtual unanimity of opinion about Bryan's attitude toward appointments in the American Foreign Service. He stands condemned as a spoilsman, one of the last out-and-out defenders of the idea that any American—in particular, any American who has contributed to his political party—is qualified to represent his country abroad. Virtually everyone who has written about Bryan has quoted with appropriate relish the notorious letter to James Sullivan in which the Secretary of State blandly wrote about the need to find jobs for "deserving Democrats."

More significant is the criticism which grows out of contemporary re-examinations of the intellectual tradition of American diplomacy. The prevailing interpretation, one which mirrors the current involvements of the United States in a world of power, severely condemns the national effort in foreign policy for having been excessively concerned with what are described as moralistic pronouncements and legalistic solutions. The realists look almost in vain for Secretaries of State who understood the operations of the balance of power, thought in terms of the national interest, or recognized the necessity of balancing commitments with a willingness to utilize the instruments of coercion if need arose. Bryan, it is scarcely necessary to say, abjectly fails to meet the realist criteria. With his rejection of power politics, his penchant for moralizing, his addiction to platitudinous speeches, and his reliance upon the tenets of Christian pacifism, Bryan seems to be the symbol of virtually every error that is condemned by contemporary critics of the American diplomatic tradition. Indeed, as one recent writer has observed, since Woodrow Wilson shared many of Bryan's mistaken assumptions, it was disastrous for his administration to have as Secretary of State a man who did not bring a different point of view to discussions of diplomatic policy and who "harbored the very attitudes that at once inspired and handicapped his chief."

There was, to be sure, one area of the world—Latin America—in which Bryan did practice a form of "realism," but, ironically, he receives no credit for this. Bryan's special brand of Latin-American intervention, which, like the policy of his predecessor, ultimately rested upon the sanction of marines and New York bankers, has long since been repudiated by the United States. Over three decades ago this approach was found to be no longer viable in the face of increasing nationalism in Latin America.

Yet Bryan may have some claims to a more respectable place in American diplomatic history. Certainly he cannot be dismissed as a mere cipher who was always bypassed and disregarded by the President. The most careful student of Woodrow Wilson has recently taken great pains to point out that Bryan and Wilson consulted with each other upon innumerable subjects and that, for both men, the collaboration was often close and rewarding. Wilson obviously had many initial reservations about the man whom he appointed to oversee American foreign policy, but, as time passed, he did develop a high respect for Bryan. It was with regret, as the correspondence over the *Lusitania* notes clearly demonstrates, that the President overruled his Secretary of State, for Wilson realized that Bryan almost instinctively reflected the attitudes and opinions of the great democracy which he represented. Moreover, within the administration Bryan was an indispensable link between the old and the new, the one Democrat who made it possible for Populists and Progressives to create a working majority and thereby write the New Freedom into American law. The passage of the Federal Reserve Act, to mention but one piece of legislation, would never have been possible if Bryan had not played this useful role. It must also be said that, whatever the merits or demerits of his attitude toward the problem of war, Bryan had the courage of his convictions. When differences of opinion became irreconcilable, he did what few American politicians have ever brought themselves to do: he resigned from the Cabinet and attempted to take his case to the country. And even within the walls of the supposedly cynical Department of State, this act of self-denial moved great numbers of government employees, some with tears in their eyes, to come to say a word of farewell to a man willing to give up the second highest position in the United States government on a matter of principle.

II

Even in an age when the qualifications for the post of Secretary of State were something less than demanding, William Jennings Bryan brought dubious credentials to that office. His principal claim was that of the elder statesman, the three-time loser as standard-bearer of his party who, over the years, had won for himself a personal following that numbered in the millions and was composed "of friends who were all but worshippers." Equally relevant was the fact that at the dramatic Baltimore convention of 1912 Bryan had played a decisive role in swinging delegates to the cause of Woodrow Wilson. It was clear that no one really wanted to appoint Bryan to the highest position in the Cabinet, but it was equally clear that no one wanted to run the risk of not including him in the new administration. Bryan, in short, was appointed as a reward for years of faithful service to the Democratic party as well as from fear that, if he were not included in the new administration, he might produce incalculable harm.

His intellectual qualifications for the Secretaryship were no more impressive than his political claims. A man of fixed ideas, Bryan had a decided tendency to oversimplify complex issues, to look upon tangled diplomatic problems as relatively simple matters of right and wrong, and to believe that controversy could be eliminated by the application of a few homely truths. Typically, Bryan's very first set of instructions, which he sent to American officials in revolution-torn Mexico, noted that "as disagreements generally arise from misunderstandings or from conflicts of interest, it is wise to remove misunderstandings by conference and to reconcile conflicting interests by mutual concessions. . . ." It was the responsibility of Americans to work for cooperation between the various conflicting factions in Mexico "upon a basis of justice to all at home and abroad."

Bryan's general outlook on the world was that of an unsophisticated opponent of anything that could be called imperialism. Indeed, much that Bryan attempted to do can be explained by pointing out that, in his political lexicon, imperialism was a cardinal sin. As a matter of strict principle, he opposed virtually everything that Philander C. Knox and the advocates of "dollar diplomacy" held dear, and he wrote fondly of his desire to replace their policies with "a system more in harmony with our nation's traditions and ideals." Dollar diplomacy, indeed, appeared to Bryan as merely the foreign policy of the same wicked business interests whose domestic policies he had long fought and opposed. At one of the first Cabinet discussions of the Mexican Revolution, the Secretary endorsed fully the proposition "that the chief cause of this whole situation," as Josephus Daniels, himself a Bryanite, phrased it, "was a contest between English and American oil companies to see which would control." When Bryan was approached about continued American participation in a Chinese loan consortium, he rejected any such action on the grounds that the consortium granted monopolistic privileges to a restricted group of American financiers. His record of continuous opposition to imperialism was clear. Although he had supported the great crusade to free Cuba in

1898 and had, for mistaken reasons, advocated ratification of the treaty which added the Philippines to the American domain, he never again wavered in his opposition to what he regarded as the naked imperialism of the Republican administrations of McKinley, Roosevelt, and Taft.

A no less significant aspect of Bryan's outlook was his pronounced moralism and his belief that the United States, as the foremost democracy in the world, had a duty to set an example for the other, less fortunate nations which had not yet scaled the heights of American achievement. When he opposed American intervention in Mexico in 1913, he rested his case in large part upon the argument that "our nation claims to stand in the forefront of the world's civilization and aspires to be the greatest moral influence in the world. We cannot hope to realize our ambition or to support our claim if we are willing to engage in war with a neighboring people merely to protect property which has been acquired with a full knowledge of the risks attendant upon it." This was not a new attitude for Bryan. In a speech delivered long before he became Secretary of State, he had envisioned a future in which the rest of the world would look upon the United States as "the supreme moral factor in the world's progress and the accepted arbiter of the world's disputes." This moral perspective affected not only Bryan's general outlook but also his daily conduct of the business of the Department of State. He was opposed, for example, to recognizing the Huerta regime in Mexico, even though this step was recommended as a matter of practical necessity. He was, as he put it, "so unaccustomed to the consideration of public questions separated from both morals and the principle of popular government that I was not able to endorse the position of those who favored the recognition of Huerta."

Bryan, of course, had had no formal experience with the business of diplomacy. He had traveled abroad, but there is no evidence that his visits to Latin America, Europe, and the Far East had provided him with insights into the state of affairs in those regions. It seems, rather, that Bryan saw what he wanted to see and that his travels only confirmed what he had suspected beforehand. Certainly his Latin-American trip merely produced speeches in which he told his Latin-American audiences that they were the victims of imperialism, and his conversations with Tolstoy in Europe simply reinforced his pacifistic convictions. His reaction to the proposed appointment of Charles Eliot, the former president of Harvard, as American Minister to the new republic of China, clearly indicated his lack of knowledge about actual conditions in foreign countries. To appoint a Unitarian to this position, Bryan immediately protested, would be an insult to China; the Chinese Revolution, he insisted, was a Christian movement conducted by men who had imbibed deeply the Christian faith.

Bryan had one principal aim: to further the work of the peace movement by negotiating a series of treaties which would make it virtually impossible for the United States to go to war with any nation. Believing that the principles of Christian pacifism were viable to meet the conflicts of nations, he had consistently preached peace on the Chautauqua circuit. There had indeed been no more fervent worker in that garden. Since 1904 he had favored a series of agreements—ultimately dubbed the "cooling-off treaties"—whereby no nation would go to war until there had been a twelve-month period of grace during which the basic facts underlying the dispute would be investigated. The plan was not original with Bryan, for he was by no means an original thinker, but it did reveal his abiding faith in the goodness and rationality of man. It was inconceivable to Bryan that any people, once the issues had been clarified and publicized, would deliberately choose the course of war and reject the possibility of compromise. Even after the European war had broken out, Bryan wrote to Lloyd George reaffirming his belief in international arbitration: "There is no dispute that must necessarily be settled by force. All international disputes are capable of adjustment by peaceful means. Every guarantee that can possibly be secured by war can be stated as a condition precedent to peace."

In March, 1913, the future Secretary's qualifications and objectives appeared sufficient to both Bryan and Wilson. Indeed, when the two men discussed Bryan's pending appointment, they considered only two matters —Bryan's desire to avoid serving alcoholic beverages at official functions and Wilson's attitude toward the projected cooling-off treaties. The new administration was primarily concerned with domestic problems and with creating the conditions for the New Freedom at home. So little were the two men aware of international difficulties that the President could remark —and it was *not* in the spirit of prophecy—that it would be ironic if his administration had to pay great attention to foreign affairs.

Certainly Bryan assumed office without any sense of deep concern for the nation's diplomatic future. He would simply reverse the imperialism of his predecessor and re-establish American foreign policy upon moral foundations. He would negotiate his long-sought peace treaties. In addition, he would reward loyal Democrats who had long labored in the political wilderness. These were modest goals which, in other times and circumstances, might have been possible to achieve. But, unfortunately for Bryan and his reputation, the future was to involve the United States in problems for which neither he nor the President was intellectually prepared.

III

Bryan was no less controversial during his Secretarial years than he had been in the days when he advocated the panacea of free silver. At the outset there was the expected quota of unflattering comment about what the newspapers called "grapejuice diplomacy"—dinners and receptions without benefit of alcohol. His penchant for leaving Washington for periodic speaking engagements on the Chautauqua circuit drew the fire of critics who charged that the Secretary lacked interest in his job and that it was improper for him to accept payment for public lectures. These tours, however, were a virtual necessity for Bryan's peace of mind. Since he took seriously his title as the Great Commoner and regarded himself as the representative of the people in the councils of government, he felt an inner obligation to speak in public of his work for peace and justice. Moreover, since his natural means of communication was the emotional address rather than the written report or the reasoned memorandum, he could not long have remained content if the opportunity to perform as an orator had been denied him.

The greatest criticism of Bryan was directed against his unabashed devotion to the tenets of the spoils system, for although the American Foreign Service was as yet essentially unreformed, there were already many who believed that diplomatic appointments should bear some relationship to merit and professional qualifications. Historians have recounted the lugubrious details of how Bryan replaced experienced diplomats with an unappetizing collection of political war horses, and there is no reason to repeat these stories here. But it should be emphasized that there was nothing malicious in this practice. Bryan, with his Jacksonian faith in the common man, honestly believed that, just as he himself was qualified to conduct the affairs of state, any average American could carry on the relatively simple task of representing his country abroad. It is also true that he and Wilson distrusted many of the officials appointed by previous administrations and believed that they represented a point of view antithetical to the ideals of the New Freedom. Even so, the work of replacement was essentially that of an American politician doing what politicians in this country have always done—finding suitable rewards for those who have served their party. At an early Cabinet meeting, Bryan reported that he was having great difficulty finding a suitable place for the brother of the chairman of the Democratic National Committee. Even Bryan admitted that the candidate, although admirably suited for government employment, was not particularly qualified for a position in the Consular Service. He therefore proposed a trade. "I will give a man a position at $4,000," he told his colleagues, "if you will give me a $4,000 job in another Department." The Attorney General rose to the bait. "All right," he answered, "I will give him a place if you will let me name the minister to Persia." Bryan just as promptly accepted. "All right, send over your man," he said.

The new Secretary of State was held in low esteem both by foreign officials and by many of his associates in the administration. Some diplomats, such as the British Minister, Cecil Spring-Rice, came close to being openly contemptuous; and the general European opinion of Bryan was summed up in a remark that Colonel Edward M. House recorded in his diary: "Mr. Asquith cast the usual slur upon Mr. Bryan." Indeed, on count-less occasions House admonished Wilson not to rely upon Bryan in his dealings with European governments. "Please let me suggest that you do not let Mr. Bryan make any overtures to any of the Powers involved," the Colonel wrote in the summer of 1914. "They look upon him as absolutely visionary, and it would lessen the weight of your influence if you desire to use it later yourself." Walter Hines Page, the American Ambassador to Great Britain, regarded Bryan as little more than an untutored frontiers-man with no understanding of the great issues of Anglo-American rela-tions. Page incessantly complained that Bryan mishandled official cor-respondence to such a degree that it was impossible for him to learn what was going on in Washington and pointless for him to try to keep the Secre-tary of State informed about events in London. Likewise, a number of Bryan's associates in the administration left behind memoirs in which they recorded their doubts about his administrative ability and his general fitness for office.

Much of this criticism can be at least partially discounted. Colonel House, cherishing his own position as the unofficial adviser behind the Wilsonian throne, had never truly respected Bryan and was always more than willing to assume diplomatic assignments which properly belonged to the Secretary of State. Although he had learned to respect Bryan's good intentions, he also clearly believed that his own outlook in world affairs was broader and wiser than that of the Great Commoner. Within the Democratic party, too, there were leaders who represented a more sophis-ticated point of view; to them Bryan's rural enthusiasms would be suspect automatically. European governments, eager to obtain American support for the policies which they pursued after the outbreak of war in 1914, could scarcely be expected to view with much favor a man devoted to strict neutrality and pacifism. Their ministers and ambassadors, trained in a tradition in which the forms of diplomacy were often as important as the content, naturally looked upon Bryan with disfavor. Thus, one should be properly skeptical about much of the criticism of Bryan which is to be found in the diaries, memoirs, and autobiographies of the Wilson era. But not entirely. The virtually unanimous disapproval of Bryan indi-cates that he lacked the qualities which alone permit an American Secretary of State to deal effectively with foreign governments and thereby to ad-vance the interests of his country.

Bryan faced certain obstacles on the Washington scene which added to his troubles as Secretary of State. There was Colonel House, who had already established his own personal influence with the President. And the

Texas colonel, whatever his faults and limitations, was no isolationist who wished merely to shelter America from European storms. He proposed imaginative schemes to avert world conflict through an Anglo-German-American agreement, he outlined a far-reaching project for Pan-American union, and he suggested many plans whereby the United States could play an effective role in the European conflict. It was therefore not surprising that Wilson, whose mind could also encompass the vision of aiding human-ity in the whole, was not only attracted by the grandiose schemes of House but also tempted—to the disadvantage of Bryan—to give important diplo-matic assignments to his unofficial adviser. Moreover, within the Depart-ment of State there was a highly competent international lawyer, Robert Lansing, whose stature with the President steadily increased and whose reasoned documents on the issues of the European war carried ever-increasing weight at the White House. As luck would have it, Bryan was absent from his post during the autumn of 1914 and concerned with the November elections at the time when the principal business of the Depart-ment of State was to establish the American attitude toward the British blockade of the Central Powers. Thus it was Lansing who handled the American response to all the issues related to the blockade and who thereby established a position for himself in the policy-making process that made him virtually coequal with Bryan.

In the last analysis, however, the crucial fact is that Bryan was Secretary of State to a Chief Executive who, despite his lack of experience in diplo-macy, firmly believed that he had both the right and the duty to direct all phases of foreign policy. Wilson's energy and direction did not reduce Bryan to the status of a mere subordinate without the power of initiative or an adviser who was never consulted. The record is quite the contrary. On many issues, such as the negotiation of the cooling-off treaties or the daily conduct of Latin-American affairs, Wilson was quite content to leave the development of policy in the hands of his Secretary. Moreover, whatever the subject, there was an extensive interchange of notes and memoranda between the two men; the sheer bulk of the Wilson-Bryan correspondence indicates that Bryan was never bypassed to the extent that Cordell Hull was during World War II. Wilson and Bryan, as Ray Stannard Baker has attested, were united by many common beliefs and had "a common devotion to a body of ideas and ideals as deep and as old as the foundations of the nation." The record again bears reliable witness to the fact that the President came to have abiding respect for his Secretary of State—"my elder son" was the epithet which Wilson used in conversations within his own family.

On such fundamental issues as the handling of the *Lusitania* notes, Bryan could not develop arguments sufficient to convince his chief to treat the Germans with leniency. But it is also clear that, even on this bedrock issue, the President felt it necessary to weigh carefully the arguments presented by his Secretary of State. On more than one occasion Bryan's advice compelled Wilson to pause, to reconsider his own ideas in the light of his Secretary's criticism, and only then to move ahead. Yet when the issues were sufficiently crucial or when the President's own emotions and intellect were involved, Wilson was clearly his own Secretary of State. Of this there can be no doubt. Bryan might be consulted, his views might be given proper consideration, but final decisions were made in the White House. Thus, the administration's policy toward Mexico, the stand taken on the Panama Canal tolls, and the handling of the German submarine problem were all the work of Wilson; Bryan was, at best, the informed subordinate. This, however, was not necessarily a reflection upon Bryan's abilities or an indication that the President did not respect his Secretary. Robert Lansing, a far more knowledgeable and able man than Bryan, received the same treatment when he succeeded Bryan as Secretary of State. If both men were subordinates, the reason lies in the character and temperament of the President—in his conviction that ultimate responsibility was his and in his confidence in his own mission.

Another characteristic of Wilson's handling of foreign affairs which adversely affected Bryan's position was the President's predilection for using special agents or personal favorites to carry on the work of American diplomacy. The already muddy waters of Mexican-American relations were further dirtied by a steady procession of Presidential agents given special assignments to report their observations to the White House. Colonel House was sent on various missions to Europe about which Bryan was not fully informed and over which he certainly had little control. That this confused the conduct of foreign policy is unquestionable. It is quite clear that on more than one occasion the British assumed that House spoke for the American government and, as a result, not only regarded some of his statements more seriously than was wise but also tended to disregard the words of Bryan. Similarly, though Page complained that Bryan did not keep him informed about developments in Washington, at least part of the reason for this situation was that Bryan was aware of the elaborate House-Page-Wilson correspondence which was conducted through unofficial channels; Bryan could assume, with more than a little justice, that he had no responsibility to tell Page about things which the Ambassador was already learning from other sources. Thus, some of the confusion attendant upon American diplomacy in these years resulted not from Bryan's lack of administrative ability but from Wilson's tendency to rely upon personal agents and to bypass normal channels of communication. But this situation lasted long after Bryan had resigned, and Robert Lansing —as any study of the Peace Conference of 1919 will reveal—labored under the same handicaps.

IV

But, whether or not Bryan was master in his own house, he can be appraised only in terms of the policies which he recommended or sanctioned during his slightly more than two years in office. What did he hope to accomplish in the Far East or in Latin America? Were his objectives in the national interest? And how, above all, did he react to the European war, for the raging conflict in Europe confronted Bryan with the gravest dilemmas that any American Secretary of State had encountered since the time of William H. Seward.

In the spring of 1913, Far Eastern problems seemed ridiculously easy to handle. It was the American purpose to aid the Chinese Revolution and to halt the meddling of American imperialists. Thus it was decided to accord diplomatic recognition to the new Chinese republic and to withdraw governmental support from the bankers' consortium. These decisions were based not upon prolonged study of the power relationships in the Orient but upon the essentially moralistic logic that monopolistic grants of financial rights were contrary to American principle and that recognition would demonstrate American approval for China's presumed evolution toward democratic institutions of government. Nor, of course, was there any apparent reason to consult the few holdover experts in the State Department; their opinions, conditioned by the years of dollar diplomacy, could be presumed irrelevant. Both Bryan and Wilson, in short, labored under the early-twentieth-century version of the "China myth"; theirs was the delusion, as Arthur Walworth has succinctly written, "that the millions of China ... were groping toward a Christian democracy patterned upon the Republic of the United States, and that it was the manifest duty of good Americans to aid them."

Far Eastern skies, however, soon became threatening and caused far more difficulty than either Bryan or Wilson had anticipated. Japan was angered by proposals before the California Legislature to deny Japanese the right to own land. As the dispute, at first underestimated by Wilson and his Cabinet, became more serious, Bryan became deeply involved. His role, from first to last, was conciliatory. He made fruitless efforts to persuade the Californians to modify their pending legislation; he and Daniels were the Cabinet members most strongly opposed to suggestions from the Army and the Navy that the United States begin taking advance military precautions by changing the disposition of fleet units in the Far East; and he continually tried to convince Baron Chinda, the Japanese Ambassador in Washington, that the United States wanted to preserve friendly relations with his country. Typical of Bryan's attitude during the controversy was his often-quoted remark—made to Chinda when that dip-

lomat apparently thought that the United States had made its "final" offer—
that "nothing is final between friends."

The crisis of May, 1913, vanished almost as rapidly as it had appeared.
But when World War I broke out, the Japanese, who had long been
thwarted in their expansionist moves, realized that the disruption of the
balance of power in the world provided them with a splendid opportunity
to resume their course of empire. When Japan began to press her claims
upon China, Bryan naturally sided with the Chinese and became involved
in the familiar American diplomatic game of note writing. One of his last
major acts in the Department of State was to reassert, in the face of Japan's
Twenty-one Demands, the traditional American insistence upon recognition by all nations of the territorial and administrative integrity of China.

It would be difficult to discover any immediately harmful consequences
of Bryan's Far Eastern diplomacy. The settlement of Japan's expansionist
claims was not worked out until after the European war was concluded,
and the touchy issue of alien-land legislation, which, like that of Oriental
immigration, had started in the era of Theodore Roosevelt, was to drag on,
with only partial alleviation, until long after Bryan had departed the national scene. In the short run, Bryan's conciliatory tactics in 1913 were
certainly beneficial; the President's military advisers were unduly alarmed,
and their military plans, if executed, might have fanned embers into flames.
Yet in point of fact Bryan did very little except offer soothing words; he
was, for example, far less severe with the recalcitrant Californians than
Roosevelt and Root had been at the time of the first Japanese-American
crisis. The quick passage of the incident owed less to Bryan's diplomacy
than to Japanese reluctance to turn it into a major issue. On the other hand,
the uncritical way in which Bryan allied himself with the Chinese added
one more important link to the chain of events whereby Americans came
to think of themselves as the chosen friends and protectors of China. Moreover, the series of notes in which Bryan indicated American opposition
to the Twenty-one Demands led to unnecessary complications in later
negotiations, for they were so imprecisely stated that they could be given
different interpretations in Washington and in Tokyo.

Bryan's record in Latin-American affairs is a far more perplexing one;
it is, indeed, a record which must forever confound the historian who
desires to fit his subject into any neat pattern of consistency. Bryan began,
as in the Far East, with the desire to undo the imperialistic wrongs of the
past, but, as his critics have noted gleefully, he ended by sponsoring as
many interventions as had his predecessor. This inconsistency between
intent and deed resulted in part from Bryan's inexperience. Since he knew
almost nothing about actual conditions in Latin America, he was compelled, in spite of himself, to listen to the advice of officials in the Latin-
American Division who had long since become convinced that only the

techniques of intervention would work effectively in the countries to the south. Then, too, although Bryan was essentially a pacifist, he was not deficient in patriotism (he had, after all, volunteered in 1898), and he was fully aware of the need to protect the routes to and from the Panama Canal. He found no conflict between his anti-imperialistic philosophy and the presumed need of the United States Navy to acquire bases protecting the Windward Passage. Indeed, as early as June, 1913, Bryan was hard at work trying to obtain from Haiti a coaling station long prized by American admirals. When the effort failed, he was no less eager than Knox to get the Haitians to promise that the potential naval base would never be leased to any other foreign country.

Bryan's interventions in Latin America can also be explained in part by the sheer lack of alternatives. Once he had decided that it was necessary to stabilize conditions in a particular country, it was obviously necessary to find the money for the task. But when Wilson would not approve some of Bryan's unorthodox financial remedies and when Congress proved reluctant to move with any celerity, Bryan found himself obliged to turn to the same banking houses which had been patronized by Knox. Finally, and more regrettably, Bryan's interventions were the result of his naïveté. His plan for the reformation of Nicaragua included provisions, comparable to the terms of the Platt amendment, whereby American military intervention would be entirely legal in the event of revolution or disorder. When Bryan argued in behalf of these provisions, he stressed repeatedly that the Nicaraguan government itself wanted to give such rights of intervention to the United States. But Bryan never asked himself why the Latin-American officials were so willing; he never considered that in Nicaragua, where revolution was then the national pastime, an unpopular, discredited regime might desire the privilege of calling on the United States Marines, seeing in their intervention the only means of remaining in office.

Yet these reasons alone could never have led Bryan to drink at the well of imperialism. There was also—indeed, there had to be—the firm belief that America was performing a service by bringing the benefits of its own successful national experience to the aid of less privileged peoples. For, as Arthur Link has persuasively argued, both Bryan and Wilson were motivated by a missionary zeal to render disinterested service. Thus, although their interventions may have been similar in kind to those of Knox and Taft, there was a marked difference in motive. Furthermore, there were more than a few scattered occasions when Bryan issued statements designed to protect Latin Americans not only from American financial interests but also from their own susceptibility to exploitation. One note, for example, declared that the Department of State had a responsibility to prevent citizens of the United States from obtaining excessive financial privileges in Latin America. It would, indeed, be difficult to imagine such

a memorandum emanating from the desk of Knox or his assistant, Huntington Wilson.

The Secretary of State was unquestionably bothered by the implications
of his "imperialism." He tried to develop new approaches or different
rationales which would make what he was doing acceptable to his conscience. His solutions were both inventive and ingenious; even if incapable
of fulfillment, they indicated that Bryan was a man who did not live entirely
by platitudes and who put much time and thought into his work at the
Department of State. One remedy which he suggested was a reworking
of the Monroe Doctrine to bring it into line with the contemporary situation. The real danger to Latin America, Bryan argued, came not from
European political or military threats but from the impact of foreign financial interests. Local rulers in Latin America, in their eternal search for
funds, turned to Europe for financial assistance and, with this foreign
help, were able to maintain themselves in power. At times the foreign
bankers themselves obtained a stranglehold upon the economy of the country. But in either case, Bryan was careful to point out, "the people are as
helpless as if a foreign army had landed on their shore." On another occasion he argued that American bankers pointed to the disordered political
conditions in Latin America as an excuse for demanding exorbitant rates
of interest or as justification for calling upon the United States Navy to
send gunboats to protect their investments. The solution for these varied
problems, Bryan contended, was for the United States government itself
to provide the necessary loans, to peg them at low rates of interest, and to
establish provisions whereby a part of the interest could be set aside for
the eventual repayment of principal. It was Wilson who found this proposal too unorthodox and who never expressed more than polite interest
in it. Yet, although Bryan's project was obviously related to his naïve tendency to place excessive blame upon "the interests," it did anticipate
methods of international financing which in more recent years have become
commonplace—the substitution of intergovernmental loans for private
business arrangements.

The problem of Mexico was second only to the European war as a
cause of diplomatic difficulties for the Wilson administration. Mexico, to
be sure, was the private preserve of the President, and American policy
toward Victoriano Huerta and Venustiano Carranza was determined by
Wilson himself. But the views of Secretary and President on the Mexican
problem were marked by only minor points of disagreement; Bryan, for
example, was unhappy about the landing at Vera Cruz and more than a
little relieved when the intervention of the ABC powers (Argentina, Brazil,
and Chile) offered Wilson a way out of his difficulties. On balance, however, the coincidence of viewpoints was more striking than the dissimilari-
ties. Indeed, when Bryan curtly rejected one of Huerta's notes during

the controversy that followed the arrest of two American sailors at Tampico, Wilson scribbled the marginal comment, "Your reply . . . is exactly what I would have wished it to be." Bryan certainly did not attempt to rock the Wilsonian boat over Mexico. It was typical of his attitude that, when the American admiral at Tampico first reported the arrest of his sailors and his demand for a public apology, the Secretary of State merely passed the message on to the President without analysis and with the uncritical comment that he could see no way that the officer could have acted otherwise. When questions were raised about the right of American sailors to land at Tampico, Bryan was quite content to accept the arguments put forth by the General Board of the Navy (which naturally put the onus upon the Mexicans) and to transmit these to Mexico City as representing the opinions of the Department of State. Bryan's contribution to the Mexican policy of Wilson thus seems to have been one of almost unquestioning support.

V

In the twentieth century, unfortunately, the ultimate test of the statesman has been his understanding of the uses—or misuses—of the instruments of coercion. In a half century of global conflict, the leaders of nations have all too often had to face the issue of whether to resort to force or to find avenues for compromise, conciliation, or appeasement. Bryan's instinctive reaction was to shun coercive methods and to search for peaceful solutions. During the controversy over the Panama Canal tolls, Josephus Daniels recorded the following entry in his diary: "England is willing to arbitrate. Mr. Burleson said he did not believe in arbitration. Mr. Bryan said he would arbitrate anything." The Secretary of State, on another occasion, resolutely opposed all suggestions that the United States provide armed protection for its citizens who had remained in Mexico to protect their own private business interests. These Americans, Bryan was convinced, were staying of their own volition in a country where they were not welcome; military protection could be tendered them only if the United States first recalled all its citizens from Mexico, requested the Mexican government to grant them safe conduct, and then learned that Mexico could not guarantee such safe conduct. Then, and then only, could the United States legitimately consider the use of force. Likewise, after he had resigned from the administration, Bryan refused to endorse the plans of the League to Enforce Peace because they called for the use of force to fight force. At times Bryan could be virtually unreasonable at the mere suggestion of the possible use of coercive methods. During the 1913 dispute with Japan, Bryan "got red in the face" when the Secretary of War merely stated that, in his opinion, officers of the Army and Navy were competent to decide whether or not naval vessels should be moved to other stations as a precaution. "He thundered out," one witness later recalled, "that Army and Navy officers could not be trusted to say what we should or should not do ... that we were discussing not how to wage war, but how not to get into war."

This is not to imply that Bryan was always consistent, for he obviously tolerated military moves against Mexico and he utilized the Navy in the Caribbean. And he was willing to go to war if the United States itself was attacked. He remained convinced, however, that there would always be sufficient time to create a nation in arms out of the millions of Americans who would volunteer to defend their country after it had been attacked. Like many Americans of his time, he felt that military preparedness was wrong, that it was a cause rather than a symptom of international tension, and that, in any event, the United States could establish a force capable of repelling any enemy after the crisis occurred.

It is not surprising, therefore, that Bryan believed at the time—and long continued to believe—that his greatest accomplishment as Secretary of State was the successful negotiation of the series of treaties whereby the United States and the signatory nations agreed to submit their disputes to an investigating panel and refrain from going to war during the period that the issues were under investigation. These cooling-off treaties, as previously noted, did not represent any original contribution on the part of Bryan and—aside from a clause which permitted disputes involving that greatest of all intangibles, "the national honor," to be investigated— were not dissimilar to various arbitration and conciliation treaties submitted to the Senate by William Howard Taft. To Bryan's credit, however, the Senate, which was normally provided with built-in mechanisms to resist such proposals, readily endorsed his treaties and subjected them to little adverse criticism. This occurred in part because Bryan carefully explained his purposes to the senators and kept them well informed and also because the chairman of the Foreign Relations Committee, being himself a Democrat of the Bryanite faith, needed little persuasion.

What was even more noteworthy was Bryan's continuing faith in the validity of his treaties. His convictions remained unchanged despite the fact—and it is, indeed, one of the central ironies of his career—that the first great holocaust of the twentieth century broke out in Europe just at the moment when his treaties were being signed. He rejoiced in the British signature, although a more suspecting Secretary of State, noting that Britain's final approval came less than a month after that nation had gone to war with Germany, might have concluded that the British had an ulterior motive and were, by signing the treaty, trying to convince the United States of England's abiding love of peace. Indeed, Bryan even convinced himself that Imperial Germany endorsed his treaties "in principle." Therefore, although he never obtained the German signature on a cooling-off treaty, he regarded the German attitude with perfect equanimity and thought that Germany's agreement "in principle" provided a viable basis for German-American negotiations designed to break the stalemate over the submarine issue. The frequently-told story about Bryan and the plowshares is revealing of both the naïveté and the sincerity of his hopes for peace: After the signing of several of his treaties, Bryan obtained a surplus Army sword from the War Department and had it melted down and recast into miniature plowshares; these he distributed personally to his colleagues at special Departmental ceremonies. On each was inscribed the Biblical quotation about beating swords into plowshares and, in addition, two maxims: "Nothing is final between friends," and "Diplomacy is the art of keeping cool."

VI

For William Jennings Bryan, as for Woodrow Wilson, the European conflict was the greatest challenge of all. Here again the basic policy was that of the President, and Bryan was the consultant whose ideas were given careful attention but, in the last analysis, were never decisive.

At the outset of the war there was no fundamental disagreement between the two men. Bryan's desire for absolute impartiality between the belligerents was matched by Wilson's insistence that his fellow countrymen should remain neutral in thought and deed. But not far beneath the surface were genuine differences. Wilson insisted that the belligerents must respect America's rights as a neutral, and as the war continued, he began to see a relationship between the issues of the war and the broader, more vital interests of mankind. But the matter of rights was never crucial to Bryan, certainly not when their enforcement seemed to demand American involvement in the conflict. Although Bryan, too, was concerned about the fate of mankind, his humanitarianism tended toward emotionalism, and he was always moved to personalize the great issues of the war and to view them in terms of the fate of individual human beings. Thus his instinctive reaction to the news of the sinking of the *Lusitania* was to declare that the British were trying to use women and children as a shield to get illicit armaments across the Atlantic. British policy, Bryan contended, was like putting women and children in front of an army. His particular brand of humanitarianism led him to believe one of the great hoaxes of World War I: the German charge that the civilian population of the *Reich* was being starved by Britain's "food blockade." And because he believed that the problem of food was crucial to Germany, he was led into a number of false moves which attempted to relate the British blockade to the submarine question.

Bryan was always certain that the European war was both unnecessary and wicked. From the very beginning of the conflict he begged Wilson to offer American mediation and to use all his influence to attempt to restore peace in Europe. He never cared about the issues which had led the powers to war or the underlying causes of the conflict. All that mattered to Bryan was the restoration of peace and the end of bloodshed. Indeed, he firmly believed that the onus of continuing the war was as great as the responsibility for initiating hostilities.

This is not to say that Bryan's ideas were entirely dissimilar to those of Wilson. The President, after all, was himself to propose mediation and on several occasions to express his opinion that the causes of the conflict were both obscure and irrelevant. But Bryan never showed any sophistication or sense of timing in his many calls for mediation; his mind never seemed to encompass any concept more complex than that of the virtue of peace and the wickedness of war; and he never suggested any feasible terms or programs whereby the blessed state of peace could be achieved. His ideas, in short, stopped at the point where Wilson's began.

In regard to American neutrality, however, the Secretary of State did offer some common-sense proposals which were not lacking in his usual ingenuity. There was, for example, his attitude on the famous issue of whether or not loans could be granted to the European belligerents—an issue whose importance was later swelled out of all proportion by the "revisionist" historians who believed that these loans were responsible for the American entry into the war. To a Bryan who had fought for free silver and who had never wavered in his hostility toward the "money power" of Wall Street, it was obvious that money was the great contraband which controlled everything else. The tenets of international law notwithstanding, there should be no loans. This outright prohibition was actually unneutral; it was founded upon distrust of the financiers rather than upon any understanding of the economics of modern war; and, as time was to prove, it was an unrealistic policy for a nation emerging from an economic recession and anxious to participate in wartime trade. Yet it had a common-sense appeal which was lacking in many of the more urbane arguments which were put forth to justify financial dealings with the Allies. There was also cogency in Bryan's contention that Americans who knowingly booked passage on Allied passenger vessels were, after Germany's formal announcement of submarine warfare, guilty of "contributory negligence." Therefore, if the ships on which they traveled were torpedoed, they were not entitled to the full protection of their neutral rights under international law. The doctrine of contributory negligence, so frequently employed in civil suits, could hardly be plucked out of Anglo-Saxon common law and applied to the more complicated structure of international law; and Woodrow Wilson, with his broader sense of the interests of both the United States and humanity, could not accept it. Yet, in retrospect, it too seems to have offered a leaven of common sense to the submarine controversies that was missing in the Wilsonian argument based on higher principle.

The split between President and Secretary became virtually inevitable when Wilson insisted upon treating German violations of American rights as more serious than those of Britain and, above all, as demanding immediate resolution. Bryan, whose concept of neutrality still demanded absolute impartiality and who wanted to avoid even the slightest chance of involvement, felt compelled to oppose Wilson at almost every step. He insisted that protests against German policy should be linked with protests against Great Britain. He could never understand the logic behind Wilson's argument that such an approach might lead the German government to temporize and to think that there was no urgency, since Anglo-American relations were also in a state of disarray. Bryan insisted that Germany must be given every opportunity to understand that Wilson's protests did not foreclose the possibility of peaceful settlement and that, indeed, the American government confidently expected a favorable response from William II. Bryan was never convinced that this would weaken the force of the American demands and perhaps convince Germany that Wilson's notes were not to be taken in deadly earnest. Above all, Bryan was afraid of any American step which could be interpreted as an ultimatum, any measure which would put the final decision for peace or war in the hands of William II and his advisers. It is true that Bryan's arguments did at least sway Wilson momentarily from his course and forced him to examine his own arguments in detail (though it is also true that Bryan weakened his own position by mishandling an interview with the Austrian Ambassador in such a way that he gave the impression of desiring peace at any price). But, throughout the weeks of the controversy, Bryan showed himself essentially unsuited to the rough-and-tumble of serious diplomacy and completely unable to be tough-minded in dealing with fundamental questions of national policy. Although his proposals had their usual quality of common sense, they were always too simple for the complexity of the issues and too liable to misinterpretation by those who would have received them.

By the time of the second set of *Lusitania* notes, there was clearly no alternative for Bryan but resignation. Wilson was absolutely determined that Berlin must realize the seriousness of the American protest; Bryan was equally determined that a conciliatory attitude must be preserved. There was a period of intense emotional strain during which the Secretary of State bluntly accused his colleagues in the Cabinet of harboring pro-British sympathies and accused the President of treating him as a mere figurehead. Unable to comprehend the attitude of the President, he went home night after night with the unanswered question, "Why can't he see that by keeping open the way for mediation and arbitration, he has the opportunity to do the greatest work man can do!" His resignation was an act of conscience, an act made necessary by his conviction that Wilson was unintentionally, but irrevocably, committing the nation to unnecessary war. He resigned to take the issue to the people.

The rest was anticlimax. Few understood the reasons for his resignation, and many a newspaper shrieked desertion. Moreover, when the second set of *Lusitania* notes did not produce the war which Bryan had feared, it was the President and not his former Secretary of State who appeared vindicated. Bryan developed no great following, and Wilson, ironically, was re-elected in 1916 as "the man who kept us out of war." But in a very real sense Bryan's failure to convince the American public was a sign not only that he had misread the popular temperament but also that his ideas were unsuited for the age in which he lived. Bryan had always assumed that, if "the people" had time to study the issues of international affairs and reflect upon them, they would always prefer peace to war. But after the election of 1916 was over and after the Germans had resumed unrestricted submarine warfare, the American public did not so react. The passage of time merely increased the sentiment for war. Thus, when April, 1917, came, Bryan was virtually a leader without troops.

VII

William Jennings Bryan left no permanent mark upon the Department of State. The significant ideas of 1913–1915 were those of the President, and it is the foreign policy of Woodrow Wilson that is studied by historians. Bryan was a stubborn man who could compel another stubborn individual, Wilson, to pay heed to his opinions, and the President valued his advice precisely because he realized that Bryan often reflected instinctively the attitudes of the average American on the farm or in the small town. But the great ideas which made these years memorable in the history of American foreign policy originated in the White House and not in the Department of State.

A Secretary of State can be too consistent. The record of Knox, for example, could have been improved by a few moralistic binges to counterbalance the drab sameness of his reliance upon dollars, investments, and marines. But Bryan's record was the worse for his inconsistency. He wanted to avoid the evils of dollar diplomacy in Latin America, but his lack of knowledge about that part of the world and his assumption that American standards of political behavior could be exported combined to produce a moralistic brand of imperialism which was even less appealing than the blunter practices of his predecessor. He wanted to stem the tide of imperialism in the Far East, but the foreign policy of morality became ridiculous when it was based on the assumption of the Christian character of the Chinese Revolution and positively dangerous when it failed to discover any way to deal with the rising power of Japan except to insist, as did the Open Door tradition, that all nations must respect the rights of China. Finally, it is impossible to reconcile Bryan's attitude toward Mexico with his insistence upon neutrality toward the war in Europe.

Bryan's most severe critics have been those who believe that America's greatest failures in diplomacy have resulted from a national inability to comprehend the role of power in international relations and from a tendency to shrink from its application. The "realists," to be sure, have often painted an exaggerated picture. They have drawn too sharp a dichotomy between realistic and idealistic approaches; at times they have conveniently overlooked the fact that precise calculations of the national interest were announced in idealistic terms in order to convince a skeptical public that the United States was really concerned with justice and morality; and they have frequently failed to realize that the ideals of a Woodrow Wilson might in fact be a form of "higher realism." But with respect to Bryan, the realist critique is unfortunately substantiated by fact. He did think that "power politics" was inherently wrong; he did believe that coercion and force were immoral; and he was convinced that American democracy was not only a unique achievement but also something to be taught to backward peoples and held up as an example to the snobbish societies of Europe. His, in short, was an essentially negative reaction to anything that can be described as "realistic."

But Bryan's greatest failure was his lack of analysis, for he approached all issues in terms of simple blacks and whites, of right and wrong, of "good" and "evil." He apparently never had command of the facts in a given situation or was aware, in advancing his own solutions, of the sharp complexities of the nettle he had grasped. Had he understood the causes of the European war or the forces which were prolonging that conflict, he could scarcely have advocated the simple remedy of mediation or have based his entire program on a foundation no stronger than the Christian belief that peace is always preferable to war. His greatest virtue, to be sure, was his love of peace—for, even in the twentieth century, the peacemakers have sometimes proved to be blessed. But his desire for peace, expressing itself in an insistence on strict American neutrality in a world at war, was also one of his greatest defects. World War I demonstrated that the world of the twentieth century is an interrelated world in which no country, let alone any individual, is an island. Bryan's simplistic conviction that America had no interest but to remain at peace was a personal attitude, not a viable policy.

It is exceedingly difficult for the historian, writing almost half a century after the event, to argue that there is much in Bryan's experience that is meaningful for America's present concerns. In an era in which intercontinental missiles can arrive on target in twenty minutes and in which the great danger is war from miscalculation, what is to be learned from a man who believed that the solution to the problem of war was to have the United States sign treaties promising to turn all its disputes over to impartial investigation and to forswear conflict for the twelve months during which the facts were being ascertained? The historian is tempted to conclude either that the lessons of Bryan's career in diplomacy are merely lessons in errors to be avoided—on the grounds, as Santayana wrote, that those who do not know the past are condemned to repeat it—or that the history of recent American foreign policy is essentially a repudiation of the principles for which Bryan is remembered. As a nation, the United States has grown, if not more sophisticated, certainly less innocent; by the seventh decade of the twentieth century, it had acquired sufficient experience to play the game of power politics in a manner to suggest that it had exorcised any Bryanesque ghost of the past.

Bryan was a representative of the old America which had to succumb before the age of steel and oil. His was essentially the outlook of rural, Middle Western America, of the small town and the small farm; it was an outlook which could not withstand the demands and pressures of the twentieth century. His career in domestic politics was itself an illustration of the fact that the agrarian, Populist virtues for which he stood were rapidly becoming outmoded. In Wilson's Cabinet, Bryan represented a point of view in domestic affairs that had already been superseded. It was the same in foreign policy. His ideas were anchored to a provincialism which rendered them even less applicable than Wilson's to the world in which he lived. Shortly after he resigned, Bryan returned to Nebraska and, in delivering an oration on the farmer's interest in peace, congratulated his cheering audience on living west of the Alleghenies. These mountains, he said, still served as a dike to keep out the heresies of the Eastern press. But Bryan was wrong. It was not the Eastern press that was corrupting the prairies from which he came. It was rather the twentieth century— with its wars and revolutions, its new weapons, its interrelated economies, its instantaneous communications, its global political issues—that was beginning to press in upon the towns and farms of his America. And, as time would eventually reveal, against these forces the Alleghenies were no barrier. In the twenties and thirties, to be sure, there would be a temporary return to many of the older, isolationist concepts, but the events of 1913 to 1915 had already indicated that the traditions which Bryan represented were unable to meet the new challenges that confronted the United States.

6

Robert Lansing

1915-1920

BY DANIEL M. SMITH
University of Colorado

Robert Lansing has emerged as one of those fortunate public men who have grown in stature with the passage of time. Although one of the ablest and most experienced American Secretaries of State of this century, he did not receive due recognition during his incumbency. The explanation, no doubt, lies largely in the realm of personalities—the reserved and proper Lansing was eclipsed by the eloquent Woodrow Wilson and by the President's well-publicized adviser, Colonel E. M. House. In the decades following the Wilson era, historians have slowly revised their estimates of Lansing's contributions to American foreign policy, until it is now generally agreed that his role in the years from 1914 to 1920 was one of great importance.

When Lansing assumed control of the State Department in 1915, he was fifty years of age—a short, distinguished-looking man, dignified and reserved in bearing, conservative in outlook. Born into a socially prominent New York family and educated at Amherst, he married the daughter of John Watson Foster, a former diplomat and Secretary of State. Lansing soon entered Foster's law practice and subsequently served as counsel for the United States at a series of international arbitrations. By 1914 he had traveled widely, had become intimately acquainted with influential foreign leaders, and had participated in more arbitrations than any other living American.

Almost painfully reserved, during his first years in Washington, Lansing found relaxation in a circle of close friends, to whom he was known as "Bert." He was famed among them for his addiction to coffee drinking

and his passion for fishing. Lansing was a prominent layman in the Presby-
terian Church. Later he took great pleasure in Washington's social functions, attending so frequently that Wilson once complained that Lansing
was ruining his health to the possible impairment of his duties.

Lansing was conservative in politics, religion, and diplomacy, but his
was a conservatism within the democratic tradition. An individualist of
the nineteenth-century vintage, he stressed freedom from governmental
controls and desired that change be made slowly within established institutions; but he was firmly committed to democratic procedures and viewed
democracy as the only cement uniting diverse peoples into the American
nation.

In the field of diplomacy and foreign policy, Lansing was a realist,
though his views were strongly tinged with idealism. He cherished the
rules of diplomacy and understood their usefulness. A perusal of Lansing's
daily desk diary impresses the reader with his meticulous observance of
diplomatic procedures. The "new diplomacy" of informal agents and of
negotiations which took the form of propaganda and debate filled Lansing
with distaste and dismay. He appreciated the virtues of cautious diplomacy
as a means of serving the national interest and protecting the national prestige. Wilson failed to understand this facet of his Secretary, mistaking
caution for dullness and lack of imagination.

Force and self-interest, in Lansing's view, were the determinants of
behavior in international politics. Sovereign states had no higher obligation
than the national interest, which Lansing understood basically as survival
and security. "Force is the great underlying actuality in all history," he
wrote, and "no nation at war, whose national safety is menaced . . . should
be expected to permit obligations of justice, morality, humanity or honor
to interfere with acts it considers necessary for its self-preservation."
He did not rule out idealism, but he believed that only by recognizing the
fundamental facts of national self-centeredness could any progress be
made toward a noble goal. For Lansing the American national interest
meant security in the Caribbean-Atlantic area, stability in the Far East,
and the preservation of the existing favorable power structure in Europe.
The mixture of realism and idealism in his thought is reflected in his belief
that the German government not only threatened American security and
economic interests but also menaced democratic institutions throughout
the world. He therefore advocated entering the war against Germany.
As the war ended, he favored a settlement based on reasonable boundaries
and a reliance on international law to prevent future wars, believing that
this approach, though it probably would not eliminate war, would at least
facilitate pacific settlement of many disputes. Skeptical of collective security and the new League of Nations, he has been incorrectly branded
an isolationist; instead, he was an internationalist of the Theodore Roose-

velt–Admiral Mahan–Elihu Root type, interested in the world, aware that nineteenth-century isolation was obsolete, but determined to preserve national sovereignty and diplomatic freedom.

The amazing feature of the Wilson-Lansing relationship is that it lasted so long. The two men were dissimilar in temperament and mental processes. Lansing was practical, skeptical, and keenly analytical; Wilson was idealistic, moralistic, and intuitive. Although many observers appreciated Lansing's gifts—foreign diplomats and statesmen acknowledged his merits— the President did not, and hence never really trusted or admired him. Wilson approved Lansing's appointment as Counselor in April, 1914, because he recognized Lansing's experience and technical knowledge; he chose him to succeed Bryan in mid-1915 primarily because he believed that he needed only a skilled lawyer to frame his policy decisions. Time revealed that Lansing was not an ardent Wilsonian and that his conservative views prevented him from giving the President the kind of unquestioning and uncritical loyalty that Wilson demanded. The President eventually regretted Lansing's appointment and considered removing him early in 1917, and again at Paris in 1919, but was dissuaded by Colonel House. Lansing, on the other hand, became disillusioned with Wilson, recording that the President was unable to brook criticism, was too intuitive mentally, and was often curt and insensitive toward others.

Despite such differences, Lansing continued in office for over four and a half years; moreover, by learning to handle his chief, he exerted considerable influence. He submitted long memoranda to the President which could be studied without a feeling of pressure, avoided references to public opinion as compelling a course of action, clothed policy advice in moralistic and idealistic terms, and worked closely with Colonel House and others in trying to sway Wilson to his point of view.

In contrast to Bryan, Lansing maintained good relations with the press, the Congress, and other members of the State Department. He was adept at handling newspaper reporters, he appreciated publicity, and he knew how to utilize the press for the benefit of the Department. His appointments were hailed with satisfaction, and as late as June, 1918, *Current Opinion* referred to him as the "most likable" head of the Department in the nation's history. Lansing appreciated fully the role and sensitivity of the Congress, bore himself well at committee hearings and in individual conferences, and remained on good terms with both Democratic and Republican congressional leaders. Within the Department and the Foreign Service, he succeeded in raising morale, which had been lowered by Bryan's spoilsmanship and inexperience. To the Foreign Service, Lansing seemed to be a nonpolitical appointee who was interested in an efficient merit career service (the Rogers Act of 1924 was in part Lansing's work). Finally, Lansing ran an orderly Department and kept himself accessible to his subordinates, conferring daily with his principal officers and advisers.

II

Lansing exerted his greatest influence during the neutrality period of 1914 to 1917. He rapidly came to the fore when war broke out in Europe, for Wilson and Bryan found it necessary to rely heavily on his knowledge of international law. His relations with the President became closer, and Bryan's absences in the fall of 1914 often left Lansing in charge of the Department. Consequently, Lansing had a large role in shaping basic policies: the tacit sanction of the arms trade; the acceptance of defensive armament on belligerent merchant ships (which Germany later claimed prevented the fragile submarine from adhering to the rules of warfare); the relaxation of the Bryan "loan ban" of August, 1914, to permit private commercial credits for the Allies; and the holding of Germany to "strict accountability" for the loss of American ships and lives within the proclaimed submarine zone around the British Isles. In disputes with the Allies, Lansing consistently conducted exchanges so that legitimate interests were protected and a legal case was made for postwar settlement, but he never allowed any issue to become so sharp as to threaten seriously Anglo-American relations or to embarrass the Allied war effort. Notes were verbose and inconclusive, and working arrangements were encouraged between private American firms and the British government to ease the impact of the blockade.

Disposed by both sentiment and reason toward the Allied cause, Lansing was not disturbed by the fact that American neutrality was benevolently oriented toward the Allied Powers. He was convinced that American policies were technically neutral, morally defensible, and consistent with the nation's economic, political, and ideological interests. Wilson and Lansing defended their strict-accountability policy not only by arguing that neutrals had the right to travel the high seas on neutral and belligerent vessels subject to the normal risks but also by proclaiming moral considerations and a determination to uphold American honor and prestige. Underlying this policy were both the realization that Germany threatened American commerce and prosperity and the consequent lack of any real desire to make an adjustment to German interests.

In the crises of the *Falaba* and *Lusitania* sinkings in the spring of 1915, Lansing carried his policy recommendations against Bryan's dogged resistance. The first and second *Lusitania* notes of May 13 and June 9 embodied Lansing's views. Asserting the illegality of submarine attacks without warning and ready provisions for rescue, Lansing insisted that Germany comply immediately with the American demands for disavowal and restitution. In effect, these notes required that belligerent merchant vessels carrying Americans be immunized from submerged U-boat attacks. Here lay the seeds of hostilities, for Germany eventually decided to ignore the risks of American belligerency for the possible gains of unrestricted undersea warfare. The strict-accountability policy was presented to the American people solely on the grounds of rights and morality.

On June 9, 1915, in the midst of the *Lusitania* crisis, Lansing was appointed Secretary of State ad interim. Much to his surprise and pleasure, this became a regular appointment on June 23, and Lansing at last was Secretary in name as he had been in fact, on European matters, since mid-1914.

Lansing adjusted easily to his new position. After moving his files into Bryan's office, he settled into an almost unvarying routine. His daily desk diary reveals his passion for order and detail; here are recorded, in his own hand, the exact times of his arrivals and departures (9:05 A.M. and 5:15 P.M.), interviews and consultations, luncheon guests, and telephone calls from Mrs. Lansing. On one occasion, Lansing utilized a leisured hour in noting, with obvious satisfaction, the details of his regular weekly schedule. Precision, order, regularity, routine—these were the characteristics of Lansing's official life.

Early in July, 1915, Lansing recorded his views on the war and on the correct policies to be followed. He had been convinced by the exchange of notes on the *Lusitania* sinking that a diplomatic rupture and war with Germany were not far distant. Increasingly he had come to believe that America's interests demanded an Allied victory and that to ensure that victory it might be necessary for the United States to enter the conflict.

Germany, the Secretary recorded in his private memoranda, was hostile to all democratic governments and sought to dominate Europe. He detected signs of German intrigue in Mexico, Haiti, and Santo Domingo, as well as in other Latin-American countries. He concluded that such anti-American activities were designed to prevent a firm American policy on the *Lusitania* and perhaps to prepare for war on the United States after the Allies had been crushed. To cope with this menace, Lansing proposed (1) to delay the present submarine controversy until the American public was ready for war; (2) to expose and suppress German plots within the United States; (3) to frustrate German intrigue in Mexico and the rest of Latin America; (4) to promote greater Western Hemisphere solidarity, especially against Germany, through emphasis on Pan-Americanism; (5) to improve relations with Mexico by recognizing the Carranza faction; (6) to purchase the Danish West Indies to forestall German acquisition; (7) to prevent German influence from becoming dominant in the Caribbean area and in the vicinity of the Panama Canal; and (8) to enter the war if necessary to prevent a German victory or even a stalemate. For Lansing, the necessity for these measures was heightened by the fact that he foresaw a possible alignment of Germany, Russia, and Japan—all absolutist states determined to divide the world among them. The American government should, he thought, subordinate all else to the possible necessity of entering the war and ensuring an Allied victory.

The Secretary's emphasis on an ideological concept of the war was sincere, for he believed that democracy was the world's best hope and that German absolutism threatened democratic institutions everywhere. But he was conscious also that ideological and moral terminology appealed both to the President and to the American people. His writings and policies reflect a deep awareness of national interests—economic advantage, prestige, and security—and he realized that the American tranquillity of the past had rested in large degree on a favorable world balance of power in which Britain had played the key role. What was now necessary was to educate the American people to the German menace and to avoid war "until the indignation . . . of the American people against Germany could be sufficiently aroused."

After the *Lusitania* crisis, Lansing consistently followed the policy of sharpening the U-boat issue but postponing drastic action until such time as the public would be ready for belligerency. The general difficulty of evaluating public opinion, the Secretary's overreliance on the pro-Ally Eastern press, and his own predilections caused Lansing on two occasions to conclude prematurely that the nation was ready for a showdown on the submarine issue, but each time he recovered and adjusted his actions accordingly.

When the British liner *Arabic* was torpedoed, with the loss of two Americans, on August 19, 1915, Lansing at first advised Wilson that the people were ready for drastic action. He tried to make such a course palatable to the President by noting that German friendship had been irretrievably lost, that a war entry would restore harmony with the Allies, and that American involvement would permit the United States to play a large role at the peace conference. Reactions from the rest of the country, however, revealed that most citizens were apparently apathetic. To escape the dilemma of attempting to pursue policies that satisfied both the doctrine of strict accountability and the will of the American people, Lansing on his own responsibility threatened Ambassador Bernstorff with a diplomatic break and eventual war if Germany did not halt attacks on enemy belligerent passenger ships. Impressed, Bernstorff helped persuade the Berlin government to promise that liners would not be sunk without warning and safety provisions.

In the winter of 1915, Lansing again believed that recent events—the series of submarine crises and the exposures of German propaganda activity in the United States—had prepared the public for action. With Wilson's approval, he revived the unresolved *Lusitania* case and demanded an admission of German liability and a disavowal of ruthless underseas tactics. Believing hostilities near, he alerted the War and Navy Departments and drafted a virtual ultimatum to Austria-Hungary, whose submarine had sunk the Italian liner *Ancona*. The note was sent, with a few Wilsonian phrase changes, and brought prompt Austrian compliance. Once more, however, Lansing was to discover that the public was not ready to fight.

On the day following the triumph over Austria-Hungary, the armed British liner *Persia* was sunk, with heavy loss of life. Instead of resulting in a widespread demand for hostilities, as Lansing had expected, the event touched off an impassioned debate on the soundness of the administration's foreign policies. Sharp criticisms were made in Congress of the alleged pro-Ally character of American neutrality, and measures were introduced to embargo the arms trade and prohibit citizens from traveling on enemy ships.

Lansing perceived again that he had misinterpreted the popular mood. Yet signs indicated that Germany was preparing a new U-boat campaign. The Secretary decided that the only solution was to seek a temporary compromise. If the Allies could be persuaded to abandon defensive arming of merchantmen, Germany would either have to agree to cease submerged submarine attacks or stand condemned before the world. Such an arrangement would not harm the Allies, he thought, and would help the American government out of a critical dilemma. It was not an unrealistic plan in conception, but Lansing did not know that Britain regarded the submerged U-boat as less dangerous than a surfaced one.

The President agreed that Lansing's proposal should be tried, and on January 18, 1916, the Secretary presented the *modus vivendi* to the Allied powers. It never received serious consideration. Great Britain angrily rejected the proposal as benefiting only Germany. Colonel House, then in Europe promoting a stillborn scheme for American mediation in the war, opposed the suggested compromise as likely to destroy Allied confidence in the United States. Germany tried to exploit the Lansing proposal to justify proclaiming ruthless warfare against all armed merchant ships. The contents of the compromise leaked to the American press, and loud demands ensued in Congress that Americans be kept off armed enemy vessels. The American government, thereupon, beat a hasty retreat and announced that the previous policy of October, 1914, was still in effect. Although the furor in Congress soon receded, the affair had been a diplomatic blunder. Regardless of the merits of the proposal—and there were some—Wilson and Lansing should have foreseen the Allied reaction and, having made the proposal, been prepared to force it through. Lansing had committed one of the few maladroit moves of his career, and it definitely diminished his stature with the President.

The ensuing *Sussex* crisis helped clarify the situation. On March 24, 1916, the vessel, an unarmed French channel steamer, was torpedoed. Viewing the attack as part of a full-scale renewal of underseas warfare, Lansing and House advised Wilson that the only step consistent with honor was to break diplomatic relations with Berlin. The President was most reluctant to act, however, resisting steps likely to lead to war. Lansing drafted a harsh note to Germany which declared that no apologies, indemnities, or disavowals would satisfy the United States. When Germany sent back an evasive reply, Wilson gave in to his advisers and completed a revision of Lansing's draft note designed to threaten a diplomatic break unless ruthless submarine warfare was halted. Upon receipt of the note, the German government re-examined its submarine policies and finally capitulated, giving a pledge on May 4 that belligerent passenger and other merchant vessels would not be attacked without warning and without safety provisions. Lansing was by no means satisfied, for he objected to the tone of the German note as insolent and equivocal; but he had helped, nevertheless, to sharpen the issue with Germany so that any renewal of ruthless submarine warfare would mean a certain break between the two governments.

In the interval between submarine crises, the State Department did not neglect its formal diplomatic duties toward the Allies. Although Lansing did not wish to interfere seriously with vital Allied measures, he believed it necessary to lodge a formal protest regarding the legality of the Allied blockade of March, 1915, and he was eager to prevent British trade on the Continent from being advanced at American expense. Wilson and House had resisted earlier, but in the fall of 1915 they agreed that a full protest was necessary. The note that was finally sent to London and Paris, on October 21, 1915, was prepared with the aid of the Joint State-Navy Neutrality Board, which Lansing had established in 1914 and which was headed by the able Dr. James Brown Scott and Counselor Frank L. Polk (later Under Secretary). Though designed as a sweeping challenge to the blockade, it was a long note and by no means a summary challenge. Britain calmly and leisurely prepared a reply, and the blockade continued. The proprieties had been satisfied.

The final barrier to an expanding war trade with the Allies meanwhile had been removed, and Lansing took advantage of another opportunity to defend that trade. In late summer, 1915, the administration was warned by American banking representatives that, unless the remainder of the Bryan loan ban was rescinded, so that the Allies could float general loans in America, the prosperity-producing purchases would soon cease for lack of credit. Lansing had never really approved the Bryan policy, and so he joined the Secretary of the Treasury in urging that the prohibition be scrapped. Wilson agreed, and in early September the ban was repealed.

A few months earlier, Lansing had persuaded Wilson to let him answer an Austro-Hungarian protest against the arms trade. The Lansing reply, admittedly designed for home consumption, defended the trade as both neutral and moral, for an arms embargo would penalize peaceful states and encourage aggressors. As Wilson suggested, the note implied a condemnation of the Central Powers as aggressors in the war.

The lowest point of American relations with the Allies was reached in the period after the *Sussex* pledge. American attention was free to concentrate on the numerous Allied interferences with neutral trade. Great Britain unwisely chose a presidential election year to add fresh fuel to the controversy by censoring neutral mails and black-listing neutral citizens, including Americans, accused of German ties. Lansing was greatly distressed lest the Washington government be pressured into sharp action against the Entente, convinced as he was that the true course of American policy was to aid the Allies and to join them in the war as soon as possible. Bending his every energy to smooth differences, the Secretary allowed the issue of censoring neutral mails to expire quietly. He was unable to dissuade Wilson from obtaining a mildly retaliatory authority from Congress, but he did rise from his sickbed, in June, to remind the American people of the essential differences between Allied acts affecting only property and submarine acts destroying precious lives. The Allies were greatly cheered by this speech, and in the autumn the number of Americans on the black list was reduced.

After his victory in the 1916 election, President Wilson made several attempts to mediate between the belligerents, aware that the United States would probably be drawn into the conflict if hostilities continued and convinced that a viable postwar world required that the war be halted short of full victory for either side. Lansing was not in sympathy with Wilson's program, believing that mediation was futile and failing to see any satisfactory alternative to American involvement in the war. Furthermore, he was afraid that an offer of mediation might seriously embarrass the Allies, for the existing war map favored Germany. The Secretary marveled at Wilson's inability to grasp the real issue and concluded that he was obsessed with a personal desire to play the peacemaker. So hostile was Lansing to mediation that he might well have resigned. Rejecting the opposition of Lansing and House, Wilson requested the belligerents, on December 18, 1916, to state their war aims. Lansing attempted deliberately to prepare the American people for war and to remove the sting for the Allies, who were opposed to mediation, by stating to the press that the President's note revealed how near the United States was to actual hostilities. The furious Wilson not only forced the Secretary to issue a semi-retraction but, for some time thereafter, refrained from taking him into the confidence of the White House. The "peace without victory" speech, delivered to Congress on January 22, 1917, was not shown to Lansing until quite late. Whatever the President's devotion to the cause of mediation, both of his peace efforts failed.

Early in 1917, there were numerous indications that a new submarine campaign was imminent. Lansing was not displeased, recording on January 28 the hope that the Germans blundered soon since the Allied cause was not prospering. On January 31, the expected blow fell, for the German government announced that all ships, neutral as well as belligerent, would be destroyed without warning in the waters around the British Isles. Lansing immediately urged the President to break relations with Berlin, if not to seek a declaration of war. Joined by Colonel House in his arguments that honor and rights were at stake, Lansing also invoked the theme that Prussian militarism threatened democracy and world peace —anticipating Wilson's subsequent invocation of the same view. In the Cabinet the Secretary restated his views forcefully and called for American involvement on the side of the Allies to secure the triumph of democracy and to protect America's security.

Persuaded by Lansing and House and constrained by his own public pledges, Wilson announced, on February 3, 1917, the severance of diplomatic relations. He was most reluctant to enter the war, however. Both his pacifistic inclination and his concern lest the balance of power in Europe and the Far East be upset by an American entry were factors in his hesitation. He insisted, therefore, on awaiting "actual overt acts" by Germany, and he apparently contemplated only limited participation in the war. Lansing, though admitting the need to prepare the public for hostilities, was sorely tried by what he viewed as Wilson's irresolution. Trying to exploit the President's interest in a prominent role at the eventual peace conference, Lansing informed him that the Allies, fearing too much generosity toward Germany, were no longer as eager for American belligerency. The Secretary joined other officials in urging the arming of American merchantmen for defense against submarines. After Wilson's request for congressional authorization of this step was frustrated by a Senate filibuster, it was Lansing who found the necessary legal basis in an 1819 statute. Lansing also utilized eagerly the intercepted Zimmermann telegram, in which Germany offered an alliance to Mexico, to arouse Wilson and the public to the necessity for war.

The sinking of three American vessels in mid-March was interpreted by Lansing as *the* awaited overt act. Finding Wilson still hesitant to act, Lansing and House cooperated to overcome the President's resistance. Lansing again exhausted his arguments for a declaration of war and cited the recent democratic Russian Revolution and signs of unrest within Germany as rendering a war entry psychologically opportune. In a lengthy letter to Wilson, he summed up the reasons for full-scale war:

the peace and welfare of mankind demanded a victory for democratic principles, a war entry would immediately strengthen liberal forces in Russia and even in Germany, the American people would be satisfied, and American influence at the peace conference would be immeasurably strengthened. When Wilson delivered his war message on April 6, it contained many of Lansing's references to the war as a democratic crusade.

Though many factors entered into Wilson's decision to request the declaration of war, there can be no doubt that he was influenced greatly by Lansing, first in shaping the strict-accountability policy and then in urging steps toward war on the basis of ideology and security. Although opinion differs somewhat on the immediate menace that Germany represented to the United States, Lansing was no doubt correct in viewing a German victory as inimical to America's long-range interest. But the subsequent peacemaking would have been smoother if Wilson had justified the war declaration on the grounds of concrete interests rather than on the basis of legal rights and morality.

III

In his policies toward Latin America, Lansing was concerned primarily with continued United States predominance in the Western Hemisphere. Wilson entrusted both Bryan and Lansing with a large degree of responsibility in directing Latin-American affairs. Lansing, in addition, was to be more active in Mexican policy, previously reserved for the President's special attention. The national interest, defined largely in terms of security, was Lansing's guide.

To frustrate German influence in Mexico, which undoubtedly existed, Lansing decided, soon after taking office, to work for greater order and stability through diplomatic recognition of the strongest of the Mexican factions. Aware of the great pressure in the United States for armed intervention in this turbulent neighbor, the Secretary resolved that everything possible should be done to preclude such a fateful step. "Our possible relations [the threat of war] with Germany must be our first consideration," he argued, "and all our intercourse with Mexico must be regulated accordingly." He appreciated the underlying social and economic causes of the Mexican Revolution and realized that progress and stability could be furthered only by dealing with the liberal groups, not with the conservative and reactionary followers of the deposed Díaz and Huerta. Furthermore, he sought to associate United States policy with that of other Western Hemisphere nations, realizing that this would not only preclude charges of unilateral intervention in Mexico's domestic affairs but also foster the Pan-American spirit of cooperation. Lansing had conceived of a concert early in 1915, and now, supported by House, he secured Wilson's consent to call to a conference on Mexican affairs the representatives of the ABC powers (Argentina, Brazil, and Chile) and also of Bolivia, Guatemala, and Uruguay. It was a sound and imaginative plan.

The records of the Conference of Ministers indicate that Wilson and Lansing realized that the Constitutionalists were the strongest of the liberal factions and had to be recognized. Lansing did hope, however, that the difficult leader, Venustiano Carranza, could be displaced by the more amenable General Alvaro Obregon. When he discovered that Carranza was solidly entrenched, he tried gently to lead the conference to the acceptance of that fact. Four of the six Latin-American representatives were outspokenly critical of Carranza, who was allegedly radical and anticlerical, and were inclined to favor the conservative faction. Astutely appealing to the "Latin mind," Lansing employed a long argument about sovereignty to reconcile the conferees to the distasteful Carranza, finally persuading the diplomats to recommend recognition of the Constitutionalist regime to their respective governments. On October 19, 1915, the United States and the six Latin-American states simultaneously extended *de facto* recognition to the government of General Carranza.

Stability in Mexico had thus been encouraged, even though Carranza personally aroused some misgivings on the part of both Wilson and Lansing. Although there were some adverse reactions within the United States, particularly from Roman Catholic spokesmen opposed to Carranza's anticlericalism, reports from Latin America indicated approval of the American course and of Lansing's personal role in coordinating this nation's policy with that of the six Latin states. Lansing himself was pleased with the resulting diminution of anti-American sentiment. Wilson's moralistic nonrecognition policy toward Mexico was at last replaced by the practical method of dealing with *de facto* regimes.

The Caribbean was another area that claimed Lansing's attention. The United States had been interested in acquiring the Danish West Indies as strategic naval bases in the Caribbean ever since the mid-nineteenth century. Aware of the failure of past efforts to purchase the islands, Lansing was nonetheless resolved to secure them, for he believed that German influence was growing in the Panama Canal area and that the German government might gain control of Denmark and force cession of the strategically situated islands. Bryan and Wilson had earlier indicated an interest in acquiring the islands as naval bases; Lansing added to this motive the importance of securing them from the German menace.

After obtaining Wilson's approval for the purchase, Lansing, in June, 1915, prepared the way for discreet overtures in Copenhagen. Then, timing his move carefully and acting solely on his own responsibility, he informed the Danish Minister that, if Denmark refused to sell, security considerations might compel the United States to seize the islands by force. The threat was apparently effective in prodding the hesitant Danish government. Wilson, subsequently informed of the exchange, approved his Secretary's action, and the Navy General Board advised that, though there was no present need for the island bases, it was desirable to secure them in order to forestall a possible hostile lodgment.

The treaty of purchase was signed on August 4, 1916, and ratified early in January, 1917. In defending the purchase before the Senate Foreign Relations Committee, Lansing argued this step was dictated by the necessity of obtaining strategic naval bases and preventing possible dangerous foreign complications. Although Lansing again had overestimated German intentions, he was justified in rounding out the Caribbean security system.

Two other measures reflected the Secretary's concern with security against a possible German threat in the Caribbean—the American interventions in Haiti and Santo Domingo. Lansing, if given a free hand, was determined to make the Caribbean an American lake. As Counselor, he had drafted an admirable analysis of the Monroe Doctrine, defining it as a unilateral security policy. He suggested that it was necessary for the United States to prohibit dangerous European economic and political activity in the Western Hemisphere. In a revised memorandum of November 24, 1915, he recommended to the President that the United States be prepared to intervene in the Caribbean to promote orderly and responsible government and thus to prevent foreign interventions. However American intervention might benefit the nations involved, Lansing believed that its fundamental purpose should be "the conservation of national interests." Wilson approved the memorandum as a guide to future national action.

Even under Bryan, events had foreshadowed intervention in disorderly Haiti. When a fresh wave of revolutionary violence occurred in July, 1915, Lansing, fearful of German commercial interests and political ambitions in the republic, warned the President that the situation required forceful measures. Naval and marine units were landed, and a protectorate was forced on Haiti.

Somewhat later, the Dominican Republic, already under American financial tutelage, was also occupied. As Counselor, Lansing had recommended drastic action for that still debt-ridden country. Although the island regime resisted increased American control, Lansing took advantage of a revolution in 1916 to secure Wilson's approval to land marines. Eventually an American-controlled military government was established in the Dominican Republic.

Though fearful of the effects of these interventions on Latin America, Wilson had reluctantly deferred to Lansing's assertion that there was no alternative. Hostile reactions did ensue, frustrating Lansing's desire for Western Hemispheric solidarity against Germany. Except for the Caribbean protectorates and friendly Brazil, much of Latin America was unresponsive to the American entry into the war against Germany. The State Department, moreover, failed to supervise closely American military authorities in Haiti and the Dominican Republic, with the result that some brutality and arrogant behavior occurred. In the name of security and a greatly exaggerated German threat, Lansing helped inaugurate occupations destined to last into the postwar decade and to poison future relations with Latin America.

IV

The war years, 1917 and 1918, were accompanied by a diminution in the influence of the State Department. No longer were international law and neutrality at issue. Now Wilson began to realize the divergence between his and Lansing's views and relied even more upon Colonel House for the delicate wartime diplomacy with the Allies and the planning of peace. The Department soon discovered that foreign affairs had to be shared with war-born agencies and commissions. Especially troublesome was the Committee on Public Information, established at the suggestion of Lansing and the Secretaries of War and the Navy and headed by the fiery journalist, George Creel. Lansing and Creel clashed repeatedly over the committee's efforts to interfere in the State Department's news releases and to establish independent branches abroad.

Lansing's earlier forbearance in protesting Allied interference with neutral commerce now paid dividends. The Secretary quickly involved the United States in activities recently at issue with Great Britain—censorship, black-listing, bunker controls, embargoes, and extensions of the contraband list. To the great distress of the Netherlands, Dutch shipping in American ports was seized temporarily as an emergency war measure. Lansing managed, however, to keep American actions within the loose requirements of international practice.

For Lansing, much of the war period was occupied with the routine functions of representing the Department on special war committees and receiving Allied war missions. Not that such routine bored him, for he apparently enjoyed the flurry of social activity attending the visits. In three major areas of the world, however, his part in policy making deserves special emphasis: the Far East, Russia, and Austria-Hungary.

The Secretary recognized that an expansionist Japan could be contained only by British-American cooperation. Long-range American interests in the Far East were dependent, therefore, upon an Allied victory in Europe which would leave British sea power intact. During the war years, however, the United States alone confronted Japan in the Pacific. The situation called for conciliation.

By the time the United States had entered the European conflict, Japan had secured Allied recognition of her recent gains in the Far East. Now the government in Tokyo sought similar approval from the United States. Determined to avoid conflict and disturbed by rumors of a Japanese-German peace, Lansing concluded that some bargaining was unavoidable. He reverted to the plan he had suggested in 1915, when Japan had utilized the war to seize the German holdings in the Chinese province of Shantung and to force on China the Twenty-one Demands. At that time he had proposed, in concurrence with E. T. Williams of the Far Eastern Division, that Japan's special position in South Manchuria and Shantung be recognized in return for a promise of nondiscrimination against foreign commerce and the cessation of protests against the California alien-land law. Wilson and Bryan had not acted on the proposal. Now in 1917, Lansing, in conversations with the Japanese Ambassador, acquiesced in Japan's "special interests" in Manchuria (excluding Shantung, where conditions seemed to favor American influence and investments) and agreed that Japan had "special and close relations, political as well as economic," with China.

In response to these intimations, the Japanese government sent Viscount Ishii on a special mission to the United States. Before Ishii arrived, Lansing secured the aid of Colonel House in an attempt to get Presidential acceptance of an arrangement whereby the United States would concede Japan's position in South Manchuria and Mongolia in return for Japanese pledges to respect the Open Door and to avoid political interference in China proper. Wilson refused to accept the concept of a Japanese sphere of influence in Manchuria. Consequently, when the Japanese mission arrived, the best that Lansing could do was to conceal all basic disagreements in the ambiguous Lansing-Ishii Agreement of November 2, 1917. The document recognized Japan's undefined special interests in China and pledged observance of both the commercial Open Door and Chinese territorial integrity.

This agreement was subject to mutually incompatible interpretations by the two governments. Lansing had tried to settle the matter on the realistic basis of concessions to Japan and preservation of existing American interests. Wilson believed that such an arrangement was contrary to America's moral responsibilities to China and the world. Had Lansing's original proposal been adopted, subsequent Japanese-American relations might well have taken a decisive turn for the better; even the vexed Shantung controversy could perhaps have been avoided.

The Russian Revolution of March, 1917, had been hailed by Lansing as a triumph of democracy. He soon became pessimistic about the pros-

pects of the Provisional government, however, for reports indicated that
the Socialists were agitating to take Russia out of the war. He therefore
recommended the dispatch of a three-man commission to encourage Russia
to continue hostilities. Receiving similar suggestions from Colonel House
and others, President Wilson agreed. The commission, headed by Elihu
Root, was appointed after consultation with Lansing. When the commission returned from Russia early in August, 1917, Lansing found its
members optimistic about the stability of the Provisional government and
the continuation of Russia's war effort. Although his own sources of information were meager, the Secretary rejected such optimism. Privately
he predicted that the Russian Revolution would follow the course of the
French Revolution, progressing from moderation to terrorism and terminating in a military dictatorship. The United States, he was convinced,
should be prepared for a steady deterioration of Russia as a military factor
in the war.

Thus Lansing was not surprised by the Bolshevik seizure of power in
November, 1917, and the subsequent Russian withdrawal from the war.
On December 4, he initiated the nonrecognition policy toward the Bolsheviks by forwarding to Wilson a memorandum describing the Communist regime as a class-hatred movement inimical to democratic institutions and coming to power by violent means. The President approved
the memorandum.

Unlike Wilson and most other Allied leaders, Lansing was aware of
the revolutionary significance of Communist ideology. In a private memorandum of December 7, 1917, he anticipated Winston Churchill in describing Russian affairs as "an unanswered and unanswerable riddle." The
Bolsheviks could not be recognized, he noted, for they sought to overthrow all existing governments and to replace them with proletarian
despotisms. To deal with the Bolshevik regime would simply encourage
the spread of the Communist virus, hostile to private property and to
democratic and autocratic governments alike. The Central Powers, in
recognizing Lenin's government, might reap immediate benefits, but the
future costs would be great. Lansing rejected the popular view that the
Bolshevik leaders, Lenin and Trotsky, were really German agents. He
termed the two men "honest in purpose and utterly dishonest in methods."
Predicting civil war and a reign of terror in Russia, the Secretary concluded that the United States should do nothing until the situation clarified and a strong anti-Bolshevik leader emerged. Although Wilson approved Lansing's recommendation that General Kaledin's Don Cossack
movement against the Bolsheviks be aided, events prevented implementation, and the policy of cautious waiting continued.

Analyzing a Lenin-Trotsky appeal to the Allied nations, Lansing pointed
out in a lengthy memorandum that the Bolsheviks threatened the world

social order and were falsely exploiting nationalistic urges for independence. The Secretary's conservative nature was appalled particularly at the prospect of proletarian rule—of government by "the ignorant and mentally deficient." After reading this memorandum to the Cabinet on January 10, 1918, Lansing urged issuance of a policy statement against Bolshevik ambition. Wilson demurred, apparently unwilling to risk weakening the effect of his Fourteen Points Address of January 8.

Wilson and Lansing were agreed in opposing the Allied schemes for armed intervention in northern Russia and Siberia. The pressure to intervene was intense, for the Western Allies wanted to restore Russia to the war. The American leaders predicted, however, that intervention would have the undesirable result of rallying the Russian people around the Bolsheviks. In addition, Lansing feared that such action would compel even non-Communist Russian factions to turn to Germany for aid. No doubt the American government was also apprehensive about Japanese designs in Siberia, although Lansing later recorded the view that Japan was justified in blocking the spread of communism in Manchuria and the rest of Asia.

Wilson agreed finally to intervention in northern Russia and in Siberia. The justification for striking at Murmansk was to safeguard supplies; at Siberia, to rescue the stranded Czechoslovak legion. Wilson and Lansing accepted the Murmansk action in the false belief that it was favored by the Soviet authorities and without realizing that the Allies planned an anti-Bolshevik operation. Siberian intervention, recommended by Department advisers, was resisted by Lansing until news arrived that the Czechoslovakian troops, then trying to move to the Western front via Vladivostok, had been involved in armed clashes with local Red forces and German-Austrian prisoners of war. On June 23, Lansing informed Wilson of the new situation in Siberia, and in a subsequent memorandum he concluded that the United States was morally bound to relieve the besieged Czech forces. Such a step would be an entirely different matter, in his view, from armed intervention for political purposes. At a special conference of Wilson, Lansing, the Secretaries of War and the Navy, and the Army and Navy chiefs—Colonel House apparently was not consulted—Lansing's cogent memorandum was read and a limited joint intervention with Japan agreed upon. Troops were landed in August, but when the intervention subsequently developed a clearly anti-Bolshevik emphasis, both Wilson and Lansing condemned it as unwise and sought to disassociate the United States from it.

Motives for the decision to intervene were mixed. If the Czechoslovak plight was the precipitative one, a more basic reason was the fear that Japan would soon act unilaterally. Although unwilling to become entangled in a drive to unseat the Bolsheviks, Wilson and Lansing evidently hoped that limited intervention would encourage the formation of a friendly anti-Bolshevik government. The entire program of intervention was based on faulty information. Apparently it was not necessary to rescue the Czechoslovakian troops, and the landing of American and Allied soldiers had the undesired effect of strengthening the Bolshevik regime and engendering Russia's enduring suspicion of American and Allied motives.

Setting aside the question of intervention, was nonrecognition wise? At one level, that policy seemed understandable and practical, for a small group of Bolsheviks had overthrown by violence an apparently democratic government, had taken Russia out of the Allied camp, and had openly declared "war" on all existing capitalist governments. Since Lansing expected the Bolsheviks to be displaced speedily by another regime, the initial withholding of recognition was realistic. But Lansing apparently did not change his mind even when the Bolsheviks demonstrated that they would retain power. Although he had accepted other disagreeable regimes —such as the Carranza government in Mexico—he found the Bolsheviks ideologically and morally impossible. The legacy of the Wilson-Lansing policy was the ostrichlike refusal of the United States in the twenties to deal officially with the Soviet government.

Wilson's administration initially favored the preservation of the multinational Austro-Hungarian Empire, convinced falsely that the subject nationalities, mainly South Slavs, Czechs, and Poles, were content with Hapsburg rule. With Lansing's support, Wilson had, in February, 1917, endeavored to avoid hostilities by detaching Austria from the war. As the key to Austrian compliance, the United States sought and obtained assurances from the Allies that the empire would not be dismembered. Nevertheless, the Viennese government was unwilling and, in view of its dependence on Germany, perhaps unable to make a separate peace. Diplomatic relations were then broken when the United States entered the war against Germany.

Although Wilson still clung to hopes of detaching Austria-Hungary from Germany and favored preservation of the empire, with autonomy for subject nationalities, Lansing gradually came to support dismemberment. Influenced by his advisers—Albert Putney of the Near Eastern Division and Assistant Secretary William Phillips—the Secretary, in the fall of 1917, recorded privately the conviction that Europe must be protected against a postwar resurgence of Prussian militarism by the establishment of strong independent states around Germany's eastern and southern borders. He was unable, however, to dissuade the President from repeating assurances against dismemberment in the declaration of war against Austria (December 4, 1917) and in the Fourteen Points Address (January 8, 1918).

After the apparent failure of another attempt to detach Austria-

Hungary, in May, 1918, President Wilson was persuaded to support dismemberment. Lansing advised that justice to the subject nationalities, the elimination of Austria-Hungary as a military factor, and future security against a German revival required American support for an independent Poland, Bohemia, and Yugoslavia. In late May, 1918, the United States publicly declared its sympathy for these national movements and in June recognized the belligerency of the Polish and Czech, and national committees.

The policy of Wilson and his Secretary was defensible on the grounds of military expediency and justice to the nationalities, and it did accelerate the collapse of the empire. The decisive factors in the disintegration of Austria-Hungary, however, were actual military defeat and the autonomous desires of the subject nationalities.

V

After the United States entered the war on the Allied side, Lansing had no definable wartime goal beyond the defeat of Germany. Only the interest of others in some type of collective-security league forced him to articulate, slowly, a larger aim.

His war speeches were rather intemperate in condemnation of "Prussian autocracy," attributing the war to militaristic and aggressive strains rooted deep in the German philosophy and character. He persistently called for a peace of no compromise with the existing German rulers. In August, 1917, when the Pope had appealed for a negotiated peace (with which House sympathized), Lansing helped persuade Wilson to reject it as merely preserving the *status quo*. The United States was fighting the war, Lansing assured the American people, not to save the Allies, but to protect this nation's security. In his address at Madison Barracks, New York, late in July, 1917, he stated: "Let us understand . . . that this is no war to establish an abstract principle of right. It is a war in which the future of the United States is at stake." This address was popularly received at home and abroad; Senator Henry Cabot Lodge hailed it as a wise reminder that America's prosperity and security were involved. The Secretary was far more successful in arousing an emotional and vindictive spirit among the people, however, than in encouraging an informed appreciation of the stakes of the war. Obviously, the Secretary was involved in an unresolved clash between idealistic and realistic concepts of the struggle, as were such conservatives as Root and Taft; for a time he came close to demanding unconditional surrender of Germany.

Lansing differentiated between a harsh and a just peace. Both he and the President became aware early of many of the secret treaties existing among the Allies, which provided for a postwar division of spoils. The

British Foreign Secretary, Arthur J. Balfour, revealed the terms of several treaties to the American leaders when he headed a special war mission to the United States in the spring of 1917. The Washington government, probably unwisely, decided to ignore the treaties in order to preserve wartime Allied unity and still reserve freedom of action at the peace conference. This decision was apparently the work of Colonel House. Lansing, unlike Wilson, was eager to learn the details of the treaties. He deplored Allied threats of postwar economic ostracism of Germany as likely to drive the middle classes into the arms of the militarists. As the Bolshevik revolution gained headway, he began to feel that communism represented a greater threat to democracy than did autocracy. He feared that harsh treatment of the defeated Central Powers would open the way for further Bolshevik triumphs. By the time of the Armistice in November, 1918, his dread that bolshevism would exploit a hungry and chaotic Europe influenced him to seek milder treatment for Germany.

Preparatory work for the peace conference was entrusted to a special body of scholars known as The Inquiry. Under Colonel House's direction, this group was formally organized under the State Department in mid-1917. Lansing earlier had discussed the need for such a group and had drawn up a memorandum to guide its work.

By the autumn of 1918, the Secretary had developed his own ideas of a desirable peace treaty. He recorded twenty-nine "essentials for a Stable Peace," all practical terms which attempted to blend considerations of nationality aspirations with those of strategy and economics. He believed that Germany could justifiably be charged with the costs of the war, but he doubted that its resources would make payment possible. What disturbed Lansing most, however, were the implications of Wilson's planned League of Nations. In February, 1917, in criticizing a Wilson memorandum entitled "Bases of Peace," he had raised practical questions about the details of collective security, disarmament, and the right of peoples to the "dynamite" of nationalistic self-determination. Lansing also had asked whether some special consideration should not be given nations with large and expanding populations and whether ethnic boundaries could really be drawn without laying the basis for future conflict.

Since democracies were inherently peaceful, in Lansing's rather questionable view, the surest guarantee of peace was the universal triumph of democracy. The projected League, ideally, should contain only democratic states—apparently Lansing had an Atlantic Union of Democracies in mind. On practical grounds, Lansing criticized Wilson's plan for a positive guarantee of the League, the provision for the use of force to defend the territory and independence of members. Specific pledges to use force, Lansing believed, were no stronger than the good faith of the members, especially the more powerful ones. Moreover, the employment of force and economic coercion would in itself raise detailed and troublesome problems. The best solution, so Lansing and his friend and adviser James Brown Scott were convinced, was to strengthen the existing world arbitration and judicial machinery. If a world society of nations must be established, let it be simple and practical. Lansing feared privately, however, that idealists and utopians would overlook the basic selfishness of nations and attempt the impossible in a league; he expected Wilson, perhaps from personal ambition, to attempt to give the projected international body many of the attributes of a world state.

Lansing was not an isolationist, unless isolationism be distorted to mean anything less than an unquestioning commitment to the Wilsonian brand of internationalism. Rather, he was a conservative internationalist, who deplored partisanship in foreign affairs and recognized that the country was not isolated from world currents. He even believed that the world was slowly evolving toward a world federal state, but until that far-off day should arrive, he preferred traditional diplomacy, with some increased emphasis on machinery for the peaceful settlement of disputes.

By the time of the Armistice, Wilson held his Secretary in rather low regard. He was well aware of their divergent views on the peace, and he dismissed Lansing's caution as obtuseness. Increasingly disillusioned with Wilson, Lansing was now more often blunt and tactless. When Lansing opposed Wilson's attending the Peace Conference at Paris in person, on the grounds that it might impair his diplomatic strength, the President apparently viewed the Secretary as guilty of effrontery and disloyalty. Whether or not Lansing's advice was correct, it was honest advice, apparently untinged by any personal ambition to lead the American delegation. Lansing was also accurate in forecasting that Wilson's decision to go to Paris would provide the Republicans with ammunition for a political assault. To prevent this, the Secretary then recommended that the American delegation include the eminent Republican Elihu Root, but Wilson rejected him as too conservative. Instead, Lansing, House, General Tasker Bliss, and Henry White (a Lansing nominee and the sole Republican) were named as the President's fellow peace commissioners.

Lansing's role at Paris was one of futility and humiliation. Always an indefatigable doodler and a caricaturist of some ability, he seems to have spent most of the time in Paris sketching and writing caustic but anxious comments in his private memoranda book. Aided by House, the President made all the important decisions and generally ignored the other three commissioners. Lansing, Bliss, and White were often reduced to the role of disillusioned and disturbed observers. The Secretary was embittered by Wilson's repeated slights and his publicly displayed preference for House's counsel and aid. Occasionally annoyed in the past at House's role, made tolerable only by the fact that the Colonel usually lived away from the

Capital, Lansing found the Paris situation almost unendurable. When
he had tried to remedy one serious defect, the lack of preparation for
the conference, by having State Department experts prepare a detailed
treaty plan, Wilson angrily ordered a halt. He would not have lawyers
drafting the peace. But at Paris the British and French delegations had
elaborate treaty plans and were thus able to maintain the initiative. The
American commissioners and delegates, isolated from the President and
without regular policy guidance, tended to flounder inefficiently.

At first Lansing sat with Wilson on the Council of Ten, and directing
body of the conference. Here his manifestation of frankness and his logical
arguments apparently angered Wilson. For reasons of efficiency, Wilson
later met with the Allied premiers—Lloyd George of Britain, Georges
Clemenceau of France, and Vittorio Orlando of Italy—in the Council of
Four, leaving Lansing and the other foreign secretaries to constitute a
clearinghouse in the Council of Foreign Ministers, known as the "Little
Five." The Secretary found himself sidetracked so completely that he
contemplated resignation. Only his sense of duty and his desire to do
nothing which might endanger the work of the American delegation restrained him.

Wilson and House monopolized the work on the League of Nations.
Lansing, not being informed of the actual content of the Covenant as it
was being prepared, recorded exaggerated fears of a diminution of American sovereignty and a loss of diplomatic freedom. Later he risked Wilson's
anger by suggesting modifications. He recommended a League based on
a "negative guarantee," in which each member would renounce aggressive
intentions against other members. The League Assembly and Council
would be occupied largely with codifying international law and facilitating
peaceful adjustments of disputes. In case of aggression, the League would
confer on measures to restore peace. It would, furthermore, be based
unequivocally on the legal equality of states—no big-power vetoes or old
balance-of-power politics—and so could not be accused of creating a
Great Power oligarchy to run the world. For all his appreciation of power
realities (he recognized that the equality of states was a legal fiction),
Lansing could not rid himself of the American legalistic approach to international relations. Although House was impressed with the possibilities
of the negative guarantee, the President ignored the suggestion. Lansing's
plan would probably have secured Senate approval. The negative guarantee might well have been as meaningless as the 1928 Pact of Paris, but at
least it had the virtue of not requesting cooperation improbable of actual
fulfillment, and the emphasis on judicial machinery was practical and valuable.

As the labors of the Peace Conference became more protracted, Lansing
became more critical of Wilson's League. Fearful of expanding bolshevism

in a war-wracked Europe, the Secretary saw the cure for Europe simply in the immediate restoration of peace. What Europe needed above all was food, for, he said, "men with full bellies are not Bolsheviks." Lansing blamed the delay in concluding the peace on Wilson's obsession with the League project. This was perhaps unfair, for Wilson usually worked on the Covenant after the regular sessions. Lansing argued for a preliminary peace with general provisions for a League, to be followed by a second and more definitive peace treaty. His effort to force such a decision through the Council of Ten was frustrated by Wilson. The President subsequently and incorrectly believed that Lansing and House had been ready, while he returned briefly to the United States, to agree to a preliminary treaty without even a brief reference to the League of Nations.

Lansing's plan was commendable. A preliminary treaty containing a simple commitment to a League would not have aroused as much controversy in the United States as did the completed Covenant. On the other hand, Wilson wanted to make the League the key to the peace and was fearful that any other method of peacemaking would, in fact, jettison the planned organization.

Troubled by the success of bolshevism in Russia and moved by a sense of fairness, Lansing opposed excessively harsh treatment of Germany. He predicted that unreasonable reparations would never be collected, and he supported the struggle of the American counsel on the Reparations Commission, his nephew John Foster Dulles, against violation of the pre-Armistice agreement to include war costs with allowable civilian damages. He denounced as preposterous the more extreme Allied plans of squeezing Germany dry, especially those which sought to deprive Germany of colonies, a merchant marine, and valuable ore-bearing lands. He opposed unsuccessfully both Wilson's decision to allow war pensions to be included in civilian reparations and House's concession, made during Wilson's illness, to base reparations on claims rather than on an estimate of Germany's actual ability to pay. Lansing scored a minor success when he persuaded Wilson to block French schemes to obtain German trade secrets and patents and to prohibit the development of commercial aviation.

The Secretary supported vigorously Wilson's opposition to the dismemberment of Germany, challenging in the Council of Foreign Ministers several moves to treat Bavaria and other German states as independent entities. Wilson defended the principle of German territorial integrity successfully, but at the price of a defensive military alliance with France. At first opposed to the "Security Treaty" on the grounds that it was inconsistent with the League Covenant and ran counter to America's non-entanglement policy, Lansing soon realized that the French need for security was understandable, especially since it was American power that had checked German expansion. Although he was warned by Lansing that the Senate would never approve the alliance, Wilson ordered the pact signed.

As chairman of the commission dealing with the question of responsibility for the war, Lansing helped attach the war-guilt clause to the final treaty—an unfortunate clause, not historically valid, which engendered much German resentment. He believed that Germany indeed had been responsible for starting the conflict; but he openly disagreed with Allied leaders on the matter of a trial of former Kaiser Wilhelm II as a war criminal, contending both that it would establish a bad precedent and that the former German ruler was not guilty of actual war crimes. If he were to be tried, the trial should be a "political" one for his moral offenses in beginning the war, nothing more. What Lansing had in mind, apparently, was not an exhibition like the later Nuremberg trials but an exile comparable to that of Napoleon on St. Helena.

On other major decisions of the conference Lansing had little influence. He opposed concessions to Italy at Yugoslavia's expense on the Dalmatian coast and, strangely for a traditionalist, approved Wilson's unsuccessful appeal to the Italian people, over the head of Orlando, for support on the disposition of Fiume to Yugoslavia. As for Japan's claims to Germany's Pacific holdings, Lansing and the American commissioners, with House wavering, supported Wilson in opposing transfer of the Shantung leasehold to Japan. Although earlier willing to bargain with Japan, Lansing was now convinced that Japan's possession of Shantung threatened China's independence and territorial integrity. He freely advised the Chinese delegates at Paris in their fight to regain Shantung and ably challenged the Japanese arguments in the Council of Ten. Finally, when it appeared that Japan would bolt the conference and not join the League, Wilson rejected the advice of Lansing, Bliss, and White and acquiesced in the cession to Japan of German rights in Shantung. In exchange, Wilson managed to secure a verbal Japanese promise to restore eventual sovereignty to China. In opposing this move, Lansing had contended that Japan was merely bluffing in its threat not to sign the treaty. It is incomprehensible that Lansing, as a realist, should have taken such a stand, for Japan occupied the areas it demanded and would not be forced out short of military action. Nothing concrete was to be gained, therefore, by humiliating a powerful state.

With the signing of the Treaty of Versailles on June 28, 1919, the greatest assemblage of statesmen since the Congress of Vienna dispersed. Surveying the work of the conference, Lansing was convinced that not all wars had been fought and that France and Italy had been wise to insist on strategic rather than ethnic frontiers. He suspected that the peace was in many particulars faulty, harsh, and unjust. He signed the treaty because he believed that the world needed peace, even a decidedly imperfect one, if the Atlantic powers were to check bolshevism and resume their former progress.

VI

If Lansing's influence reached its nadir at the Peace Conference, it experienced a sharp resurgence in 1919–1920, when Colonel House fell at last from Wilson's esteem and the President himself became ill. Upon his return to the United States, Lansing sought a speedy Senate approval of the treaty. Yet his effort mattered little, for the President set the pace in the noncompromising struggle with the Republican opposition. It is true that Lansing, in his testimony before the Senate Foreign Relations Committee, revealed much ignorance of the actions of the Big Four and admitted his disagreement with the President on Shantung, but he made an effective case for approval of the treaty and the restoration of peace. When William C. Bullitt, a disillusioned member of the peace delegation, related to the committee a distorted version of Lansing's private criticisms of the treaty in Paris, the Secretary attempted to repair the damage in a public address which stressed the need for Senate approval of the treaty in its original form. Later, during Wilson's illness, Lansing entered the struggle actively and tried to draft reservations satisfactory both to Republican moderates and to the Allied governments. It was the White House that vetoed any compromise. Lansing, confident that he could have secured Senate approval of the treaty with moderate reservations, was greatly distressed at the defeat of the treaty in November, 1919, and in March, 1920.

Early in October, 1919, President Wilson had suffered a paralyzing stroke or cerebral thrombosis, virtually incapacitating him for at least two months. Aware of the need for active executive leadership and believing Wilson to be disabled within the meaning of the Constitution, Lansing considered having the Cabinet advise the Vice President to act as President temporarily. He was thwarted in this endeavor by the jealous and protective Mrs. Wilson and by White House officials. Lansing then called and presided over regular meetings of the Cabinet, both to transact some business and to reassure the public that the executive was still functioning. Symbolically, the President's chair at the head of the Cabinet table was always left vacant.

Lansing was now largely on his own in managing the State Department. He enjoyed his new position and even adopted a patronizing attitude toward the now out-of-favor Colonel House. He was denied direct access to the President and for months received responses from the White House in the handwriting of Mrs. Wilson. Despite the counsel of Department advisers, the Secretary decided not to extend recognition to the anti-Bolshevik regime of Admiral Kolchak in Siberia. He discounted the reported Japanese designs on the maritime provinces of Siberia and noted privately that Japan quite reasonably should attempt to halt the spread of bolshevism into Manchuria and adjacent areas. In November, 1919, he concluded that American forces in Siberia should be withdrawn, for the Bolshevik advance threatened to involve them in armed clashes. The ailing President indicated approval, and the troops were evacuated by April, 1920. Lansing handled the explosive clash with Mexico over the arrest of Consular Agent William O. Jenkins. After alerting the War and Navy Departments, Lansing virtually threatened Mexico with war and compelled a release of the agent.

By early February, 1920, Wilson had recovered a measure of his strength. The recovery was signaled publicly by his demand for Lansing's resignation. Ostensibly the President requested the resignation because Lansing had called unauthorized meetings of the Cabinet during his illness. Wilson believed apparently that Lansing had disloyally tried to usurp his office. But the underlying cause was the widening rift between the two officials over basic foreign policy, a rift which dated back to early 1917 and was revealed clearly at the Paris Peace Conference. Having disagreed with the President sharply over peace goals and the League of Nations, Lansing no doubt should have resigned earlier. He had frequently considered such a step in the fall of 1919, especially when Mrs. Wilson almost forbade him to enter the White House premises. His diary entries indicate that he remained in office only out of a sense of duty to his country and his President. There is no need to question his sincerity.

As Lansing left office, on February 13, 1920, he could feel reasonably well satisfied with his tenure. Judged by the outline of policies he hoped to establish when he began his term, his record shows that he had been a successful Secretary of State. By helping to make the Caribbean an American lake, he had been instrumental in securing the Panama Canal; he had helped recognize a Mexican government and, despite the Caribbean interventions, had made some progress in encouraging the Pan-American spirit. Above all, he had defended the nation's security by achieving those commitments to war which had assured the defeat of Germany. In the Far East, he had attempted to adjust American security and economic interests to power realities by seeking some *modus vivendi* with the Japanese government. He had initiated the policy of nonrecognition toward Bolshevik Russia. If the League of Nations had never really been his goal, Lansing's advice to Wilson both at Paris and later at Washington, if adopted, might well have spared the President his ultimate failure.

Although Lansing was an able Secretary of State, he fell short of greatness, partly because of his own conservative limitations and partly because of the conditions under which he worked. Granted the personality of Woodrow Wilson and the President's reliance on Colonel House, it was remarkable that Lansing left as significant an imprint on the office as he did. In retrospect, one of the many tragedies of the Wilson years was the President's failure to avail himself more fully of Lansing's talents.

7

Charles Evans Hughes

1921-1925

BY JOHN CHALMERS VINSON
University of Georgia

Charles Evans Hughes presided over the return of American foreign relations to "normalcy" during the early twenties. It was consistent with the times that the Secretary of State should have been charged with the essential responsibility for the nation's diplomacy. Between 1921 and 1925, he served under two Presidents, Warren G. Harding and Calvin Coolidge, neither of whom was famous for his energy as Chief Executive. When reporters asked Harding about his foreign policy, his standard reply was, "You must see Mr. Hughes about that." He did not exaggerate. Hughes, after slipping past the crowds that swarmed the White House office, customarily presented the current issues to the President every day. More often than not, Harding, shaking his head in bewilderment, would remark sadly, "Hughes, this is the damnedest job!" Cabinet meetings were equally barren of advice. From the beginning of Harding's administration in March, 1921, the Secretary learned to work out his own solutions and to put them in final form for the President's acceptance or rejection. Generally Harding accepted his Secretary's recommendations without question, permitting Hughes to describe him as "a most agreeable chief." Under Coolidge, who was concerned primarily with domestic issues, this formula was not substantially altered. Both Presidents contented themselves with the constitutional necessity of signing their names, leaving to Hughes the task of determining both the substance and the details of policy. Neither chief put the weight of Presidential authority, either political or constitutional, on the State Department's side in the endless conflict with Congress.

128

Thus for Hughes the Senate was a major challenge. Long suppressed by Woodrow Wilson, the Senate was in revolt against any form of executive direction. In particular, the Senate's Republican "irreconcilables," solidly united against the League of Nations, were troublesome. They sought to block Hughes's appointment as Secretary in favor of some hollow figurehead. Failing in this, they adopted, in accepting Hughes, the philosophy of Senator Boies Penrose that it mattered little who was Secretary of State, since the Senate would run foreign policy anyway. The animosity of the politically powerful irreconcilables placed Hughes at a marked disadvantage. He could not afford to offend this bloc of senators, who were strong enough to veto the administration's measures in domestic as well as foreign policy. Always conscious of this liability, Hughes prudently avoided any open battle with the Senate that might paralyze the orderly processes of government. At the same time he was aware of his responsibilities for maintaining the President's dignity and prerogatives. By careful study and meticulous planning, he occasionally outmaneuvered his senatorial opponents. Routine business moved smoothly. More treaties were passed under Hughes, seventy-one in all, with less time devoted to debate, than in any other administration since Elihu Root's. Still, the specter of Senate revolt ruled out some programs and sharply limited the scope of others.

As Secretary, Hughes discovered an additional burden in an American public disillusioned with diplomats and anxious to establish popular control of foreign policy. At the same time, this public, caught up in the fabled foppery of the roaring twenties, was not genuinely concerned with the mechanics of foreign relations and refused to admit, much less attempt to understand, its complexities. National security was hardly an issue, for scientific progress and diplomatic attrition had not as yet placed the United States on the front line in the event of war. There was no overpowering sense of urgency. Hughes, for example, could spare over a month's time from Washington for a cruise to the centennial celebration of Brazilian independence. The State Department remained inadequate when judged in terms of this nation's growing impact on world affairs. The budget was only 2 million dollars, and the Department's home staff numbered just over six hundred. The time-honored tendency, strongly endorsed by the public, was to maintain the *status quo* and to ignore foreign affairs except for those issues too insistent to be avoided.

During the early twenties, both the Congress and the public were devoted passionately to the purpose of escaping from everything concrete. The perils of isolationism were obscure; the advantages of untrammeled sovereignty were evident. Within the limits imposed by this situation, Hughes worked superbly. If he sometimes envisioned the larger task of bringing national policy into harmony with national responsibility, he saw even more clearly the impracticability of achieving those ends against the apathy of the public and the hostility of Congress. The storms of time revealed that even his house of policy was built on sand, but in its day it often appeared to be an admirable structure indeed.

Perhaps the most pressing need facing Hughes was to clear the atmosphere of the partisanship that had marked the last days of the Wilson administration, had stalemated the League of Nations issue, and then had disposed of it completely in the campaign of 1920. In addition to this chaos, described by Hughes as the "worst possible tangle," a ruinous naval race endangered the peace between the United States and Japan in the Pacific. There was still no peace treaty with Germany, and a new European conflict threatened to erupt from the bitterness engendered by disagreement over reparations and war debts. Maturing Latin-American states were growing restive under the paternalistic American interpretation of the Monroe Doctrine. In Hughes's words, there were opportunities for dispute on every hand.

Setting this disrupted house in order was the task for a practical, realistic administrator. It required a statesman who viewed the national interest in the precise terms employed in the diplomacy of a forgotten past. In large measure, Hughes appeared to answer the stringent needs of the time. Though his stern and bewhiskered face gave him the look of a prophet, he never sought to be one. Wholly dedicated to the art of "achieving the possible," he defined his duty as that of doing the best he could to meet the immediate problems stemming from the recent war. Perfection, in his opinion, was a distant goal, to be reached in decades, not days. Fifty-nine years of age when he became Secretary, Hughes brought to his office ideas and attitudes firmly engrained by time and experience.

II

Born in Glens Falls, New York, in 1862, Hughes revealed early the brilliance of mind and precision of habit that marked his entire career. In later years he denied that he was a child prodigy but admitted that he was precocious. According to one family legend, at eight years of age he drew up The Charles E. Hughes Plan of Study to accelerate his school work. He graduated as fourth honor man from Brown University in 1881, when he was only nineteen. Three years later, having acquired a law degree from Columbia University and a Master of Arts degree from Brown University, he began the practice of law with a diligence described well by his own remark that "life is only work, and then more work, and then more work." During the next two decades he won wide recognition in his profession and acquired a measure of wealth.

Suddenly, in 1905, he was thrust into public life as counsel for committees of the New York Legislature. His brilliant work in prosecuting life insurance companies made him a national figure and built the foundation for a distinguished political career. By 1916 he had served as Governor of New York, associate justice of the United States Supreme Court, and unsuccessful Republican candidate for the Presidency. His return to private law practice was interrupted by duty as special assistant to President Wilson's Attorney General in the wartime inquiry into the aircraft industry.

Despite his unusually broad background in law and politics, only as a presidential candidate, in 1916, and briefly as an instructor in international law at Cornell University, in 1893, had he come into direct contact with problems of foreign affairs. His qualifications for the office of Secretary of State, therefore, lay more in his general characteristics of high intelligence, unquestioned integrity, and political availability than in any expert knowledge of international relations. As a consequence, his approach to foreign policy was determined, not by any particular theory of world politics, but rather by the intellectual and political milieu in which he worked.

Hughes was determined to achieve the same success as Secretary that he had enjoyed in his previous endeavors. In part, his emphasis on success was dictated by politics. He wanted to confront the nation with Republican achievements which would contrast favorably with Democratic failures. At all times he felt compelled to prove that he knew where he wanted to go and how he planned to get there. But to an equal degree, Hughes's will to succeed stemmed from his own character. For all his stern aloofness, he was intensely human. Highly sensitive, he was irritated by criticism, especially on those occasions when national security made it impossible for him to explain and defend his position. When he was attacked sharply for doing nothing on reparations at a time when he was devoting much quiet effort to the problem, he told a friend, "I wish I were a woman so that I might weep." Under fire from the pro-League faction, he once mused that it would be "a wonderful thing . . . to wear a mantle of complacency so thick and warm that you would never feel the cold comments of the world." Ambitious, proud, and conscientious, he was willing to drive himself unstintingly, but he expected acclamation to be his reward. Unlike Wilson, who extolled the glory of failing in causes that would ultimately succeed, Hughes preferred immediate, if smaller, triumphs. It was Hughes's tragedy that he could not accept defeat; too often he was content with the appearance rather than the substance of diplomatic progress.

Hughes's experience as Governor of New York had schooled him in caution and had confirmed his opinion that progress must be achieved by short and painful steps—that reforms could not be built on sweeping pronouncements alone. On becoming Governor, he had confidently asserted his independence of press and politicians. On one occasion he had predicted that his program would be carried even though he probably would not have enough Republican friends to give him a decent burial. But gradually he discovered that his personal zeal for reform was no match for political maneuvering. To his astonishment, some of his most cherished plans failed. As his term as Governor wore on, Hughes became more cautious and conservative, less enthusiastic and willing to undertake a fight for a cause that might lose. His critics attributed the change to overweening ambition—the desire to avoid mistakes. His friends assessed his conservatism as the harvest of wisdom reaped from the fields of practical experience. Applying the knowledge he had gained in domestic politics to the problems of foreign policy, Hughes moved slowly and carefully, doubtful that any single agency or agreement among nations would secure world peace. Moreover, he appeared at all times to be as conscious of the galleries at home as he was of the nations with which he was negotiating.

It was inevitable that Hughes would adopt a narrow, factual, and legalistic view of the office of Secretary of State. He was once characterized as the "diplomat of legalism, the diplomat of constitutionalism." His mind, in fact, seemed created by nature for the practice of law. As Secretary, he clung to the lawyer's methodical definition of problems and the rendition of final decisions in strict conformity with the rules of logic, law, and precedent. He was limited, in addition, by his judicial acceptance of decisions that went against him. Hughes believed that a Secretary of State should be a servant of the people and of Congress, operating the machinery of government as efficiently as possible but not undertaking to remake it. His objective in the office, he said, was the establishment of "a policy which protects American rights, maintains a candid and direct diplomacy, is in accord with the genius of our institutions, and gives cooperation wherever there is a sound basis for it. It is a policy which yields results. . . ." There would be under Hughes no bold bid to remake the world, no comprehensive reforms undertaken at the risk of failure.

Wilson had talked of universal ideals; Hughes talked of national interests. "Foreign policies are not built upon abstractions," the Secretary once said. "They are the result of practical conceptions of national interest arising from some immediate exigency or standing out vividly in historical perspective." The surest guides to the achievement of such limited goals, he added, were time-tested traditions and the canons of international law. Yet there was a marked ambivalence in Hughes's realism, for he could not escape the rationalism of Wilson completely. In large measure Wilson's fundamental concept of a world order based on law merely reinforced Hughes's legalism. For Hughes believed, as did Wilson, that the world's respect for the rights of the individual state was "the foundation of international justice, the basis of enduring peace, and the mainstay of reasonable diplomacy." Sound international order could be built, therefore, only on the willingness of nations to respect formal contracts and to observe international rules of good conduct.

Hughes accepted the obligation, established for him by his predecessors, to protect American interests, primarily economic interests, abroad—a policy which the *Nation* attributed to "oil and the almighty dollar." Within this circumscribed area, Hughes sought limited and obtainable objectives. Conferences succeeded, he said, in direct proportion to the success in limiting the number of participants and the scope of the subjects discussed. This philosophy was completely in character, for despite his brilliant intellect, Hughes was singularly lacking in imagination and wholly uncreative in social thought. The content of his ideas, critics lamented, in no way matched his magnificent mechanism for thinking. As a reporter of the day expressed it, Hughes would be easy to beat at poker, impossible to beat at chess. He relied on logic, almost never on intuition or emotion. Consequently, he was masterful in executing ideas, mediocre in producing them. His analytical talents permitted him to simplify even the most complex issues and reduce them to formulas. Optimism and unswerving faith in the efficacy of logic were so marked in Hughes that Justice Louis D. Brandeis attributed to him "the most enlightened mind of the eighteenth century." The great danger in Hughes's methods of thought was what one contemporary called "a fatal habit of oversimplification."

From March, 1921, onward, Hughes was involved in the debate on the League of Nations. His views on the League conformed to Republican orthodoxy. His fundamental cautiousness was challenged by the apparent obligations which membership imposed. Quite correctly, he judged that Article X, which contained the principle of collective security and the mutual guarantee of territorial and political integrity, would stir up the greatest opposition to the League in the United States. Hughes, furthermore, did not believe that this article could be reconciled with the Constitution. It represented, he said, a binding commitment which was unwise, unnecessary, and unenforceable. Article X merely flew in the teeth of experience, for, he said, peace could not be achieved by the "attempted enforcement of an inflexible rule." Rather, peace must be ushered in by firm friendships based on a community of interest and purpose. Such friendships were more likely to grow from voluntary conferences than from "hard and fast engagements." These convictions, stated early in 1919 before the Union League Club of New York, guided Hughes during the years that he was Secretary of State.

Along with many other Republicans of legal bent, Hughes favored judicial organizations for world peace. As a presidential candidate in 1916, he had stressed the advisability of establishing a world court and holding periodic conferences "to formulate international rules, to establish principles, to modify and extend international law...." In subsequent speeches, during 1917 and 1918, Hughes reminded the nation that it had outgrown its former isolation and emphasized the need of building an organization for international justice through the judicial instruments of a court, conciliation, arbitration, and conferences. Hughes was, therefore, a vigorous exponent of the internationalism of the twenties. His search for legal and judicial substitutes for power in world affairs made him far more the critic than the exponent of the principles of Woodrow Wilson. He simply had no interest in a political league based on collective security. Like most other internationalists, Hughes favored a maximum of security with a minimum of commitment.

This ambivalence toward Wilson's concepts accounted for Hughes's reaction to the Treaty of Versailles. His natural aversion to extremes and his interest in the economic advantages of the treaty led him to repudiate the irreconcilables' demand for the outright rejection of the League. In March, 1919, even before the final draft of the League was completed, Hughes sent seven proposed reservations to Wilson. During the Senate debate, he advocated the retention of those features of the Covenant that provided for a judicial approach to peace, the elimination of all possible threats to American independence, and the restoration of the economic community to its prewar status. These three goals, he believed, could be achieved through a League with reservations. "There is a middle ground," he insisted, "between aloofness and injurious commitment." At every opportunity during the League debate and the campaign of 1920, Hughes demanded that Article X be nullified. One of his typical observations was that the article had "no place in a proper covenant for an association of nations to promote peace." To Wilson, who placed chief reliance on the League of Nations rather than on the World Court, Hughes was guilty of sheer heresy. Theodore Roosevelt once called Hughes "a whiskered Wilson," but on the League issue the two men were separated by far more than a hair. Although some Republicans classified Hughes as pro-League, the reason was not that he embraced Wilson's ideal of collective security but merely that he rejected the irreconcilables' demand for total opposition to Wilsonism.

Hughes studied the League issue carefully from the viewpoint of practical statesmanship. Wilson had failed, he believed, because of his unyielding insistence on nonessentials, such as Article X. "Under a leadership more sensitive to public opinion and wiser in discerning the limits of practicability," he wrote, "our government would have taken its place in the League...." As Secretary, Hughes was determined to avoid the error of ignoring the political factors within the nation upon which the successful conduct of democratic policy depended.

When the Secretaryship was offered to Hughes in December, 1920, he restated his position on the League to Harding. As a signer of the celebrated Declaration of the Thirty-one during the presidential campaign, Hughes had attempted to bind the Republican party "by every consideration of good faith to bring the United States into a League purged of the unnecessary and useless Article Ten." Harding appeared to be in full agreement with Hughes that an amended League could be ratified by the Senate.

But when Hughes assumed office, he quickly discovered that even his moderate views on the League were anathema to the Republican irreconcilables in the Senate. Recognizing the limits of practicability, he asserted that the Senate would not agree to League membership. Harding, whatever his views before he entered the White House, refused to employ the power of his office in any campaign to overcome the Senate's opposition. Hughes dropped his campaign pledge to promote United States membership in a modified League of Nations, rejecting the suggestion of some of his cosigners in the Declaration of the Thirty-one that he push the League issue until it was defeated and then resign in protest. "I think," wrote Hughes, "that it would have been wholly unjustifiable for me to have resigned the responsibilities that I had assumed simply because the President did not undertake what I was convinced he could not accomplish.... I accepted office to do the best that I could for the country and I have remained in office for the same reason."

More than this nation's membership in the League of Nations was at stake here, for the irreconcilables threatened to wreck all the work of the administration during the next four years if it supported the League. Through direct interviews with the senators themselves, Hughes found that this was no idle boast and that his pro-League classification made him suspect in their eyes. To challenge this opposition by championing or even condoning the League would have terminated his influence before his career began and would have made it impossible for him to discharge his "imperative obligation" to serve the country as Secretary of State.

Hughes was an advocate of international cooperation. He would engage in conferences, but he believed, as did the irreconcilables William E. Borah and Hiram Johnson, that cooperation must not jeopardize the independence and sovereignty of the United States. Although his personal feelings were not, according to his theory of office, of paramount importance in formulating policy, he consistently disagreed with those who believed that armed force could be employed successfully to preserve peace. Even if it could, the American people and the Senate would reject military means to promote peace and would refuse blanket commitments to cover unforeseen contingencies abroad. In denying the efficacy of force in maintaining the nation's interests abroad, Hughes was not only at odds with Wilson's concept of collective security but also in tune with the deepest convictions of the American people.

Thus Hughes had neither the temperament nor the convictions to become a martyr for the League of Nations, even with reservations. The real issue of 1921, he believed, was to end controversy and establish a spirit of cooperation at home and abroad. Only then could the nation resolve the dull and inglorious, but totally inescapable, issues of international affairs. Among the immediate challenges facing the nation abroad were the revival of trade and the formal ending of the war with the Central Powers. Hughes set out to protect the national interest, considerably limited by his own ideas and by the dominant political forces of the decade.

III

Hughes's first major problem was that of securing for the United States the rights which the defeated Germany guaranteed to the victorious Allies in the rejected Treaty of Versailles. He hoped to purchase the benefits of the settlement without committing the United States to its Siamese twin, the League Covenant. When the Senate blocked access to the treaty by way of the League, Hughes sought another means of establishing formal peace with Germany. Meanwhile, the Senate, without consulting the State Department, adopted its own resolution for a separate peace which would guarantee the United States all the benefits granted to the signatories of the Treaty of Versailles. To implement this resolution would, it appeared, require tedious negotiations with Germany for a new treaty. After much thought, Hughes decided to eliminate this irksome duty by lifting verbatim from the Treaty of Versailles all the sections dealing with rights due the United States and incorporating them into a new treaty. Germany agreed to this arrangement, as did the Senate. Probably this Treaty of Berlin mirrored more closely than any other document of Hughes's time the aims of the Senate to acquire all the privileges but none of the responsibilities accruing to the victors in the war. Although Hughes admitted that the treaty had to be swallowed with a "wry face," he believed that the unpleasant effort was necessary. "Those who have sense enough to appreciate the facts," he wrote, believe "it is the best that could be done."

With this immediate issue removed, Hughes was ready to consider the broader problem of establishing world order. He turned automatically to the World Court. Permanent peace, he declared, was to be achieved, not "in forms of mere engagements," but only as the spirit of justice prevailed and men came "sincerely to prefer the processes of reason to the struggles of force." Thus he proposed United States membership in the Court more from personal conviction than from any assurance that his program would meet with success in the American political arena. The strong popular sympathy for the Court, he knew, was not reflected in the Senate. For this reason, he made no move toward the Court until the last treaty of the Washington Conference of 1921–1922 was approved by the Senate. Then Harding urged even further delay, wishing to transact business of his own with the Senate before executive-congressional relations had a chance to become strained over a tough decision in the realm of foreign affairs.

Hughes, with scrupulous consideration for the wishes of the Senate, sought to meet its principal objections to the World Court with four reservations, presented in the form of a protocol in February, 1923. The Senate Foreign Relations Committee kept the protocol off the floor of the Senate for another year. Meanwhile, Borah and other irreconcilables branded the Court a creature of the League and led a running fight against United States membership. Hughes had left office before the Senate debated and disposed of the issue.

Hughes's policies in meeting the challenge of world cooperation achieved little and pleased few. They were too radical for the irreconcilables and too conservative for the liberal Republicans. Hughes was excoriated by the pro-League faction for failing to redeem his promise to support a modified League. Milder internationalists denounced Hughes for ignoring his pledge to pursue some alternative association of nations if his League plan failed. His critics were all the more caustic because they were convinced that Hughes, supported by his known abilities and the prestige of his office, could have swept all opposition aside. Hughes insisted, in his defense, that he followed the only practicable course available, for none other would have been satisfactory to the majority of Americans.

IV

During its first months in office, the Harding administration faced pressure from several directions to arrange a conference of world powers to resolve some of the problems remaining in the wake of the great war. Eventually this pressure led to the Washington Conference and Hughes's most celebrated activity as Secretary of State. Such a conference was demanded, first of all, by those editors and senators who were intent on armament limitation, or disarmament as it was optimistically and inaccurately called. By 1921 the United States Army had already been reduced from its 2,000,000 of 1918 to about 200,000. The Navy, on the other hand, escaped the first cut, and the ambitious and expensive building program of 1916 was still under way. The superior British fleet and the ever-expanding navy of imperialistic Japan lent plausibility to demands for continued American naval expansion. Furthermore, the Anglo-Japanese Alliance of 1902 appeared to link the two rival fleets against the United States in the event of war in the Pacific. For American naval experts, also desirous of some better arrangement on the question of naval power, the only alternative to breaking the Anglo-Japanese Alliance was building an American fleet equal to the combined navies of England and Japan.

Few Americans saw much logic in these arguments. By the spring of 1921, it was clear even to such an ardent naval expansionist as Senator Henry Cabot Lodge that naval appropriations must be cut, regardless of the naval policies of other nations. If America's relative naval strength was to be preserved, therefore, a mutual reduction of fleets by the naval powers was an immediate and vital necessity.

During 1921 Hughes was confronted with the proposition that American naval strength was being threatened by the Senate. A big-power conference might mitigate the effect of congressional action, but the prerequisites of such a meeting were British acquiescence in naval parity and an agreement which would neutralize the Anglo-Japanese Alliance. The difficult task of driving a bargain with foreign powers while fencing off the importunities of an aroused public had to be completed within a few weeks after Hughes became Secretary of State.

Hughes approached this Herculean task with considerable determination, meeting the diplomatic issues involved and skillfully salvaging from near eclipse the executive initiative in directing foreign policy. He managed to delay the passage of a disarmament resolution introduced by Borah. Harding had no desire to oppose the will of the Senate, but he withheld as long as possible the approval that regular Republican senators demanded before they would support the Borah resolution. Utilizing to the utmost the three months of time gained before a restive public drove the resolution through the Senate, Hughes concluded a series of tentative understandings with the British which granted the principle of naval parity, some modification of the Anglo-Japanese Alliance, and support for a naval conference in Washington. Even before the President's signature gave the Borah resolution the status of law, Hughes had issued the formal invitations for the Washington Conference. Perhaps it was true, as the press insisted, that the conference was forced on the administration by Borah, the Senate, and the American people. Nevertheless, the Secretary had gained control of the movement for naval limitation and rescued the executive prerogatives so completely that when Harding announced

the forthcoming conference the press described him as a farsighted statesman.

Hughes's struggle with the Senate was not over. To prevent senatorial interference with the Washington Conference, he took special precautions not to antagonize the irreconcilables. He rejected the persistent
British demands for a preliminary conference on Far Eastern affairs because he knew that the Senate would not approve of it. He selected the
official American delegation to the naval conference with great care, excluding the recalcitrant Borah but including the Senate's majority and
minority leaders, Lodge and Oscar W. Underwood. By consulting the
two senators on every important decision, Hughes made it almost impossible for the Senate to make effective protest against any of the conference
treaties. He even pared the conference agenda carefully, omitting provocative questions such as Japanese immigration and the limitation of
land armies. The questions he did include he defined very narrowly. Naval
limitation, for example, applied only to battleships. The Far Eastern treaties deliberately excluded such trouble spots as China and India from their
jurisdiction. All the treaties, in fact, were drafted with the prejudices and
predilections of the Senate in mind. Hughes was not intent on reaching
maximum goals. His paramount objective at the Washington Conference
was to demonstrate—as Versailles had failed to do—that the United
States could meet with other nations and draft agreements acceptable to
the Senate. For him it was essential that American leadership re-establish
the confidence of the world in the good intentions and good faith of the
United States. Another American failure at the peace table would be cat-
astrophic.

As a negotiator, Hughes drove toward reasonable agreements as directly as possible. Ignoring the diplomat's rule of keeping national objectives vague at the outset, he began by stating the American position
frankly. With the possible exception of Britain, the nations represented
at Washington were offended by the Secretary's well-intentioned disregard for traditional methods of diplomatic exchange. Critics at home
argued that Hughes, by stating his objectives less specifically in his opening address to the conference, might have tested his opponents for every
possible concession and seized advantage of any sign of weakness. But the
Secretary never doubted, then or later, the wisdom of his course.

In his famous opening-day speech, Hughes not only demanded naval
limitation but also detailed the names and number of American battleships to be destroyed. By so candid a disclosure of the American position
he probably lost tactical ground in negotiation. He could not force the
British to give up cruisers by threatening to utilize America's potential
superiority in battleships. On the other hand, his bold statement of what

this nation was prepared to do, coupled with his clear inference that other nations could do no less, brought him at once the overwhelming support of the press both at home and around the world. This assured success for some program of naval limitation and silenced the administration's critics in the Senate. If the mere assurance of some agreement was a valid objective, Hughes's speech was a masterful performance, his finest hour as Secretary. So adroitly did he press the advantage afforded by widespread public support that the English delegate, Arthur Balfour, traced the achievements of the conference from Hughes's initial speech on naval limitation.

For his industry and direction of the Washington Conference, Hughes deserved the nation's acclamation. The confidential memoranda of meetings from which the Five-Power Naval Treaty and the Four-Power Pact developed reveal that Hughes was the true architect of these agreements. His unique ability to assimilate ideas and make them his own was demonstrated repeatedly in the negotiations. He mastered the briefs prepared for him by experts on Far Eastern affairs and by Navy Department personnel so completely that he was able to defend the American positions superbly through the extemporaneous discussion that led to the treaties.

Hughes's task as chief negotiator at the Washington Conference was comparatively simple. First of all, the principle of naval parity required the approval of only three nations—the United States, England, and Japan. Second, the will of these three powers was all that mattered in the crucial questions of the abrogation of the Anglo-Japanese Alliance and the reassertion of the Open Door in China. Perhaps Hughes's major achievement at the conference was the Five-Power Treaty, which established the 5:5:3 ratio in naval strength among the Big Three. Yet this agreement ignored the important category of cruisers in limiting naval tonnage. The Four-Power Pact, signed by the United States, England, France, and Japan—the four primary powers in the Far East—established the principle of mutual security in the western Pacific and abrogated, in the process, the long-standing Anglo-Japanese Alliance. This removed the danger that England might be obligated at some future date to support Japan in a war against the United States. It removed as well the implication that Britain was underwriting Japan's obvious aggressiveness toward China. In the Nine-Power Pact, the third of Hughes's achievements at the Washington meetings, all the nations represented at the conference sanctioned the principle of the Open Door for China. Since the Japanese were in a minority position, they could not seriously threaten to disrupt the conference over this issue, but they did seek concessions, such as the nonfortification of the Pacific islands and the retention of the *Mutsu*, their prize battleship.

In appraising the obvious, if temporary, achievements at Washington, too many Americans detected the dawn of a new era in international affairs. The conference, they declared, had inaugurated a wholly new method of open diplomacy, had replaced distrust with good will among nations, and had created a permanent basis for peace. In the words of one Republican senator, "the very angels in heaven sang at the work of that conference." Hughes was acclaimed a national hero, the greatest Secretary of State in a century. The public accepted the Five-Power Treaty, not as a temporary naval arrangement at best, but as the final substitute for the irksome necessity of naval expansion. Hughes himself asserted that the naval treaty "ends, absolutely ends, the race in competition in naval armament...we are taking perhaps the greatest forward step in history to establish the reign of peace." This statement was taken as final proof that there had indeed been a "miracle in Washington."

But Hughes was far too wise to take his own words seriously. In meeting the naval problem, he had succeeded in casting a cloak of rationality over the nation's naked determination to stop paying for armament. He had gained British and Japanese agreements to reduce their battleship fleets in accord with reductions which the United States would have taken even without such agreements. Hughes warned the nation in 1922 that national security demanded a navy kept at maximum treaty strength, for otherwise a policy of mutual arms limitation was meaningless. Furthermore, he made it clear that this nation's bargaining position at future conferences depended upon the actual naval strength it maintained. Unfortunately, the American people ignored his advice and abandoned his program of cooperative naval limitation in favor of irresponsible unpreparedness. By 1934 the United States was 102 ships, or about 380 million dollars, short of treaty strength. Thus the country's lack of preparedness in 1941 was less the result of the destruction of vessels in 1922 or of excessive naval building by Britain and Japan than the fruit of the insidious idea that the Five-Power Treaty rendered further preparedness unnecessary.

Hughes recognized the flaws in the Far Eastern settlements which, within a decade, became unmistakably clear. It required more than a year of negotiations to achieve the final annulment of the Lansing-Ishii Agreement of 1917, in which the United States, under the pressure of war, had conceded in part the principle of Chinese territorial integrity. The Japanese asserted repeatedly during the negotiations that their ambitions in China stemmed from inexorable necessity and were not subject to modification by treaty. Even in the Washington treaties of 1922, the Japanese, ironically, managed to strengthen their position in the Far East. The Four-Power Pact neutralized those islands, including both Guam and the Philippines, from which an offensive campaign could be launched against Japan. It is true that the Japanese recognized the Open Door in China, but the United States refused to assume any responsibility in the treaties for enforcing this policy.

After the Washington Conference, Hughes became more than ever enamored of laudatory public opinion. Believing that the American people should be educated on the issues of foreign policy, he inaugurated the weekly press conference as a means of informing the nation of the problems facing the administration abroad. Yet he strayed widely from his fundamental precepts of realism in the news that he gave, for too often it had a political, rather than an educational, purpose. Hughes's unfounded optimism, so apparent in these conferences, fostered complacency and induced apathy.

V

Hughes's unwillingness to face unpleasant realities, especially when Congress was involved, was evident in his handling of the Japanese immigration problem. Never did he seem more resigned and weak than in his attempts to meet this baffling question. Its significance could not have escaped him, for obviously the permanent impact of the Washington Conference depended upon the satisfactory settlement of the troublesome problem of Japanese immigration. Postwar nationalism in the United States produced the provisional immigration act of 1921, which limited immigration from all nations to established quotas. During the next four years, fourteen states passed alien-land laws, directed at the Japanese, similar to those adopted in California. Anticipating a crisis with Japan, the Wilson administration had recalled Ambassador Roland Morris in 1920 to discuss with Baron Shidehara methods of resolving the issue. After thorough investigation of the problem, these two men compromised their major differences in a model treaty. This treaty reached the Senate Committee on Foreign Relations shortly after Hughes became Secretary. Hiram Johnson simply pigeonholed it.

Hughes never made any attempt to utilize the Morris-Shidehara formula. It would, he explained to the Japanese Ambassador, nullify state laws on alien land ownership. The employment of the treaty-making power to enhance Federal over state authority, he said, would set a most unpopular precedent. When the Japanese sought to put immigration on the Washington Conference agenda, Hughes refused, asserting that it was a purely domestic issue. After the conference adjourned, Hughes, still reluctant to act, advised the Japanese to reduce their immigration to a minimum while developing a spirit of good will toward the United States. Attitudes, observed the Secretary, were far more important than formal agreements in determining affairs among nations. If Japan could become friendly enough, suggested Hughes, a settlement on Japanese immigration might follow.

For two years the matter drifted without benefit of diplomacy, while the Japanese government, fearing exclusion as the ultimate American policy, warned the Secretary of State from time to time that exclusion would dissipate whatever moral force the United States still retained in the Orient, destroy the party of conciliation in Japan, and drive Japan and China into an alliance against the West. Still Hughes took no stand. In December, 1923, and again in January, 1924, the Japanese urged measures to avoid the inevitable crisis. But it was not until February 8, 1924, weeks after the congressional debate on immigration had begun, that the Secretary acted.

At this point Hughes demonstrated his complete grasp of the dangerous implications of a Japanese-exclusion policy, thus making his former passive attitude seem mystifying indeed. He warned members of Congress that exclusion would jeopardize the work of the Washington Conference by exciting Japanese belligerence. As an alternative to what he regarded as a needlessly dangerous course, he suggested the continuance of the Gentlemen's Agreement and the provision of a quota for Japan. This fair and logical program did not appeal to Congress. And with the immigration bill nearing a vote, there was no longer enough time for the Secretary to explain and promote his plan.

Hughes's hurried effort to remove congressional misunderstanding of the Gentlemen's Agreement by submitting a letter of explanation from Japanese Ambassador Hanahira resulted in catastrophe. The Secretary was immediately termed pro-Japanese and rebuffed by a Senate vote of 70 to 2 that ratified the bill excluding aliens ineligible for citizenship. In a desperate bid to save face for Japan, Hughes proposed a reciprocal treaty establishing exclusion in both countries. It was merely a gesture, for even as he proposed reciprocity, he warned the Japanese that it was not worthwhile to promote a plan which would inevitably be doomed in the Senate. Hughes, in his remorse, bitterly charged the Senate with undoing the spirit of friendship engendered by the Washington Conference and "in a few minutes" spoiling the "work of years." There was no note of self-condemnation. Yet it is difficult to believe that the man who managed to dominate the Washington Conference could not have struck more telling blows in what amounted to a defense of his major policies in the Far East. Perhaps like other Secretaries of State, he was more fearful of United States senators than he was of foreign diplomats.

VI

If Hughes seemed inept in handling immigration policy, he showed considerable dexterity in resolving the reparations issue. Again it was Congress that stood in the path of an easy and sound solution. In this instance, however, Hughes reacted with resourcefulness and determination, pushing his program to adoption. The Senate, in the separate peace with Germany, included a reservation forbidding American participation in the work of the reparations commission. Hughes accepted this reservation, although he did not agree with it. Thereafter, without challenging Congress directly on the question, he proceeded by devious and unofficial means to correct what he believed to be a mistake. First he urged privately, in conversations with French and British diplomats, the establishment of a reparations commission of financial experts from the countries concerned. This informal commission could invite private American citizens to participate; Congress could not interfere.

When this approach did not yield results, Hughes turned to another. In a speech before the American Historical Association at New Haven in 1922, he presented the essence of his plan for an informal reparations commission. In this manner he brought his ideas before the American public. Continuing his private conversations with foreign statesmen, Hughes eventually managed to circumvent the Senate and arrange a reparations conference to meet in England. Then, by coincidence, the American Bar Association held its meeting in London in 1924 at the same time that the reparations commission met. Hughes, by an even more striking coincidence, was president of the bar association. So it was that the American Secretary of State could cloak himself in unofficial capacities in order to work for the success of the reparations commission. The Dawes Plan was the distinguished result. Senators chafed, unable to restrain the president of the American Bar Association, although he looked and acted like the American Secretary of State. The Dawes Plan itself, while not a lasting solution to the reparations problem, was a constructive beginning, and its very existence was a monument to Hughes's resourcefulness. Even the most formidable barriers could not, in this case, restrain him from what he believed to be his duty.

But the Secretary failed again to impress the nation with the unpleasant but important realities in foreign affairs. Although he reflected the popular notion that war debts must be paid, he stood firmly with his party in opposing the lowering of American tariffs to make payment possible. His policy helped to confirm the fatal, superficial optimism of the times. An unthinking Republic merely assumed that the settlement of a few immediate differences between nations, without ever touching fundamental issues, was all that mattered. Perhaps it is true that neither Hughes nor any other Secretary of State could have altered the course which the American people persisted in following during the twenties. But on many occasions Hughes shied away from giving publicity to unpleasant truths and overstated the effectiveness of his own policies. His defense for misleading the nation was that a Secretary must retain the confidence and cooperation of the Congress and the people. Hughes simply refused to antagonize either group. The Secretary, moreover, was a devoted member of his party. Confidence and optimism could serve the Republicans better than fear and doubt.

VII

At the heart of the opposition to the League in the United States during Hughes's Secretaryship was the fear that no reservation could prevent the Covenant from destroying the Monroe Doctrine. With the entire Western Hemisphere under the League, European states would be bound to intervene in Latin-American affairs and to stand in judgment of United States policies. These suspicions reflected not only a sentimental loyalty to honored traditions but also a recognition of economic realities and the exigencies of defense.

Hughes subscribed to these anti-League theories. Even before the Covenant was completed, he demanded reservations to protect the doctrine and insisted on settlement of American disputes by the cooperative action of American states alone. Only by the joint request of these nations would Europeans be permitted to participate. Hughes followed these precepts consistently as Secretary, beginning with the 1921 Panama–Costa Rica boundary dispute. He was so ardently opposed to League participation in Western Hemispheric affairs that he prevented League observers from attending the 1923 Pan-American Conference. When the Geneva Protocol was proposed in 1924 to strengthen the League's powers of enforcement, Hughes set forth strong objections to it. If the Protocol carried out its objectives, he argued, a concert of powers could intervene whenever they "considered that the United States had committed some act of aggression. . . ." This would be true even though this nation believed its action "entirely justified" and "in accordance with its traditional policies." The Protocol, in Hughes's estimation, was nothing short of a reincarnation of the Holy Alliance of Alexander I that had originally called forth the Monroe Doctrine.

Actually Hughes again was overcautious. The League had shown no disposition to coerce nonmember or even member states. The British, whose fleet would be the chief instrument of any such coercion, would not have jeopardized the friendship of the United States on any question arising under the Monroe Doctrine. As usual, however, Hughes was on solid ground in surmising the status of public and Senate opinion. There was no disposition in the United States to tolerate any threat to the sacrosanct credo of Monroe.

Though standing foursquare for the doctrine, Hughes was aware of the dangers of blatant insistence on American rights in the Western Hemisphere, and the passing of the war crisis permitted the Republican platform of 1920 to call for a policy of forbearance. Rising nationalism in the "sister republics," as Hughes called them, lent weight to the critical notion that the Monroe Doctrine was nothing more than a cloak of piety concealing a ruthless plan of United States imperialism. The need to counter this charge, Hughes's devotion to legal precision, and the occasion of the doctrine's centenary during his term in office afforded him justification for restating the doctrine's meaning. This was a task that he enjoyed.

The doctrine, Hughes asserted many times, was nothing more than a policy of self-defense, limited in scope and never intended to be "our sole policy in this hemisphere." The most serious consequence of this blanket interpretation, he said, was the effort to trace a sanction for intervention to the Monroe Doctrine. Such a relation did not exist. Intervention was a right derived from the broad body of international law, specific treaties, self-defense, or the need to protect the interests of humanity. Consequently, intervention was not a crime in itself. It might be justifiable or unjustifiable. If nonpolitical in nature and undertaken by a nation for the protection of its citizens, it was justifiable. In the technical phrase that Hughes liked to quote, it was not intervention at all, but "nonbelligerent interposition." Intervention became unjustifiable when it degenerated into an aggressive use of military force for imperialistic purposes.

Hughes realized that even legally sound theories did not meet Latin America's fundamental objections to intervention. These proudly independent and intensely nationalistic nations could see no justification whatsoever for American intervention. Whatever its origin or purpose, intervention impaired their sovereignty and independence. Yet the United States, in Hughes's opinion, could not sacrifice the rights and property of its nationals to the pride of nations plagued with anarchy. The optimum plan, Hughes believed, was to "limit our interposition to a pressing exigency well established" and to emphasize on such occasions that "we are not seeking control of the peoples of other lands or to interfere with the governments they desire." At all times the United States stood ready "to make available its friendly assistance to promote stability in those of our sister republics... afflicted with disturbed conditions...." The right to extend protection ought not to be a shield for economic penetration, but neither should that right be forfeited where protection was actually needed. The problem was to avoid abusing the valid right of intervention. The American objective in the Western Hemisphere, declared Hughes, was "by friendly cooperation with the nations concerned to eliminate the causes for unrest, and thus prevent the growth of conditions prejudicial to the interests of the United States." Rather than subverting political and economic strength, he said, the United States desired "to have prosperous and independent neighbors with whom we can deal in peace to our mutual advantage." Anyone who really understood the American people, Hughes concluded, must realize that the last thing in the world they wanted was to assume responsibility for other people.

In seeking to liquidate the charge of American interventionism in Latin America, Hughes moved in his chosen way through a series of limited acts. He presided over a convention in Washington in 1922 during which five Central American states renounced the right of intervention in one another's internal affairs. The United States did not sign this agreement, but all understood that this nation was bound by it. Over some Senate protest, Hughes managed the ratification of a treaty which reimbursed Colombia 25 million dollars for the loss of the Canal Zone. Cuban anarchy invited intervention in 1923, but the Secretary held to his policy of forbearance. American marines were recalled from the Dominican Republic in 1924 and from Nicaragua the following year. These were substantial signs of a new day in inter-American relations. But Hughes was not willing, at the Pan-American Conference at Santiago in 1923, to give any support to indirect proposals limiting the right of intervention. He argued that American rights could not be upheld or American property protected if intervention were prohibited.

Hughes rejected all Latin-American demands that the Monroe Doctrine be made multilateral. It was his fundamental principle that the United States should not accept any binding commitments to a course of action which might contain unforeseen contingencies. This nation, he declared in 1923, "reserves to itself the definition, interpretation, and application of the Doctrine." This policy did not flow from "suspicion or estrangement." Unhampered discretion, he said, was required to assert the fundamental right of self-defense. To meet Latin-American insistence on a cooperative policy, Hughes urged each nation of the area to incorporate a Monroe Doctrine into its own foreign policy. "In this way," he continued, "without sacrifice by any American state of its particular interests, the doctrine would have the support of all the American republics." Hughes proclaimed repeatedly the equality of all nations in the Western Hemisphere.

Hughes's theories were illustrated clearly in his policy toward Mexico. The Mexican Constitution of 1917 confiscated the holdings of many American investors. The Secretary moved with firmness and dispatch to protect these interests. Although he had criticized Wilson's Mexican policy during the presidential campaign of 1916, Hughes had aimed his fire more at the failure of Mexico to protect American rights than at American intervention itself. Like Wilson, Hughes refused to recognize the Mexican government, now under Alvaro Obregon, demanding as the price of recognition nothing less than a treaty guaranteeing American rights. After two years of negotiation the treaty was dropped, but the

Mexican government accepted an executive agreement which protected American property under the 1917 Constitution. Critics insisted that this agreement was the most drastic form of intervention—a revision of the Mexican Constitution itself. Hughes denied these charges. The Mexican Constitution remained untouched. All that he had done, he said, was to encourage Mexico to adopt an interpretation which would bring that Constitution into harmony with long-established principles of international law.

After granting recognition to the Obregon government, Hughes proceeded to supply it with arms, while withholding them from the revolutionary forces of General de la Huerta. Instantly the cry of intervention in Mexican affairs was raised again. The Secretary dismissed the charge with the explanation that the Huerta forces did not deserve arms because they did not represent the "aspirations of an oppressed people." Hughes admitted that his policy influenced "proceedings in other lands," but he maintained that such interference was wholly justifiable. The nation had always acted to uphold "normal rights" and to accomplish "good ends." Hughes never delayed when American rights and property were in danger. Although his duty to his country may have required nothing less, he could not convince the Mexican government that his policies were just. Improved Mexican-American relations could not be built on legal justification alone. But to his credit Hughes remedied some of his predecessors' worst abuses of authority and presented a reasonable explanation of his nation's actions.

Charles Evans Hughes, as Secretary of State, was guided by strong convictions which often limited the scope of his responses to a narrow legalism. Hampered by the intellectual and political liabilities of a weak administration, an ambitious Senate, and a thoughtless public, he supplied much of the illusive energy to be found in the executive during Harding's Presidency. He brought some order to the nation's foreign relations. Yet there was something unrealistic in his beliefs that problems abroad were identical in nature to domestic questions and amenable to domestic law written on a world-wide scale, that a universal will to order existed, and that all conflicts must inevitably yield to reason and justice. With the passage of the years, Hughes's seemingly practical approaches have taken on an air of utopianism, and his concrete measures have assumed the abstractness of Wilsonism. An efficient administrator, Hughes fell short of true statesmanship because he lacked boldness, imaginativeness, and, even more, an auspicious era in which to perform.

8
Frank B. Kellogg

1925-1929

BY L. ETHAN ELLIS
Rutgers University

Frank B. Kellogg was well below the top level of Secretarial practitioners in the twentieth century, and the period of his incumbency was
one of less than crucial importance. From 1925 to 1929 a run-of-the-mine
Secretary of State, teamed with a modestly equipped President, coped
industriously, if less than brilliantly, with problems for the most part
originating prior to Kellogg's appointment and climaxing after his departure. In retrospect, it can be seen that the United States relations with
Latin America, with the Far East, and with Europe were in a sort of
interim period and that American dealings with these areas were tentative rather than determinative. The Kellogg-Briand Pact, the development bearing the Secretary's heaviest personal imprint, would soon topple
from its lofty but precarious perch in the face of the concussions of war
in Manchuria and Ethiopia. Perhaps the most constructive policies which
Kellogg developed were those which inched inter-American relations
toward a sounder base and which led to a restoration of China's tariff
autonomy. The result was a workmanlike but unimpressive Secretaryship;
the shop was kept running, but few new goods were put on the shelves.
The verdict on its effectiveness will therefore depend somewhat upon
which aspect of merchandising the observer considers more important.

Born in New York, Kellogg moved to Minnesota at the age of nine.
His formal education was confined to the "common school," and his
sensitivity about this circumstance is reflected in the somewhat stilted
phraseology that characterizes the occasional documents he drafted during his Secretaryship. Admission to the bar in 1877 launched him on a

149

long and impressive career in law and public service. Although his early reputation was derived in part from serving as government prosecutor in antitrust suits, he had a more lasting and lucrative connection with the corporate side of the business-government equation. It was this phase of his experience that won him membership in the Universal Congress of Lawyers and Jurists (1904), brought him to the presidency of the American Bar Association (1912 and 1913), provided him with the competence to serve in public office, and created a bent of mind which had important repercussions upon his career as Secretary of State. Failing re-election after a term as Senator from Minnesota (1917–1923), he served as a delegate to the Fifth International Conference of American States in 1923 and then became United States Ambassador to the Court of St. James's. From this post Calvin Coolidge called him to the Secretaryship at the outset of his own full term. His predecessor, Charles Evans Hughes, pointed out that this background gave Kellogg "a much more intimate knowledge" of Departmental problems than most of his predecessors had had.

Temperamentally, Kellogg brought varied and not always useful equipment to his task. What was probably a lifelong habit of caution sometimes stood him in good stead and sometimes stood in the way of needed action. An occasional streak of naïveté shows up in his documents and in his relations with his colleagues, but it seldom found its way into the public records. Coolidge's aversion to Washington's unique combination of heat and humidity led him to indulge in long vacations in the hinterlands. This condemned Kellogg to close confinement during the most unpleasant season. Much of this confinement would doubtless have been self-imposed anyway, for the Secretary once boasted that he "read every word of the reports from our ambassadors and ministers." His devotion to duty was matched by his irascibility in its performance—a perennial quality not dependent upon climatological factors. His associates varied in their estimates of the importance of the Kellogg temper, perhaps in some sort of ratio to the immediacy of their exposure to it, but it would probably be fair to say that its effect on the policy-making process was enlivening and mildly retarding rather than significant.

There is no doubt, however, of the results of hard work and close confinement upon Kellogg's health. Late in December, 1926, while some of his major problems were in an acute stage, one of his close associates observed that the Secretary was "wildly inaccurate, intolerably rude, unwilling to read memoranda or to listen to an oral statement.... He thinks he bears on his shoulders the whole burden of the Department, complains that no one gives him any support or assistance and totally fails to grasp the fact that we are the only people who accomplish things by getting him, often with difficulty, to sign what we have prepared." A

month later the President virtually ordered him out of Washington for
a vacation, but it was only at the end of February, 1927, that he consented to leave his desk for a rest. This relief worked a considerable
restoration and aided him in seeing his assignment through to its conclusion.

Kellogg's service did not coincide with an outreaching period in his
country's history. The United States was barely beginning to emerge
from the trough of isolationism which followed World War I. A desire
to avoid too close or formal a contact with "the League at Geneva" (a
phrase often repeated in the documents) bespoke a compulsion to remain
independent of European politics, despite earlier involvement with European powers in the Washington Conference of 1922 and the later disarmament discussions at Geneva in 1927. Latin America was a disturbed
and disturbing area, whose resentful stirrings did not invite a venture-
some approach. And the Far East was very far away indeed.

Moreover, any venturesomeness on Kellogg's part would have faced
the double obstacles of Calvin Coolidge and American introversion. A
President whose training and experience had been primarily domestic,
Coolidge had neither any knowledge of nor any concern for foreign
affairs beyond the bare obligations inherent in his office. His autobiography, for example, contains no mention of foreign relations. The country, too, was domestically oriented. Prosperous business and industry,
expanding under the aegis of Secretary of Commerce Herbert Hoover
and basking in the light of judicial favor, was intent on greater and
greater profits. Not-so-prosperous workers in agriculture, coal, and tex-
tiles were equally intent upon bettering their lot. Bankers and specu-
lators were busy with their own concerns, which also were mainly domestic, despite the siphoning of surplus dollars into overseas investments.
On the whole, it was not a time conducive to new and experimental commitments.

Kellogg's views on the broad aspects of American foreign policy
were always conditioned by the events and moods of the twenties. In
general, he reflected the nation's rather reluctant awareness of the world
scene and its somewhat greater awareness of hemispheric affairs; accepted
involvement in particular directions and upon certain issues but remained
firmly resolved against any wholehearted commitment; recognized his
country's power but hesitated to accept international responsibility. Altogether, his attitude may be likened to that of a timorous young lady
who, observing her contemporaries cavorting in a pool, tries the water's
temperature and, finding it not to her liking, looks about nervously for
deep holes and refuses to get wet above the ankles.

One other matter, of conditioning significance rather than of fundamental importance, was the repercussions of the Rogers Act of 1924 on the

Department of State. This law was designed to consolidate the diplomatic and consular services, hitherto sharply separated, into a single Foreign Service, with personnel interchangeable between the branches. Operations under this law were still in a shakedown stage in the days of Kellogg, so that slight irregularities could produce disproportionately abrasive effects, especially when sharpened by political complications.

As time passed, friction arose over promotion procedures. Prior to the bill's passage, the consular branch had acted on the basis of carefully compiled efficiency ratings; the diplomatic branch had formulated no such system, and seniority and various pressures had played a considerable role in its advancement procedure. Under the new law, Departmental action on promotion recommendations culminated in a Personnel Board which developed and used two efficiency lists, one for each branch. By the spring of 1927, this system had resulted in the promotion of 63 per cent of the diplomats and only 37 per cent of the consuls, who outnumbered the diplomats by about three and a half to one.

Disgruntled consuls gained the ears of Congress and of the press, stimulating the Personnel Board to adopt a single efficiency list and to take steps to narrow the promotion gap between the two branches. In 1928 a senatorial subcommittee held hearings and rendered a report sharply criticizing the record of promotion. A bill was introduced providing for a personnel bureau, to be headed by an Assistant Secretary and staffed from outside the Foreign Service, but it failed of enactment, and the Kellogg period ended without further important developments. There is little indication that the Secretary involved himself deeply in this family quarrel, but there is abundant evidence that the promotion issue occupied an inordinate amount of the time of many of his top-ranking assistants and that it was sufficiently disturbing to the rank and file to have an appreciable, though not an easily measurable, influence on the efficiency of both the Department and the Foreign Service.

II

Like all Secretaries of State, Kellogg functioned in a complicated executive environment, which included the President, professional assistants, and unofficial advisers. The denizens of this environment, moreover, were not an isolated group acting in a vacuum. Congressional and public scrutiny, registered in a vocal and not always friendly press, dogged their every step and re-enforced the caution which was one of Kellogg's principal characteristics.

In performing his constitutional function of advising the President on foreign affairs, Kellogg funneled policy proposals to the White House; these normally emanated from Departmental channels but occasionally bore a personal fillip. With the circumspect, aloof, and domestically oriented Coolidge in the Presidency, Secretarial advice usually determined policy, although an occasional upsurge of Presidential determination engendered Kellogg's respectful, sometimes even abject, acquiescence. Generally, however, Coolidge agreed, laconically, both with what had been done and with what was proposed. In these circumstances, the charting of day-to-day operations moved from the working staff through the Secretary to the White House without great emotional or intellectual involvement on the part of the President.

Coolidge's usual reaction to a lengthy Secretarial exposition was a brief, unqualified acceptance. A typical example was his reply of July 31, 1928, to Kellogg's long account of current church-state turbulence in Mexico: "Thank you for your personal and confidential letter . . . regarding conditions in Mexico. It is very interesting." His occasional interventions in policy matters generally had a negative force, designed to head off proposed excursions into what he deemed dangerous waters. By no stretch of the imagination can it be said that Coolidge at any time sought to be his own Secretary of State.

Although Kellogg was accustomed to taking the initiative in proposing policies, he was ever alert to ascertain Presidential wishes and to shift course upon evidence of Presidential dissatisfaction. For example, he went through a period of vacillation in the early summer of 1926 regarding the policy to be adopted toward cooperation with the powers in dealing with China's demands for revision of unequal treaties. At first he tentatively favored a united front, but he finally decided that, although his government should act with the other powers "as far as possible," independent action would be warranted in certain circumstances. Coolidge, agreeing with this view, instructed his Secretary, on July 4, to "use your own judgment and keep in harmony with the powers concerned." Kellogg, however, was careful to explore the new gambit with the President, interrupting a leave to travel from Minneapolis to Swampscott, Massachusetts, to lay the matter before Coolidge at the Summer White House. There he obtained the President's approval of a conciliatory policy toward China.

Another episode showing Kellogg's deference to the President developed in connection with the Secretary's proposed journey to Paris in the summer of 1928 to sign the Kellogg-Briand Pact. Shortly before his departure, Britain and France announced signature of a naval agreement possibly inimical to United States interests. His suspicions aroused by this act, Coolidge began to doubt the advisability of subjecting his Secretary to the sinister influences that he would encounter at Paris. Although Kellogg had always believed the antiwar pact to be the capstone of his career, he promptly and dutifully wrote the President that he was "very sorry" that he had promised to go to Europe to sign the agreement.

Privately, however, he threatened to resign if Coolidge interfered with his departure.

Given the personalities of the President and the Secretary, it would seem likely that subordinates in the Department would be in a position to wield extensive influence. This was indeed true, but the situation hardly manifested itself according to what might be considered a normal pattern, since Kellogg's personal attitudes played no small part in affairs. The first factor of moment was his predilection for lawyers, which had considerable effect on the tenancy of the Under Secretaryship during his term in office.

After some hesitancy, Kellogg decided to retain Under Secretary Joseph C. Grew, a seasoned and knowledgeable professional who had served Hughes ably in this capacity. But neither principal was entirely happy in this relationship. Kellogg's failure to keep Grew fully informed on policy matters created problems when Grew was left in charge in the Secretary's absence. Moreover, Kellogg felt that on such occasions Grew spent too much time on personnel matters. When, finally, Grew returned to the field in 1927 as Ambassador to Turkey, there was obvious relief on both sides.

This shift made it possible to elevate to the second position in the Department Kellogg's former law partner, Robert E. Olds, who had been an Assistant Secretary since the autumn of 1925 and who provided the legal talent which the Secretary felt he needed. From preparing legal matters for Kellogg's consideration, Olds moved easily into policy formulation and, by the time of Grew's departure, had taken over much of the latter's function in this area. In addition to acting as legal adviser, Olds involved himself actively in Mexican affairs. These two somewhat extracurricular activities tended to disturb the organizational balance of the Department, to the discomfiture of some professionals. But Olds's legalism contributed an element of decisiveness which was useful both to the Secretary and to the career men.

When Olds followed a not unusual pattern and left the Department to enter more lucrative private employment, the position went to another lawyer, J. Reuben Clark, who had recently been in Mexico on Dwight W. Morrow's personal staff. This appointment continued the high level of legal competence in the Department which the Secretary prized. Clark's interests were restricted, however, and aside from the Clark Memorandum on the Monroe Doctrine, he seems to have contributed little to the policy-making process. All in all, it would seem that Kellogg's preoccupation with lawyers resulted in his being less well served by his assistants than he might have been and that the machinery of policy making operated at somewhat below the top level of effectiveness.

Eight men occupied the four Assistant Secretaryships between 1925 and 1929. Of these, three went into the field, and Olds was elevated to the Under Secretaryship. Only Wilbur J. Carr served throughout Kellogg's term. The three new incumbents were Nelson T. Johnson, an old China hand and a graduate of the Consular Service, who had great influence upon Kellogg's Far Eastern policy; Francis White, whose broad knowledge of Latin-American affairs was somewhat overshadowed by the fact that successive Under Secretaries and Dwight W. Morrow played such large roles in Mexican affairs; and William R. Castle, who moved up from the Western European Division.

Castle, a career man in the Department, as distinguished from the still hardly amalgamated Foreign Service, occupied in many ways a unique position during the Kellogg period. He could observe the personnel problems mentioned above with at least a modicum of detachment. The accidents of neighborhood and a common love of exercise often brought him and the Secretary together on morning walks to the Department, and a further coincidence placed his office next door to the Secretary's, so that consultation was easy. These fortuitous circumstances were supplemented by a comfortable personal competence, which freed a naturally independent judgment to perform the highly important function of listening to, and sometimes moderating, Kellogg's extravagant first thoughts on many matters. The present account owes much to Castle's long-time habit of confiding his keen and often caustic comments to a diary, which he has made available to the author.

Kellogg's incumbency occurred during a period when a resurgent Congress, long restive under the restrictions imposed by Woodrow Wilson's wartime dominance, was still manifesting its prowess over a succession of weak executives. This constant flexing of congressional muscles tended to exaggerate the tender regard with which any executive department views the source of funds upon which its day-to-day existence depends. To this general situation was added the necessity of maintaining the maximum degree of good relations with William E. Borah.

This powerful, voluble, and often unpredictable chairman of the Senate Committee on Foreign Relations was a constant distraction to the Secretary of State. Borah's reactions to any problem were certain to be vigorous; to anything savoring of international entanglements they were likely to be violent. Kellogg was probably more sensitive to this menace than either his predecessor or his successor. The respect, not to say fear, with which Kellogg treated Borah is abundantly clear from the Secretary's communications with the chairman—the frequent letters, telephone conversations, and invitations to the Department for consultation, explanation, and justification of plans which were in process either of formulation or of implementation. Kellogg once made the remark (as paraphrased by Castle) that "you never have any idea what Borah is going to jump on and it is just as well to get his approbation in advance." This "ringing of

Borah's doorbell" was sufficiently common and obvious to cause wide comment.

Kellogg's relations with the press were less formal and more pleasant than those of his chief. Unlike Coolidge, who insisted upon written questions from newsmen, Kellogg invited oral interrogation on the memoranda which he read to the reporters, whom he met four times weekly. He did not permit direct quotation, except after specific authorization, but the press emerged fairly well briefed from the free give-and-take of discussion. Some experience with this approach encouraged him to distribute mimeographed summaries of these sessions to Foreign Service officers in the field. He tried, on occasion, to influence important organs of opinion, particularly the Hearst press, to support his policies and sometimes took to task any newspapers that opposed him.

III

At times Kellogg abdicated his policy-making function to men in the field. This was not inconsistent with his usual meticulous attention to the minutiae of operations, for in each instance he surrendered authority only after he himself had been deeply involved in the issue and even then he continued to keep a close watch over the proceedings.

One example of Kellogg's abdication of authority is provided by Henry L. Stimson's mission to Nicaragua. By the time that Kellogg took office in 1925, the American occupation of that republic, which had been in effect for over a decade, had been reduced to token form in a legation guard of United States Marines. This pressure had been sufficient to underwrite a series of unofficial fiscal relationships which had amply satisfied Nicaragua's creditors. The ill-advised removal of the guard in August, 1925, unleashed barely submerged forces of unrest.

Emiliano Chamorro, a member of the traditionally pro-American Conservative party, ousted the incumbent Chief Executive and emerged as President out of a confused and confusing welter of events. The techniques of his accession to power not only disturbed Nicaraguan domestic affairs, giving the Liberal party no cause for joy, but also did violence to a treaty of 1923 by which the Central American republics had bound themselves not to recognize presidents-by-revolution. The United States, though not a signatory, had indicated adherence to its principles. Chamorro's fiscal operations, moreover, endangered the republic's stability and raised the possibility of complications under the Roosevelt Corollary of the Monroe Doctrine. Finally, though not often mentioned, there was the underlying danger of political upheaval in a potential canal site.

The United States refused, in January, 1926, to recognize Chamorro, though Kellogg was apparently willing to have him continue in power if he could do so without the imprimatur, and his administration prospered briefly. Embarrassments developed quickly, however, despite the favorable treatment accorded Chamorro by Americans involved in the operation of the Nicaraguan fiscal machinery. At home, American anti-imperialistic forces became vocal at this support of an alleged dictatorship. Liberal-fomented hostilities developed on the Nicaraguan east coast in May, and by mid-summer it was apparent that the revolution was being helped from Mexico, whose relations with the United States were anything but amicable. With his fiscal situation deteriorating, Chamorro beat an orderly retreat, offering to resign in September and asking American cooperation in choosing his successor.

Adolfo Díaz, a Conservative more acceptable to the United States, though hardly more eligible than Chamorro, was chosen President in November and promptly recognized in Washington as the legitimate head of the republic. Continuing east-coast hostilities were enlivened by the appearance on Nicaraguan soil, in December, 1926, of Juan Sacasa, the Vice President whom the Chamorro regime had also superseded. He proceeded to proclaim himself constitutional President of the republic and continued hostilities, with Mexican assistance, under the banner of José Maria Moncada, a former pedagogue who came more and more to supplant Sacasa as representative of the Liberal opposition to Díaz.

Events moved rapidly in early 1927. American business interests were pressing for "active" measures. Coolidge refused to heed Borah's loud demands for support of Sacasa but publicly pointed out that Mexican connivance at Nicaraguan events cast a dark shadow over both American investments and the canal site. Borah's Senate committee interrogated Kellogg vigorously, and the Secretary gave it for publication a statement on Bolshevik Aims and Policies in Latin America, which, it was charged, was a red herring designed to implicate the Kremlin, via Mexico, in Nicaraguan affairs. A hostile Latin-American press piled up sarcasm, while hostilities, spreading to the west coast in February, seemed to render the renewal of formal intervention the only immediate answer. This occurred before the end of the month.

It was only a partial intervention, however, since it was limited to the west. Moncada's forces, meantime, were fighting merrily westward through well-nigh impassable mountains, creating an imminent threat to the American-supported Díaz regime. By mid-March the Department was faced with the necessity of taking decisive action. A memorandum favored complete and outright intervention on behalf of Díaz. It was in these circumstances that Kellogg—after conferring with Olds and former Senator Walter E. Edge of New Jersey, who had just returned from Central America—made his decision to send Stimson to Nicaragua in an attempt to avoid the full-scale intervention recommended in the memorandum. Before Stimson left, Coolidge instructed him point-blank: "If you find a chance to straighten the matter out, I want you to do so." Thus the initiative on Nicaraguan policy matters was formally shifted from the Department to the field.

Stimson took full advantage of his carte blanche. In the face of Departmental instructions to try to avoid responsibility for managing the Nicaraguan presidential election of 1928, he concluded that supervision was essential. He posited his early negotiations with the Conservative Díaz government upon this premise and made similar implications in his first approach to the Liberal leaders, undertaken before he had Washington's permission to negotiate on the basis of supervision. He made full use of Departmental permission to intimate to the Liberals that "forcible disarmament" might be the alternative to negotiation. At the well-known Tipitapa Conferences with Moncada, on May 4, 5, and 11, Stimson, having recently received Departmental assurances that he had "the widest discretion in handling the entire situation," successfully demanded that Moncada and his troops submit to the abandonment of their titular leader and accept retention of Díaz in the Presidency, pending the election of 1928. A more thorough delegation of authority, in a situation fraught with dangerous possibilities of aggravating the severe Latin-American tensions already in existence, could hardly be envisioned.

Another episode, with a similarly complicated background and an equally complete surrender of the conduct of operations, occurred in Mexico. The Mexican Revolution was almost a decade and a half old when Kellogg entered office. Having passed through its initial phase of blood, it had begun to concentrate on social and economic adventure under the Constitution of 1917, a principal objective of which was to re-establish Mexican mastery over the land and natural resources which had been largely alienated to foreigners under the regime of Porfirio Díaz. This adventure drew the frowns of Americans who had invested in the resources, particularly land and oil, which Mexico was seeking to reclaim.

Kellogg's attitude reflected initially the point of view of Ambassador James R. Sheffield, whose concern for American vested interests equaled his obtuseness about Mexican realities. Kellogg's pronouncement of June 12, 1925, drafted after consultation with Sheffield, contained the widely publicized and irritating charge that the Mexican government was "now on trial before the world"—a statement hardly calculated to evoke enthusiasm on the part of Plutarco Elias Calles, a tough-minded revolutionary whom the exigencies of domestic politics had elevated to the Presidency.

His riposte to the Kellogg pronouncement was to launch Mexico, in the autumn of 1925, on a legislative program implementing the Constitution's provisions for restoring Mexican control of subsoil minerals and of land useful for the re-establishment of the village communities which had disappeared in the face of foreign onslaughts on the land supply. By the time the laws had passed, Kellogg was beginning to shy away from the extremes of Sheffield's position, and the bewildering exchange of notes which characterized 1926 was largely devoted to reiterating opposed positions. The notes persuaded no one and ended in a stalemate, but the lengthy discussion preserved the peace in the face of determined pressure by the American oil companies for a more vigorous policy. Anti-Mexican pressure erupted again toward the end of 1926, when Mexican interference with Nicaraguan affairs stirred Departmental interest in alleged Communist infiltration into Mexico and Central America.

Early 1927 witnessed both a near crisis and the beginning of its resolution. The administration, continuingly sensitive to the alleged Communist threat, was also subjected to vitriolic press criticism and the lobbying of oil companies. On the other hand, it was becoming increasingly apparent that influential members of Congress opposed drastic action. Mexico, moreover, was beginning to feel a pinch caused by declining revenue from oil, a situation which could only continue and grow worse until political relations were stabilized. By March 21, Calles instructed his Minister in Washington to ask Coolidge to send a "personal representative" to Mexico for a *sub rosa* interview which would enable him to assure the United States of his "absolute sincerity and friendliness in all of his dealings with the American Government." Though this plan to short-circuit Sheffield did not materialize, the ambassador failed to receive adequate support for a stronger Mexican policy. Coolidge, furthermore, made a placatory statement, on April 25, to the effect that "we do not want any controversy with Mexico. We feel every sympathy with her people in their distress and have every desire to assist them."

This peaceable composition of several potentially explosive incidents indicated that by mid-1927 both sides were moving from belligerency toward caution. The aftermath of Kellogg's enforced holiday in February and March found Olds playing a larger role in Mexican matters, and this paired well with Coolidge's statement. It is probably fair to conclude that the decision to adopt a more conciliatory policy toward Mexico had been hammered out of the months of acrimonious discussion which preceded Dwight W. Morrow's assumption of control in the autumn of 1927.

His appointment to Mexico in July, 1927, afforded Morrow a bridge from thirteen years of private employment with J. P. Morgan & Company back to the public service to which his restless energies had so often been devoted. The magnetism of his personality seems to have captivated the dour Calles and to have made it possible for both countries to recede from positions in which each was feeling increasingly uncomfortable.

Morrow's frame of reference was a broad one. At an interview at the Summer White House in the Black Hills, Coolidge told Morrow: "My only instructions are to keep us out of war with Mexico." An Olds memorandum of October 10 suggested that he "work out a *modus vivendi* enabling oil production to go on and the Government to get the revenue which it needs, pending a final settlement of the controversy either by a decision of the Mexican Supreme Court or otherwise." It dealt also with claims, the agrarian question, and an arms embargo which had been troublesome, but Morrow gave relatively little attention to these matters, concentrating on the oil problem. Here, relying upon his privately retained expert, J. Reuben Clark, and upon friendly personal relations with Calles, he operated mainly through personal and oral negotiations and without further instructions from Washington.

In a meeting on November 8, 1927, Calles asked Morrow bluntly how he thought the oil controversy could be settled. Morrow replied promptly that he had been expecting a favorable Mexican judicial decision in pending cases similar to the 1921 ruling in which the courts had sustained the contentions of the Texas Company against governmental efforts to curtail its activities. Such a decision, he pointed out, would open the door for a satisfactory settlement. After some further discussion, Calles promised that it would be forthcoming within two months; the courts, ever sensitive to executive pressure, were more obliging, for the decision was rendered in less than two weeks. Though considerable further negotiation was necessary, Morrow later said that in his judgment this action "substantially settled the oil controversy."

That the settlement eventually arrived at was only temporarily successful and that other and ancillary questions continued to exercise Morrow's ingenuity do not negate his diplomatic achievement. Both Olds and Kellogg congratulated Morrow upon his management of affairs. Morrow's letters had been sequestered in Olds's personal files, to be read only by Kellogg, his personal assistant, Spencer Phenix, and by Olds himself. The evidence is overwhelming that the development of policy had been transferred from Washington to Mexico City.

The principal accomplishment of Morrow's tour of duty, the temporary reconciliation of the bitter Mexican church-state controversy, dealt with a problem of such a delicately domestic nature that it foreclosed entirely any resort to ordinary diplomatic channels. Morrow was completely on his own, although he used official channels of communication and received unobtrusive Departmental assistance. He acted upon his own conviction that the future stability of Mexican affairs, both foreign and domestic, depended upon a genuine solution of the problem.

Matters were in a bad state when Morrow arrived. A series of national measures had, in 1926, resulted in the nationalization of church property, the closing of church schools, and the curtailment of the teaching functions of the religious orders. The Mexican hierarchy, with papal sanction, had closed the churches, on July 31, in a protest against a final demand that all priests register with the political authorities. A subsequent series of unpleasant incidents had inflamed Mexican feelings, which were at a high pitch when Morrow arrived in the autumn of 1927.

Within a few weeks, Morrow had obtained Kellogg's permission to try his hand at a settlement, the Secretary writing on December 17 that success in this quarter "would have a tremendous moral effect in this country and render our task very much easier." This was, apparently, Kellogg's sole formal contribution to the matter, for he wrote in August, 1928, "I have never had any written communications with Mr. Morrow on the subject." Morrow's technique was to bring American representatives of the church to Mexico for secret meetings with Calles in April and again in May, 1928. These conferences resulted in a great improvement in relations and in the elaboration of a tentative basis for settlement. For reasons not ascertainable from presently available documents, Rome failed to accept the proposals, and though Morrow kept active in the affair, he made no further headway during Kellogg's incumbency. The whole episode, when carried to its temporarily successful conclusion after Kellogg's departure, illustrates aptly the Secretary's permissive policy which, in allowing a trusted agent a free hand, transferred out of the Department responsibility for a potentially explosive operation.

Taken together, the Nicaraguan and Mexican episodes comprised a virtual surrender of Departmental management of policy operations, not only in relation to particular nations, but in regard to the position of the United States vis-à-vis Latin America. This surrender was preceded in each instance by close personal interest on Kellogg's part and was accompanied by his continuing interest and decreasing involvement. The fact that, in both cases, American interests were well served by the surrender illustrates again the superiority of private and personal negotiations in the settlement of complex diplomatic questions.

IV

Kellogg often leaned heavily upon outsiders for counsel. He frequently conferred by telephone or letter with Charles Evans Hughes, his predecessor as Secretary of State; Elihu Root, another former Secretary; and Henry L. Stimson, his successor in the State Department. Underlings in the Department often acted as messengers between the Secretary and the first two men, carrying papers for their examination or picking up their observations on problems which Kellogg had submitted to them. Kellogg repeatedly expressed his personal gratitude to them for services rendered.

Hughes was most frequently consulted. This was perhaps to be expected, since he had bequeathed to Kellogg an organization whose collective admiration and respect for its departing head were bound to rub off on his successor, whose *esprit de corps* was at a high level, and whose many tangled problems had been brought into focus by Hughes's able mind. One of the early issues that brought the two men into close contact involved the long-standing controversy over the boundary between Tacna and Arica, a line through desolate country left undetermined since Chile's defeat of Peru and Bolivia in the War of the Pacific, waged between 1879 and 1884. President Coolidge, as arbitrator, issued an Award proposing that the dispute be settled by a plebiscite. It became Kellogg's unhappy task to implement this well-nigh unenforceable decision in a framework established by his predecessor's actions. The resulting complications brought him to a higher degree of uncertainty and a closer dependence upon others for advice than did any other episode during his tenure of office. Although he ultimately failed to reach a solution, he contributed largely to the answer which emerged shortly after he left office.

As early as September, 1925, a Kellogg messenger carried the Tacna-Arica correspondence to Hughes with a request for his advice on the extent of the powers of the plebiscitary commission then in process of trying to carry out the Coolidge Award. Adopting Hughes's interpretations as his own, Kellogg promptly passed them along in the form of instructions to General John J. Pershing, chairman of the commission. As matters deepened into crisis, Kellogg issued an important policy statement, on October 31, which was based in outline, and sometimes in exact phraseology, on Hughes's letter of two days earlier. Again in December he sought Hughes's advice, by which time Kellogg was reportedly "hot with Mr. Hughes for ever getting mixed up in the matter at all."

Except for its potentially explosive elements, the situation developing in early 1926 was reminiscent of comic opera. Through it all Kellogg relied continually upon Hughes, who was kept "cognizant of every message" passing between Washington and those in the field. In April, Hughes was called into personal conference, along with Stimson, who had been engaged as a paid consultant. In these talks Stimson found Kellogg ill, confused about the issues, and critical of Hughes as the instigator of his troubles. He described Hughes as making the necessary decisions, veiled politely as "advice," which Kellogg gratefully accepted. At the end of a year of frantic activity, Kellogg confessed sorrowfully to his wife that this was "the first big job I have ever undertaken and made a failure of." His later moves, which emerged from renewed diplomatic relations between Peru and Chile, seem to have been taken without dependence upon Hughes's advice.

The Sixth International Conference of American States, held at Havana early in 1928, afforded Kellogg another occasion to lean upon Hughes, who served as head and dominant member of the American delegation. The meeting afforded a sounding board for Latin-American restiveness against the alleged imperialism of the United States, with questions of intervention furnishing ground for an overt attack, which Hughes parried dramatically, if ineffectively, in one of the last such stands by an American spokesman.

The Havana Conference adopted a resolution calling for an inter-American study of arbitration and conciliation questions, the management of which would be in the hands of the United States. Within a minimum interval after the conference adjourned, Kellogg was at Hughes's doorstep seeking advice on the timetable for the proposed study sessions and urging that Hughes serve as his fellow delegate at the meetings. Accepting, Hughes promptly issued advice, based on earlier experience, regarding the preliminary-stage management of the sessions and dictated to the President and the Secretary of State, as a condition to his serving on the delegation, a significant alteration in the United States position on important substantive proposals. After the meetings, Kellogg wrote to Hughes: "I do not know what I could have done without your help."

Kellogg consulted Elihu Root less frequently, but still to a substantial extent. He asked Root, during one of the warmer periods of the Tacna-Arica episode, for an opinion about the possibility of a plebiscite in the area, with Root returning a negative opinion. In December, 1927, Kellogg wrote him at length concerning a proposed arbitration treaty with France designed to perpetuate an expiring agreement of 1908 which Root himself had negotiated as Secretary of State. He carefully, almost apologetically, indicated certain tentative changes in the new draft. He turned then, and more emphatically, to a discussion of the current Franco-American negotiations which were to eventuate in the Kellogg-Briand Pact and which had then reached the stage where the original proposal of a Franco-American agreement was evolving into the idea of a multilateral engagement. Eager for Root's judgment on both matters, but loath to intrude upon his ill-health, he was hopeful that Olds, who would be in New York over the following weekend, might have an opportunity to wait upon Root for his opinion.

Root was also drawn into the maneuvers attendant upon repeated American failures to adhere to the Statute of the World Court. Root had evidently urged Kellogg not to put an irrevocable quietus on membership. This gave Kellogg an opportunity to write him in November, 1928, indicating that Root's advice had governed his own earlier action, insisting that the door to negotiation still remained open, and hoping that Root's health was equal to devoting some time to considering Court problems. This request was made shortly before a French delegate to the League of Nations moved establishment of a committee to revise the Court Statute, a task in which Root was to participate as one of his last public services.

Kellogg did not call upon Stimson for assistance as often as he did Hughes and Root, but Stimson's proconsular activities in Nicaragua were of considerable significance. Kellogg had originally planned to send him to "study and report" upon the convolutions of the Tacna-Arica problem, but he was dissuaded by advice that such action would jeopardize the position of American agents already in the field. He compromised by hiring Stimson as a paid consultant to study the documentary evidence and to render an opinion on the practicability of holding a viable plebiscite in the two provinces.

V

The multilateral Kellogg-Briand Pact for the renunciation of war as an instrument of national policy was signed at Paris on August 27, 1928. Kellogg's involvement in it, though reluctant in the early stages, was marked toward the end by an almost fanatical determination. This effort brought him the Nobel Prize and the greatest satisfaction of his Secretaryship, but its built-in limitations ensured its ineffectiveness in the face of the first determined challenge. This was administered by Japan within Kellogg's lifetime.

The pact stemmed originally from Aristide Briand's proposal of April 4, 1927, that France and the United States sign a bilateral agreement outlawing war. Kellogg, beset with numerous other problems, suspected this move as a nefarious scheme to involve his country in a political alliance and hence shied away. Presently, however, the normally isolationist Borah suggested in May, 1927, that the proposal be broadened to include other nations. Borah's modification was not likely to attract France, since it would destroy the preferred position which a bilateral agreement would ensure that nation. The first Departmental move of June 11 was an obviously dilatory tactic, offering to move the matter into the diplomatic channel of "informal" conversations, whose logical termination would be a treaty—a more formal document than Briand had in mind and one, moreover, which would at best involve time-consuming discussions. Briand picked up the hint promptly and presented the draft of a bilateral agreement, but Kellogg was as yet in no mood for action.

Various pressures, the exact contributions of which cannot be measured accurately but among which that of Borah was probably not the least important, came to bear on the Secretary during the summer and autumn of 1927. Kellogg decided, late in December, on a multilateral treaty for the renunciation of war. Notes of December 28 went to five nations in addition to France; they recommended generalizing Briand's Franco-American proposal to all the world. Thus Kellogg sought adroitly to gain the initiative by suggesting an arrangement which, by its promise to make peace universal, vitiated a nexus of French treaties designed to deal with war and, likewise, avoided the dangers of American involvement in that treaty complex.

Having tardily espoused multilateralism, Kellogg became exceedingly vigorous in its defense. There ensued several months of maneuvering during which he gradually gained the tactical advantage by acceding in roundabout fashion to certain French reservations concerning the right of self-defense, recognition of the validity of existing treaty engagements, and release from obligations to treaty violators. These capitulations were carefully obscured, partly by reference to a public statement made by Kellogg on April 28, 1928, partly by including the Locarno powers among the original signatories, and partly by the verbiage of the treaty's preamble. Thus Kellogg was able to maintain intact the strong language whereby the contracting parties agreed to renounce war as an instrument of national policy. The limitations which in practice would demonstrate the Pact's inherent futility were less obviously displayed.

Both the American and the French governments attained limited objectives: Briand tied the United States into the peace machinery, albeit on a less exclusive pattern than he had projected, and Kellogg gained a day of glory by developing an agreement whose benefits were more apparent than real. The whole episode is a rather remarkable illustration of the evolution of an idea into something entirely different from the original concept and of a process whereby a reluctant dragon was turned into an ardent champion. The change in Kellogg, his obvious conversion to the idea of outlawry, disturbed Castle, for he had never regarded the Secretary's involvement as any more than an effort to satisfy the American enthusiasts for the Briand proposal. In February, 1928, Castle wrote hopefully in his diary that "we have done what we set out to do. We have made a big, peaceful gesture and we have public opinion fairly solidly behind us." But as the Secretary revealed ever-greater enthusiasm for the vision of a peaceful world built on a multilateral pact, the no-longer-amused Castle confided to his diary again: "For weeks the press has chorused approval of F.B.K.'s exchange of notes with Briand on outlawing war ... actually it is futile. It appealed enormously to the Pacifists and the Earnest Christians but ... I think it is about time for the correspondence to stop. The political trick has been turned and now we should take a well deserved rest. *The funny thing is that Olds and the Secretary seem to take it all with profound seriousness....*" The pact itself aptly exemplified an agreement whose shortcomings, though less obviously manifested than its potentialities, were fully recognized and carefully shepherded by both parties to its promulgation.

Amid the ubiquitous expressions of gratitude for Kellogg's apparent moral conquest of war, more realistic writers and observers wondered whether the Secretary's treaty was merely meaningless or genuinely injurious to the cause of peace. Somehow it did not face the fundamental questions of world politics—the conflicting interests of nations that remained unresolved. It created a magnificent vision, but nothing more. One young American Naval officer wrote: "There is no evidence, even in religion, to prove that the world can outlaw war any more than it can outlaw the weather. Either scheme is so absurdly impractical that none but fanatics advocate such futility." Another officer, Rear Admiral William V. Pratt, Naval adviser to the Washington Conference, observed that the belief that war could be abolished with a statement was "to belie the facts of recorded history and to underestimate the human element." Some critics, in search of something more concrete, termed the Pact of Paris little but a partisan effort to direct the nation's peace sentiment away from the League of Nations. John Bates Clark, the noted economist, warned that the pact would paralyze the existing military arrangements which alone could prevent war. Henry Cabot Lodge, Jr., regarded the pact as absurd. "It seems to me," he wrote in *Harper's* of December, 1928, "that this attempt to get something for nothing ... entrenches war more solidly than ever. War fears truth and realism; only understanding and mutual sacrifice can end it. Is it not apparent that the Kellogg treaty, with its many textual dangers, only thickens the haze, deepens the pitfalls, and once again postpones the day when some really clear thinking is done?"

As the Senate debates wore on into 1929, Carter Glass of Virginia admitted that he would vote for the treaty but hoped, he said, that no one in Virginia would think that he regarded it as worth a postage stamp. Hiram Johnson of California declared that he also would vote for the pact but that "he did not want to be considered as under the delusion that it would cure war." Apparently other opponents of the treaty followed the same reasoning, for the final vote in the Senate was 85 to 1. It was left for Senator Johnson to close the debates with eight lines from François Villon:

> To Messur Noel, named the neat
> By those who love him, I bequeath
> A helmless ship, a houseless street
> A wordless book, a swordless sheath
> An hourless clock, a leafless wreath
> A bell sans tongue, a saw sans teeth,
> A bed sans sheet, a board sans meat,
> To make his nothingness complete.

For Kellogg, the years of his Secretaryship were years of extreme busyness. They were years of mixed frustration and achievement, with some problems remaining far from solution and others seemingly terminated.

For the country, they were years in which domestic matters were the primary concern and foreign affairs generally took a back seat. Whatever advances resulted from Kellogg's leadership could be chronicled quite modestly: the Peace Pact, some amelioration of inter-American tensions, and some slight improvement in China's international position. These advances were accomplished with Presidential cooperation but without strong Presidential leadership, through Secretarial industry and the able counsel and assistance of advisers and agents both inside and outside the Department. They were accomplished, moreover, without essential disturbance of the *status quo*—a highly important factor in the twenties.

9
Henry L. Stimson

1929-1933

BY RICHARD N. CURRENT
University of Wisconsin

Henry L. Stimson was well past sixty when he took office as Herbert Hoover's Secretary of State. He did not look his years. His black hair and mustache showed only traces of gray, and his outdoor habits kept his body trim, his shoulders square. The impression he gave of vigorous health was a bit misleading, for he had his troubles with high blood pressure, lumbago, biliousness, indigestion, and other infirmities of age. He could not put up with more than two or three hours a day at a desk, nor could he endure even that stint for many days at a time. He had to have frequent exercise and relaxation, preferably in the open air.

Except with intimates, he was reserved and cold; yet he could be hot-tempered at times, especially in dealing with his inferiors. He liked punctilio and protocol. A man of decided opinions, he held to those opinions with the "greatest imaginable tenacity," as it seemed to his admiring successor in the State Department, Cordell Hull. His determination was evident in his firm lips and hard-set jaw. Once he had made up his mind, he seldom, if ever, doubted the rightness of his course.

He had a sense of mission, which may have come in part from his ancestral background. One Stimson after another had achieved some degree of eminence, at least within the confines of the State of New York, and Henry L. Stimson, happily married but childless, was the last of his line. He seemed always conscious of a duty, and perhaps a destiny, to live up to the family name. He was a rich man. On his Long Island estate he lived somewhat after the manner of an English squire who, because of his advantages of birth and breeding, recognizes an obligation of generosity

168

and service toward less favored humanity. As an artillery officer in World
War I, he had seen three weeks of actual fighting—three weeks that he
remembered as "wonderfully happy." Always afterward he thought of
himself as a soldier, "on active service," even when in civilian office. He
kept his hair close-cropped, in military style, and he prided himself on
what he called his "combat psychology." His sense of soldierly duty reflected his philosophy of *noblesse oblige.*

A graduate of Phillips Academy at Andover, Yale College, and the
Harvard Law School, Stimson had to his credit a very good academic
record. He was a highly successful lawyer, a member of the New York
firm of Winthrop, Stimson, Putnam & Roberts, which originally had been
headed by Elihu Root. From Root he had learned more of law and government than from any of his professors. From Root's friend Theodore Roosevelt, once his own Long Island neighbor and intimate, he had acquired
some of his deepest political convictions. By 1929, he had already had
considerable experience in public affairs, having served in various capacities under three presidents. Under Roosevelt he had been a Federal district
attorney; under Taft, Secretary of War; and under Coolidge, a legal adviser on Latin-American problems, a special trouble shooter in Nicaragua,
and governor general of the Philippines.

Thus, on the whole, he had a reasonably good preparation for his Secretarial post, whether or not he had the personality and the stamina for the
job. The office was to bring perplexities, however, that no man could have
foreseen in the halcyon days of early 1929. "Of all the assignments to which
he was called in his years of public service," the Stimson memoirs long
afterward confessed, "the appointment to the State Department was the
one for the difficulties of which Stimson was the least prepared."

These difficulties were compounded by the Great Depression, which
fell like a withering blight upon the nation and the world before Stimson
had been a year in office. The tasks of American diplomacy remained more
or less routine for yet another year. In Latin America and the Far East
all was comparatively, though not completely, quiet; and in Europe no
problem seemed desperately urgent, since a reassuring equilibrium of
power appeared to prevail. Then, in 1931, came financial collapse in Europe
and a Japanese military adventure in the Far East. Soon the world balance,
and with it the prospects for general peace, began visibly to crumble. It
was Stimson's lot to head the State Department at a time when, as seen in
retrospect, a "postwar" period ended and a "prewar" period began.

II

Stimson was not President Hoover's first choice for the position.
Hoover would have preferred to keep Coolidge's Secretary of State, Frank

B. Kellogg. When Kellogg declined, Hoover made overtures to three other men in succession. Finally he turned to Stimson in response to strong and repeated urging from several prominent Republicans, among them Elihu Root. It was not that the new President had anything against Stimson but simply that he was not well acquainted with him. In fact, the two had the highest respect for each other, and as they began to work together, they got along quite well at first and agreed upon most issues of foreign policy.

Yet, in spirit and personality, they were decidedly different, and eventually their differences began to tell. Hoover was a man of simple tastes and modest manners, a man who often questioned and doubted himself, a man who believed in and practiced a gospel of hard and unremitting work. His and Stimson's habits of thought, as well as their habits of work, were basically incompatible. As Stimson recorded in his diary (late in 1930), he once discussed "the President's peculiarities" with Root, at the latter's home near Clinton, New York. "I told him [Root] frankly that I thought the President being a Quaker and an engineer did not understand the psychology of combat the way Mr. Root and I did." On another occasion (early in 1932), when Stimson wished to "bluff" Japan by threatening naval action, he noted the "great difference and difficulty" he was having with Hoover. "He has not got the slightest element of even the fairest kind of bluff."

For the first two years, Stimson maintained fairly harmonious relations not only with the President but also with his own advisers, or at least with the most important of them. He brought from the Philippines his personal military aide, Eugene Regnier, who, in the uniform of an Army captain, attended him at home, at the office, and on horseback rides through Rock Creek Park. (The Secretary did not think it funny when Washingtonians referred to Regnier as the "Grand Vizier.") For the post of Under Secretary, Stimson chose Joseph P. Cotton, a brilliant lawyer and an old friend. Cotton seemed a rather undiplomatic diplomat to some State Department visitors, who resented his wisecracks. But to Stimson he was a "godsend"—kindly as well as witty and, besides, wholly loyal and completely frank. He became Stimson's "alter ego." "In many of his qualities," the Stimson memoirs later said, "he was a most valuable complement to Stimson, who knew that he sometimes seemed stern and aloof to his subordinates."

Stern and aloof he did indeed appear at times. Often he ignored the permanent officers of the Department, who found it hard to get a hearing for their views. He could be disagreeable to men he looked upon as underlings. Occasionally, in a fit of anger, he threw books and papers at his secretary. "There is no blinking the fact," another subordinate was moved to say, "that Stimson is an unlovable character, a very hard man to work under."

His ways must have led to a certain loss of efficiency in the functioning of the State Department, fond though he was of the words "team" and "team-work."

Teamwork suffered a blow in 1931, at the very time when the world situation was about to worsen and when divided counsels were to be all the more dangerous for the United States. In that year Under Secretary Cotton died. To replace him, Hoover suggested the promotion of Assistant Secretary William R. Castle, the scion of a pioneer American family in Hawaii, who had given up a promising position at Harvard to become a career diplomat. Stimson accepted Castle willingly enough but afterwards regretted having done so. "The two men were not fitted to make a team," as the Stimson memoirs put it. After this experience, Stimson resolved that "he would freely recognize the right of the President to veto any proposed appointments to major positions, but he would vigorously oppose any attempt to select his subordinates for him."

During the critical years from 1931 to 1933, the rift in the State Department grew. More and more, Stimson depended for advice upon the men of his own choice, especially Assistant Secretaries James Grafton Rogers, a former dean of the University of Colorado Law School, and Harvey H. Bundy, an attorney from Boston. Stimson was influenced also by the permanent chief of the Division of Far Eastern Affairs, Dr. Stanley K. Hornbeck. Occasionally the Secretary and his advisers listened to the counsel of experts from outside, such as Professor George Hubbard Blakeslee, of Clark University. Occasionally, too, Stimson gave heed to the views of the new Under Secretary, Castle. But, as time passed, he and Castle found themselves again and again in fundamental disagreement. Stimson might not have had to concern himself a great deal about this, except for the fact that, on the points in dispute, the opinions of Castle were usually the same as those of the President.

Castle was a personal friend of Hoover's. He had direct access to the White House, lunched with Hoover from time to time, and visited him at his summer camp on the Rapidan. When Stimson left the country to go to Geneva early in 1932, Castle, as Acting Secretary, considered himself Hoover's representative, not Stimson's. Stimson resented this. Before Cotton's death, the Secretary had been able to go abroad "with complete certainty that a first-rate man was boldly and responsibly doing what he believed Stimson would want done," as Stimson said in his memoirs. "After Cotton's death, when he was again abroad on major missions, Stimson was never able to feel this sort of confidence in the Acting Secretary."

As Stimson lost confidence in Castle, Hoover came to have more confidence in Castle than in Stimson. Though an "able Secretary," Stimson was at times "more of a warrior than a diplomat," Hoover afterward reflected, dryly. In the summer of 1932 the President told Castle, as Castle recorded in his diary, that "he was always afraid Stimson would get us into real trouble through his earnest and entirely laudable desire to support the various peace treaties." After his defeat for re-election, Hoover spoke with Castle about Castle's writing a book on the foreign policy of the administration. He said Stimson would feel that *he* ought to write it. "But," observed Castle, "the President does not want Stimson to make himself the center of the book because, as he said, 'he would have had us in a war with Japan before this if he had had his way.' "

Politics added to the estrangement of the President and his Secretary. In the newspapers, the administration's policy of refusing to recognize Japan's conquest of Manchuria was called occasionally the "Hoover-Stimson doctrine" but more often the "Stimson doctrine." The President felt that he himself deserved credit for the idea, and he wished it to be known as the "Hoover doctrine." More than his self-esteem was at stake. Running a rather hopeless race for re-election, he needed all the help he could get, and he had reason to think that the nonrecognition policy was a popular *démarche*, a political asset. He hoped that Stimson would speak out, stress the President's role in policy making, and capitalize the doctrine for Hoover's benefit. At first Stimson declined to speak at all, on the grounds that it was improper for members of the State Department to make political speeches. At last, reluctantly, he took the stump, but not to campaign in the forthright way that Hoover had desired.

After the election and before the inauguration of Franklin D. Roosevelt, Stimson found himself in a delicate and indeed an anomalous position between the incoming and the outgoing Presidents. With Hoover's permission, he visited Roosevelt at Hyde Park (January 9, 1933). Several days later he met with him again, in a Washington hotel. "We are getting so that we do pretty good teamwork, don't we?" Roosevelt then remarked. Stimson laughed and said, "Yes." Indeed, he was getting along better with his new acquaintance than with his chief. At a press conference soon afterward, he said (though not for publication), "I am Roosevelt's acting Secretary of State." Later, in a kind of apology, he told Hoover that "the only thing that upset" him was the thought that Hoover "felt that he was being humiliated" by what Stimson "had done with regard to Roosevelt."

Another man in Stimson's circumstances might have resigned, but apparently the thought of resignation never occurred to Stimson. Another man in Hoover's place might have removed his Secretary, but Hoover gave no evidence that he ever considered such a step. Privately, he made it clear, however, that if he had been re-elected to the Presidency, there would have been a new man heading the State Department for the second term.

The strained relations which became so painful to both men toward the end should not obscure the fact that, for at least three of their four years in office, Hoover and Stimson worked together fairly well. During that earlier time it was generally true, as Stimson afterward said, that "both understood that Mr. Hoover's views would always be controlling, and neither allowed differences of opinion to do more than cause occasional very short-lived outbursts of temper."

Necessarily, the President gave much thought to domestic problems arising from the Depression; yet questions of foreign policy never were far from his mind. This was to be expected, for he had brought to his office a wide experience in world affairs—a wider experience than Stimson's, a wider one, indeed, than that of any other President since John Quincy Adams. He frequently raised questions of diplomacy for discussion in his Cabinet meetings. He listened to advice and urging, from Stimson and from others, and sometimes he was swayed. But he always kept the final decision, the ultimate responsibility, as his own.

III

Skill in the art of politics may or may not be an asset for a State Department head. In any case, Stimson was not a politician, not a vote getter, not a man of the kind that can appeal to crowds. Once, in 1910, he had run for governor of New York and had been soundly beaten. In all his life he held only one elective job, as a delegate to a state constitutional convention in 1915. Thus he brought with him to Washington little experience in dealing with Congress, the press, or the public.

Congress presented a challenge to him as Secretary of State. During the difficult years from 1931 to 1933, the opposition party, the Democrats, controlled the House of Representatives. True, the Republicans maintained a majority in the Senate, and so a Republican continued to head the Committee on Foreign Relations. But that Republican was William E. Borah, something of a party maverick and one of the three men who had declined to be considered for Secretary of State before Hoover finally appointed Stimson. With strong opinions of his own, Borah could have made trouble for Stimson and the State Department.

From the outset, Stimson carefully cultivated Borah's friendship and support. In 1931, when the isolationist Senator Hiram Johnson waxed sarcastic about Stimson, the latter took Borah aside to explain the State Department's views on the Manchurian situation. Again, in 1932, Stimson tactfully told the Senate leader that he had not consulted him in advance about a certain step because he did not wish to saddle him with the blame for it. On more than one occasion, by prearrangement with Borah, he issued policy announcements in the form of public letters to him. Such attention to personal susceptibilities was rewarded. In the main, Stimson succeeded in gaining and holding the cooperation of the Foreign Relations Committee, and thereby the support of the Senate as a whole.

Stimson did not do quite so well in dealing with the press. True, soon after taking office, he was given a good send-off by Anne O'Hare McCormick, who interviewed him for the *New York Times*. She described him as an able man who was alive to the delicate requirements of diplomacy. He told her that a diplomat was like a man carrying a long ladder on a crowded street: if he swung one end aside to avoid hitting someone in front of him, he was almost sure to bang someone behind him with the other end. Before long he himself was being criticized for the way he carried the ladder.

Stimson was acutely sensitive to criticism. In 1930, while he was at the London Naval Conference, a news leak revealed him in a position quite opposed to that of President Hoover, and he resented the publicity. He was indignant when Walter Lippmann wrote a column disagreeing with him and again when the *New York Herald Tribune* printed an anonymous letter and an editorial contending that his use of the Kellogg Pact against Japan was both ineffective and dangerous. The *Herald Tribune*, he complained to his diary, had "chosen just the time when everybody else was so satisfied with my policy" to make an unjustified attack upon it.

The more suspicious and resentful he became, the more the newspapermen tried to bait him. In the beginning he felt that he gave as good as he got at his press conferences. At one of them he had a "rosy time," as he put it, in struggling to justify his support of a Brazilian regime that suddenly had been overturned. "As I felt very confident of our position, however, and that it had been right and taken in accordance with grounds which were justifiable whatever the result, I stood my ground under a pretty heavy cross-examination and finally got the Press fairly well to understand the situation and around to my side." Eventually he tired of exposing himself to the free-for-all of the regular press conference. So he discontinued it and, except for routine handouts, dispensed the news privately at luncheons in his Washington mansion, Woodley.

Here he talked with editors and publishers as well as with selected reporters; he aimed to influence journalism at the top level. When, for example, the Scripps-Howard newspapers were, in his words, "pounding the government for not being more aggressive toward Japan," he invited Roy Howard and his chief editorial writer to lunch and tried to make them "see the folly of taking an aggressive step" too soon. Whatever luck Stimson may have had with arranged interviews of this kind, he did not succeed in stopping the flow of State Department news to unauthorized reporters and columnists. He was unflatteringly described as "Wrong-

Horse Harry" in the gossipy book *Washington Merry-go-round* (1931), written by reporters Drew Pearson and Robert S. Allen. Pearson, a rather shrewish critic of the Secretary, continued to get confidential information from some source inside the State Department.

From time to time Stimson undertook to play upon public opinion by other means than direct appeals to journalists. For weeks he kept quiet about the interchanges between the United States and Japan on the Manchurian question, so as to prevent undue excitement, and then, early in 1932, he decided to publish the correspondence in order to wake the people up. His famous letter to Borah on Japanese violations of the Open Door policy (February 23, 1932) was intended partly to "get public sentiment behind us in this country," as Castle noted. To find a forum for stating his case, Stimson telephoned Walter Lippmann to ask whether the Council on Foreign Relations, in New York, would like to hear a speech from him. The speech, of course, was arranged, and it was afterward published as a special supplement to the magazine *Foreign Affairs*.

In this address, as well as in other statements, Stimson emphasized the unique importance of public opinion in the affairs of the contemporary world. Yet he never undertook to define public opinion as a general concept or to measure it in a specific case. He depended upon rather random indications of popular feeling. At one of his dinner parties, for instance, he found it "very interesting" when James Grafton Rogers, just back from a trip to the Pacific Coast, gave his impressions of what people in that part of the country were thinking.

Though concerned about public support, Stimson did not view diplomacy as an expression of the popular will. Rather, he thought of himself and his work as being above the clashes of interest that occurred in politics. He did not, and probably could not, dramatize either himself or his office. Though a "doctrine" was named for him, he was not widely known as a person—not nearly so familiar to the American people as some of his successors in the State Department were to be. His comparative remoteness from the public was quite all right with him and quite in keeping with his conception of his job.

IV

In considering policy formation, it is not always easy to distinguish between the contributions of a President and those of his Secretary of State. Stimson brought to the State Department certain ideas that were in accord with Hoover's, but he changed some of these in the course of his four years in office. He brought other ideas that differed from, but were modified to fit, those of his chief. And Hoover, in cases where his thought diverged from Stimson's, was persuaded occasionally to change his own position. At other times, however, he stood firm and, failing to convert Stimson, only frustrated him.

So far as general principles went, both men at the outset held the view that "moral" force should be relied upon to achieve the ends of diplomacy in a balanced world, though Stimson held this belief with somewhat less conviction than Hoover did. Both were enthusiastic about the Kellogg Pact renouncing war, but Stimson was more eager than Hoover to put "teeth" into the pact, to give it sanctions more concrete than the mere conscience of mankind. Both, at first, resisted "involvement" with the League of Nations, then changed their minds to approve the official representation of the United States at a sitting of the League Council. Soon Stimson began to feel that the United States was not going far enough, and Hoover that it perhaps had already gone too far, in cooperating with the League. Though both had favored disarmament in principle, Stimson held back while Hoover went ahead with his drastic arms-cut proposal of 1932. An imperialist by conviction, Stimson wished to keep the Philippines forever, but Hoover believed that freedom for the islands should be the ultimate goal, though at Stimson's urging he vetoed a Philippine-independence bill. Before the end of his term, Stimson concluded that international law had been revolutionized (by the Kellogg Pact), that the concept of neutrality was obsolete, and that in future wars assistance to the victims of "aggression" was a duty as well as a right. Hoover clung to more traditional notions of neutrality for the United States.

Regarding Latin America, the views of Stimson and Hoover coincided, and the two men cooperated in a policy of good neighborliness. The initiative must have come mainly from the President, who, well before his inauguration, had dedicated himself to a program of winning friends within the hemisphere. The Secretary, by contrast, had previously supported and participated in diplomacy that, however well intentioned, had the effect of alienating Latin Americans. He was once an advocate of the Roosevelt Corollary, which justified the intervention of the United States, by force if need be, to forestall intervention on the part of European powers. As Coolidge's peacemaker in Nicaragua, in 1927, he had used the blunt threat of force to bring about a truce between the warring factions. He had favored the recognition of none but constitutionally legitimate regimes. As Hoover's Secretary, however, Stimson reversed himself. He issued the Clark Memorandum, which officially severed the Roosevelt Corollary from the Monroe Doctrine. Helping to liquidate the interventionist policy, he succeeded finally in withdrawing the marines from Nicaragua. Also, he announced a return to the old principle of recognizing *de facto* governments (except where treaty obligations stood in the way).

With respect to European affairs, Stimson developed some ideas of his own but was not permitted to see them carried out. He was willing, at the time of the London Naval Conference and at other times, to give ear to French demands for a "consultative pact," in the hope of persuading France to limit her naval armaments. Moreover, he was a forthright "cancellationist," believing that the European debtors could not pay and should not be made to try. But Hoover insisted upon collecting, not canceling, the "war debts," though he finally arranged his emergency moratorium. And he stood pat in opposition to all proposals that the United States bind itself to "consult" with France or any other nation.

It was in dealing with the Far East that the sharpest differences between Stimson and Hoover arose, and it was here also that the most significant policy decisions were made. When the Manchurian crisis originated, in 1931, Stimson was still fairly well disposed toward Japan, as he had been during the previous few years, when the Chinese rather than the Japanese had seemed a threat to Asian peace. Time and again he was to be disappointed in his hopes that the civilian authorities in Tokyo would get control of the rampaging army in Manchuria. Ultimately, however, he grew angry with Japan. Hoover, on the other hand, though never approving the Manchurian conquest, persisted in believing that there were two sides to the Sino-Japanese question. He and Stimson agreed upon most of the actual steps that the United States took in response to Far Eastern events, but they did not always agree upon the inner meaning of these measures.

In particular, the two men collaborated on the policy which Secretary of State William Jennings Bryan had adopted in 1915, of refusing to recognize territorial changes made in violation of American treaty rights. Hoover suggested the idea, and Stimson elaborated upon it, tying it to the Nine-Power Treaty of 1922 and the Kellogg Pact. With the full approval of both men, identic notes went off to China and Japan on January 7, 1932.

How the policy was to be enforced and what it was to lead to—on these issues the men did not see eye to eye. For the President, nonrecognition was a final and sufficient measure, a substitute for economic pressure or military force, a formula looking toward conciliation and peace and relying on the moral power of public opinion for its effect. That was the Hoover doctrine. For the Secretary of State, nonrecognition was not an alternative to economic and military sanctions but a preliminary measure, a way of sharpening the issue between the United States (along with the League of Nations) and Japan, a means of laying down the ideological grounds for war if, as he expected, war eventually should come. That was the Stimson doctrine.

A few important steps were taken, beyond the dispatch of the nonrecognition notes. Ships were sent to Shanghai when fighting broke out there, Stimson hoping that the Japanese might thus be intimidated, Hoover intending that Americans in China would thus be protected. The famous Borah letter was published, hinting strongly that, if Japan persisted in violating the Open Door principle, the United States would consider itself free to refortify its Pacific possessions. The Lytton Commission, with an American member, investigated the Manchurian dispute and reported to the League of Nations. The League accepted the Lytton Report, adopted the nonrecognition idea, and passed a resolution formally censuring Japan. And the United States declared itself to be in "substantial accord" with what the League had done.

If Stimson had had his way, Japan would have suffered more than a mere rebuke. The United States would have made clear its willingness to supplement League sanctions with an embargo of its own. With American encouragement and cooperation, the League, so Stimson hoped, would actually have imposed sanctions on Japan, and under the resulting economic pressure the Japanese supposedly would have had to abandon their Manchurian conquest. But Hoover, in August, 1932, compelled Stimson to omit from a scheduled speech three pages in which, as Castle reported Hoover's saying, Stimson "went the whole limit, expressed our willingness to join in sanctions, etc." In the opening months of 1933, Hoover again checked Stimson's efforts to associate the United States closely with the League. Stimson, at the close of his term in the State Department, could only look to the future for the vindication and the implementation of his views.

V

In some respects the United States followed Stimsonian policies more thoroughly *after* he had left the State Department than it did while he was Secretary of State. Before his death, in 1950, he had the satisfaction of seeing put into practice a number of the principles for which he had contended, more or less vainly, between 1929 and 1933. And after his death some of his spirit continued to infuse American diplomacy.

His idea of economic pressure eventually was applied against Japan. As a private citizen, in the late 1930s, he made himself the outstanding American champion of the Chinese cause, serving as honorary chairman of the American Committee for Non-Participation in Japanese Aggression and taking every opportunity to declare that the Japanese should be disciplined with a boycott. As Secretary of War in the Cabinet of Franklin D. Roosevelt, in 1940 and 1941, he used his official influence in the same direction. All along, he insisted that stopping trade would not bring war but, on the contrary, would deprive Japan of the means of carrying on hostilities. Successive embargoes were at last imposed, and Roosevelt's "freezing order" finally ended all opportunity for Japan to buy from the United States. The Japanese response came on December 7, 1941.

Stimson's view of nonrecognition was accepted by his successor, Cordell Hull. "I knew he had had a difficult time getting President Hoover to agree to his policies on Manchuria," Hull wrote in his memoirs. Before taking office, Hull had a series of "elaborate talks" with Stimson and was deeply impressed by him. Hull found him "to measure up to his reputation as a very able, broad-gauged, patriotic statesman," and the future Secretary "readily assented to his position." Hull and Roosevelt continued to apply nonrecognition to the Japanese conquest of Manchuria and, in 1936, extended it to the Italian conquest of Ethiopia. The principle, though left out of the United Nations Charter, remained a tenet of American diplomacy. In 1945, President Harry S. Truman declared: "We shall refuse to recognize any government imposed upon any nation by the force of any foreign power." Truman's successor did not reverse this stand.

The Kellogg Pact, with the interpretation Stimson had placed upon it, was cited as the basis for the Nuremberg trials of 1946, involving Nazi leaders accused of war crimes. The gravamen of the charge against these men was conspiracy to wage aggressive war in violation of the pact. "Unless this pact altered the legal status of wars of aggression," declared the chief American prosecutor at Nuremberg, Justice Robert H. Jackson, "it has no meaning at all and comes close to being an act of deception." He went on to say: "In 1932 Mr. Stimson, as Secretary of State, gave voice to the American concept of its effect. He said: 'War between nations was renounced by the signatories of the Briand-Kellogg Treaty. This means that it has become illegal throughout practically the entire world.'"

In the Korean conflict the United States undertook the sort of enterprise to which Stimson would have liked to commit the country, with respect to Manchuria, about twenty years before. "The history of the Nineteen Thirties is now influencing the approach of the United States to the aggressions of the Nineteen Fifties," James Reston of the *New York Times* observed in early 1951. "To Secretary of State Dean Acheson, Mr. Stimson was much more than an illustrious predecessor. He was a personal hero, carefully studied and perhaps unconsciously followed." Acheson was carrying on in the spirit of his hero. "Like Mr. Stimson, he is determined to punish the aggressors in Korea and China as much as possible."

The Eisenhower-Dulles, as well as the Truman-Acheson, aim of resisting aggression, by force if necessary, was similar to the purpose that much earlier had animated Stimson. In fact, the whole idea of "collective security," which was taken for granted by most mid-twentieth-century Americans, owed a great deal to his championing of the concept at a time when it was by no means an accepted thing.

VI

To some, the course of events after 1933 seemed to justify the
position that Stimson had taken, or tried to take, before that time. With
the passage of the years, the adverse publicity that once had plagued him
was largely forgotten, and he came to have a reputation for almost pro-
phetic vision. In retrospect it appeared that World War II had come because the "peace-loving nations," in particular the United States, had failed
to join forces in due season for resistance to "aggressors." There had been a
few Americans who, like watchmen on the ramparts, dutifully sounded the
alarm, and Stimson had been one of them. *If, when he seeth the sword come
upon the land, he blow the trumpet, and warn the people: then whosoever
heareth the sound of the trumpet, and taketh not warning, if the sword
come, and take him away, his blood shall be upon his own head.*

As Stimson himself, from the vantage point of 1947, looked back upon
his State Department career, he felt that perhaps he should have been
even more forthright in advancing his views than he had been. In 1932
and 1933, he was handicapped by the very tools with which he had to
work. Though he did not consider economic or military pressure as itself
"immoral," the "only weapon" actually available to him in those years
was public opinion. That this weapon would prove effective, however,
"was a vain hope, as he always feared it would be," his memoirs said. "And
in this respect his advocacy had been harmful: if people were taught that
public opinion was 'irresistible,' they might the more easily excuse themselves from using stronger weapons. This was a mistake which Stimson
himself never made, but he was afraid, in 1947, that in his attempt to make
the best of what he had, he had perhaps given aid and comfort to the very
irresponsibility he hated. Such were the difficulties of arousing Americans
to action without frightening them into a deeper isolation than ever."

Yet, despite the ineffectiveness of "moral condemnation," Stimson believed that his "success in securing a unanimous judgment against Japan"
had been perhaps the "greatest constructive achievement" of his public life.
Thus Stimson attributed this nation's victory in World War II to his
moral opposition to Japanese aggression when he was Secretary of State.

> The United States, with him as spokesman [he wrote] had taken a
> leading position in organizing the opinion of the world, and by this
> leadership there had been secured a united front against approval of
> conquest by military force. This united front did not prevent aggression
> or punish it or even act as an effective discouragement to further ag-
> gressors. But it prevented any acquiescence by peace-loving powers in
> a return to the jungle law of international diplomacy before the First
> World War. If it were true, as Stimson believed in March, 1932, that

Japanese aggression must inevitably lead to war, it was also true that the doctrine of nonrecognition laid the cornerstone for a righteous stand on principles of law and order by the nations which in the end combined to win the Second World War.

If indeed the war was bound to come, and it was foreseen as early as 1932 by those who had the eyes to see it, then Stimson's statement of his case is quite convincing. And if "aggression" adequately explains the causes of the war, his argument becomes indisputable. But there is another way of looking at these matters. If policy makers assume that violence is inevitable, their very assumption may help to make it so. And if they think in terms of "punishing" the "aggressor," they may be disinclined to seek and to eradicate the roots of lawlessness.

Even Stimson, in certain of his moods, would probably have agreed with this. He once wrote:

This world of ours is a growing, developing community. In such a world a reign of law, however desirable, cannot be used as a strait jacket to prevent growth and change and still less to protect injustice and perpetuate hardship. Any attempt to make use of such a system of war prevention will ultimately cause explosions which may well destroy the system itself. I fear Europe will never achieve a permanent system of war prevention, no matter how sound a judicial system she may devise, until she has provided methods of relieving fundamental causes of pressure resulting in discontent.

The relieving of such pressure—the appeasing of discontent—was once considered as a proper task for diplomats. "Appeasement" then was an honorable word. It fell into disrepute when it was misused to describe the paying of diplomatic blackmail, that is, the granting of concessions at the last minute, without a fair *quid pro quo,* in response to terrifying threats.

It is conceivable that, during the years Stimson was Secretary of State, there were "fundamental causes of pressure resulting in discontent" in Germany and Japan. If there were, he spent comparatively little of his energy in trying to identify and to relieve them. At times he apparently recognized that the Germans had a case against the Versailles Treaty, and he once agreed with President Hoover that the treaty ought to be revised. If it had been, possibly Hitler and the Nazis would have had less appeal for the German people, and some of the worst aggressions of the 1930s might never have occurred. In any event, Stimson did not stay long with the subject of treaty revision. Instead, he toyed with the idea of a Franco-American "consultative pact," which would have had the effect of endorsing the Versailles settlement and solidifying the *status quo.* As for the Japanese, they claimed that treaties concerning China, especially the Nine-Power Pact of 1922, no longer fit the facts a decade later. Hoover was inclined to agree; certainly he thought Japan suffered from pressures that ought to be relieved. But Stimson, losing all patience with the "aggressors" of the Far East, refused to concede a thing to the Japanese demand for treaty reconsideration.

As Stimson saw it in 1931 and 1932, the treaties, including the Kellogg Pact, were the law, and the law must be upheld, whether it accorded with reality or not. "The peace treaties of modern Europe made out by the Western nations of the world no more fit the three great races of Russia, Japan, and China, who are meeting in Manchuria, than, as I put it to the Cabinet, a stovepipe hat would fit an African savage," he wrote in his diary late in 1931. "Nevertheless they are parties to these treaties... and if we lie down and treat them like scraps of paper nothing will happen, and in the future the peace movement will receive a blow that it will not recover from for a long time." Admittedly the hat did not fit, but Stimson was determined to jam it on anyhow.

The more the Japanese flouted the Open Door policy, the more he looked upon it as a thing of value—indeed, as an almost sacred dogma. He was dismayed to find that Hoover lacked "appreciation of the real nobility of the traditional and standard American doctrine towards China of the 'Open Door.'" Stimson was a lawyer, as almost every Secretary of State had been. In the State Department he surrounded himself with lawyers. And he took an attorney's view of international conflicts. The law was the law. There was a right and a wrong in every case. Trespassers must be prosecuted.

These attitudes of Stimson were examined and found wanting in George Kennan's critique of American diplomacy, published in 1950, though Kennan said he would be most unhappy if any of his observations should be taken as "a mark of disrespect for such men as John Hay, Elihu Root, Charles Evans Hughes, or Henry Stimson." According to Kennan, the United States should never have pursued the will-o'-the-wisp of the Open Door in China or tried "to achieve our foreign policy objectives by inducing other governments to sign up to professions of high moral and legal principles." The "legalistic-moralistic" approach to foreign affairs, especially with respect to the Far East, eventuated in serious problems that a more realistic and less self-righteous approach might have avoided. "The Japanese," Kennan noted,

> are finally out of China proper and out of Manchuria and Korea as well. The effects of their expulsion from these areas have been precisely what wise and realistic people warned us all along they would be. Today we have fallen heir to the problems and responsibilities the Japanese had faced and borne in the Korean-Manchurian area for nearly half a century, and there is a certain perverse justice in the pain we are suffering

from a burden which, when it was borne by others, we held in such low esteem.

There are, then, at least two points of view from which Stimson's record in the State Department may be judged. And there are at least two possible verdicts. Either he helped to lay the legal and moral basis for a war which, in turn, strengthened the legal and moral foundations of international society—and thus he served America well by serving the cause of world peace—or, in so far as he influenced events, he contributed to the tensions and instabilities of the world, to the onset of a kind of never-ending crisis.

10

Cordell Hull

1933-1944

BY DONALD F. DRUMMOND
Eastern Michigan University

Cordell Hull served eleven years and nine months as Secretary of State—approximately half again as long as any predecessor in that high office and nearly double the term achieved by the most enduring of his twentieth-century forerunners. Already past sixty-one when he took the Cabinet oath on March 4, 1933, he had to learn the duties of his post in the midst of an economic crisis that eroded the footings of world peace. From this beginning to his retirement on November 27, 1944, he faced a succession of the most grueling tasks in the history of United States foreign policy.

The man who completed this marathon performance at the age of seventy-three was born on October 2, 1871, near Byrdstown, Tennessee, just below the Kentucky border about a hundred miles northeast of Nashville. The area belongs to the foothills of the Cumberlands, where political forces generated in the mountains of eastern Tennessee mingle with the preferences of the less isolated and more sophisticated west. In Hull the two strains were nicely blended. His basic political philosophy embodied a kind of latter-day Jeffersonianism modified by the attitudes of the post-Reconstruction South: frugal, agrarian, and self-reliant; willing to use Federal authority against the more assertive forms of economic privilege, yet jealous of state rights, instinctively distrustful of the urban liberal, and slow to approve untried experiment. Though Hull lived half his life in a much larger world, his home section of Tennessee remained a fixed reference point in his mental outlook.

Thanks to a relatively prosperous family—his father, William Hull,

184

ultimately built an estate worth $300,000—the future Secretary of State had no difficulty obtaining a decent education, which culminated in a year's study at the Cumberland Law School, in Lebanon, Tennessee. Thereafter, he practiced law sporadically, but politics was always his real career. During his twenties and early thirties, he spent two terms in the state legislature, served briefly as a captain of volunteers in the Spanish-American War, and held a circuit judgeship for about three years. He left the bench in 1906 to enter the United States House of Representatives, and there he stayed. From 1906 to 1930, when he successfully ran for the Senate, he was re-elected every two years, except in the Republican sweep of 1920. Between 1921 and 1924, he gained both administrative experience and a special kind of political prominence as chairman of the Democratic National Committee.

Believing that effective participation in the legislative process requires an expert knowledge of detail, Hull chose fiscal policy as his own specialty. At first he dealt with general problems of taxation, and was prominent in framing the Federal income tax law of 1913. Thereafter, the tariff got most of his attention. Long before his congressional career ended, he was recognized as one of the nation's ablest and most persistent champions of tariff reform. Naturally his proposals emphasized the lower prices, improved business volume, and other domestic benefits of tariff reduction. But soon his advocacy developed broader perspectives. He argued that economic competition between nations was a major cause of war, that commercial cooperation had become prerequisite to other forms of cooperation. For him the key to the international political instability of the early thirties lay somewhere in the nationalistic tariff schedules then proliferating on every hand.

Thus Hull's interest in world affairs and his prescription for their betterment moved outward from a set of economic theories solidly rooted in nineteenth-century liberalism. He admired Woodrow Wilson—perhaps somewhat uncritically, though he thought him dangerously prone to ignore Congress—and he spoke up strongly for the League of Nations. In the moralistic fervor and legalistic tone of Wilsonian internationalism he discovered a lasting appeal, and his sense of identification with Wilson's proposals embodied a ready acceptance of their idealistic content. But Hull's own experience as a dedicated internationalist lay far in the future. Once he got outside the economic sphere, his grasp of ways and means, as distinct from concepts of principle, evolved slowly and haltingly.

II

Some turnings of the path which led Hull from Congress to the Department of State always remained hidden in the complex mind of

Franklin D. Roosevelt. It may be admitted that the Tennessean's long congressional career gradually became a kind of apprenticeship in international relations. As his tariff studies matured and his ideas concerning reciprocal trade agreements took final form, Hull devoted more time to other aspects of world affairs, especially the disarmament movement. During the 1920s, he was, in a fairly accurate sense, a minority spokesman on foreign policy. But he was totally lacking in diplomatic experience, and it is hard to believe that his appointment to the Roosevelt Cabinet was solely, or even mainly, in recognition of his technical competence for the post. It seems perfectly safe to say that his selection involved considerations founded in the expediencies of domestic political maneuver.

A powerful figure in Democratic councils throughout his final decade of congressional service, Hull was strong enough to have real influence in the kingmaking process and, as a leader of the party's entrenched Southern wing, was closely identified with the reaction against Alfred E. Smith following the electoral debacle of 1928. A big-city politician, a Roman Catholic, an outspoken critic of Prohibition, the favorite of the Northern immigrant groups, Smith was never popular in the South. Moreover, some observers, Hull included, believed that the New Yorker was veering to high-tariff policies under the guidance of conservative advisers, and the future Secretary of State made no secret of his role in turning the party to Roosevelt. Although there is no evidence of a prior understanding between the two men, Roosevelt's heavy initial dependence on Southern support made Hull, already a tariff expert and a professed Wilsonian, a compellingly logical choice for the first position in the Cabinet. It is certainly true that an extension of the same logic furnished one major reason for his prolonged continuance in office.

Hull's assertion that he hesitated before accepting the appointment rings true enough. But it was not modesty that deterred him, for Hull seldom lacked confidence in his own ability; rather, it was an unwillingness to accept a part less significant than his existing one. Deeply entrenched with his colleagues and experienced in legislative procedures, he knew something of what he might reasonably hope to accomplish in the Senate, whereas the Department of State was unknown terrain. A strong-minded senator, between elections at least, can function as a kind of sovereign entity, but a Cabinet member must live, to some extent, in the Presidential shadow. Unless he could expect a relatively free hand in Departmental administration and a strong voice in the determination of policy, Hull preferred to remain where he was. He accepted Roosevelt's offer only when he felt assured that he would help make decisions as well as implement them.

This is not to suggest that Hull entered the Cabinet without misgivings. He was always something of an anachronism in the new administration, and no one realized this more clearly than Hull himself. Although his Jeffersonian values ratified much of what he saw, the reform movement was, in many respects, already passing him by. He instinctively distrusted the New Deal's paternalism. Its fiscal policies violated his notions of sound finance. He deplored the speed with which decisions were made. Often during the early New Deal days he felt that reckless whim had supplanted sober reason. Yet the battle against the Depression conformed to no single philosophy. The Roosevelt administration harbored many anachronistic elements, and Hull found reassurance in this diversity.

As Secretary of State, moreover, Hull did not consider domestic affairs his province. Realizing that a man's time and energy are limited, he decided at the outset to concern himself with internal matters only when their bearing on foreign policy was clear and direct. In any event, he tended to believe that many actions taken by the early New Deal had little permanent significance. Like world peace, recovery from the Depression called for an effort that transcended national boundaries. In the long run, international economic adjustments—supplemented by a general revival of morality and law—offered the real solution to both problems.

It was a narrow formula at best. But Hull, though he usually distrusted panaceas, had great faith in his own single-minded remedy. And his confidence that he possessed answers which others were still seeking furnished him with a kind of insulation against much that happened about him.

To say that his views on foreign policy survived twelve years in office without change would do Hull a serious injustice. As he well knew, implementation is an essential part of any political program, and his heavy emphasis upon the lowering of world trade barriers made implementation a major problem. He never disavowed the rightness of his principles, but he did come to recognize the difficulty of persuading others to accept them.

It was Hull's misfortune to assume responsibility for the management of foreign affairs at a time when most Americans, including the President, gave domestic needs an almost unassailable priority. The massive economic nationalism of the New Deal's initial recovery plan ruled out immediate tariff reductions and continued to act as a brake even after passage of the Reciprocal Trade Agreements Act in June, 1934. Equally frustrating was the basic isolationism of many progressives, who resented any new departure in external affairs as a possible interference with domestic reform. The heterogeneous character of the forces underlying the New Deal—an unstable coalition of varied political groups and special interests, constantly pulling in different directions—offered a third drawback. To obtain agreement on any consistent design of long-term application was all but impossible. Hull could rail, and with some justice, at the blindness of individuals and the selfishness of factions. But much of his difficulty was inherent in the circumstances of his time.

Developments abroad played Hull false in a somewhat equivalent fashion. When he took office, he viewed the international future with apprehension, but it required a clairvoyance that Hull did not possess to anticipate in detail the Gargantuan problems of the next twelve years. His prescriptions were based upon a much simpler and more optimistic assessment of world affairs than subsequent events could justify. As it was, his belief that a relatively limited economic and moral initiative on the part of the United States would halt the decline of international stability proved utopian. By 1933 the initiative was passing into other hands. Hull's sense of objective broadened out under the pressure of events; long before the first shots of World War II, he was prepared to admit that the situation required something more than a free-flowing world trade. Yet he seemed always to believe that his ideas would have been vindicated if the United States had moved a bit faster, or the dictatorships more slowly.

III

When Hull made his somewhat labored decision to exchange his legislative career for a place in the Cabinet, he necessarily assumed a dual role. As executive head of the Department of State and the Foreign Service, he was not only chief adviser to the President in the conduct of foreign relations but also a busy administrator, charged with the effective operation of a far-flung bureaucracy.

Hull proved himself no administrative reformer, though the need for reform certainly existed. In 1933 the Department was small, placid, comfortably adjusted to the lethargic diplomacy of the preceding decade, and suffused with habits of thought that reached back to a still earlier day. What was true of the center was equally true of the circumference. The Foreign Service—genteel, slow-moving, and complacent—also cherished its ties with the past. Able men could be found in both jurisdictions. But individual competence is seldom proof against outmoded procedures and relaxed standards of accomplishment.

Meanwhile, the administrative structure was buffeted by rapidly changing demands. The foreign-policy establishment grew tremendously in size and responsibility during Hull's term of office, especially through the war years. Between 1939 and 1945, the Department's personnel roster burgeoned from less than 1,000 to more than 3,700 names; the Foreign Service increased from 3,700 to approximately 7,000 persons; the management of diplomacy became more complex, the avoidance of error more urgent. Yet there was no general reorganization until 1944. Even then

Hull's role was largely passive, the moving force being supplied by Edward R. Stettinius, Jr., the newly appointed Under Secretary of State.

Hull recognized the importance of administration. It was scarcely in his nature to take anything lightly, and he took his administrative responsibilities very seriously indeed. But time eluded him. Problems never came singly in those troubled years. Reform, if attempted at all, had to be completed swiftly—often in a crisis atmosphere and always without the hours needed for comprehensive reflection. Actually, the Department's experience with the reorganization of 1944 suggests that Hull displayed a certain wisdom in avoiding the issue so long. Though the plan embodied some real advances, especially in the creation of the Policy Committee, it was badly conceived in some respects and was amended a number of times in the course of the year.

For Hull, the press of daily business offered just one of several obstacles to basic administrative improvement. He was limited also by scant experience outside the legislative field and, even more, by a certain weakness of imagination. He failed to envisage the benefits that might come from broadly conceived innovations. Viewing the Department of State and the Foreign Service with a kind of paternalistic approval, he instinctively defended the *status quo*. He knew that the quickening pace of international relations required some adjustments in the system. But since his concern, on the administrative side, was specific rather than general, his organizational tinkerings usually came piecemeal. Selecting problems on an *ad hoc* basis, he built the walls higher at points of weakness. Sometimes he even looked in new directions. But his emphasis was upon repair, not reform.

Some changes were made simply to accommodate new functions. The Division of Trade Agreements was established in 1935 to administer the newly authorized reciprocal trade program. The special Neutrality Act of August 31, 1935, with its mandatory embargo of arms shipments to foreign nations engaged in war, produced the Office of Arms and Ammunition Control. The Office of Philippine Affairs, also created in 1935, was established to carry out the provisions of the Philippine Independence Act, passed about a year earlier.

The Division of Cultural Affairs, founded July 28, 1938, constituted a real addition to Departmental machinery. Heretofore the American missions abroad had not been staffed with cultural or press attachés, nor had the United States maintained any other agency to promote international cultural relations—a most unfortunate lack in an age of vehement ideologies which made the contest for men's minds an essential part of the political process. Less fundamental but equally pressing were the special tasks imposed by war. An immediate result of the European fighting which began in September, 1939, was the formation of a special division to oversee the repatriation of Americans living abroad and to represent the interests of friendly belligerents—Great Britain, France, Canada, and others—in Germany. The burden of temporary wartime duties grew heavier as the conflict spread, and after Pearl Harbor there was an amazing proliferation of special agencies to cope with such problems.

In addition to the establishment of new services, some adjustments were made to secure greater efficiency in the discharge of customary responsibilities. The year 1937, for example, produced several minor consolidations. The Division of Latin-American Affairs and the Division of Mexican Affairs were joined to form the Division of the American Republics, thus promoting administrative unity in a region of growing significance to the United States. Reorganization of three other political divisions—the Western European, the Eastern European, and the Near Eastern—as two components, the Division of European Affairs and the Division of Near Eastern Affairs, moved toward the same objective in another vital policy area. An order dated July 6, 1937, centralized control of the Department's financial operations in a new agency, the Office of Fiscal and Budget Affairs; and the Division of International Communications, created the following year, helped coordinate activity in the fields of aviation, shipping, and telecommunications. In 1939 the foreign services of the Department of Agriculture and the Department of Commerce were transferred to the Department of State and consolidated with the regular Foreign Service.

It is hard to be specific about Hull's personal contribution to these changes. The detailed planning that went into the adjustments of 1937–1939, for example, was largely the work of Assistant Secretary George E. Messersmith, an experienced career officer. But it seems clear enough that Hull approved and supported these moves and that he took a highly personal interest whenever proposals for reorganization looked beyond the question of mere bureaucratic efficiency.

Whatever his success as a maker of policy, Hull was always concerned about the policy-making function, eager both to emphasize its importance and to separate it, as far as possible, from the routine management of Departmental affairs. The problem was that of giving a limited number of senior officials the opportunity to study major policy questions with some degree of single-mindedness. A solution was projected in 1937, when Herbert Feis, formerly Chief of the Office of Economic Affairs, received a new and less specific designation as Adviser on International Economic Affairs. The idea seemed to promise well, and later on several other chiefs of divisions were released from managerial assignments to concentrate on analytical and advisory duties. In practice, however, these men never managed to shed all their earlier functions, so that they gave policy matters less time than expected. Yet the device itself underlined one of the

Department's grave weaknesses and pointed to a significant line of future development. It bore a logical relationship to the Advisory Committee on Postwar Foreign Policy, which Hull created in 1942, and it clearly adumbrated the Policy Committee established in the general reorganization of 1944.

With a few notable exceptions, Hull liked and respected the officials who served under him. Hostile criticism of his subordinates usually aroused his protective instinct, and it was hardly surprising that personnel questions should become one of his major concerns. He recommended appointments with great care, favored quicker and more regular promotions, urged that a greater proportion of the top diplomatic assignments be reserved for career men, and sought to improve salaries for everyone and to obtain better allowances for persons serving overseas.

Hull had his way, within limits. President Roosevelt did not share altogether the Secretary's complacency regarding the diplomatic establishment. Both procedure and personnel sometimes aroused the President's impatience. Occasionally Hull's advice went unheard. Not so many professionals received ambassadorships as the Secretary thought desirable; a few appointments were made over his express disapproval. But Roosevelt directed no structural reforms and almost never interfered in questions of a purely administrative nature. Inside the Department of State, Hull enjoyed a free hand. What he made of his role there was largely his own doing.

Though Hull conceded that his desk was seldom clear of unread papers, it is beyond question that he worked hard throughout his years as Secretary of State. No one could have worked harder. From the outset he avoided all but the most essential social activity, and he took remarkably few holidays, considering his age and health. He later testified that croquet playing at Woodley, the Washington estate of Henry L. Stimson, formed his only regular diversion. His working day reflected a manifest effort to observe a schedule, and despite the increasing demands on his time he tried to hold a daily press conference. Nor did his labor end when he closed his office in the evening. He nearly always carried work home, and he frequently arranged after-dinner interviews with foreign representatives at his apartment. Not even Sunday was completely free. Though the Under Secretary, the Assistant Secretaries, and the divisional chiefs met regularly each Monday in the Secretary's office, Sunday morning was usually pre-empted by still another meeting of key subordinates. Few of the Sabbath conferences were elaborately planned, but Hull felt that they encouraged the expression of new ideas.

Hull's record of selfless absorption in official duties was one that few of his predecessors could have matched. But the Secretary's diligence did not always produce efficiency in action. The truth is that Hull moved

slowly. Both the number of problems he had to face and their complex
interrelationships encouraged deliberation. His innate caution furnished
another retarding influence. But a third source of weakness was the administrative failure to organize for effective staff work. It appears that
Hull, in his perfectly legitimate resolve to act only upon the fullest possible data, took responsibility for a great deal of study, consultation, and
analysis which should have been performed by lesser officials. He made
the mistake of trying to do more than one man is capable of doing, and
his work could not fail to suffer as a result.

IV

Though Hull's management of his administrative function con-
stitutes one basis for judging his performance, administration is never an
end in itself. His primary task as Secretary of State was the synthesis and
implementation of policy. It is with reference to this purpose that his
final dimensions must be established.

In principle, Hull's views on foreign policy were clear enough. In application, they were marked by a kind of obfuscating generality that threatened to leave him without a yardstick for measuring progress. His conviction that a better world might be achieved relatively soon gave him a sense
of mission and defined his goal, but it tended to blur the shape of intermediate objectives. What he contemplated was a peaceful, prosperous future
based upon cooperation among states and right thinking among peoples.
Rejecting balance-of-power concepts on moral grounds, Hull felt that
they would have no place in the new world that he envisioned. In his
memoirs, he summarized his deep attachment to the principles of Wilson:
"I was not, and am not, a believer in the idea of balance of power or
spheres of influence as a means of keeping the peace. During the First
World War, I had made an intensive study of the system of spheres of
influence and balance of power, and I was grounded to the taproots in
their iniquitous consequences. The conclusions I then formed in total
opposition to this system stayed with me." For Hull it was essential that
international trade barriers be reduced to a minimum. Unselfishness, law,
and morality were the ingredients of the enlightened self-interest toward
which mankind was striving. The United States had to assume leadership
in this transformation, and the forward movement had to start at once if
disaster was to be averted. Essentially Wilsonian, these concepts reached
straight back to Hull's apprenticeship in foreign policy.

On the side of practical action, Hull considered economic reform the
most realistic approach to international stability. Great consequences
could be expected to flow from the reciprocal trade program if its principles were applied with sufficient energy and understanding. But even

this objective presupposed a kind of moral regeneration among men. "Today nearly all the nations of the world, including our own, have no fundamentals, either political, moral, or economic," he declared in his first speech as Secretary of State. "The nations and their peoples everywhere are in a large sense prostrate without a definite program of ideas and ideals for the rehabilitation of their political, economic, and other affairs."

Certainly this assertion was no complete statement of foreign policy, nor did Hull intend it as such. Yet it indicated a great deal about the man. It revealed a kind of negativism, a tendency to stress what was wrong rather than what might put things right. It also suggested his capacity for moral indignation. The ends Hull sought were not easily related to the means at hand. In his despair of bridging the gap, he sometimes forgot the urgency of his task and simply stood still—refusing to postulate new remedies himself, demonstrating why the cures envisaged by others would not work, and blaming his frustration on a human perversity that lay entirely outside his control. Too often he thought in clichés; the main trouble with international affairs, he seemed to feel, was man's reluctance to adopt the attitudes and procedures that he recommended for their betterment. It is true that Hull had some positive concepts of method— as illustrated in his advocacy of the reciprocal trade program, in his development of inter-American relations, and in his postwar planning, especially in his work as organizer of the United Nations—but generally he was much better at holding the line than at formulating new departures.

This is not to argue that Hull's views carried little weight in the decisions of his time. Often negative influences can leave as deep an imprint as positive ones. It is clear that he achieved no ultimate objectives, but any useful judgment of his work must employ more lenient standards. The real problem is that of evaluating his contribution to American foreign policy as it actually developed during the Roosevelt period.

Hull's personal estimate of his role was high. His inward and outward satisfaction with his career as Secretary of State is hardly open to question. Doubtless this feeling owed something to his monolithic prestige. He inspired public confidence. With his sparse white hair, high forehead, large nose, dignified bearing, and benign aspect, he looked the part of a Secretary of State. His native conservatism, his habit of speaking in moral absolutes, and his talent for scolding foreign diplomats in homely language struck millions of his countrymen as the essence of things American. Very little of the criticism endured by so many figures in the Roosevelt administration was ever directed at him, and for the most part he retained the freely acknowledged esteem of the political opposition.

But Hull's attitude embraced more than a confident reaction to public approval. His belief that he directed American policy into some very rewarding efforts and steered it away from many dangers is written large everywhere. Direct evidence of this complacency is reinforced by the circumstances of his long tenure. Notwithstanding his manifest disappointment on certain issues and his frequent talk of resignation, he stayed in office nearly twelve years. Even then his retirement was dictated primarily by ill-health and advancing age.

Hull was not immune to self-deception. Always inclined to emphasize the verbal aspects of foreign policy, he found it hard—especially in areas of strong feeling—to distinguish between words and deeds. Since his policy-making ambition was a subjective impulse, only Hull could measure its fulfillment. But it seems fair to suggest that he valued his impact somewhat too highly. The heart of the problem of assessing Hull's Secretarial accomplishments lies in his relationship with the President.

This relationship was neither close nor particularly sympathetic. Although the two men certainly respected each other and held many beliefs in common, they were not cronies or even intimate friends. They had little social contact. Though frequent, their conferences were almost always limited to official business. Political exigency, the force that brought them together, remained their strongest tie. That a degree of aloofness should exist between them was not, in itself, surprising. Hull was self-contained by nature, and Roosevelt's famed affability masked a reticence that few men were able to penetrate. There is widespread agreement that the President rarely, if ever, gave his full confidence to another person. It is doubtful that even Harry Hopkins shared his inmost thoughts, and at one time or another practically everyone who knew him well confessed an inability to trace the processes by which he made up his mind.

On Roosevelt's part, this reserve was more than instinctive. It also embodied a reasoned evaluation of the Presidential office and helped determine his administrative techniques. Jealous of his prerogatives and deeply conscious of his responsibilities, he felt himself bound to exercise a firm control over policy—no easy task in the sprawling executive establishment of the mid-twentieth century. Within the administration his first objective was not efficiency but power. Only by countering the tendency of subordinates to create independent satrapies could he maintain an appropriately sovereign position, and, as many observers have pointed out, he found the means he sought in a kind of ordered chaos. Lines of authority that stopped short of his own person received no clear definition. Departments, agencies, and individuals had overlapping functions. Cabinet officials were set in conflict with their own staff members and with one another. "Divide and rule" became the governing principle. So long as the President's advisers could resolve their differences and assuage their uncertainties only by appeal to the President, they remained dependent on him.

This highly personal administrative system all but precluded organized staff work, for it reserved nearly all serious discussion of policy matters for the private conference, called when the President wanted information and counsel or when an adviser requested an interview in order to urge his own point of view. Such talks, moreover, rarely produced significant written records; the real connection between them was known only to Roosevelt. Though it is almost impossible to extract from this procedure the detailed evolution of any major policy, it is obvious that the President was well situated to resist any advisory influence he found distasteful. He was no doctrinaire; he seldom had his mind made up in advance. Highly sensitive to his environment, he heard advice and often followed it. But his decisions were his own.

Although no Cabinet member or lesser official found the President an easy mark, it should be emphasized that Hull's efforts to direct Roosevelt's thoughts labored under some special disadvantages. Essentially, the two men were very unlike each other. Their educational and social backgrounds differed significantly, and they had risen to political eminence by widely separated routes. In temperament, they stood at opposite poles. The cautious, plodding Tennessean never quite appreciated his chief's superb political artistry or understood his brilliant improvisation. And Roosevelt could find little basis for intellectual harmony with a Secretary who often seemed less eager to act than to discover reasons for inaction. This was particularly true in the area of foreign policy, where the President enjoyed both a strong natural interest and impressive qualifications. Hull admired the President, respected his leadership, and approved the major trends of his policy. Roosevelt shared Hull's ideals, respected his monumental diligence, valued his ability to see the defects in almost any new proposal, and found his excellent relations with Congress and his influence with party leaders nearly indispensable. But the intellectual gap between them remained, and Roosevelt filled it with ideas drawn from many quarters.

Of course, Hull knew he was not Roosevelt's only mentor in foreign policy, and to a degree he appreciated the factors that kept them apart. He prided himself on his superior caution. He thought his custom "of being deliberate, while also being on time, resulted in a record containing less of error than would otherwise have been the case." He seldom waxed enthusiastic over Roosevelt's habit of sending personal representatives abroad. He resisted the tendency of other Cabinet members to seek the President's ear with recommendations on foreign policy. He deprecated the assignment of overseas functions to agencies for which the Department of State was not responsible. The liberty exercised by a few of his subordinates—particularly Sumner Welles, who became Under Secretary in

1937—to confer directly with the White House sometimes excited his wrath. And he strongly resented his own omission from the delegation that accompanied Roosevelt to Casablanca, Cairo, and Tehran.

Hull was fully conscious of his difficulties with the President, but in evaluating them, he usually emphasized symptoms rather than causes and effects. Although he admitted that Roosevelt worked around him, he seldom recognized this practice as a significant limitation of his policy-making role. To him the essence of foreign policy was the verbalization of general principles, and in this domain he usually enjoyed a free hand. His recurring failure to distinguish appearance from reality not only impaired his performance as Secretary of State but also diverted his attention from the fact that an impairment existed.

Yet Hull's strongly subjective view of his activities was supported by a number of objective circumstances. The rift between the Secretary and the President never became an open chasm. To Roosevelt, the Presidential responsibility for major policy decisions was exact and, in the final analysis, exclusive. His administrative practices were effectively designed to meet this responsibility. But he never became his own Secretary of State in any real sense. Though Roosevelt controlled foreign policy and personally conducted a large segment of it during the war years, Hull never lost the basic functions of his office. On the positive side, he exercised the greatest influence when he and the President thought alike. But his negative advice was also potent. Again and again his talent for raising objections forced his more sanguine and imaginative associates to re-examine hasty proposals, and occasionally he prevailed even when Roosevelt himself was initially disposed to act differently. Because the President found in his Secretary both a supplement and a foil, Hull performed a valuable service to the day of his retirement.

V

On the whole, American foreign policy reflected Hull's ideas and personality much more accurately during his early years in the Department of State than at any subsequent period. His authority was always limited by other forces bearing upon the White House and by the President's own judgment. As a practical matter, it varied inversely with the tempo of developments overseas and with Roosevelt's desire to assume a strong initiative in the direction of external affairs. Circumstances permitted Hull the greatest latitude at the outset of his diplomatic career.

In 1933 American isolationism ran strong and deep. That the international system created by the peace settlement of 1919 had a somewhat ephemeral quality was widely recognized, but only the most acute observers of the spreading unrest in Europe and Asia perceived a real threat to American security. Economic depression was the concern of the moment; economic recovery absorbed the nation's energies throughout Roosevelt's first term. Though the President's interest in foreign affairs broadened rapidly as time went on, prior to 1936 or 1937 diplomatic problems were secondary and were left largely in the hands of the Secretary of State. Hull's disappointments at this stage resulted less from opposition to his foreign policies than from the preferential treatment enjoyed by domestic questions.

The delay encountered by the reciprocal trade program illustrates the point. Hull's plan for reviving world commerce called attention to the economic basis of international politics at a time when nations everywhere were seeking economic panaceas by political means. He thought that the World Economic Conference, meeting in London in June, 1933, offered a most favorable opportunity to encourage widespread tariff reform, provided that the United States presented clear evidence of leadership. But the early New Deal considered firm domestic prices more important than a rising foreign trade, and the legislation needed to activate the principle of reciprocity was not passed until June, 1934, a year after the London talks broke up in failure.

This postponement Hull neither forgot nor totally forgave. Its real significance is debatable, for the remedies most governments then sought were inspired by economic nationalism. But in the reciprocal-trade idea Hull found a deep reality. That the principle later achieved a modest success was largely owing to his firm advocacy, and its entire history proved that he was not easily discouraged when his concept of ends was supported by a clear view of means. Though Roosevelt never gave international trade the weight it deserved, Hull promoted the cause of lower tariffs as long as he remained in office. He criticized the Democratic platform of 1936 for its ambivalence on the trade question and undertook to ignore the high-tariff overtones he thought he detected. He repeatedly expressed dissatisfaction with the statement on international trade in Article 4 of the Atlantic Charter because it appeared to sanction the British system of imperial preferences. During the war years he not only used his influence with Congress to keep the Reciprocal Trade Agreements Act in force but also favored the use of America's wartime bargaining power to make other governments acknowledge the underlying principle. He personally launched such an effort in the lend-lease negotiations of 1942 with Great Britain, and he flattered himself that Article 7 of the resulting agreement committed the British to a generalized acceptance of his philosophy. The same formula, or one very like it, was used in subsequent lend-lease understandings. Hope of extending the good work figured prominently in Hull's labors on behalf of the United Nations.

If one judges by the immediacy of results as well as by the nobility of intention, Hull appeared to even greater advantage in his management of relations with the Latin-American states. Here his motives were similar to those underlying the reciprocal trade program, for he viewed the Good Neighbor policy both as a means of extending the network of trade agreements and as a chance to implement Wilsonian ideals. His success owed much to a congenial environment. He was aided not only by the President's consistent approval and active support but also by many other favorable circumstances.

Actually the United States had been turning to Good Neighborism's most essential principle—nonintervention in the domestic affairs of independent countries—for the better part of a decade. The nation's systematic and sometimes gratuitous coercion of neighboring republics on the plea of hemispheric security had overtones of imperialism that always left many Americans uncomfortable. Despite his highhanded methods, Woodrow Wilson sought to emphasize values higher than naked self-interest. A more distinct reaction set in after World War I, when European weaknesses seemed to guarantee the safety of the Western Hemisphere. It gained force as the search for new business opportunities in the area likewise counseled a gentler treatment of the Latin-American peoples. The change became evident as early as the Coolidge administration and was rather clearly defined under Hoover. All that remained for the New Deal was to give nonintervention the status of a systematic policy.

For Hull the new practice had attractions beyond its appeal to his democratic and anti-imperialistic principles. Fundamentally it was passive, a course of inaction that could be pursued to the advantage of national interests. Yet it also had a positive side, a creative effect which gained real significance when the practice of nonintervention was transmuted into a structure of inter-American cooperation. Before the United States entered World War II, many principles underlying both the Monroe Doctrine and the general concept of hemispheric security had been accepted by the American republics as a joint responsibility.

To the success of this development Hull's contribution was invaluable. His modesty and self-effacement in dealing with touchy Latin-American diplomats were displayed to advantage at the Montevideo Conference of 1933. His persistence in moving toward a planned objective bore rich fruit in the Declaration of Lima of 1936 and in the Act of Havana of 1940. His careful study of economic sensibilities helped the program's political aspects gain acceptance. Reciprocal trade arrangements were of great value to countries like Cuba, which depended heavily on markets in the United States. Tolerance of such nationalistic moves as the expropriation of American oil holdings in Bolivia and in Mexico also helped create a friendlier mood throughout the region. Even after 1942, when the stresses of war gave hemispheric cooperation a special urgency, Hull strove to maintain the spirit of the Good Neighbor. Though he considered it most important that Argentina and Chile follow their sister republics in breaking relations with the Axis—and was ready to exert considerable diplomatic pressure to achieve that end, especially if British support could be obtained—he twice blocked Treasury proposals for the freezing of Argentine assets in the United States, on the ground that so drastic a reprisal would be offensive to the whole Latin-American community.

The Good Neighbor program never belonged to Hull exclusively. Roosevelt was personally identified with the effort throughout his administration. Sumner Welles, whose expert knowledge of the area was exceeded by no one else in public life, also made an impressive contribution. But to the popular mind, both at home and abroad, Hull unquestionably symbolized the movement. And with his vast legislative experience, he was much better fitted than anyone else to interpret the program to Congress and attract its support.

The strength Hull exhibited in carrying out the most distinctive foreign policies of the early New Deal was not evident in his approach to the major aggressions of his time. Although both the reciprocal-trade principle and the Good Neighbor movement served highly useful purposes, neither could contribute much toward arresting the course of events in Europe and Asia. The diplomatic problems created by Germany, Italy, and Japan led him onto new ground, where power had to be recognized as the ultimate sanction. Here Hull was always somewhat lost.

The truth is that Hull, like most other Americans of the epoch, had an essentially naïve view of how power functions in world politics. He did recognize, however, the significance of raw military preparedness. "I thought for a time, while talking to Axis diplomats, that they were looking me in the eye," he noted, "but I soon discovered that they were looking over my shoulder at our armed forces and appraising our strength." As World War II approached, he realized that an unfavorable balance of military power imposed serious limitations on American diplomacy, and he came out for substantial rearmament as early as 1935. The externals impressed him; he always counted soldiers, warships, and planes. Power was a short-run consideration of great importance. But he never quite understood its relevance to long-range political planning.

In view of the world situation developing during the thirties, Hull argued that both the United States and its potential allies must rearm before the administration could accept new commitments outside the Western Hemisphere; meanwhile, he maintained, the nation should restrict itself to observing what transpired overseas. Thus his preparedness thesis was used for conservative purposes, a means of keeping the imagination in check. The failure of the democracies to rearm at the pace he considered appropriate became an excuse for his standing still. As he waited, he could enlarge upon the legalistic generalities and moralistic rebukes that came so readily to his tongue.

This negativism was especially marked during the tentative reorientation of foreign policy which occurred in 1937 and 1938. By this time President Roosevelt, with some help from Sumner Welles, was studying the possibility of diplomatic intervention at a number of points. Although his famed "quarantine" speech of October 5, 1937, must be regarded primarily as an effort to arouse and test public sentiment in the United States, it also suggested a new line of action overseas. Alarmed beyond measure, Hull vehemently protested the implications of the "quarantine" passage. In his view, any kind of initiative was too hazardous.

A short time later he was equally appalled to learn of another plan, presumably worked up in talks between Welles and Roosevelt, for calling a White House conference of the Washington diplomatic corps to explore the possibility of creating an anti-Axis diplomatic front. Contending that the democracies were unprepared for such an undertaking, Hull urged postponement, at least until Great Britain had been consulted. Roosevelt yielded, and then Prime Minister Neville Chamberlain proved so cool to the idea that the President allowed the project to wither and die. In September, 1938, during the Munich crisis, Roosevelt sent personal messages to leading European statesmen emphasizing his hope for peace. But Hull opposed even these gestures. As he later remarked, "Welles kept pushing the President on, while I kept urging him to go slow." Hull sensed, rightly enough, that acceptance of appeasement had become the only possible basis for American cooperation with Britain and France. Yet one suspects that he also preferred inaction for its own sake.

Elsewhere Hull viewed appeasement with more enthusiasm. On the Pacific side, the United States did not lie behind a screen of friendly powers. Since it faced Japan more or less directly, its position here was somewhat analogous to that of Great Britain and France in Europe, and its policy reflected the same lack of rashness. For years the American government did little more than refuse to sanction Japan's grosser violations of the Open Door, while patiently reiterating the legal and moral principles on which that nation was expected to act. But this attitude was not based on caution alone. Curiously enough, Hull used the same argument employed by the European democracies in their dealings with Germany and Italy; he professed to hope that such restrained conduct would persuade Japan that she had nothing to fear from the United States and would thus discredit the militarists who had seized control of the Japanese government. Doubtless the hope was sincere. But it also furnished a rationale for the *modus operandi* in which he felt most at home. Until well after the European war started, he remained free to lay down principles for the Far East which, however admirable as statements of objectives, largely ignored the question of means.

Hull gained useful experience between 1933 and 1939. If he still lacked a truly sophisticated grasp of international realities, he at least recognized some of them as obstacles. Essentially, however, he remained unchanged, confusing attitudes with policies and regarding words as a substitute for action. "The President and I had certainly made the position of the United States limpidly clear to the Axis Powers," he wrote in review of prewar diplomacy. "They could have no doubt as to where our sympathies lay. They may have doubted whether Congress would support the Administration or whether we could effectively support the democracies, but they could have no uncertainty that our hearts were with the victims of aggression." It was a strangely complacent summary, everything considered. But at this stage American foreign policy could still be outlined primarily in terms of what Hull had accomplished.

Hull's status began to change following the German invasion of Poland in September, 1939. Not only did the European war push the New Deal's concern with domestic issues into the background and give international affairs a clear priority, but it led President Roosevelt to make the direction of foreign policy his own personal endeavor. As he concentrated the resources of his extraordinarily fertile mind upon the security problems stemming from hostilities overseas, he became much less dependent on his advisers—particularly those who were too cautious or too disillusioned to approve the rapid movement he considered necessary. He still consulted Hull, but now his deep sense of urgency placed a heavy discount on the Secretary's hesitations. Most diplomatic business continued to be routed through the Department of State, but for special purposes Roosevelt came to prefer less roundabout methods, involving the use of special emissaries and personal meetings with foreign leaders.

The decline of Hull's influence cannot be measured exactly. With respect to such areas as Latin America and the Far East, where the war was slow to produce major changes in United States policy, he remained the chief spokesman on American objectives. It is more difficult, however, to assess his role in guiding official reaction to the problems which emerged from the European conflict. For a time, he had few open differences with anyone. Though he opposed the European mission of Sumner Welles in February and March, 1940, lest it create an impression that the United States government favored a negotiated peace, it is certain that he approved the general lines of Roosevelt policy. In relations with Vichy France and with Spain, where the administration sought to achieve its ends by exerting heavy economic pressures, Hull played a most active part. But the extent of his responsibility for initiating such policies is, and will probably remain, the subject of guesswork. It would seem, however, that his major contribution to the European policy of the United States is to be found in implementation and in detail rather than in creative concept.

In essence, diplomacy by 1940 had entered a semimilitary phase, and foreign policy was now affected directly by many factors that were not the exclusive prerogative of the Department of State. More and more regularly, diplomatic questions were submitted to the so-called War Council, composed of the Secretaries of War and the Navy, the Chief of Staff, and the Chief of Naval Operations, as well as the President and the Secretary of State; and the President himself played an increasingly dominant role. There was no abrupt change in Hull's status between 1939 and 1941—merely a slow attrition. But when Pearl Harbor brought the semimilitary phase to an end and all diplomatic business became inseparable from the conduct of the war, Roosevelt settled heavily into his part as Commander in Chief and relegated the Department of State to a secondary position in regard to most aspects of planning. Thereafter Hull did not sit as a member of the War Council. Although it appears that little was done without his knowledge, there was a notable tendency to make decisions without his prior agreement.

Though Hull admitted the primacy of military considerations, he did not concede that war planning and diplomatic planning could be effectively separated. He resented having to cope with the diplomatic consequences of military decisions over which he had exercised no control, and he believed that the Department of State should remain the prime avenue of communication with foreign governments. He seriously contemplated resignation as early as January, 1942, following the unauthorized seizure by Free French forces of St. Pierre and Miquelon, the two French islands off Newfoundland. It is true that he was motivated in part by his ill-health, but he was also provoked by the President's failure to insist on British cooperation in checking the headstrong policies of Charles De Gaulle, the Free French leader. Already Hull felt himself badly used, and it is hardly too much to say that the threat of resignation was never fully dissipated thereafter.

Especially bothersome after the United States entered the war was the problem of maintaining centralized control over diplomatic operations. By early 1942 the Treasury, the Coordinator of Inter-American Affairs, the Office of Lend-Lease Administration, the Petroleum Coordinator, the Coordinator of Information, and the Board of Economic Warfare were all dealing with foreign governments independently of the Department of State. Hull insisted that every representative abroad should work in close union with regular Foreign Service personnel and under the supervision of the resident minister or ambassador. Finally, in May, 1942, the President issued an order embodying this principle. Thereafter, Hull acknowledged some improvement, but he continued to have difficulty of the same general character.

Hull was distressed at the obvious influence that other government administrators exerted over foreign-policy decisions. He blamed Vice President Henry A. Wallace, head of the Board of Economic Warfare, for the inability of the State Department to work effectively with this new wartime agency. He was deeply disturbed that Henry Morgenthau, Jr., his Cabinet colleague, never ceased to inundate the White House with advice on foreign policy, much of it unrelated to Treasury business. Hull observed that Roosevelt's continued employment of special representatives, responsible to the President alone, kept the State Department from exercising the scrutiny over diplomatic procedures that he considered desirable. His relations with Harry Hopkins, the chief Presidential agent, were generally good. He conceded that Hopkins performed valuable services, although he frequently disagreed with him on matters of substance. He was exceedingly irritated, however, by the fact that highly important liaison functions were assigned to Hopkins, since this seemed to reflect a distrust of the Department's ability to seal off information leaks. As Secretary of State, he was equally annoyed at Wallace's personal diplomatic ventures. He thought that the Vice President's tour of Latin America in 1943 did more harm than good and regarded Wallace's trip to China in 1944 as a positive disservice to United States foreign policy. Most serious of all, to Hull, was Sumner Welles's habit of carrying proposals directly to the President without first consulting the Department.

Hull was not a man to suffer in silence. On occasion, when his protests were firm enough, he carried his point. By almost literally forcing Roosevelt to choose between himself and Welles, he obtained the latter's resignation in the summer of 1943. Aided by Henry L. Stimson, the Secretary of War, he successfully opposed an outright endorsement of the cataclysmic Morgenthau Plan for Germany. As indicated above, he likewise blocked Morgenthau's proposal to freeze Argentine credits in the United States. More often, however, his defenses against encroachment proved inadequate. Though Hull apparently recognized no serious diminution of his influence so far as major policies were concerned, it seems clear that after Pearl Harbor he saw himself fighting a rear-guard action to preserve the integrity of his role.

VI

Those concepts of foreign policy which Hull carried through the war were entirely consistent with his philosophy and temperament. Like Roosevelt, he thought the major threat to American security emanated from Europe. He entertained no doubt whatever that Germany was the real enemy. For all his caution, he never resisted the administration's effort to bring American resources to bear against the German cause. On the contrary, in the fall of 1939 and the spring of 1940 he opposed any move tending to create an impression that the United States would look favorably upon a negotiated peace. To his mind, a decisive victory over Germany was essential. Italy he took less seriously, not only because her limited war potential rendered her less dangerous but also because he thought the Italian people gave the conflict no firm support. On this ground he felt that Italy should be treated more leniently than the other Axis nations. But the nature of the German threat, which so clearly dictated a "Europe-first" strategy, made it easier for Hull to observe a restraint in Asia that was somewhat out of harmony with his moral rejection of Japanese conduct. The wisdom of postponing a break with Japan in order to direct American capabilities toward Europe helped to justify the slow-moving Far Eastern policy the United States had adopted years earlier.

Hull's views toward Russia followed a reasonably clear line of expediency. The thesis that the United States should not break completely with the Soviet Union, even during the period of Russo-German collaboration in 1939 and 1940, he accepted as fundamentally sound. He sensed, though perhaps dimly, that the democracies would have trouble beating the Axis unless Russian help could be obtained. Believing that conflicting ambitions would eventually drive Germany and Russia apart, he felt that the United States must maintain a position from which such differences could be exploited. The outbreak of the Soviet-German war in June, 1941, he considered a vindication of this judgment, and the subsequent program of active collaboration with Russia gave him no serious qualms.

Hull had few illusions, however, concerning Soviet expansionist ambitions. In May, 1942, he helped kill a proposed Anglo-Russian agreement approving Stalin's demands for new frontiers in Eastern Europe. He believed that Russia would enter the war against Japan only to seize Manchuria and other areas in northeastern Asia during the final weeks of conflict. In 1944 he opposed Roosevelt's acceptance of an agreement establishing Russian and British spheres of influence in the Balkans. Hull also expressed doubt concerning the purported dissolution of the Comintern in 1943; he never believed that Russia would become a democracy overnight. On the other hand, he advocated full consultation with Russia and professed to believe that an "era of fruitful working together" lay ahead.

Of Great Britain, Hull was critical more often than not. Before Pearl Harbor he fully approved the President's determination to aid Britain by all means short of war. After Pearl Harbor he stressed the importance of Anglo-American cooperation in all military and diplomatic endeavors. Yet he traced many of his troubles directly to London. Although he appreciated the Gargantuan war effort of the British people, he was almost morbidly suspicious of British policy. Winston Churchill's brisk practicality and unabashed imperialism nearly always set Hull's teeth on edge. He believed that the Prime Minister was more intent upon salvaging his country's traditional place in world affairs than in establishing a new order based on the principles of the Atlantic Charter.

Churchill's reluctance to abandon imperial preferences outraged Hull's low-tariff philosophy, and his apparent determination to keep the British Empire intact ran counter to Hull's principle of self-determination for colonial peoples. The Prime Minister's indulgence toward De Gaulle, his desire to preserve the Italian monarchy, his readiness to approve territorial agreements with Russia, his partiality for marking out spheres of influence violated some of Hull's deepest prejudices. The Secretary believed that Churchill's refusal to sanction stronger economic measures against Spain, Portugal, Sweden, Switzerland, and others encouraged the European neutrals to supply Germany with vital war materials much longer than necessary. He also thought that this reflected a selfish determination not to block off commercial channels that were important to Great Britain in time of peace.

Most of the wartime decisions that Hull found unsatisfactory were made at a level just beyond his reach and involved a balancing of forces which were beyond his experience. Though he had many personal contacts with the Prime Minister, he seldom attended the Roosevelt-Churchill discussions even when they occurred in Washington. Stalin he knew solely from his visit to Moscow in late 1943. Generally he could study the exchanges of the three leaders only from a distance. Hull understood that Roosevelt shared most of his reservations concerning British policy and nearly all his views on Russia. But he thought the President vulnerable to overpersuasion.

Nevertheless, the basis for Hull's disapproval of the compromises made by the Big Three went much deeper than his exclusion from the major wartime conferences. As the road to victory opened up, Hull reverted more and more to his Wilsonian vision of a new world, tending to judge each decision in terms of the objective toward which he was striving rather than in terms of the circumstances which gave it birth. His views on wartime diplomacy were highly congruent to the objective in that they emphasized higher standards of international conduct, but they offered no viable analysis of the political realities from which the new world must emerge.

Hull knew that the war could not fail to produce some drastic changes in the power relationships on which the future rested, and he made some reasonably direct recommendations for dealing with this problem. He considered it essential that China be strengthened to fill the power vacancy in the Far East created by the defeat of Japan. He urged the rebuilding of

France so that it might resume its traditional place in the international state system, and he opposed the dismemberment of Germany as fatal to European economic stability. He thought the unconditional-surrender dictum not sufficiently flexible and likely to prolong the war beyond need. Perhaps this was also a way of saying that power disturbances should be minimized.

But if Hull sensed danger, his misgivings were haphazard, and he was unable to define the problem in its broader aspects. Above all, he seemed to have only a slight appreciation of the tremendous advantages Russia stood to gain from the destruction of Germany and Japan, her two most formidable neighbors. He agreed that the future international organization would have to begin with the concert of anti-Axis powers, but he made no allowances for the pressure to be created by selfish national interests. His rejection of the old diplomacy—with its emphasis on spheres of influence, partition, and other balance-of-power techniques—precluded his acceptance of the only methods by which an adjustment to the emerging results of the war could be achieved.

Yet, from this very single-mindedness Hull derived great strength. While most of his contemporaries still lacked a purpose beyond military victory, his own thought patterns made him see the war as the supreme opportunity of his epoch to build a lasting peace organization. He seized the initiative promptly and then, with monumental persistence, charted the course leading to Dumbarton Oaks and San Francisco. If he cannot be considered the father of the United Nations, he must at least be regarded as a presiding midwife.

Postwar planning in the Department of State began in January, 1940, with the establishment of the Advisory Committee on Problems of Foreign Relations, under the chairmanship of Sumner Welles. A year later the Division of Special Research was added to collect and analyze data. Immediately after Pearl Harbor these activities were centered in the new Advisory Committee on Postwar Foreign Policy, which included congressmen, senators, and experts drawn from private life, as well as officers of the Department. As chairman of this group, Hull pushed ahead energetically, his heart now set on the formulation of definite proposals. He quickly brought the United Nations project under public discussion and thereafter lost no chance to urge his views on interested parties. At the Moscow Conference of Foreign Ministers, in October, 1943, he successfully carried the fight to the international level. The details of organization kept him heavily occupied throughout his final year of Cabinet service.

On questions of substance Hull was remarkably faithful to the Wilsonian prototype. His proposals regarding form, function, and scope reflected the ideas he had nourished since World War I. Above all, he stressed the wisdom of giving the peace organization a universal character. As late as the spring of 1943, Roosevelt favored the creation of several more or less independent regional councils, with other separate agencies to assume specialized tasks in the field of economic and social cooperation. According to this formula, all nations would be disarmed except the United States, Great Britain, Russia, and China, and general security problems would be handled by direct consultation among the heads of these four states. Churchill shared many of the President's ideas, especially his preference for regionalism. But Hull felt that such an approach vitiated the one-world concept, and he strongly resisted every suggestion that tended to make the parts greater than the whole. The new society of states could not begin with division and discrimination, he argued, and his triumph was registered in the clauses of the Four-Power Declaration that called for "a general international organization, based on the ... sovereign equality of all peace-loving states, and open to membership by all such states, large and small. ..." Though the principle of Great Power dominance gained recognition in the structure of the United Nations Security Council, Hull could point out that the Security Council of the League had been similarly constituted.

But if Hull stood firm on Wilson's philosophy of international relations, his procedural doctrines honored the former President more in the breach than in the observance. His long political experience told him that Wilson had erred badly on the home front—first, by holding Congress at arm's length until the postwar settlement was far advanced and, second, by permitting foreign policy to become a partisan issue. Wilson's failure to grant Congress an effective role in the development of the peace program not only had cost him a valuable and possibly willing ally but had fatally discounted the Senate's truly commanding position in all business relating to treaties. His apparent willingness to identify the program with the Democratic party had compounded the initial error by bringing to bear upon an external question all the resentments, jealousies, and expedients associated with a domestic political maneuver. Practical politics on Capitol Hill was a field Hull understood thoroughly, and he was determined that the gaucheries of 1918 and 1919 should not be repeated.

The attitudes Hull had acquired in his three decades as Congressman and Senator again served him well. He understood the deep-rooted sense of congressional prerogative, and with his generally high regard for the leadership in both houses, he found it easier to seek cooperation than to demand compliance. From the moment he became Secretary, he had gone out of his way to propitiate his erstwhile colleagues, and he had concluded long since that the results justified the effort.

The appointment of congressional representatives to the Advisory

Committee on Postwar Foreign Policy early in 1942 served notice that peace planning would not be treated as an executive monopoly. Among other things it helped clear the way for the Fulbright resolution and the Connally resolution, which committed the House and the Senate, respectively, to support American participation in the future peace organization. Such gestures as Hull's acceptance of an invitation to address a joint session of Congress on the results of the Moscow Conference also helped keep a trustful spirit alive.

But the threat of excessive partisan debate remained strong until March, 1944, when Hull invited the Senate Committee on Foreign Relations to establish a special group of members from both parties to assist the Department of State in carrying out plans for an international organization. Republican leaders agreed, with the understanding that other aspects of foreign policy should also come before the new committee. A few months later Hull attacked the same problem at a different level by negotiating an agreement with John Foster Dulles, foreign-policy adviser to Republican presidential candidate Thomas E. Dewey, not to make the international organization an issue in the campaign of 1944. Whether this established a "nonpartisan" or a "bipartisan" treatment of foreign policy has been the subject of much debate. As a practical matter, however, the differences between the two parties were reduced to negligible proportions during the months in which the United Nations changed from concept to reality.

VII

The election of 1944 was the real terminus of Hull's public career. As the voting statistics disclosed another victory for Roosevelt, every significant force in the Secretary's personal world conspired to bring about his retirement. Physically, Hull was no longer equal to the office, and the purposes which had kept him active despite failing health and advancing age seemed close to execution. Triumph over the Axis was clearly, if not immediately, in sight, and the United Nations had been given a firm promise of birth and the assurance of American membership. The ancillary problems of foreign policy had already passed into other hands. For months, even years, Hull had been settling into the role of elder statesman. Now he could play that role most effectively from outside the Cabinet.

Hull's prestige was never greater than at the moment of his resignation. The years of responsibility which ended on November 27, 1944, had brought many satisfactions: reciprocal trade, the Good Neighbor program, a victorious war coupled with moral idealism and the beginning of a new international order. Even the negative aspects of Hull's temperament had served a useful purpose.

But Hull's negativism had also constituted his fundamental weakness as Secretary of State. In the decade just past, world events had speeded up tremendously, whereas Hull's pace had remained the same. Grown to adulthood in the generation following the Civil War, the Secretary had never come fully abreast of the twentieth century. His aims had been high, his motives unselfish, his impulses humane. He had helped crystallize some of Franklin D. Roosevelt's basic preferences in the area of foreign policy. But his assumptions had remained those of an earlier and simpler world. In his thinking, ends and means had never achieved a realistic balance.

11

Edward R. Stettinius, Jr.

1944-1945

BY WALTER JOHNSON
University of Chicago

Early in October, 1943, just after the Senate confirmed the appointment of Edward R. Stettinius, Jr., as Under Secretary of State, President Roosevelt told Mrs. Stettinius: "Ed is going to raise Hell in the State Department . . . and he will do it with my blessing." By that autumn, the reputation of the Department was at a low point. Everywhere it seemed to be under sharp attack. Thus, Joseph M. Jones wrote in *Fortune* (September, 1943): "Notwithstanding the personal prestige of the Secretary of State, the organization that he heads has only to be mentioned in almost any circle, American or foreign, to arouse either doubt, despair, or derision."

The first task Cordell Hull assigned to the handsomely silver-haired, forty-three-year-old Under Secretary was a reorganization of the Department. Stettinius brought to this formidable task the experience of a successful career in both business and public administration. Although the fact that his father was a partner of J. P. Morgan & Company was an obvious asset to the son, the younger Stettinius's ability to get things done and his administrative skill quickly won him recognition and advancement in business on his own right. In 1926 he became an assistant to John L. Pratt, a General Motors vice-president, and was placed in charge of employee welfare activities; in this capacity, he negotiated a group insurance plan for the corporation's employees—the largest plan ever written until that time. Later, as assistant to Alfred P. Sloan, Jr., president of General Motors, he handled institutional advertising and publicity, and in 1931 he was named vice-president in charge of industrial and public relations. Three years later, he joined the United States Steel Corporation and, in 1938, at the age of thirty-eight, was made chairman of the board of directors. One of his first actions was to oppose a suggestion that wages be reduced in proportion to the reduced price of steel. Immediately thereafter, President Roosevelt, in a fireside chat, congratulated the company for its "statesmanship."

In August, 1939, Roosevelt appointed Stettinius Chairman of the War Resources Board. Ten months later, Stettinius resigned from U.S. Steel to join the National Defense Advisory Commission. As the dimensions and fury of the war overseas mounted, so the hitherto somewhat indifferent United States began to look to its defenses. In January, 1941, Stettinius became Director of Priorities of the newly created Office of Production Management. Soon a few self-righteous New Dealers snidely suggested that this former big-business man was a "go-slower" on converting industry to production.

Stettinius, however, had become a close friend of Harry Hopkins, a prince of the New Dealers, and this friendship was influential in Roosevelt's appointment of Stettinius to the hugely important lend-lease program in September, 1941. Here he obtained invaluable experience in the delicate art of how to deal with Congress, and his administrative ability won the respect of congressmen of both political parties.

The genial Stettinius, who radiated warmth and enthusiasm, liked people. But, strangely, some of his Washington critics sourly insisted that his affection for the human race was a substitute for tough-mindedness —a dubious proposition that equates the dour face with strength. But even these critics reluctantly agreed that he was a man of good will and enormous energy, and his subordinates, whether top assistants or lowly typists, admired him as a hard-driving administrator infallibly touched with grace.

Though a serious man, Stettinius was no "egghead." As a student at the University of Virginia, he showed little interest in the art of gentlemanly conviviality prevalent on the campus, but neither did he evidence any scholarly passion or reflective qualities that might eventually lead to a Phi Beta Kappa key. On the contrary, he neglected his studies to help the poor living in the slums of Jefferson's Albermarle County, he taught Sunday school, and he devoted himself to YMCA work.

It is not surprising that such a young man should have considered entering the pulpit or that he should have decided against doing so only because he felt that he could be more useful to society through industry than through the ministry. He seems to have subscribed to the view of Romain Rolland that "when a man is young he must be under the illusion that he is recreating the life of humanity." But the saving illusion was still strong upon Stettinius in his maturity. Hence, in 1937, he declared that the instruments of production should "in the future be conducted with more statesmanlike emphasis on the welfare of all involved—employees, stock-holders, consumers, and the public—that the goal of production shall not be profit alone, but material, social, and spiritual betterment for all groups and all classes."

II

When Stettinius became Under Secretary in 1943, the Department of State had expanded its activities as a result of the pressures of the war and the necessity of planning for the postwar era. But in form and personnel it was still essentially the Department that Hull had presided over since 1933. As Under Secretary and later as Secretary, Stettinius introduced an organizational structure which made it possible for the Department to assume responsibilities which would have been difficult under the old system.

As Under Secretary, he noted in his diary that a serious defect of the Department was the haphazard manner in which various duties had been assigned; as a result, one man was often in charge of widely disparate functions, and the responsibility for one function was divided among different divisions. Another weakness was that the Department was set up almost entirely for day-to-day decisions, so that problems were often handled on a strictly *ad hoc* basis without regard for over-all policy and the need for long-range planning. The Department was further handicapped by inadequate methods for gathering and disseminating information and hence lacked the machinery for a sound public relations program.

The reorganization Stettinius announced on January 15, 1944, attempted to group similar functions within the same divisions. All international economic matters were concentrated under Assistant Secretary Dean Acheson; all important administrative and public relations functions were placed under Assistant Secretary G. Howland Shaw; and relations with Congress were made the special responsibility of Assistant Secretary Breckenridge Long.

To lighten the administrative load on the Assistant Secretaries and the Under Secretary and to leave them more time for broad policy questions, twelve offices were created, each with a director and a deputy director. Seven Directors reported to specified Assistant Secretaries. The four Directors of the geographical offices—American Republic Affairs, European Affairs, Far Eastern Affairs, Near Eastern and African Affairs—the Director of Special Political Affairs, which included the International Organization Division and the Security and Territorial Studies Division, reported to the Under Secretary.

To meet the requirement of long-range planning, two top-level committees were created—the Policy Committee and the Committee on Post-war Programs. The Secretary served as chairman and the Under Secretary as vice-chairman of both committees. The Policy Committee was to meet three times a week and to assist the Secretary in the consideration of "major questions of foreign policy."

The creation of the Office of Public Information was a significant innovation. With John S. Dickey as Director, it included two older divisions, Current Information and Research and Publication, and two newly created divisions, one for motion pictures and radio and the other for science, education, and art. In July, 1944, the Division of Science, Education, and Art was renamed the Division of Cultural Cooperation. It handled the exchange of professors and students with other nations and all international cultural matters. The strengthening of this division was most important in the light of the subsequent expansion of such activities under the Fulbright and Smith-Mundt programs.

In December, 1944, when Archibald MacLeish was appointed Assistant Secretary of State in charge of Public and Cultural Relations, Dickey's office was renamed the Office of Public Affairs. This office established a close working relationship with private groups interested in foreign policy and, in addition, carefully analyzed public attitudes toward policy. Through publications and radio programs it made a determined effort to explain the Department's work and to present its policy on major issues.

Some of the old State Department people scoffed at the new ways and were particularly scornful of the insistence on better public relations. The *New York Times* remarked later, however, that Stettinius "brought a breath of fresh air to the somewhat musty corridors...." Graham H. Stuart, in his book *The Department of State*, criticizes the haste with which the reorganization was carried out, but the President gained greater confidence in the Department as a result of the changes.

III

On November 21, 1944, Under Secretary Stettinius explained to Roosevelt that the State Department must be revitalized with new leadership, and he presented the President with a list of possible appointees, being careful, however, not to suggest replacement of any of Hull's key advisers. Six days later, when Cordell Hull's resignation was announced, Roosevelt asked Stettinius to be Secretary.

Stettinius immediately recommended the selection of Joseph C. Grew as his successor; the appointments of William L. Clayton, Nelson Rockefeller, and Archibald MacLeish as Assistant Secretaries; and the retention of Dean Acheson. The need for two additional Assistant Secretaries had been agreed to earlier, and after the President received congressional approval, James C. Dunn and Julian Holmes were appointed to these posts. The members of Stettinius's new "team," as he referred to them, were an able group of men who gave strong policy leadership and supplied the Secretary with substantive programs. "In many ways," John S. Dickey has written, "it was one of the most creative periods that the Department has known, at least in modern times."

The two major tasks facing the Department, the new Secretary believed, were to push forward the proposed world security organization and to strengthen the Department itself. On December 20, 1944, Stettinius made several major changes in the Department. The Policy Committee and the Committee on Postwar Programs were replaced by the Staff, or Planning, Committee, whose function was to "advise and otherwise assist the Secretary in determining current and long-range foreign policy." It included the Secretary, the Under Secretary, the six Assistant Secretaries, the Legal Advisor, and Leo Pasvolsky, the Special Assistant planning the proposed international organization. At a lower level, a Coordinating Committee was established to give prior consideration to matters of policy and to deal with interoffice relations. An important addition was a Joint Secretariat to serve both committees by collecting and preparing material for policy decisions and to implement promptly the actions which were authorized. There was also a redistribution of Departmental activities among the Assistant Secretaries. Thus the geographic offices now reported directly to Assistant Secretaries Dunn and Rockefeller rather than to the Under Secretary. The greatest improvement, Graham Stuart has written, "lay in the channeling of reporting, which reduced very considerably the flow of policy problems to the top-level officers, thus giving more time for consideration of the most vital questions and overall policy."

Disturbed over the wide gulf which had existed between the White House and the Department under Hull, Stettinius secured the appointment of career diplomat Charles E. Bohlen to the White House staff to serve as liaison officer. And in order that the Under Secretary and the Staff Committee would be apprised of the President's attitudes, Stettinius made a practice of having Grew sit in his office while he dictated his memoranda of talks with Roosevelt. Grew was always informed, as well, about the Secretary's talks with ambassadors. Grew, who had served in the same post for Hughes and Kellogg, later remarked that Stettinius "was the best chief I ever had."

Stettinius also made a genuine attempt to be easily accessible to the chief officers of the Department. In addition, he cultivated the chiefs of foreign missions; a notable example is the series of group meetings he held with Latin-American ambassadors to discuss the Dumbarton Oaks proposals for the United Nations Organization. To improve the Department's public relations, he met informally with leaders of national opinion-forming groups. Seeking closer cooperation with other governmental agencies, he held a series of meetings with fellow Cabinet members and high executives. Whereas Hull had been antagonistic to the Bureau of the Budget, Stettinius, even as Under Secretary, through free and full discussions, had obtained its support for greatly increased appropriation requests. Then, by cultivating close relations with Congress, Stettinius was able to secure larger appropriations for the Department than had been granted in the past. He and Assistant Secretary Acheson devoted themselves to keeping leading members on Capitol Hill informed about major policy questions, and both gave sufficient personal attention to these senators and congressmen to keep them well disposed toward the Department.

IV

In appointing Stettinius as Secretary, Roosevelt made it clear that he himself would continue to work closely with Churchill and Stalin. He wanted someone, he added, who could work harmoniously with him. For that reason, he had discarded James F. Byrnes as a possibility. When Stettinius remarked, "In other words, Jimmy might question who was boss," Roosevelt replied that this was "exactly the point." Readily assenting to Roosevelt's determination to be the formulator of policy, Stettinius felt that his own responsibilities consisted in re-enforcing the Department, implementing decisions, and serving as a two-way "messenger" between the Department and the President.

To Roosevelt, Stettinius may have seemed a desirable choice not only because he had no aspirations to encroach on Presidential power but also because he had no association with party politics. Since Roosevelt was advocating American entrance into a world organization as a nonpartisan issue, Republican opposition to a Democrat could have precipitated a fight like that of 1919–1920 over the League of Nations. In addition, the proliferation of government activities in wartime Washington required a Secretary associated with this expansion and familiar with the influential personalities and the power structure that had evolved.

Although Stettinius did not have the training or experience in world politics to originate substantive foreign policies, he presented the recommendations of the Department to the President ably and forcefully. To save Roosevelt's time, Stettinius regularly prepared a two-page memorandum for the President which never included more than seven or eight questions, each summarized in a succinct paragraph. Approval and disapproval columns were provided, so that when Roosevelt reached a decision, he had only to initial the appropriate column.

Beginning in the fall of 1944, Roosevelt paid more attention to the Department's ideas than he had during the preceding three years. Although he did not always accept its suggestions, it seems clear—from the Stettinius diaries, unpublished archival material, and the records of the Yalta Conference—that the President relied heavily on the Department's position papers on a number of vital questions. James F. Byrnes was quite wrong when he stated in *Speaking Frankly* (page 23) that Roosevelt ignored the briefing papers prepared by the Department for the Yalta Conference. Roosevelt himself said, at the close of the meeting in the Russian Crimea, that the assistance of the Departmental representatives had been so important that he would not attend another conference without them. The Far Eastern agreement signed there was, however, a conspicuous example of the President's favoring a policy advocated by the Joint Chiefs of Staff. Stettinius was not consulted on this question and was merely informed by the President of the decisions reached.

On the other hand, the plans for a world security organization provide a notable instance of the President's acceptance of Departmental recommendations *in toto*. The work initiated by Hull was energetically forwarded by Stettinius. He continued Hull's efforts to win bipartisan support for the world organization, consulting regularly with leading congressmen of both parties, as well as with interested citizen groups. And he was insistent on securing British and Russian agreement.

The United States had taken the initiative in calling the Dumbarton Oaks Conference, which met from August 21 to September 28, 1944. The American proposals were accepted by Great Britain and the Soviet Union as the basic documents for the negotiations. Stettinius, as Under Secretary, headed the American delegation, and he, Sir Alexander Cadogan, and Andrei A. Gromyko formed the Joint Steering Committee directing the meetings. During the conference, representatives of the three great powers drafted the document that became the basis of the discussions at the San Francisco Conference of April, 1945.

The three nations were unable to agree at Dumbarton Oaks on the voting procedure to be followed in the Security Council on questions concerned with maintaining peace and security. Although they decided that the permanent members would have to be unanimous for any action involving sanctions, they could not settle on the voting procedure to be adopted on other substantive issues in case one of the permanent members was a party to a dispute. The United States opposed the Soviet insistence that the veto should apply. The American delegation also refused the Russian request that all sixteen Soviet Republics be admitted as members of the world organization.

With the public preoccupied by the war, Roosevelt and Stettinius decided to launch a massive campaign to generate public understanding of the Dumbarton Oaks proposals. Archibald MacLeish was persuaded to resign as Librarian of Congress to take charge of it. Aided by Adlai E.

Stevenson—recently Assistant to Secretary of the Navy Frank Knox—
MacLeish distributed several million copies of the proposals, issued comic
books and cartoons to reach the less literate, sent speakers around the
country, and arranged numerous radio appearances by informed officials.
By thus capturing the initiative, the State Department prevented any
demagogues from creating the type of misunderstandings that had so
complicated Wilson's struggle for the League of Nations.

By early 1945, the unsolved differences over the Charter of the United
Nations, the impending defeat of Germany, and the question of Russia's
participation in the war against Japan propelled Churchill, Roosevelt, and
Stalin to their second wartime meeting. Stettinius headed the State Department group that accompanied Roosevelt to the Yalta Conference, February
4–11, 1945. In addition to the daily afternoon meetings of Churchill, Roosevelt, and Stalin, the foreign secretaries and their advisers held morning
sessions and worked on items for the afternoon agenda. Although Roosevelt was the dominant figure in presenting the American position on most
issues, Stettinius explained the American formula on the voting procedure
in the Security Council of the world organization. After a lively discussion of his statement, there was a brief intermission. Churchill told Stettinius that, as a result of his analysis, "now he—and he thought Stalin—
really understood it for the first time." Eden and Churchill both agreed
that progress had been made and that they now had high hopes that there
would be a world organization after all. The following day Stalin announced that, "as a result of the clear explanation given the previous day,"
the Soviet Union accepted the American proposal. It was also agreed, at
that point, to call a United Nations conference at San Francisco on
April 25.

After Yalta, Stettinius visited Brazil to conclude an agreement on an
atomic question and then flew to Mexico City to attend the Inter-American
Conference on the Problems of War and Peace. The American delegation
included thirty-five members from the Department and the Foreign
Service, two senators and three congressmen, and several businessmen.
Some Latin-American representatives were dissatisfied with the Dumbarton Oaks proposals and insisted upon a strong regional system that would
guard against aggression in practical independence of the world organization. And they wanted it created before the conference met at San Francisco. This and other objections to the Dumbarton Oaks proposals required
lengthy private discussions outside the conference rooms. Skillful drafting
by Leo Pasvolsky and Harley Notter and careful diplomacy by Senator
Warren Austin, Stettinius, and Nelson Rockefeller achieved the following
workable compromise: "The above Declaration and Recommendation
constitute a regional arrangement for dealing with such matters relating
to the maintenance of international peace and security as are appropriate

for regional action in this Hemisphere. The said arrangement ... shall be consistent with the purposes and principles of the general international organization, when established."

Although some delegations would have preferred more explicit autonomy for the Inter-American system, they received assurance from Senator Austin's statement that, if the world organization were not established or if it failed to provide security and peace in the Western Hemisphere, then the regional arrangement "would be competent and able to take care of security and peace in the Western Hemisphere so long as the war lasts and in subsequent peacetime by special treaty."

When Stettinius returned from Mexico City on March 13, 1945, he began a series of discussions with the American delegation to the San Francisco Conference. Roosevelt had appointed Stettinius as chairman of the delegation, adding as members Senators Tom Connally and Arthur H. Vandenberg, Congressmen Sol Bloom and Charles A. Eaton, former Governor Harold E. Stassen, and Virginia C. Gildersleeve, Dean of Barnard College. In addition, a large number of Departmental officers were chosen to assist the delegation. And at Stettinius's suggestion, Roosevelt had appointed Alger Hiss, Deputy Director of the Department's Office of Special Political Affairs, to the post of Secretary-General of the conference. After Roosevelt's death on April 12, President Harry S. Truman asked Stettinius to remain in office and push ahead with preparations for the San Francisco Conference on April 25.

Before leaving for San Francisco, Stettinius continued the practice he had followed with Roosevelt of bringing a daily summary of important diplomatic developments to Truman. In addition, he presented the President with a recently completed reference book on the major points of American foreign policy. Such a compilation had been conspicuously lacking when Stettinius took office as Under Secretary, and he had insisted that an intensive effort be made to prepare it. With Truman largely uninformed on wartime policy, this volume served him well in his first trying days in the White House.

Just before Truman became President, relations with the Soviet Union had begun to deteriorate. The Russians had begun to renege on certain of the Yalta decisions. When Molotov met with Truman and Stettinius on April 23, the President expressed forcefully his displeasure at the Russian failure to carry out the agreement that a reorganized Polish government would be formed. Truman added that the United States was prepared to abide by the entire Yalta protocol but "not on the basis of a one-way street." And when Molotov demanded that the puppet Lublin Polish government be represented at San Francisco, Truman bluntly refused.

Stettinius told Molotov that future aid to Russia depended on the mood, temper, and conscience of the American people and that the San Francisco Conference was Molotov's last chance to prove that the Soviet Union deserved such aid. On April 27, the third day of the conference, the Czechoslovakian delegation advocated the admission of the Lublin government. Stettinius took the floor and with great emphasis delivered a statement that Senator Vandenberg had quickly prepared. After the proposal was defeated, the Michigan Senator recorded in his diary his gratitude for the "prompt and whole-hearted consideration Stettinius gives me upon all occasions. . . ."

Several weeks later, the Russians nearly disrupted the proceedings by insisting that a dispute could not even be discussed by the Security Council without the unanimous vote of the five permanent members, unless the situation was one that could be settled by peaceful means. Stettinius told Gromyko that the United States would not join a world organization on such a basis. The Russian position confronted the conference with its most serious problem. Many delegations began to lose confidence that a United Nations could be formed and expressed the desire to return home. Stettinius decided on a dramatic step to force the Russian delegation to change its position. He phoned President Truman on June 2 and read him a prepared cable to Ambassador Averell Harriman and Harry Hopkins in Moscow, which instructed them to warn Stalin of the gravity of the situation and to explain the necessity of adjourning the conference unless the Russian demand was withdrawn. Truman approved the message. Four days later, Stalin accepted the American position, and the conference completed its work on June 26.

Although Stettinius kept the President well informed on developments throughout the conference, the Secretary was in a nearly impossible position. He did not know Truman well. And Truman did not have the confidence in Stettinius that Roosevelt had had. Sometime in April, Truman had resolved to appoint James F. Byrnes as Secretary, but he had decided not to announce the Cabinet change until after the close of the conference. It was not a well-kept secret. Stettinius sensed the accuracy of the rumor, which must have caused him a certain degree of humiliation at San Francisco. In addition, there were difficulties within the American delegation. With the exception of Harold E. Stassen, all the members were older than Stettinius; they were individualists with no experience in delegation teamwork at an international meeting, and two of the members were potential candidates for the Presidency. Although the delegation liked Stettinius personally and supported him well at the public sessions, in private several members disparaged him.

Vandenberg, at the outset of the delegation's work, was highly critical of the Secretary. He noted in his diary that Stettinius was an excellent "general manager" of the Department and got things done but that he was not firm on policy. "I urged him to take hold ... with a firm hand and *to be the Secretary of State* in fact as well as in name," the Senator wrote. Gradually, in the next few weeks, Vandenberg's attitude changed. When Truman appointed Byrnes as Secretary on June 27, the Senator was indignant. Stettinius, he wrote, "deserved better treatment after his rare performance at Frisco.... Just as we have, at long last, got Russia to understand (through Stettinius) that we occasionally mean what we say, Stettinius gets the axe...."

But during the first weeks at San Francisco, Stettinius's position with the delegation was an unhappy one. For all his ability in teamwork and public relations, he now had in his group skilled politicians unwilling to accept him as their leader in all activities. Vandenberg and others refused to authorize Stettinius to speak to the newspapermen on behalf of the delegation. And to compound this difficulty, the delegation, after each morning's session, could not agree on a statement to issue to the press. As a result, the American correspondents went to the British and French delegations to obtain information on the American position. The American press became more and more restless and critical of Stettinius. Arthur Krock told the Secretary that someone had to be appointed to brief the press, even if he was only an unofficial spokesman whom the delegation might repudiate. Krock insisted, however, that it had to be a person trusted by the correspondents. On May 10, Stettinius called Adlai E. Stevenson to San Francisco and assigned him this task. Then, with the strong backing of both Vandenberg and the Secretary, aided by Thomas K. Finletter, Stevenson attended the delegation meetings and used his own judgment about what to say to the twenty-odd reporters who were admitted to his "leak office." As a result, relations with the press improved, and there was better reporting of the American position.

Despite Stettinius's difficult position with the President, his predicament with the American delegation, and the troublesome problems created by the Russians, his sense of purpose at San Francisco was impressive. His devotion to the United Nations' idea communicated itself to other delegations and to the American public, as did his determination that the conference could not be allowed to fail.

On June 27, the day after the conference closed, Truman accepted the resignation that Stettinius had submitted at the time of Roosevelt's death. According to the President, a major factor in his decision to replace Stettinius was that the Secretary had never held an elective office. Under the Presidential-succession law then in operation, the Secretary of State was next in line to Truman. "It was my feeling," Truman has written, "that any man who stepped into the presidency should have held at least some office to which he had been elected by a vote of the people."

Truman prevailed on Stettinius to go to London that autumn as chairman of the United States delegation to the meetings of the United Nations' Preparatory Commission. Stettinius recruited an able group to help develop the rules of procedure for the organization, but illness forced him to turn the direction of the American delegation over to his deputy, Adlai E. Stevenson. Upon his recovery, Stettinius served as a member of the American delegation to the first session of the General Assembly of the UN, which began in January, 1946. In addition, he represented the United States on the Security Council until he resigned from government service on June 2, 1946.

V

As Secretary of State, Stettinius made a major contribution in reorganizing the Department. With diligence and dispatch he performed his administrative responsibilities, and this was essential to achieving results not only within the Department but with the White House, the Congress, and the public. His tenure can be viewed as the dividing line, from an organizational standpoint, between the old and the new Department. Under his leadership the Department was able to assume responsibilities that could not have been handled adequately before. The new organization created a more rational structure, permitted the appointment of many more highly qualified people, gave recognition to the new dimensions that were necessary in the conduct of foreign relations, and enabled the Department to adjust to the new power position that the nation had assumed during the war.

Both as Under Secretary and as Secretary, Stettinius enhanced public understanding of the role of the Department. And his honesty, idealism, and energy gained him the respect of many congressional leaders. This helped the Department to secure larger appropriations for its work. Stettinius's reorganization and the new men he brought into the Department improved the Department's relationship with President Roosevelt. The White House frequently had ignored the Department on wartime policy questions, except for the planning of a world organization, but now Roosevelt paid greater attention to other Department recommendations.

Although Stettinius did not himself originate substantive foreign policy, and on occasion displayed a lack of confidence in dealing with major policy perplexities, he knew how to select strong men as his associates and had a talent for getting them to work together. He conceived the idea of the Department's Planning Staff, brushed aside opposition to it, insisted on daily meetings, and presided at as many of its sessions as possible. His determination to reach decisions and his skill in curbing endless conversation and irrelevant discussion brought to fruition the ideas of men like Grew, Acheson, MacLeish, Rockefeller, and Pasvolsky. He vigorously recommended their ideas to Roosevelt and, at the same time, kept the policy men informed about the President's views.

A large portion of Stettinius's time was devoted to the conferences at Dumbarton Oaks, Yalta, Chapultepec, and San Francisco. The warm and informal manner in which he conducted meetings eased these conferences over some difficult moments. Although he, like Roosevelt, held too high hopes of what the United Nations could achieve in helping to win Russian cooperation in the postwar world, the enthusiasm he had for the UN, coupled with his organizing and promotional ability, contributed immeasurably to its formation before the war ended.

When Stettinius died in 1949, the Secretary-General of the United Nations observed that he "will live in history as one of the chief architects of the United Nations." Its creation, Trygve Lie added, owed much "to his utter devotion to the United Nations cause and to his courageous determination in the face of every obstacle to bring the United Nations into being as a world organization in which all the great nations, as well as other countries of the world, would participate."

12

James F. Byrnes

1945-1947

BY RICHARD D. BURNS
Los Angeles State College

No other American Secretary of State ever assumed the burdens of office at a more critical time in the nation's history than did James F. Byrnes in mid-summer, 1945. The international community was awakening to the harsh realization that the old power structure of the interwar years, so beneficial to the Western democracies, had been destroyed. Before the war there had been seven great nations; now statesmen could find only three—the United States, the U.S.S.R., and Great Britain. Time would reveal shortly that Britain's stature was largely dependent upon the United States. France and Italy had not stood the test of aggression and war. The Big Three had reduced Germany to impotence, managing in the process to endanger the whole tradition of Western influence in Eastern Europe. The impending defeat of Japan, plus the internal weakness of China, created vast sources of instability in the Far East. Conscious of the collapsing authority on both her eastern and western flanks, the Soviet Union was prepared to avail herself of unforeseen opportunities, armed and guided by long-standing ambitions. Victory over the Axis would not in itself return America to an accustomed world of stability and security.

Wartime relations between the United States and England had been promising. These two nations, through the combined Chiefs of Staff, joint military operations under single field commanders, and various joint commissions, had, in the words of Winston Churchill, become "somewhat mixed up together." No one in 1945 doubted that this wartime cooperation would continue into the postwar world. With the Soviets, however, the United States had maintained what General John R. Deane termed a "strange alliance." This relationship was clouded by suspicion and, more importantly, by persistent conflicts of interest and principle. Although President Franklin D. Roosevelt had recognized these differences, he believed that a sincere recognition of Russia's security interests and the involvement of that nation in the United Nations would both prevent the U.S.S.R. from withdrawing again into isolation and lay the foundation for world peace through Big Three unity. Unfortunately, at the moment of victory over Germany, the Soviet determination to gain something more tangible than the triumph of principles as the result of her war effort was already challenging all the wartime assumptions of the American people.

On July 2, 1945, President Harry S. Truman formally recalled from retirement the "painless statesman," James F. Byrnes, to head the Department of State. Weeks earlier Truman had decided to appoint Byrnes to replace the youthful Edward R. Stettinius, Jr., and had been waiting for the appropriate time to make public Stettinius's resignation, which he had held since the death of F.D.R. The successful termination of the San Francisco Conference, which created the United Nations, on June 26, 1945, provided such an opportunity. At last Truman could have the Secretary of State that filled his requirements.

Byrnes was no novice in American politics or public life. He had observed the government at first hand "from the floors of both the House and Senate, from the vantage point of the Supreme Court [and] from inside the White House." His rise to political prominence was in large measure a typical American success story. Byrnes was born of immigrant Irish stock at Charleston, South Carolina, in 1879, a few weeks after the death of his father. At fourteen, he left school to work as an office boy in a local law firm. He served briefly as stenographer in the local district court, entering the bar in 1903. In 1908 he was elected to the office of circuit solicitor and two years later to Congress.

Genial, humorous, and charming, Byrnes was frequently described as a man who "hasn't an enemy in the world." To associates the friendliness, even temperament, and informality of this small-featured man were his most striking personal characteristics and, no doubt, a major factor in his political success. Coming to the Senate in 1931, he quickly became so renowned as a compromiser of conflicting interests that he was termed "a veritable Cardinal Richelieu of the cloakroom." As a reward for his efforts in promoting New Deal legislation, Roosevelt named him to the Supreme Court in June, 1941. Sixteen months later, in October, 1942, Byrnes willingly resigned from the Court to head the Office of Economic Stabilization. As Director of this agency, he became known as the "assistant president." Byrnes demonstrated such outstanding administrative ability that Roosevelt turned over to him much of the management of domestic affairs and thus freed himself to concentrate on foreign issues and the winning of the war. Impressed by Byrnes's broad knowledge of the domestic situation and its relationship to postwar economic questions, Roosevelt invited Byrnes to accompany the Presidential party to Yalta. Here Byrnes met Stalin for the first time and viewed the inner working of big-power diplomacy. Shortly after his return from Yalta and just prior to Roosevelt's death, Byrnes resigned his White House position to return to his home in Spartanburg, South Carolina.

During the New Deal years Byrnes was never regarded as a great social or economic thinker. He was not a theoretician. Rather he enjoyed the reputation, when supporting F.D.R.'s measures in Congress, of being the administration's chief legislative trouble shooter. *Time* magazine described Byrnes as a "catalytic agent" whose "talents are those of a compromiser; his friends call him a harmonizer; his enemies, a fixer." Yet Byrnes was not without convictions. A study of his record reveals far too much consistency to permit the judgment that he was concerned only with political appeasement. One contemporary has written that "in all of the things he advocated or opposed, Byrnes had always been three things: a realistic politician, a Southerner, and a loyal Democrat." In practical maneuvering, however, his creed was expediency, and his energies, both in Congress and in the Roosevelt administration, were always directed toward attaining the best solution within reach. Byrnes once said that he subscribed to the doctrine that "politics is the art of the possible." But he would soon discover that maintaining such a realistic philosophy in the conduct of American foreign policy vis-à-vis the Soviet Union was exceedingly difficult.

II

Although Byrnes was accorded the unusual honor of unanimous approval by the Senate, without either a hearing or a debate, his appointment evoked mixed feelings. This dichotomy in the American reaction was a clear measure of the confusion in national thought about the diplomatic future. The American people had been assured throughout the war years that the defeat of Germany and Japan would terminate the age-old problems of power politics. It had been easy, given the American tradition of viewing international relations in ethical terms, for their leaders to turn the war into a giant crusade against "the makers of war, the breeders of hate." Rejecting in 1945 the material and moral cost of maintaining a traditional foreign policy based on power politics, the balance of power, spheres of influence, and even alliances, many American leaders pointed to the United Nations as the sure hope for future peace. Convinced that the experience of war would continue to promote cooperation among the victors, much of the public looked no further than Byrnes's political acumen and his enthusiasm for the United Nations in assessing his qualifications for the Secretaryship. They liked what they saw.

Ernest K. Lindley observed in *Newsweek:* "If Truman had chosen anyone else for Secretary of State, it would have been astonishing." In length and breadth of experience in public life, Byrnes was "unquestionably the No. 2 Democrat of today." Lindley admitted that the new Secretary probably knew no more about foreign affairs than did any other intelligent citizen, but he added, "Byrnes is a man of steady judgment." Endorsing this evaluation, the *New York Times* commented, "A sense of realism is a definite part of his philosophy." What mattered to many observers was that Byrnes had been a very able and successful parliamentarian, thus demonstrating qualities which they believed were needed in the State Department. If foreign policy in the future would consist of carrying international legislation through the Assembly of the United Nations, the South Carolinian certainly seemed to be the man for the job.

For many Americans the United Nations had become the ultimate end of foreign policy, and its proper use the chief challenge of a Secretary of State. Thomas F. Reynolds, writing in the July, 1945, issue of *The New Republic,* pointed out that the new era was at hand when world opinion, at last, would have its way. In a world, he added,

> where peace is maintained by a Security Council, an Assembly and an International Court of Justice, it is important that nations be governed in their decisions by their own interpretations of the universal concept of justice, equality and law. While the United States, Russia, Britain, France and China, as the Big Five, maintain peace on the precious knife-edge of their unanimity, it is well for them to know that the other nations of the world are making judgments and that they will be held to ultimate account before the moral bar of the opinion of the men and women who people this world.

There were those on Capitol Hill, however, who saw little relationship, in 1945, between foreign affairs and the legislative process. Many leading congressmen, fearing that the world was returning to an era of power politics in which compromise was not the only answer, evinced private concern over Brynes's appointment. Senator Tom Connally, chairman of the Senate Committee on Foreign Relations, observed coldly that Byrnes "was not trained in foreign service and knew little about foreign affairs." Although he did not voice his reservations to the President, Connally was worried about the South Carolinian's lack of breadth in precise situations and his devotion to expediency. Another Senator, Arthur H. Vandenberg of Michigan, was even more alarmed. "Jimmy Byrnes is a grand guy," he wrote to his wife, "for *any* other job down here. But his life has been a career of compromise...." Would he face up to the Russians, the Michigan Senator wondered, would he insist upon American principles, and would he be immovable when a principle was at stake? For the new Secretary the issue was clear: one day he would be forced to choose between expediency and principle.

But that moment of decision still lay in the future. On July 3, 1945, Byrnes took the oath of office. To friends and well-wishers who had gathered on the rose-covered east portico of the White House for the occasion, Byrnes said:

> The making of enduring peace will depend on something more than skilled diplomacy, something more than paper treaties, something more even than the best charter the wisest statesman can draft. Important as is diplomacy, important as are the peace settlements and the basic charter of world peace, these cannot succeed unless backed by the will of the peoples of different lands not only to have peace but to live together as good neighbors. . . .
>
> Today there can be no doubt that the people of this war-ravaged earth want to live in a free and peaceful world. The supreme task of statesmanship the world over is to help them to understand that they can have peace and freedom only if they tolerate and respect the rights of others to opinions, feelings and way of life which they do not and cannot share.

This initial statement indicated clearly that the new Secretary viewed his task as largely that of seeking compromise among conflicting ideas and interests on the world scene. Indeed, he seemed prepared to deal with the Russians much as he had dealt in the past with Republican Senators. He looked upon the United Nations as a world congress which provided the best means of preventing wars and ensuring peace. "If we and the other powers are prepared to act in defense of law," he remarked, "the United Nations can prevent war." There was ample room in the world, he said, for more than one ideology, more than one way of life, more than one honest opinion. Open diplomacy was essential for airing these differences. Byrnes admitted that there might be some occasions for secret conferences, but he insisted that attempts to keep all important negotiations confidential would result in misleading and sensationalized newspaper accounts which in the long run would be more detrimental to settlement than open diplomacy.

For Byrnes, bipartisan cooperation in Congress was another essential element in the creation of adequate foreign policy. To build a people's foreign policy, he said, required that it be "bi-partisan in its origin and development [and] national rather than political in its conduct and its character." Although he tended to minimize the importance of Republican support at the London and Moscow Conferences of 1945, Byrnes recognized fully the need of bipartisan backing when peace negotiations began at Paris the following year. He assured Republican leaders that the administration would not ask them to share responsibility for the conduct of the nation's foreign relations unless they were advised fully both of the government's decisions and of its purposes. The record of Byrnes's relations with Senator Vandenberg measures his success in maintaining bipartisan cooperation. This relationship, which started in mid-1945 in a doubtful and even critical mood, terminated in mutual confidence and respect. To Vandenberg, in January, 1947, Byrnes had become a "very great American."

III

If Byrnes intended through compromise to maintain the grand alliance and achieve thereby a peaceful and stable world, he soon discovered that the Russians were more demanding than had been his Republican opponents in the Senate. For the Russians harbored ambitions and fears, not shared by the West, which placed the divisive issues of Eastern and Central Europe beyond the realm of compromise—at least on terms which any American Secretary of State could accept. Yet within the limits imposed on him by established principles, Byrnes attempted to face the Soviet problem realistically.

The growing dichotomy between Soviet and American purpose which plagued Byrnes and the nation in 1945 had its inception during the war years. Stalin had made it clear as early as 1943 that the U.S.S.R. would demand some control of Slavic Europe because it had fallen into Nazi hands so easily. It was equally certain that the Soviet Union, having been subjected to a destructive German invasion, would be far more vindictive than Britain and the United States in dealing with the defeated Axis Powers. In response to these clear designs of the Kremlin, the United States government pursued the contradictory policies of encouraging the Soviets to destroy Nazi power in Eastern Europe and, at the same time, of assuring the American people that they could anticipate a world-wide peace settlement based on the principles of the Atlantic Charter. Actually the contradictions were even more precise. During the war Stalin made no secret of his determination to foster governments in Eastern Europe friendly to the Soviet Union. Roosevelt and Churchill proclaimed that the nations freed from German domination would be allowed to choose their own forms of government, but they assured Stalin, at the same time, that they had no intention of supporting anti-Soviet forces along the Russian periphery.

The total incompatibility of such purposes was becoming clear by 1945, and the illusion of Big Three unity at Yalta, in February, scarcely concealed it. Having lost control of Slavic Europe to Russian armies, the Western Allies attempted to salvage what they could of the Atlantic

Charter in the form of a Declaration on Liberated Europe. Under it the Big Three pledged themselves to assist the former Nazi satellites "to solve by democratic means their pressing political and economic problems" and to acknowledge "the right of all peoples to choose the form of government under which they will live." This Yalta Charter was Roosevelt's eleventh-hour effort to prevent the creation of a Soviet sphere of influence in Eastern Europe.

Much of American leadership remained optimistic. Shortly before he died, Roosevelt wired to Churchill: "I would minimize the general Soviet problem as much as possible because these problems, in one form or another, seem to arise every day and most of them straighten out...." Two years later, Byrnes recalled: "I had assumed that at the end of hostilities an era of peace would be so deeply desired by those nations that had fought the war in unity that the inevitable differences of opinion could be resolved without serious difficulty." Unfortunately, in 1945 there no longer existed a vast body of mutual wartime interests which would permit American leadership to put off the ultimate necessity of recognizing the Soviet determination to maintain some tangible evidences of victory.

Europe's future was being determined in 1945 less by Allied diplomacy than by the westward advance of Soviet armies along the collapsing German lines. Russia's military and geographic advantages on the Continent, aided by the fortunes of war, crucial military decisions, and the refusal of Secretary of State Cordell Hull to negotiate the Eastern European question during the war, permitted Soviet leaders to create a vast sphere of influence across Eastern Europe by the spring of 1945. This sphere was separated from Western Europe by a line running from Stettin to Trieste and along the northern border of Greece. Churchill, totally conscious of what was occurring, wired Truman on May 12, 1945:

> I am profoundly concerned about the European situation. I have always worked for friendship with Russia, but like you, I feel deep anxiety because of their misinterpretation of the Yalta decisions, their attitudes toward Poland, their overwhelming influence in the Balkans... and above all their power to maintain very large armies in the field for a long time.... Surely it is vital now to come to an understanding with Russia, or see where we are with her, before weakening our armies mortally or retiring to the zones of occupation.... Of course we may take the view that Russia will behave impeccably, and no doubt that offers the most convenient solution. To sum up, this issue of a settlement with Russia before our strength has gone seems to me to dwarf all others.

Joseph E. Davies, Truman's special envoy to London, reported that Churchill was too pessimistic. He accused the British leader of being more concerned over the future of England's position in Europe than over the future of peace. Stalin's knowledge of Western hostility toward Russia,

Davies concluded, was responsible for much of the aggressiveness in Soviet policy after Yalta. The President, with his advisers concurring, informed Churchill that the United States would not use for bargaining purposes the matter of retirement to agreed zones of occupation.

At Potsdam, in July, Byrnes faced the Soviet leaders for the first time as Secretary of State. He set out immediately in search of a formula to bridge the differences between Russia and the West. The result was frustrating. Although Byrnes achieved quick agreement on the establishment of the Council of Foreign Ministers, the Russians were more adamant on the concrete issues of Germany and Eastern Europe. The United States, the Secretary assured a mystified and suspicious Molotov, "sincerely desires Russia to have friendly countries on her borders, but we believe [the U.S.S.R.] should seek the friendship of the people rather than of any particular government." His government, said Byrnes, did not wish to become involved in the elections of other countries; it merely desired to join other nations in observing elections in Italy, Greece, Hungary, Rumania, and Bulgaria. Vigorous Western protests against Stalin's unilateral violation of the Yalta agreements resulted in some revision of procedural matters but left all fundamental issues substantially untouched. Byrnes left Potsdam in good spirits, but less hopeful than he had been at Yalta. If much hard bargaining remained, he still was not convinced that realistic settlements of mutual benefit were beyond the realm of possibility.

At the Council of Foreign Ministers meeting at London, during September, 1945, the breach in the wartime alliance continued to widen. Here, indeed, world power relationships entered a new, more disturbing phase. Shortly after the conference opened, the observant London correspondent of the *New York Times* reported: "The diplomatic tussles in San Francisco were shadow-boxing compared to the sparring for position developing as the Council of Foreign Ministers gets down to cases. At the Golden Gate conference, the great debates were on general principles of world organization. Here they involve concrete questions of national interest."

From the outset, the negotiations were deadlocked over the nature of the Rumanian and Bulgarian governments and the right of France and China to enter the treaty negotiations with the former German satellites. Soviet intransigence drove the other four powers into a solid opposing bloc and accelerated the trend toward a bipolar world. Foreign Minister Molotov made it clear that Russia's price for cooperation was Western recognition of the Soviet's Eastern European satellite governments. The Soviets were determined to erase the so-called *cordon sanitaire* which had been constructed along Russia's western borders at Versailles. Byrnes assured Molotov again that the United States was not interested in seeing anything but governments friendly to the Soviet Union in Eastern Europe. Molotov replied that this could not be true. This conclusion, he continued, was based on the fact that the Radescu regime in Rumania, which had been hostile to Russia, had received cordial American and British support. Yet, he said, when the Groza government, which was friendly to the Soviet Union, was established, the Western powers had withdrawn their recognition. Molotov charged that any government in Eastern Europe satisfactory to the West would be hostile to Russia. Byrnes replied that Soviet pressure had forced the Groza government on the Rumanian people. "Our objective," the Secretary explained to the quizzical Russian, "is a government both friendly to the Soviet Union and representative of all the democratic elements of the country." American leadership refused to agree with Molotov that these aims might be mutually exclusive.

Molotov persisted in his accusations that the American demand for self-determination in Eastern Europe reflected a hidden hostility toward the Soviet Union; nothing that Byrnes could say would dissuade him. To the Russian's continuing demand for security against Germany, Byrnes countered with an offer binding the United States to keep that nation demilitarized for twenty-five years. Such a security measure appeared to the Russians less substantial than one based on their own power. Eventually Byrnes returned to the United States, unable to modify the Soviet stand on any of the fundamental issues that were dividing the world. Truman and Byrnes viewed the disagreements as a breakdown in communications. Most American writers regarded the setback as temporary.

Byrnes refused to accept the notion of a divided world. In his radio address of October 6, he stressed the exploratory nature of the London talks, the procedural advances made, and the agreements on such substantive issues as the internationalization of Trieste's port facilities. Byrnes, convinced that peacemaking could not be the exclusive concern of the big powers, was cautiously optimistic that Russia would eventually permit all the Allies to assist in negotiating the final settlements.

Before the *New York Herald Tribune* Forum on October 31, Byrnes acknowledged again the central conflict between interest and principle in Russian-American relations. Said the Secretary:

> Far from opposing, we have sympathized with, for example, the effort of the Soviet Union to draw into closer and more friendly association with her Central and Eastern European neighbors. We are fully aware of her special security interests in those countries and we have recognized those interests in the arrangements made for the occupation and control of the former enemy States.
>
> We can appreciate the determination of the people of the Soviet Union that never again will they tolerate the pursuit of policies in those countries deliberately directed against the Soviet Union's security and way of life. And America will never join any groups in those countries in hostile intrigue against the Soviet Union.

Having recognized the Soviet security interest in Eastern and Central Europe, Byrnes turned to the American principle of self-determination. People, he said, "should be free to choose their own form of government, a government based upon the consent of the governed and adapted to their way of life. . . . The whole-hearted acceptance of this principle by all the United Nations will greatly strengthen the bonds of friendship among nations everywhere." Then the Secretary warned the Soviets that the United States would not recognize a system of regional arrangements as a substitute for a world system, for such spheres of influence would be a threat to world peace. "We live in one world," he said, "and in this atomic age regional isolationism is even more dangerous than is national isolationism. We cannot have the kind of cooperation necessary for peace in a world divided into spheres of exclusive influence and special privilege."

During the autumn of 1945, Byrnes and other American leaders questioned the nation's rapid demobilization. Japan's unexpected surrender had thrown into confusion the military plans calling for the gradual scaling down and redeployment of the American Armed Forces. The crusade was over. Who would tell the citizens of the United States that a large military force was now required to check a former ally? Americans who had watched postwar diplomacy with unconcern greeted demobilization with enthusiasm. Suspicion of Soviet intentions was still sufficiently limited to prevent any political group from resisting the popular demand to "bring our boys home." Actually many politicians clamored for even greater rapidity in demobilization.

Not until mid-October did high-ranking administration officials protest publicly against this unplanned dissipation of military strength. On October 16, Byrnes, Navy Secretary James V. Forrestal, and General George C. Marshall agreed that "it was most inadvisable for this country to continue accelerating the demobilization of our Armed Forces at the present rate." Two weeks later, Marshall reminded the nation that during the critical year of 1940, in which France fell, the United States spent almost four times as much on sporting events, tobacco, and alcoholic products as it did on the Army and Navy. Viewed in the light of the clear warning of the late thirties, he added, "it would seem that the tragedy of our unwillingness to maintain what Washington called a respectable military posture becomes monstrous." The American people, Marshall observed, might do well to give sober thought to the problem of national defense again before it was too late. Forrestal suggested that the President go before the American people with the details of Western differences with the Russians. Byrnes demurred on this point. He was dubious, he said, about giving the Russians "an excuse for claiming that we had furnished provocation which justified their action." The administration's fears regarding demobilization had no effect on the general tendencies of the times. Perhaps it mattered little, for the Soviets were already in possession of all the areas in question. Nothing less than the threatened use of military force would have driven them back. A mere state of preparedness would no longer secure a settlement on Western terms.

There remained one partially compensating source of military power in American hands—the atomic bomb. In December, 1945, Byrnes informed the Senate Committee on Foreign Relations that he had prepared a formula for resolving the atomic-energy issue between the United States and Russia. This plan, suggesting as its first step the exchange of atomic information, shocked the senators, for inspection and control under the United Nations had become the *sine qua non* of any agreement. Although they were willing to concede that the Russians would probably discover the atomic secrets in time, the senators were reluctant to part with them unless there was absolute and effective agreement on control. Byrnes had not rejected the necessity for inspection and control, but the senators considered his formula too liberal. Molotov had warned Byrnes that the Soviet Union was not reconciled to a position of military inferiority. He said that Russia would soon have atomic energy "and many other things." So confident was the Kremlin that it would offer nothing, not even safeguards, as a condition for receiving technical information from the United States.

At the Moscow Conference of late December, 1945, Byrnes succeeded temporarily in breaking the Soviet-American impasse. Without special preparation or Republican advisers, the Secretary went to Moscow against the judgment of veteran diplomats and correspondents. "I believed," Byrnes has written in his defense, "that if we met in Moscow, where I would have a chance to talk to Stalin, we might remove the barriers to the peace treaties. The peace of the world was too important for us to be unwilling to take a chance on securing an agreement after full discussions." Although he eventually gained Stalin's acceptance of a peace conference, he was forced to compromise on his London stand.

Both Byrnes and his advisers, chiefly Ambassador Averell Harriman and career officer Charles E. Bohlen, were convinced at Moscow that the indefinite nonrecognition of the Soviet position in the Balkans would achieve nothing tangible for the United States. (The United States had extended recognition on October 20 to the provisional government of Austria and two weeks later to the provisional government of Hungary.) At Moscow, without openly rejecting American principles, Byrnes accepted the existing Rumanian and Bulgarian governments. Stalin agreed to a token representation of pro-Western parties and pledged early free elections. If these agreements represented a considerable retreat from the previous American position, they recognized essentially that the United States had few choices remaining. Harriman and Bohlen, among the best versed of American diplomats on Soviet affairs, believed that the Secretary had secured a more specific agreement than had been made at Yalta. The general reaction in the United States and elsewhere was one of relief. At least the negotiations would continue.

IV

Byrnes received a cold reception in Washington. Sumner Welles denounced the Balkan settlements as a betrayal of the Balkan peoples and of Roosevelt's ideals. "Byrnes, I concluded after studying the entire record," Truman wrote in his memoirs, "had taken it upon himself to move the foreign policy of the United States in a direction to which I could not, and would not agree." The President charged that the successes of the Moscow Conference were unreal. The Iranian and atomic-energy issues were untouched. In a semiauthorized biography of the President, Jonathan Daniels quoted him as saying that "Byrnes lost his nerve at Moscow." Later, Truman would date his break with Byrnes over his displeasure at his Secretary's actions in Moscow.

Although resistance to the Secretary's policies had been mounting within the administration, the chief demand for a tougher policy came from Byrnes's political opposition. Congressional Republicans had supported the wartime policies of Roosevelt, but they were not hesitant in their criticism of Democratic leadership when the great hopes for the postwar world failed to materialize. Despite its tremendous wartime effort, the nation somehow had realized far less security than the sacrifice and expenditures seemed to warrant. Republicans eventually would demand of Truman the fulfillment of what Roosevelt had promised—an international settlement based on the principles of the Atlantic Charter.

Republican pressure on Byrnes to concede nothing to the Russians began with the failure of the London Conference. John Foster Dulles, his Republican adviser, cautioned a national radio audience on October 6 that the United States dared accept only those territorial settlements which conformed to the wishes of the people concerned. Soviet intransigence, he said, was designed to determine whether this nation would really hold to its principles. For Dulles, the beginning at London had been satisfactory because American leadership had not deserted its principles. Looking to the future, Dulles added:

> We are emerging from six years of war, during which morality and principle have increasingly been put aside in favor of military expediency. The war has now ended and with that ending principle and morality must be re-established in the world.... It devolves upon us to give leadership in restoring principle as a guide to conduct. If we

do not do that, the world will not be worth living in.... For we now know that this planet will, like others, become uninhabitable unless men subject their physical power to the restraints of moral law.

Upon his return from London, Byrnes received an admonition from the Senate Foreign Relations Committee to "get tough" with Stalin. Less than a month later, the House of Representatives, with only two Republicans opposing, attempted to bar the use of American funds in the Russian satellites. These actions indicated a decided shift in Congress, particularly among Republicans, toward a new, anti-Soviet attitude. Then, on December 5, a joint committee of House and Senate Republicans endorsed a policy declaration chiding the Truman administration's Eastern European policy:

> We believe in fulfilling to the greatest possible degree our war pledges to small nations that they shall have the right to choose the form of government under which they will live and that sovereign rights and self-government shall be restored to those who have been forcibly deprived of them. We deplore any desertion of these principles.

This was a declaration of hope, not a plan for action. Unfortunately, for many Americans, unwilling either to concede principles or to employ any force stronger than argumentation, the promise of success lay only in the continued search for some magic phraseology which might turn the Russians out of Eastern and Central Europe.

When it became obvious that the new Polish regime was involved in political reprisals against non-Communist leaders, Byrnes instructed the American Embassy in Warsaw to "inform the Polish government that we are relying on that government to take the necessary steps to assure the freedom and security which are essential to the successful holding of free elections." Vandenberg objected at once, declaring that it was not enough to rely on the Polish government to "vindicate the honor and the pledge of the United States of America." We must rely, he said, "on our own moral authority in a world which, in my opinion, craves our moral leadership." Such firmness did not mean war, he insisted in a passage reminiscent of the internationalism of the interwar years:

> It means, first, that we must insistently demand prompt and dependable assurances that the Yalta and Potsdam pledges in behalf of free elections be effectively fulfilled. It means, in other words, that we shall lift the powerful voice of America in behalf of the inviolable sanctity of international agreements to which we are a party. If this does not suffice, it means, then, that we shall scrupulously collect our facts; draw our relentless indictment if the facts so justify; and present it in the forum of the United Nations and demand judgment from the organized conscience of the world.

Few Republicans would have demanded actions more explicit than those suggested here by their acknowledged congressional spokesman on foreign affairs.

During the first two months of 1946, American foreign policy was subjected to both careful scrutiny and redefinition in successive speeches by Vandenberg, Byrnes, and Connally, all of whom had witnessed Soviet tactics at first hand. Vandenberg led off the series late in February in a direct criticism of Byrnes's stewardship:

> I assert my own belief that we can live together in reasonable harmony if the United States speaks as plainly upon all occasions as Russia does; if the United States just as vigorously sustains its own purposes and its ideals upon all occasions as Russia does; if we abandon the miserable fiction, often encouraged by our fellow travelers, that we somehow jeopardize the peace if our candor is as firm as Russia's always is; and if we assume a moral leadership which we have too frequently allowed to lapse.

Somehow the Senator seemed to overlook the fact that the Russian purposes and ideals were supported by the actual occupation and control of all areas in conflict.

Byrnes, the following evening (in what one wit termed the Second Vandenberg Concerto), acknowledged that conflicts of interests existed between the former allies. The difficulty was, he declared, "that the path to permanent peace is not so easy to see and to follow as was the path to victory." Whereas he advocated a firm policy toward Russia, he warned that ideological barriers should not prevent the United States and the U.S.S.R. from living together in the same world. But, the Secretary added, "we will not and we cannot stand aloof if force or the threat of force is used contrary to the purposes and principles of the [United Nations] Charter. America is a great power, and we must act as a great power." Connally supported Byrnes's new emphasis on strength by recommending a return to universal military training. Any policy of patience and firmness, he said, must be anchored to "an adequate Army, a superior Navy and a superlative air force ... to sustain our international rights and obligations."

To re-establish a bipartisan approach to American policies, Byrnes invited Senators Vandenberg and Connally to accompany him to the first of the Paris Peace Conferences in late April, 1946. Connally was the chairman of the Senate Foreign Relations Committee, but Vandenberg controlled the Republican votes necessary for successful senatorial action on any negotiated treaty. According to Connally, the Secretary almost ignored him at Paris and gave his attention to Vandenberg. This assured bipartisan support in the Senate, but to the complaining Connally it gave the Michigan Republican a disproportionate voice in policy decisions.

At Paris the first conference recessed on May 16 without showing much diplomatic progress. Byrnes seemed determined to make no concessions to the Russians. One high French official recognized the new toughness in the Secretary. Byrnes in London, he said, had given the "impression of sincerity and willingness to negotiate; in Paris he gave the impression of a clever politician determined not to give an inch. . . ." Instead of attempting to draw compromise from the Russians, he seemed to be involved only in putting the onus of deadlock on the Soviet government. Byrnes, the official concluded, "seemed most interested in convincing the Russians that the sucker season has ended, and that henceforth the Americans would be tough."

As late as the Moscow Conference, Byrnes appeared to be seeking realistic solutions to the questions posed by the Soviet Union, assuring the Russians that the United States wanted only governments friendly to that nation along its European periphery, searching for guarantees against the resurgence of German aggressiveness, and even accepting situations over which the United States had no control. But at Paris the political and public pressure against compromise destroyed most of the alternatives for American diplomacy and moved it from the realm of action to the realm of words. Byrnes could no longer practice the give-and-take for which he was renowned. In the House and Senate, he was to write in 1947, "the art of legislating is the art of intelligent compromise. No one congressman can have his way; the spirit of compromise is necessary to secure the essential majority." Those obstinate people who insist upon their solutions to issues, he added, would attempt to justify their course "by asserting there can be no compromise when a principle is involved, and [they are] likely to see a 'principle' in every issue. . . . In my experience there were really few bills in which a great principle was involved; the issues were usually matters of policy, not principle." By the spring of 1946, Byrnes could only deny that there was any relationship between domestic and international politics. For him and for the nation, diplomacy had become a matter of principle, not policy.

After one heated session at Paris, a member of the Soviet delegation told Bohlen, who was attending the conference as an adviser to Byrnes, that it was impossible for him to understand the Americans. They had such a good reputation for trading, he said, and yet in speech after speech the Secretary of State spoke only about principles. With all sincerity, the Soviet delegate added, "Why doesn't he stop talking about principles, and get down to business and start trading?" When Byrnes admitted finally that international relations were governed by principles, not issues, the conflict between the United States and Russia entered another, more vituperative, less promising phase.

Vandenberg applauded the Secretary's new firmness. "I do not consider that our American position was at all inflexible," he told the Senate upon his return from Paris. "We did relentlessly decline to surrender our principles. We can compromise within principles, but we cannot compromise principles themselves." Byrnes's concept of policy, Vandenberg added, was founded on the "moralities of the Atlantic and San Francisco charters." This kind of foreign policy, the Senator concluded, he would support under any administration.

Winston Churchill's "Iron Curtain" speech at Fulton, Missouri, in March, 1946, added to official American policy statements, triggered all shades of criticism of the new "get tough with Russia" posture. Harold E. Stassen, former Governor of Minnesota, charged Churchill with saber rattling and the administration with trying to destroy the United Nations. Commerce Secretary Henry A. Wallace caused a furor when he said that the American air base in Iceland was being maintained solely as a military threat to the U.S.S.R. Harold L. Ickes, former Secretary of the Interior, demanded that Truman pursue the policies of President Roosevelt. The people, he warned, "do not feel comfortable with the sniping at Russia which is being indulged in." In the Senate, Claude Pepper of Florida took the lead in denouncing the new anti-Sovietism. "Not a morning passes," he told a New York dinner audience in February, 1946, "but that I read in the newspapers some new conscienceless attack on our great ally ... which for nearly two years singlehandedly held the line against the Nazi juggernaut." Greatly annoyed at these outbursts, Byrnes complained that he was being "shot in the back" by his own friends and colleagues.

Wallace forced the showdown within the administration with his famous Madison Square Garden address in September. While Byrnes was still in Paris, Wallace, announcing that he spoke with the President's consent, told his New York audience that the "real peace treaty we now need is between the United States and Russia." What he would do with Russian intransigence he was not sure, except that he would rule out the use of force. He was equally doubtful that any rhetorical device would work. "We are reckoning with a force which cannot be handled successfully by a 'get tough with Russia' policy," he said. "The tougher we get the tougher the Russians will get." The nation, he concluded, must be firm and patient but must never permit the British to return the world to the old balance-of-power manipulations.

Byrnes was distressed at what appeared to be a complete reversal in the President's position. When Vandenberg announced to the press that perhaps the foundations for bipartisan unity no longer existed, the Secretary complained to Truman that all their efforts to build a solid foreign policy had been destroyed overnight. Byrnes became even more distraught when a Wallace memorandum, written several weeks earlier, was published. This document accused the Democratic leadership, in its effort to obtain bipartisanship, of giving in "too much to isolationism masquerading as tough realism in international affairs." Herein Wallace was pointing to the growing discrepancy between ends and means in American policy, but his assumption that Vandenberg was dictating the anti-Soviet attitudes of the United States government rendered his position untenable. Byrnes made it clear that either he or Wallace must leave the administration. On the following day the President announced that he had accepted Wallace's resignation.

Neither two months of debating nor two weeks of voting solved any of the major East-West issues at Paris. Yet Byrnes, despite his growing impatience, won substantial concessions from the Russians on Italy, notably, a free city of Trieste and British control of the former Italian colonies. He took the conference's recommendations on Italy, Bulgaria, Rumania, and Hungary to the United Nations in New York for its approval. The treaties, Byrnes admitted in a radio address, were "not written as we would write them if we had a free hand." But he was convinced that they were as good as any the Western powers would extract from a reluctant Russian government.

V

Byrnes's concentration on Soviet affairs made it impossible for him to devote much attention to Latin America or the Far East. This was unfortunate, for the western Pacific particularly was confronting the nation with a series of urgent and difficult problems. The forces against stability in this area became more intense with the collapse of Japan in August, 1945. As early as May, Forrestal warned that it was time for the United States to determine with some precision what political objectives it hoped to achieve in the Far East. "How far and how thoroughly do we want to beat Japan?" he asked. "What is our policy on Russian influence in the Far East? Do we desire a counter weight to that influence? And should it be China or should it be Japan?" From Moscow, Ambassador Harriman reminded the administration in Washington that it must decide on a strong or a weak China. For him a strong China was required to limit Soviet influence in the Far East. The administration agreed, but how to achieve a strong China was not apparent.

Japanese occupation of Chinese territory from 1937 to 1945 had provided a temporary interlude in the internal strife which had plagued China since the twenties. When the Japanese threat was removed, the struggle for power between Chiang Kai-shek's Nationalists and the Chinese Communists broke out with renewed vigor. General Albert C. Wedemeyer recommended, on November 20, 1945, that the United States either withdraw from China at once or announce its intention of continuing military and economic support for Chiang. At the same time, he warned the administration of the consequences of involving itself in the Chinese civil war. "If the unification of China and Manchuria under Chinese Nationalist forces is to be a U.S. policy," he wrote, "involvement in fratricidal warfare and in war with the Soviet Union must be accepted and would definitely require additional U.S. forces far beyond those presently available in the theater to implement the policy." The question of Chinese politics, believed Wedemeyer, should be decided by the State Department and not by the military leaders.

Byrnes adopted the ambivalent policy of supporting the Nationalists diplomatically but of denying them military aid to carry on their civil war against the Reds. With the approval of Army and Navy officials, Byrnes suggested that "perhaps the wise course would be to try to force the Chinese government and the Chinese Communists to get together on a compromise basis, perhaps telling Generalissimo Chiang Kai-shek that we will stop the aid to his government unless he goes along with this."

Although Byrnes was concerned primarily with European affairs at London and Moscow, he succeeded, against the pressure of Stalin and Molotov, in establishing the concept of American predominance in occupied Japan. The United States government, underestimating Soviet interest, assumed that the Russians were simply being obstructive when they demanded the establishment of a powerful Allied Control Council for Japan. The Secretary, who was promoting the creation of the Far Eastern Advisory Commission, rejected Molotov's proposal. In October, 1945, Stalin complained to Harriman that in Far Eastern affairs the United States was behaving as though the Soviet Union were a satellite state rather than an ally. He objected to General Douglas MacArthur's "one-man" rule in Japan and said that the Soviet representatives in Tokyo were being treated like pieces of furniture. Nevertheless, the United States–sponsored Far Eastern Commission, approved by Stalin at the Moscow Conference, began to function in Washington in February, 1946. This commission quickly gave formal sanction to the preemptive control of the Japanese occupation by the United States.

Ambassador to China Patrick J. Hurley's sudden resignation in November, 1945, which came as a great surprise to both Byrnes and Truman, brought the China question into focus. Hurley charged that the President and the Secretary of State had failed to make public their purposes for China. Byrnes replied to Hurley's accusations on December 7. "During the war," he said, "the immediate goal of the United States in China was to promote a military union of the several political factions in order to bring their combined power to bear upon our common enemy, Japan. Our longer-range goal, then as now, and a goal of at least equal importance, is the development of a strong, united, and democratic China." The Secretary called for the dissident elements within China to "approach the settlement of their differences with a genuine willingness to compromise." The most satisfactory base for democracy in China, he insisted, was Chiang's government, but he recognized that it would require broadening to include representatives of large groups which did not have a voice in Chinese affairs.

Hurley's hearing before the Senate Foreign Relations Committee and Byrnes's rebuttal constituted, until 1947, the only real political debate over the State Department's China policy. But unfortunately these investigations of Chinese affairs did not clarify the major issues in the Far East for the public, the Congress, or the executive. Nor did the decisions relative to China become part of the Byrnes-Vandenberg bipartisan policies. Hurley accused his Foreign Service personnel of undermining his policies. Some American officials, he charged, appeared too eager to promote unity between the Nationalists and Communists, even at the expense of Chiang's government. Byrnes defended the State Department and Foreign Service officers. When he promised an investigation of those associated with China policy, the Senate committee voted to discontinue the hearing and to dispense with a report. Yet Hurley had focused sufficient attention on the American dilemma in China to induce the administration to dispatch General George C. Marshall to China to seek a coalition government.

On December 15, Truman released a portion of Marshall's instructions. These set forth in concrete terms the steps by which a united, democratic China might be established: (1) a military truce; (2) a national conference of the Nationalists, the Communists, and the liberal groups; (3) the creation of a broadly constituted provisional government; and (4) the integration of Communist military units into the Chinese National Army. Truman made it emphatically clear that only the Chinese could carry out these suggested reforms; the United States would not intervene to force either the Nationalists or the Communists to make any concessions. At the Moscow Conference, two weeks later, Molotov agreed to the need "for a unified and democratic China under the National Government, for broad participation by democratic elements in all branches of the National Government, and for a cessation of civil strife." Byrnes and Molotov reaffirmed their mutual intentions to abstain from interference in China's domestic politics.

During 1946, Marshall pursued the illusive object of securing some reconciliation between the Nationalists and the Communists in China. In fact, after December, 1945, Byrnes turned over the direction of American Far Eastern policy to this soldier-statesman. By January, 1947, when Marshall returned to succeed Byrnes as Secretary of State, the general had concluded that both the Nationalists and the Communists were hopelessly intransigent. The future of democracy in China, believed Marshall, hinged on the success of that nation's liberal elements.

VI

Secretary Byrnes's tenure of office spanned roughly the first eighteen months of the postwar disagreements between the United States and the U.S.S.R. The President, himself, except for his brief appearance at Potsdam, left foreign affairs largely in the hands of his Secretary of State. It was Byrnes, acting under occasional instructions from the President, who defined this nation's role in an uneasy world. Temperamentally, the Secretary was not inclined to share his responsibilities with his subordinates. He left no doubt that he intended to be the Secretary of State in fact, not merely a spokesman for Departmental ideas. Whatever the successes or shortcomings of American policies during the months after Potsdam, they belonged largely to Byrnes.

Byrnes conceived of his office and his Department as constituting a policy-making agency. He therefore resisted the efforts of the military to transfer to the State Department the control of American-occupation organizations. Whatever time the Department or the Secretary devoted to such operations, Byrnes declared, would necessarily be taken away from the consideration of important policy decisions. "The State Department is not adapted for such work," he wrote. "If the burden of carrying on shipping, maintenance of transportation, policing, inspection and all the myriad duties of occupation forces were transferred to the State Department, its capacity to define wisely important foreign policies would be seriously hampered."

Recognizing that the Foreign Service was still inadequate for the tasks assigned to it, Byrnes favored legislation to improve, strengthen, and expand it—legislation which was passed eventually in 1947. But as Byrnes spent 350 of his 562 days as Secretary at international conferences away from Washington, he could not have claimed credit for many fundamental changes in State Department procedures.

Byrnes left an indelible mark on the evolving American response to the vast power revolution of World War II. For him future peace demanded no less than the preservation of Allied unity in the postwar world. Yet his months in office witnessed the total collapse of that unity. The problems he faced were geographical as well as moral. As a Continental power without any tradition of Western liberalism, Russia refused to concede its predominant position in Eastern and Central Europe out of deference to the principle of self-determination of peoples. The Soviet leaders refused to entrust the security of their nation to others. Stalin's determination to occupy the vacuum created by the deflation of German power in Europe presented Byrnes, and the American nation, with two fundamental alternatives: either to recognize Russia's new hegemony or to build the power and policy to undo it. The first alternative required the desertion of principle; the second required war. Byrnes chose neither. Responding to the pressures from the right, he accepted the new posture of toughness—a toughness anchored, not to military and economic strength, but to a moral rhetoric which created the illusion of ultimate success. As a substitute for some concrete plan of action, this approach to the Soviet problem constituted little more than an escape from the necessity of bringing the nation behind a clear decision. In December, 1946, Walter Lippmann analyzed succinctly why the American response would prove essentially futile:

> Mr. Byrnes, Mr. Vandenberg, Mr. Connally, and Mr. Truman had been schooled in the Senate, and Mr. Bevin in the Trades Union Congress and in Parliament. Unable to induce or compel M. Molotov by what they regarded as diplomacy, they sought to outvote him, and to arouse public opinion against him. The theory of this procedure was that by bringing issues to a public vote an aroused public opinion would do to the Russians what it has done now and then to Tammany Hall and Mayor Hague, to Mr. Joe Martin and Senator Taft.
>
> But to apply the methods of domestic politics to international politics is like using the rules of checkers in a game of chess. Within a democratic state, conflicts are decided by an actual or a potential count of votes—as the saying goes, by ballots rather than bullets. But in a world of sovereign states conflicts are decided by power, actual or potential, for the ultimate arbiter is not an election but war.

National agreement on a "get tough" attitude toward the U.S.S.R. had been reached by the time Byrnes retired from the Secretaryship in January, 1947. Yet what this entailed, other than a disinclination toward further compromise with the Kremlin, was not clear. Toughness alone was not a policy. If the West could not evacuate Soviet forces from Eastern and Central Europe through appeals to principle, it could not do so through words of disapprobation. Unlike American ambitions in the Slavic states, those of the Soviet Union were based on the substantial factors of physical occupation and military power.

But for Byrnes the realization that the world was divided was not the end of hope. He felt that the conflict was still sufficiently limited to rule out the rearming of Germany or Japan, and he continued to express confidence that the Soviets and the West would agree on the concept of a demilitarized Germany. He would not break off negotiations with the Kremlin. If past experience had been hard on the nerves of diplomats, he wrote, war would be harder on the lives of millions. That diplomacy no longer offered any panaceas was clear. To build a lasting peace required far more diligence and effort than suggested either by the optimists who trusted only in faith or by the pessimists who anticipated the achievement of their illusive hopes only at the end of another war. But the fundamental question of whether the United States, in its new role as leader of the Western bloc, should seek to stabilize the postwar *status quo* in Europe or to pursue the cause of the Atlantic Charter had not yet been faced.

13

George Catlett Marshall

1947-1949

BY ALEXANDER DE CONDE
University of Michigan

Early in 1946, during a temporary return to Washington from his China mission, General George C. Marshall was approached by President Truman: "If Byrnes quits me," the President said, "I want you to be Secretary of State." The general replied dutifully that he would do whatever the President wished. In May, Truman broached the subject to Marshall again, this time through General Dwight D. Eisenhower, Chief of Staff, who was then on a Far Eastern inspection trip. Eisenhower informed the President that Marshall would accept the position of Secretary of State, but only after he had completed his assignment in China. On January 7, 1947, several days after Marshall returned from the Orient, the President announced the general's appointment as Secretary.

Marshall brought to the office of Secretary a record of distinguished service to the nation, but a record limited uniquely to military affairs. Indeed, Marshall received his commission as second lieutenant in the Army as early as February, 1902, shortly after his graduation from the Virginia Military Institute. After a brief tour in the Philippines, he returned to the United States to attend several Army schools. During World War I, he served in France and the United States, attaining the temporary rank of colonel. In June, 1920, he reverted to his permanent grade of captain but immediately thereafter was promoted to the rank of major. While serving as General John J. Pershing's aide from May, 1919, until the summer of 1924, he won the general's respect and friendship, became familiar with official Washington, and learned to know well such men as Charles G. Dawes and financier Bernard Baruch.

245

During the next nine years Marshall made the usual moves of a peace-time Army officer, finally receiving the permanent rank of colonel in 1933. Thereafter promotions came faster. In October, 1938, as a brigadier general, he became Deputy Chief of Staff. In less than a year he advanced to Acting Chief of Staff. Three months later, on Pershing's recommendation, President Franklin D. Roosevelt promoted him, over thirty-four senior officers, to General and Chief of Staff. The day he was sworn in, on September 1, 1939, Adolf Hitler's army invaded Poland. Five years later, in December, 1944, Marshall, as General of the Army, attained five-star rank.

As Chief of Staff, Marshall became the professional head of the nation's military establishment, commander of the field forces, and the President's chief military adviser. Second only to the President and the Secretary of War, he controlled the country's military forces in a period of unprecedented expansion. Not long after the United States entered World War II, President Roosevelt made Marshall directly responsible to himself in matters of strategy, tactics, and operations. With direct access to the President and in frequent conference with him, Marshall climbed to a position of unique authority. He accompanied Roosevelt to the Atlantic Conference with Winston Churchill in August, 1941, and to the wartime conferences at Casablanca, Quebec, Cairo, Tehran, and Yalta. In 1945 he also went to Potsdam with President Truman. Although at these conferences Marshall concerned himself primarily with military matters, in effect he also had a voice in diplomatic decisions. The war blurred the line between military and diplomatic issues; sometimes the line did not exist at all.

In November, 1945, Marshall retired as Chief of Staff and looked forward to a long rest that did not come. A week later, on November 27, General Patrick J. Hurley resigned as the United States Ambassador to China, with a public blast at the Truman administration's Far Eastern policy. The President went immediately to the telephone and called Marshall. "General," he said, "I want you to go to China for me." Marshall accepted the assignment, flying to China on December 19 as the President's special emissary with the personal rank of ambassador and with instructions to help bring peace in the burgeoning civil war between Chiang Kai-shek's Nationalists and Mao Tse-tung's Communists. He spent a year in China, interrupted by a brief return to the United States in March and April, 1946, but failed to arrange a peaceful settlement. The frustrating China mission gave him an unforgettable experience in the tortuous diplomacy of Asia.

Truman had long been one of Marshall's stanchest admirers. During the war Marshall had frequently appeared before congressional committees to discuss and explain military matters. Among the senators who worked closely with him in various hearings and in regular weekly conferences was Harry S. Truman of Missouri. Out of these continuous contacts,

Truman said later, "grew my high regard for him as a man and as a soldier." So impressed was Senator Truman by General Marshall that, in an interview with the *Kansas City Star,* he acclaimed the general—and this was while Roosevelt was still alive—as "the greatest living American." That veneration, which Truman apparently never lost, explained in part his willingness to break with tradition by naming a professional soldier to the nation's highest appointive office. No career military man had ever before been Secretary of State.

Marshall's appointment brought prestige to the Truman administration at a time when its political fortunes were low and foreign affairs were a foremost concern. In the elections of November, 1946, the Democrats had lost control of Congress. For the next two years the President's policies would face a hostile Republican majority in the legislative branch. Even before the elections, however, Truman and the Republican leaders in Congress had committed themselves to a bipartisan foreign policy, especially in matters relating to Europe. Marshall had qualities that would permit him to function well as Secretary of State under those conditions. Foreign statesmen, most of whom had met him during the war, respected him. At home he carried immense authority with Congress and the public as a man of wisdom, integrity, and world-ranging views. All of this stemmed from his reputation as the Chief of Staff who had been the architect of victory.

Marshall's appointment, moreover, had come after forty-five years of active service in the Army, during which he had taken no part in politics. Like many other professional soldiers, he had never voted. Without any record in politics or foreign affairs to defend, he could work easily with both Democrats and Republicans. He could, in other words, bring to the office of Secretary of State the attitude of an independent "nonpartisan," one who relied on the confidence of legislators of both parties for support of his policies.

Nonetheless, Truman's announcement aroused immediate speculation about the Secretary's political future. Many assumed that, since the Secretaryship of State had traditionally been a political office, it would continue to be so and that Marshall might become a prominent presidential candidate in 1948. On January 21, 1947, however, only two weeks after his appointment had been announced, the general terminated the political speculation. "I will never become involved in political matters," he told reporters, "and therefore I never can be considered as a candidate for political office." He stressed, with an air of finality, that he "never could be drafted" for the Presidency. "I'm assuming," he said, "that the office of Secretary of State, at least under present conditions, is nonpolitical, and I will govern myself accordingly."

Marshall, in fact, showed no desire for the office of Secretary of State, preferring to retire from public life. "Undoubtedly, this appointment is a great honor," he told newspapermen. "But I would rather have had it the other way." He took the post as any good soldier accepted an assignment, out of a sense of duty and public responsibility. Duty to his country, he felt, was the first rule of a soldier's life.

The Senate received Marshall's nomination for the Secretaryship at noon on January 8, 1947, and disregarded precedents and rules to act upon it at once. Arthur H. Vandenberg of Michigan, the Republican chairman of the Senate Committee on Foreign Relations, had quickly called the committee together and in twenty minutes received its unanimous consent to recommend confirmation. He then asked the Senate to give its unanimous approval and to notify the President immediately. Taking only a minute or two to make the recommendation, the Senate leaders even dispensed with the formality of a voice vote. That afternoon, in a gesture of bipartisanism and in an amazing tribute to Marshall himself, the Senate, under Republican control, swiftly and unanimously confirmed his nomination.

With Marshall's appointment, Truman's status with the conservative press rose quickly. Byrnes had told the President that the appointment would receive general approval, and he was right. Most Americans lauded it. Yet, some criticized the selection of a professional soldier to head the Cabinet, and liberals were alarmed by what they called a trend toward "militarism" in the conduct of foreign policy, particularly since Truman had already appointed a number of generals to important diplomatic posts.

The *Nation*, representing one wing of critical opinion, avowed its admiration for Marshall as a soldier and admitted that he was qualified to serve as Secretary of State, but expressed disapproval of the administration's action "in breaking the tradition of civilian leadership in the conduct of foreign affairs." The *Christian Century* voiced the same criticism, charging that the President "revealed his incapacity to perceive the sharp line which was drawn between the military and civilian functions of government by the writers of our Constitution" and condemning the Senate's hasty approval as "an act of uncritical sentimentalism which gave no evidence of responsible statesmanship." Marshall himself indignantly denied that the military were trying to grab control of foreign policy. "It is not with the brass hats but with the brass heads," he said, "that the danger to our country lies."

Although Marshall's name and face, as a result of his wartime accomplishments, were familiar throughout the world, very few persons knew him intimately or understood his personality. For several weeks after his appointment, foreign diplomats and newspapermen scurried around Washington trying to find out what kind of a man he really was. They discovered that he had deliberately tried to avoid publicity, saying at one time that "no publicity will do me no harm, but some publicity will do me no good." At his press conferences, where he had chosen his subjects carefully and had stuck to them, he had usually been surrounded by attentive junior generals and had retained an air of aloofness. In fact, he apparently never encouraged familiarity. Even those who had worked closely with him knew little of Marshall the man. They described him as cool, courteous, and impersonal, a man with an orderly mind, a clear sense of authority, and a great capacity for work.

Even President Franklin D. Roosevelt, who had a penchant for calling those around him by their first names, addressed Marshall as "General." Only a handful of men in the Army, friends of long standing, called him George. Soon after his appointment, Marshall let the protocol section of the State Department know that he wished to be addressed, not as "General," but as "Mr. Secretary." The new title did not take easily. He surrounded himself with men of military background who still called him "General." Even President Truman continued to address him as "General." At first when someone spoke to Marshall as "Mr. Secretary," he would look around as though trying to find the man being addressed.

II

Since Marshall wanted to take a short rest after his return from China, the President had asked Byrnes to remain in office a while longer. Byrnes had agreed, and Marshall was not sworn in until January 21, 1947, two weeks after his appointment. After the ceremony, he and Byrnes went to lunch at Blair House, the temporary White House, and the departing Secretary explained some of the problems that awaited Marshall in his new assignment.

One of Marshall's first tasks as Secretary of State was to reorganize the top command in the Department so as to clarify the lines of authority. As an Army commander, he had not devoted himself to detailed planning. Instead, he had been accustomed to fixing objectives and entrusting his staff with the problem of recommending means of attaining them. He carried that habit into the State Department. Demanding orderly staff procedure, he strengthened the position of Under Secretary of State Dean G. Acheson and in effect made Acheson his chief of staff. Like an Army commander, Marshall kept himself remote from the workings of his subordinates. Only major questions were to be submitted to him for decision. Under Marshall's command, Acheson ran the Department of State, with authority over administration and the formulation of policy. Acheson discussed policy with Marshall and sought his decisions on important matters, but the orders that went through the Department came from the Under Secretary. "The Secretary," Acheson said, "makes a sharp distinction between the realities of foreign policy and mere descriptions of them. He is more interested in facts than in the words it takes to talk about them."

Marshall disliked long discussions on policy, believing that they were mostly "hot air." "Gentlemen," he would say, "don't fight the problem; decide it." He left staff discussions to Acheson, requiring complete analyses and alternatives on matters of policy placed before him in writing. He would accept, reject, or revise. He established the rule, as in the Army, that all decisions were to be made at proper levels in the chain of command and that the Secretary of State would determine only the broad objectives. On those occasions when Marshall had to make a routine decision, a subordinate would draw up a report covering the main issues, dividing it into three sections headed facts, conclusions, and recommendations. At the bottom would be two small boxes, one marked yes and the other no. After reading the report, Marshall would indicate his decision by checking one of the boxes. If he dissented, he usually added a phrase or a sentence.

On paper that system appeared admirably efficient, but in practice it was not necessarily so. Often composed of intangible problems requiring minute analysis and refinement, diplomatic issues could not always be ruthlessly summarized and handled in a yes-or-no manner. This method, critics said, sometimes made Marshall a virtual prisoner of his staff, particularly of the Foreign Service Officers who prepared the memoranda and made the recommendations. It was alleged that he sometimes went to foreign conferences poorly prepared because he did not fully understand the complex issues at stake, having to rely mainly on information he had received from his staff in digest form. Yet in the major decisions he did not use the box system. Whenever he could, he talked with his Under-Secretaries and probed as deeply and carefully as his busy schedule would permit. President Truman was impressed by Marshall's orderly approach to the conduct of foreign policy, considering it remarkably effective.

Marshall's reliance on his staff and on Under Secretary Acheson is reflected in his handling of his first major crisis. Almost as soon as Marshall became Secretary of State, he devoted virtually his full attention to preparing himself for the meeting of the Council of Foreign Ministers. The conference was to be held in Moscow early in March, 1947, and was to deal with the future of Germany. He carefully arranged for bipartisan support by inviting John Foster Dulles, the Republican spokesman on foreign policy, to accompany him to Moscow as an adviser. Dulles, in fact, accompanied him to foreign conferences throughout 1947. Acheson, meantime, took over all but the most important matters of policy. Before Marshall could complete his preparations, the British confronted him with a crisis in the eastern Mediterranean.

Since the end of the war, Great Britain had maintained troops in Greece and had subsidized Turkey, two nations in danger of falling to communism. The Greeks were fighting a civil war, with Communists on one side and a conservative government on the other. On the morning of February 24, 1947, the British Ambassador in Washington called on Marshall and delivered two notes, one on Greece and the other on Turkey, saying that Great Britain could no longer afford to aid those countries and would withdraw its troops from Greece by April 1, that is, within five weeks. The British hoped that the United States would assume the burden they were relinquishing. Marshall promised to give the situation his immediate attention and to discuss it with the President.

Still engrossed in preparations for the Moscow meeting, Marshall entrusted the Greek and Turkish problem to Acheson, attending staff meetings only when his presence was absolutely required. The Under Secretary kept him informed on the main details and obtained his approval for all decisions. After the State Department staff had analyzed the problem, Marshall and President Truman agreed that American intervention was the only alternative to Soviet control of Greece and Turkey. The President, on February 27, called a White House conference of congressional leaders from both parties. Marshall, in cold, cryptic terms, explained that he thought Greece and Turkey could be saved and that the United States should take over Britain's role. He and Acheson then persuaded the legislators to support a program of intervention. All agreed that President Truman should explain the crisis to the American people and should ask Congress for authority to aid the Greeks and Turks.

Marshall and his advisers realized that the President's message, scheduled to be delivered shortly after the opening of the Moscow Conference, would anger the Russians and would increase his problems at Moscow. Yet, the Secretary did not seek to have the Moscow Conference postponed, either to avoid embarrassment at Moscow or to remain in Washington to take personal command of the new policy. Unflinchingly, he went ahead with established procedure, sending word to his staff through Acheson to draw up the program for Greece and Turkey and to draft the President's message without regard to any adverse effect it might have on his position at Moscow. Then, on March 4, he left for Europe.

The Moscow Conference opened on March 10. Two days later, Truman delivered his speech, read and approved by Marshall during a stop at Paris, to a joint session of Congress. The President announced that the United States must aid peoples who were resisting armed Communist subversion, a policy that came to be known as the Truman Doctrine. To provide this assistance, he asked Congress for an appropriation of 400 million dollars for Greece and Turkey and for authority to send American personnel to supervise the aid program there.

Truman's speech dispelled even faint hopes of accomplishment at Moscow. At that conference Marshall became convinced that the United States and the Soviet Union could not reconcile their objectives for Germany or for the rest of the world. Marshall found the dilatoriness, the vagueness, and the needling tactics of Russian diplomacy almost too much even for his carefully controlled temper. The Soviet tactics placed him under great strain. "In diplomacy," he was reported as saying, "you never can tell what a man is thinking. He smiles at you and kicks you in the stomach at the same time." The Russians seemingly did that. Marking the virtual breakup of the wartime coalition, the Moscow Conference ended on April 24, 1947, with nothing decided except that the Ministers would meet again in London in November.

Congress, meantime, accepted the Truman Doctrine, and a month later, on May 22, the President signed the program into law. The failure of the Moscow Conference and the enactment of the Truman Doctrine heralded a new departure in American foreign policy, the beginning of what came to be known as the "cold war," a term made popular by the widely read journalist Walter Lippmann. The cold war, meaning a nonshooting political and ideological conflict between the Soviet Union and its satellites, on one side, and the United States and its friends, on the other, seemed an ironically appropriate name for the battles that Marshall, a soldier and statesman trained to fight wars, found himself waging. The diplomatic strategy he adopted in the cold war during the remainder of his term in office was called "containment," a policy that committed the United States to the prevention of further Communist expansion.

Before Marshall left for Moscow, he had been disturbed by what he considered a lack of central planning in the conduct of foreign policy. He believed that those who uncovered facts should be separated from those who made policy. The War Department had such a separation and had long supported a Strategy and Policy Section that concerned itself with long-range planning. Again reaching into his military experience, the Secretary, with the President's approval, had undertaken to correct the deficiency by creating a small group of specialists, named the Policy Planning Staff, who would work directly under him but outside the usual hierarchy of the State Department. That group would analyze trends in foreign affairs and formulate policy for some ten to twenty-five years into the future for the guidance of those who made the decisions. On the basis of that staff's central planning, he felt, his subordinates in the State Department could think and speak about policy while he was abroad. Before leaving Washington, he had asked George F. Kennan, a Foreign Service Officer with a scholarly bent and a deep knowledge of Russia, to organize and head the Policy Planning Staff. It was agreed that Kennan would take on this responsibility in May, as soon as his temporary assignment at the National War College ended.

At Moscow, Marshall became convinced that Germany formed only a part of the larger problem of Europe. Some plan, he believed, was needed to prevent the possible economic and social disintegration of Western Europe and the triumph of communism. In the middle of April, 1947, therefore, he began sending messages to the State Department, demanding the establishment of the Policy Planning Staff without delay. Kennan then spent a few hours each day at the State Department, considering minor matters, such as organization and budget, and assembling a staff.

While flying home from Moscow, Marshall and the senior members of his delegation agreed on an idea that had been advanced by planners within the State, War, and Navy Departments: the United States should attempt to foster Europe's rehabilitation through economic aid. On April 28, two days after his return to the United States, Marshall addressed the nation by radio. Europe's recovery from the devastation of war, he said, had been slower than expected. "The patient is sinking while the doctors deliberate." Action to meet Europe's problems, he emphasized, "must be taken without delay." On the following day he outlined the problem of Europe to Kennan and asked him to take it up with the Policy Planning Staff, a staff that did not yet exist. Within ten days, perhaps two weeks, the Secretary said, he wanted a paper with ideas and recommendations for action. Kennan asked whether there were any other instructions. "Avoid trivia," Marshall replied. On May 2, 1947, the Policy Planning Staff was formally established, and three days later it held its first meeting.

President Truman, meanwhile, asked Under Secretary Acheson to make a speech for him at Cleveland, Mississippi, a little town deep in the cotton country. There, on May 8, Acheson gave definite indications of the trend of thinking within the administration on the problem of European reconstruction. Stressing Europe's economic needs, he said that public discussion of the Truman Doctrine had overemphasized its military features. Marshall congratulated him on the speech and said that he wanted to develop the concept of economic aid more fully.

The Under Secretary of State for Economic Affairs, William L. Clayton, had been equally concerned with the plight of Europe. He and those who worked under him believed that Europe's economy should be reconstructed through a Continental program rather than through many individual national programs. On May 19, while flying home from Geneva, Clayton prepared a four-page memorandum suggesting that the President and the Secretary of State urge the American people to sacrifice to save Europe from starvation and chaos and to launch a program of aid. About a week later Clayton circulated his memorandum among State Department planners, brought it to Marshall's attention, and, in conversations with the Secretary, vividly described Europe's needs and urged immediate action.

On May 23, Kennan's Policy Planning Staff completed its recommendations for a program of massive economic aid for Europe. Five days later, Marshall called a staff meeting in his office to consider the recommendations, apparently impressed especially by Clayton's pleading. At the meeting, after he had summarized all the views, the Secretary went around the table asking for individual comments. Then he said, "Are we safe in directing such a proposal to all of Europe? What will be the effect if the Soviets decide to come in?" Some suggested that Russia might interfere to block the aid plan and hence that it would be too risky to undertake. The Secretary was convinced, however, that to "sit back and do nothing" would involve an even greater risk.

Yet Marshall agreed that any public announcement of the plan had to be timed carefully. It had to break with "explosive force," he believed, to overcome isolationist opposition. "The feeling seemed to be," he explained in a later memorandum, "that any new proposal for more funds to be appropriated would be ruthlessly repulsed. Therefore, the manner of statement, the first approach, and similar factors had to be most seriously considered. It is easy to propose a great plan, but exceedingly difficult to manage the form and procedure so that it has a fair chance of political survival."

The Secretary insisted that primary emphasis be placed on European initiative in determining requirements rather than on American assistance. "I thought it imperative," he said in an interview, "that the European countries 'come clean'—that is, that they come up with a workable plan based on actual requirements beyond the existing resources at their command, not on what they thought the United States would give." To prevent leaks and premature criticism, Marshall kept consultation within the government to a minimum and did not inform the Europeans about his plan or indicate when he would make an announcement. Finally, taking the ideas expounded by his subordinates, particularly those of Clayton and the Policy Planning Staff, and adding his own, Marshall prepared a speech on European reconstruction. Delivered at the commencement exercises of Harvard University on June 5, 1947, this address announced the European Recovery Program, or the Marshall Plan.

"It is logical that the United States should do whatever it is able to do to assist in the return of normal economic health in the world, without which there can be no political stability and no assured peace," Marshall said. "Our policy is directed not against any country or doctrine but against hunger, poverty, desperation and chaos." The key to his proposal was the suggestion that the Europeans themselves should draft a joint program of recovery that the United States could support.

In his memoirs, Harry S. Truman wrote that he had referred to the idea of European economic aid in staff meetings as the Marshall Plan because he wanted "General Marshall to get full credit for his brilliant contributions to the measure which he helped formulate." Although, as we have seen, the plan had emerged from the staff work in the State Department, it was Marshall who launched the staff planning that led to the program and who made the basic decisions. He accepted the idea of the economic unity of Europe, made it his own, gave speeches in support of the European Recovery Program, and held numerous conferences with influential members of Congress to gain its acceptance. History, Truman believed, would always associate Marshall's name with the salvation of Europe. "I believe the fact that a man of Marshall's world standing made the proposal of this policy," he wrote, "helped greatly in its eventual adoption."

Truman was right, but Marshall's inexperience in politics, his curt soldierly demand for action, at one point placed the plan in danger. In asking Congress in January, 1948, to appropriate 6.8 billion dollars to finance his European Recovery Program for its first fifteen months, he said bluntly that anything less would be inadequate and a waste of resources. "Either undertake to meet the requirements of the problem," he demanded, "or don't undertake it at all." Marshall had used such ultimatums during the war and they had worked, but he had forgotten that Congress had changed. Congressional leaders now resented this tactic. "I don't think the State Department is justified in presenting these absolute alternatives," a prominent Senator said. Marshall's demand, he added, was "not a proper statement to make before the legislative branch of the Government."

Despite the Secretary's mistake, Congress, a few months later, voted funds for the Marshall Plan. This plan became Marshall's outstanding contribution as Secretary of State, bringing him greater prestige and fame than had his wartime accomplishments as Chief of Staff.

III

At the end of June, 1947, Under Secretary Acheson left the State Department to return to his law practice. For his new chief of staff, who took office on July 1, Marshall chose Robert A. Lovett, a Republican and a Wall Street banker who lacked diplomatic experience but who had made a good record during the war as Assistant Secretary of War for Air. Under Secretary Lovett shared Marshall's military outlook on foreign affairs, saying at one time that foreign policy was like a war plan. Conservative in his background and thinking, Lovett naturally selected similarly minded subordinates. Although conservatism can often be a virtue, in this instance it upset some of the liberals in the administration, who felt that the State Department already had more than its share of conservatism. Despite this criticism, Lovett proved an asset to the administration. Able to get along with fellow Republicans and conservative Democrats, he worked effectively with Congress in carrying out Marshall's bipartisan foreign policy. Since the Secretary of State relied as heavily on him to manage administrative tasks as he had on Acheson, Lovett ran the State Department and exerted considerable influence on Marshall's policies.

Some of the President's closest political advisers believed that Marshall was excessively influenced by his staff, particularly by men such as Lovett, and that the Secretary persisted in upholding them even when their views clashed with those of the President himself. A number of Truman's White House advisers, in fact, did not share the President's implicit faith in Marshall. Although they did not question Marshall's devotion to the President, they thought that he was given too much authority and too much control over policy and that his subordinates employed his prestige to thwart Presidential decisions. A case in point, they felt, was the Department's stand on the new state of Israel.

President Truman favored a homeland for the Jews, and in November, 1947, supported a United Nations plan for the partition of Palestine between Arabs and Jews, a policy that committed the United States to the principle of an independent Jewish state. Truman's political advisers and intimate members of his White House staff had urged that policy, but specialists on the Middle East and other career men in the State Department disliked it. Believing the partition plan unworkable, the Policy Planning Staff, for instance, recommended withdrawal of American support for it. The State Department specialists contended that Truman's political advisers championed the idea of a Jewish state, not because of any concern for foreign policy or national security, but in the interests of gaining Jewish votes and winning an advantage in domestic politics.

Arguing that the opposition of the State Department career men to partition flowed largely from anti-Semitic biases and not from diplomatic considerations, the President's political advisers warned him that those men were trying to undermine his policy, a warning he could not believe. "I know how Marshall feels and he knows how I feel," Truman said. A short time later the President was surprised when Senator Warren R. Austin, the American representative on the Security Council, in March, 1948, seemingly reversed the President's policy by proposing a suspension of the partition plan and agreeing that Palestine be placed under a temporary United Nations trusteeship. "How could this have happened?" Truman asked Clark Clifford, his personal adviser, instructing him at the same time to find out how it did. Truman probably was disturbed more by the timing of Austin's proposal than by its substance, for he previously had told Marshall that he would go along with the trusteeship idea.

At the time, Marshall was in Los Angeles. Lovett, who was equally surprised by Austin's timing, offered an explanation. Before leaving Washington, Lovett said, Marshall had approved a memorandum calling for the trusteeship proposal if partition failed, so that there would be no vacuum in American policy. Although partition had not failed, it had faltered, and its opponents had taken this opportunity to use the Marshall memorandum and advance the Austin proposal. Truman then called Marshall in Los Angeles, and the Secretary issued a statement that alleviated the difficulty a bit. Marshall pointed out that he had given Austin's proposal careful consideration, had believed it "the wisest course to follow," had recommended it to the President, and had secured the President's approval. The Jews in the United States castigated the President for his apparent reversal in policy.

The next clash over policy toward Palestine came in May, 1948, when the British were to terminate their mandate there and the Jews were preparing to proclaim their independent state of Israel. The President favored immediate recognition of Israel, but Marshall opposed it. Truman's White House advisers, particularly Clark Clifford, believed that Marshall's opposition stemmed from the views of his State Department specialists. Clifford, therefore, persuaded the President to call a conference of State Department leaders and the White House staff. At that meeting, on May 12, Marshall asked Lovett to explain why recognition was inadvisable. Clifford in turn argued that the President had already committed himself to an independent Jewish state and that to pretend that it did not exist was unrealistic.

"Marshall's face flushed," Clifford reported later. "Mr. President," the Secretary began, "this is not a matter to be determined on the basis of politics. Unless politics were involved, Mr. Clifford would not even be at this conference. This is a serious matter of foreign policy determination and the question of politics and political opinion does not enter into it." "He said it all," Clifford maintained, "in a righteous God-damned Baptist tone." Marshall was an Episcopalian.

"I think we must follow the position General Marshall has advocated," the President said. That seemed to settle the matter, but soon Lovett raised the issue again. Two days later, he told Clifford that he and Marshall believed that the United States should recognize Israel but should not rush headlong into recognition. But Clifford persuaded the President to recognize immediately. Eleven minutes after the Jews, on May 14, 1948, proclaimed their independent state of Israel, Truman's press secretary announced that the President had granted it *de facto* recognition.

"I was told that to some of the career men of the State Department this announcement came as a surprise," Truman recalled in his memoirs. "It should not have been if these men had faithfully supported my policy." Although he lashed out at the State Department officials, the President carefully excluded Marshall himself from criticism. "I wanted to make it plain," he wrote, "that the President of the United States, and not the second or third echelon in the State Department, is responsible for making foreign policy, and, furthermore, that no one in any department can sabotage the President's policy." Since Marshall had persisted in his opposition to immediate, though not ultimate, recognition, the question of Israel proved to be one of the few instances in which Truman overruled his Secretary of State.

Even though the Palestine problem had revealed differences of opinion between the President and his Secretary of State, Truman was satisfied that Marshall understood his position and agreed with him in general policy. Their differences, moreover, were rare. Regardless of how his political advisers felt about Marshall, Truman usually followed his Secretary's advice, often without question. Marshall, Truman believed, was the Secretary of State that suited him. He stressed that with Marshall the Secretaryship was in "safe hands." Not being familiar with foreign policy, Truman, despite his impatience with the State Department specialists over Palestine, had an unusual faith in "experts," and to him Marshall was an outstanding expert.

Another conflict between Marshall and the President's political advisers —one which showed the Secretary's great influence over Truman—grew out of a crisis with the Soviet Union over Berlin. In June, 1948, the United States, Great Britain, and France, over the opposition of Russia, introduced a reformed currency in the sectors of Berlin they occupied. Since Berlin was deep inside the Soviet zone of occupation, the Russians retaliated by clamping a tight land blockade on the Western sectors of the city. West Berlin, with a population of some 2,500,000 and only limited supplies of food and coal, could not survive without American assistance. President Truman and Secretary Marshall would not retreat, but fearing a third world war, they also rejected the idea of forcing an entrance into Berlin with armed convoys. Instead, they decided on an airlift, a continuous shuttle service into West Berlin that Americans called "Operation Vittles."

"We are in Berlin as a result of agreements between the Governments on the areas of occupation in Germany and we intend to stay," Marshall said on June 30. He added that "maximum use of air transport will be made to supply the civilian population. It has been found, after study, that the tonnage of foodstuffs and supplies which can be lifted by air is greater than had at first been assumed." Throughout the summer, tension over Berlin mounted. In September, the United States, supported by Britain and France, brought the issue of the Berlin blockade before the United Nations, meeting at that time in Paris. The Security Council, despite Soviet objections, voted on October 5 to take up the question.

The President's political advisers, meanwhile, were disturbed not only by the people's fear that a war might erupt out of the Berlin crisis but also by the use Henry Wallace's Progressives were making of that fear in the 1948 presidential campaign. They were upset, too, by stories, seemingly seeping from the State Department itself and used to advantage by Republicans, which suggested that Truman had little to do with foreign policy. The bipartisan foreign policy, some leading Democrats argued, had been watered down or captured by Republicans. What was needed to raise Truman's prestige and help win the election, they agreed, was a striking and perhaps desperate gesture that would show that the President himself was in fact, as well as in title, the maker of foreign policy and the leader who sought the American ideal of peace.

Two of Truman's speech writers suggested the dramatic move of sending Chief Justice Fred M. Vinson to Moscow as the President's special peace envoy to find some way of easing cold-war tensions in direct talks with Josef Stalin, perhaps even to persuade the old Bolshevik to lift the Berlin blockade. They wrote a speech in which Truman would tell the nation by radio about the Vinson mission. At the President's urging, Vinson, on October 3, agreed to make the long trip. "Of course I assured the Chief Justice," Truman wrote later, "that this mission in no way constituted an action to circumvent the Secretary of State, the United Nations, and most certainly none of our allies." Before acting, the President decided to discuss the mission by telephone with Marshall in Paris. "I am sure," Truman said, "that he will be for it, as he always is for any constructive move to advance the cause of peace." On the following day, before the President had talked with Marshall, Truman's press secretary made arrangements with the national networks for the broadcast.

When the President, on October 5, telephoned Paris, he found his Secretary of State flatly opposed to the Vinson mission. It would, Marshall indicated, undercut his difficult negotiations in the Security Council over the Berlin crisis. As usual, the President immediately decided to follow his Secretary's advice by canceling the whole project. Truman's political advisers urged him to overrule Marshall, pointing out that the real choice lay between making the Secretary's task more difficult and making his own election virtually impossible. Marshall, they insisted, did not realize that nothing was more important to the success of his policy than the preservation of the administration that had made it. Truman listened. "I have heard enough," he said quietly. "We won't do it." Marshall had won again.

Arrangements for the special broadcast, meantime, had gone too far to prevent serious leaks and adverse publicity. The story of the abandoned peace mission appeared in the newspapers on October 8. On the following day, Marshall, who had been called home by Truman to help repair the damage and to clear up any misunderstandings, returned to Washington. He talked with Truman and then issued a statement deploring reports that the Vinson episode had caused a split between the President and himself. Since the Republicans had not been consulted about the proposed Vinson mission and since it had originated as a partisan political maneuver, few could deny that the episode had not dealt a blow to Marshall's bipartisan approach to foreign policy.

IV

During the period that Marshall held office, both American foreign policy and its conduct underwent momentous changes—changes that affected the rest of the world. Marshall himself played a major role in the development of new administrative devices to meet the challenge of the cold war. In July, 1947, the National Security Act became law, creating a new agency, the National Security Council, to coordinate military and foreign policy in the interest of national defense and security. Although that agency recognized the supremacy of the civilian authorities in the determination of foreign policy, it gave new importance to military factors. The Secretary of State was a member of the Council, but he was seemingly outflanked by the military departments, for the Secretaries of Defense, the Army, the Navy, and the Air Force were also members. Since Marshall himself was a soldier and since other soldiers held important diplomatic posts, it appeared to critics that the military had indeed captured control of foreign policy. In the presidential campaign of 1948, Thomas E. Dewey, the Republican candidate, gave voice to some of the public misgivings by attacking the predominance of military figures among those who shaped foreign policy. Ultimately, when the Secretaries of the Army, the Navy, and the Air Force were dropped from the Council, the military influence in national policy appeared less conspicuous.

As part of his uncompromising opposition to Russian communism, Marshall, in his first appearance before the General Assembly of the United Nations in September, 1947, proposed a plan to help mitigate the Soviet abuse of the veto. "The United Nations," he said, "will never endure if there is insistence on privilege to the point of frustration of the collective will." He suggested the creation of a standing committee, or "Little Assembly," that would hear disputes brought to its attention and would remain in session when the General Assembly was not. Unencumbered by the veto, the "Little Assembly" would broaden the machinery for peaceful settlement of disputes by placing the responsibility for peace on all members. Because Marshall's proposal was a direct challenge to the Soviets, it appeared to some delegates that the Secretary of State seemed intent on driving the Soviet Union from the United Nations. In November, the General Assembly overrode Russian objections and passed a diluted version of Marshall's proposal.

In Latin-American affairs, Secretary Marshall ended a feud between the

State Department and Argentina's dictator, Juan D. Perón, thus reversing his predecessor's "tough" policy toward Argentina. In August and September, 1947, at a special Inter-American conference at Petrópolis, outside Rio de Janeiro, Marshall won a notable diplomatic victory by persuading the Latin-American republics to sign the Inter-American Treaty of Reciprocal Assistance, an alliance known as the Rio Treaty and the first regional arrangement under Article 51 of the United Nations Charter.

Violent rioting, which Marshall attributed to Communist activity, threatened to disrupt the next important inter-American meeting that the Secretary attended, the Ninth International Conference of American States, held in Bogotá in April, 1948. Despite the fear and chaos, Marshall insisted that the conference continue. Under his leadership the delegates adopted an anti-Communist resolution. He contributed to the creation of the Pact of Bogotá, which established a reorganized inter-American system called the Organization of American States, the conference's major achievement. Still Latin Americans felt that the United States was neglecting them. Under Marshall, critics pointed out, Latin-American affairs were "in temporary eclipse."

The North Atlantic alliance, a revolutionary departure from America's tradition of avoiding European entanglements, had its beginnings under Marshall. Russia's resistance to the Marshall Plan; its extravagant use of the veto, which virtually paralyzed the work of the Security Council; and the failure of the London Conference of Foreign Ministers in December, 1947, had finally convinced him and other policy makers that something had to be done for the military protection of Western Europe. Encouraged by Marshall, Great Britain, France, Belgium, the Netherlands, and Luxembourg took the first step toward military preparedness in March, 1948, when they signed an alliance known as the Brussels Pact.

Marshall then indicated a willingness to discuss additional security arrangements, a step that would commit the United States to participation in the defense of Western Europe. In April he, Lovett, Senator Vandenberg, John Foster Dulles, and other leaders met with the President in a conference at Blair House. Lovett suggested that the best solution would be a pact modeled after the Rio Treaty. Vandenberg said he thought that the Senate would go along with the idea of a regional treaty for collective defense. With Marshall's support, Lovett and Vandenberg, working in close cooperation, then completed a draft resolution embodying the regional idea. Vandenberg introduced his resolution, and the Senate, on June 11, 1948, approved it, with only four dissenting votes. Congress, in other words, agreed in advance to support American entrance into a military alliance. This cleared the road for the North Atlantic Treaty.

Less than a month later, Marshall and Lovett began intensive negotiations with the nation's future allies in Europe. Nothing definite was concluded until after the presidential elections, and the North Atlantic alliance itself did not become a reality until after Marshall had left office.

Such bipartisan cooperation in foreign policy stemmed in part from Marshall's desire to develop national policies without regard for party considerations or political issues. During his first year in office, in fact, there were no major conflicts between the Republican majority in Congress and the administration. Even during that year, however, trouble in the Far East raised issues which threatened interparty harmony.

After Marshall had returned from China in January, 1947, the fighting there burst into one of the great civil wars of modern times, affecting nearly a quarter of the world's population. In his final report on his mission, Marshall had blamed both sides, the Communists and the Kuomintang, for the fighting. As Secretary of State, he made no public statement of American aims or policy toward China, seeking to avoid commitments that might involve the United States in the civil war. He followed a policy of letting "the dust settle." Nevertheless, the United States continued to be tangled in Chinese affairs because it continued to aid and advise Chiang Kai-shek's government, not providing enough assistance to be effective against the Communists, but enough to infuriate them.

Prominent Republicans, the influential Luce publications, which included *Time* and *Life* magazines, and the Scripps-Howard newspapers, urged a policy of vigorous support for Chiang. The Secretary of State and his advisers resisted, wishing to avoid any commitment in China that might weaken the policy of containment in Europe. They felt, moreover, that American aid, even in massive quantities, could not save Chiang. Early in July, 1947, for instance, Marshall bluntly told Chiang that "the fundamental and lasting solution of China's problems must come from the Chinese themselves."

Marshall and Truman, however, bent somewhat to the Republican pressures. In July, 1947, with the President's support, Marshall asked General Albert C. Wedemeyer to go to China to investigate conditions there and to make recommendations for future policy. Returning to Washington in September, Wedemeyer submitted an inconclusive report, suggesting among other things increased economic and military aid for Chiang. Believing the report inadequate and impractical, Marshall urged its suppression. "It seems to me mandatory that we treat Wedemeyer's report strictly top secret," he told the President on September 25, 1947, "and that no indication of its contents be divulged to the public. This will allow us time to review our policy in the light of the report, giving due consideration to it in balance with our policies in other parts of the world." Truman agreed. Later, Marshall admitted that he disagreed with Wedemeyer on some points and said that publication of the report would embarrass both the Chinese and the American governments. It was finally published in 1949.

Since they had not committed themselves to bipartisanism in Far Eastern affairs, Republicans now lustily attacked Marshall's politically vulnerable China policy. In November, 1947, Thomas E. Dewey of New York denounced it as bankrupt, declaring that the United States needed a strong policy in Asia as well as in Europe. He and others urged that the Truman Doctrine be extended to the Far East to save China from communism.

Despite the attacks, Marshall persisted in his policy of watchful waiting, coupled with limited assistance to Chiang to help avert economic collapse. The strategy of containment suited Europe, Marshall's advisers argued, but not China. After all, China's territory was forty-five times that of Greece and her population eighty-five times as large. Many billions of dollars and perhaps millions of American troops would have been required for an intervention on the Greek pattern. Success, moreover, seemed unlikely. The Democrats in Congress, reposing personal confidence in Marshall or relying on his tremendous prestige to protect them politically, supported his policy.

During the debate over the Marshall Plan, the administration partially gave in to its critics and asked for funds for China. In the Foreign Assistance Act of May, 1948, Congress appropriated 338 million dollars for economic aid and 125 million for military aid for one year, essentially a Republican commitment to the Nationalist side in the civil war. Then, as Dulles has written, Marshall reversed his earlier position toward China. During his mission of 1946, Marshall had urged a coalition government for China. On August 12, 1948, he told the American Ambassador in China that the United States "must not directly or indirectly give any implication of support, encouragement or acceptability of coalition government in China with Communist participation." Still, Marshall and Truman would not sanction the intervention the Republicans demanded. And in December, 1948, when Madame Chiang Kai-shek visited the United States, they were cool to her last-minute plea for help.

Despite the partisan bitterness over China policy, Marshall escaped direct personal criticism during his term of office. Only later, after he had resigned and the Communists had won China, did he become the subject of scathing and even scurrilous personal attacks. Senator Vandenberg perhaps expressed the feelings of some of his colleagues when he later told his wife, "I dislike to say *anything*, however indirectly, which reflects on anything George Marshall ever did . . . I think he was somewhat misled by the boys on the Far East desk in the State Department. In any event, our China policy has been a tragic failure and, now that the chips are down, I can't help saying so."

In 1948, at sixty-eight years of age, Marshall was no longer in sufficiently good health to withstand the constant demands of his office. The inescapable pressure to make vital decisions and the strain of innumerable negotiations made it doubtful that he would continue as Secretary until the end of the term. In December, 1948, he underwent a kidney operation, and in the following month he resigned. The President announced Marshall's resignation on January 7, 1949, to be effective on January 20, when Truman began his second term.

V

Any attempt to make a fair assessment of Marshall as Secretary of State encounters contradictions. Critics, and friends too, have pointed out that he never grasped foreign relations as thoroughly as he had military affairs. He did not, in fact, pretend that he had mastered the art, or even the rules, of diplomacy. Once, when a newspaperman asked him whether he regarded the Secretaryship of State as the peak of his career, Marshall frowned and said, "I was a professional soldier for forty-five years." That remark, perhaps, offers some insight into his concept of the Secretaryship. It seems probable that he considered his tenure of office much as a soldier would consider any important assignment, as a tour of duty for the Commander in Chief.

Marshall tried to run the State Department as he had the Army, retaining the aloofness of a commanding officer in his daily relations with his subordinates. His mind continued to function along military lines; he even gave orders in military phraseology. And, like a military commander, he relied on information and proposals that reached him through the chain of command he had established in the State Department. Critics said that he was the prisoner of a "military mentality," but close associates in the State Department claimed that his "military mind" extended only to orderly procedures and did not obscure his broad grasp of problems in foreign policy. Marshall had the ability, in most instances, to judge what was important and to separate it from what was not, a quality that had helped him rise to the top in the Army.

As Secretary of State, Marshall spent most of his time abroad or in negotiations with foreign statesmen in the United States. Up to October 15, 1948, for example, he had devoted 228 out of his 633 days in office to international conferences. In such circumstances, even if his military training had not led him to do so, it seemed wise to rely on Under Secretaries Acheson and Lovett to run the State Department and to share in the making of policy.

Marshall was not only the nation's most notable nonpolitical Secretary of State but also one of its most powerful. That power stemmed from his relationship with President Truman, who virtually adored him but who, ironically, was awed by him and never seemed relaxed with him. Yet, Truman said, "Marshall's entire personality inspired confidence," and in his memoirs he recorded that "General Marshall is one of the most astute and profound men I have ever known." Even though the two men on a few occasions differed over details of foreign policy, their relations were never marred by fundamental disagreement or personal conflict. The President never bypassed his Secretary of State. Marshall had a voice, probably the decisive one, in every major decision of foreign policy during the years of 1947 and 1948.

Truman's confidence in Marshall was not misplaced. In Marshall he found integrity coupled with ability and prestige. He knew that his Secretary of State, in his conduct of office, had no interest other than safeguarding the security of the United States. Certainly he had no interest in the Presidency. Nor did Marshall consider himself, as had Byrnes, the assistant president in charge of foreign affairs. Marshall had a deep loyalty to his Commander in Chief and a reverence for the Presidency. Both men shared a common feeling for history. Shortly after becoming Secretary of State, Marshall told a Princeton graduating class that "one usually emerges from an intimate understanding of the past, with its lessons and its wisdom, with convictions which put fire in the soul."

When Truman, fighting against great odds, started on his lonely whistle-stop presidential campaign in 1948, Marshall was one of the Cabinet members who went to bid him farewell. The President did not forget that. During that seemingly forlorn campaign, as at other times, Marshall resisted the suggestions of some of his career subordinates that foreign policy was independent of the President. Unlike some of Truman's other advisers, Marshall remained loyal to Truman the President and Truman the man, and was not reluctant to express his admiration for him. "The full stature of this man will only be proven by history," he said of Truman at a later time, "but I want to say here and now that there has never been a decision under this man's administration, affecting policies beyond our shores, that has not been in the best interest of this country. It is not the courage of these decisions that will live, but the integrity of them."

Marshall's personal loyalty to the President at times irked some of his associates. In his memoirs, Senator Tom Connally, a prominent Democrat on the Foreign Relations Committee, wrote that Marshall, as Secretary of State, "was not very assertive or aggressive. He tried to find out what the President wanted and then do it. Ideally the secretary of state should be the best-posted man in the country on foreign relations; he should keep the President apprised of what is going on abroad and he should advise him on formulating policies." Connally's appraisal of Marshall reveals that the role of the Secretary of State in government is often misunderstood, even by those close to the office. That role, powerful or weak, aggressive or passive, depends upon the Secretary's relations with the President. Marshall's tenure showed how much those relations reflect personal factors and, despite the growth of big government and sprawling, complicated commitments in foreign policy, how little they have to do with techniques or procedures of administration.

In December, 1953, Marshall received the Nobel Peace Prize. He was the first soldier to win that honor, and some people saw a serious inconsistency in awarding a peace prize to a military man. Marshall, however, was given the award, not for his accomplishments as a soldier, but for his work as Secretary of State, a civilian office, in launching the Marshall Plan. It signified that Marshall, even if he was not a great Secretary, had recognized the role which the United States could play in the economic reconstruction of Europe and, as Secretary of State, had given his name to one of the most statesmanlike policies in the nation's history.

14

Dean G. Acheson

1949-1953

BY NORMAN A. GRAEBNER
University of Illinois

Early in 1949, Associate Justice Felix Frankfurter attempted to define the tasks of a Secretary of State and the qualifications required to fulfill them. "What we are seeking to preserve, in order to improve," he wrote,

> is "the fair sum of six thousand years' traditions of civility." Nothing less is at stake. They are the issues that underlie the items appearing in the daily press as the business of the State Department.
>
> The greatness of these issues requires capacity appropriate for dealing with them. Expert knowledge, suppleness in argument, and felicity of speech are inadequate. They call for character, self-disciplined by training and habit, a mind steeped in historic knowledge but aware that history never quite repeats itself, a confidence born of humility and a consciousness of the human limitations due to the inherent conflict between the forces of good and evil in all men—above all, they call for an understanding of the difference between greatness and bigness and for a will that acts on that difference in the exercise of power.

What provoked Mr. Frankfurter's words was the nomination of Dean Gooderham Acheson to the office of Secretary of State, and many American and European observers shared his convictions that the new appointee satisfied such rigorous standards. In a sense Acheson did not fit the pattern of the past. Lacking an established reputation in political or military affairs, he was not a public figure in the sense that his two predecessors had been. But he had been around the State Department since the days before Pearl Harbor. To those who knew him, his qualifications were impressive indeed. James Reston, the veteran Washington reporter, observed that Acheson seemed to combine the strongest assets of the four Secretaries under whom he had served—the experience of Cordell Hull, the handsomeness of Edward R. Stettinius, the style of James F. Byrnes, and the mental discipline of George C. Marshall. In intellectual artistry, Acheson was the superior of all of them. His considerable elegance went beyond his appearance; it included his dress, his manners, his words and ideas. Whether a discussion involved matters of state or matters of food, his argument had precision and grace.

Alistair Cooke, writing in the *Manchester Guardian*, attributed to the new Secretary one of the most creative political minds of the time. He predicted that homesick European diplomats, who believed that a diplomat should look like one, would admire Acheson's vivacity, irony, and sleek tailoring. Perhaps, thought Cooke, the Secretary might even pioneer the development of a new type of American statesman. If some United States senators distrusted him, as they would any brilliant professional diplomat, they would learn to appreciate his grasp and intellect. Granted Acheson's training and character, ran Cooke's conclusion, "he must become the most impressive Secretary of State since Elihu Root."

Acheson was a man of strong convictions. Beyond that, his essential qualities of personality were complex and illusive. He was idealistic, puritanical, sarcastic, intense, and even intolerant. But he could be equally cynical, earthy, humorous, relaxed, and patient. An unshakable allegiance to a strict personal code of honesty and loyalty determined most of his decisions. When he retired from public life in 1947, he was offered a fortune to write his memoirs, but he refused: he would not, he said, exploit either public documents or private conversations for personal profit. When he was nominated for the Secretaryship, he admitted before the Senate Foreign Relations Committee that he knew Alger Hiss, the former State Department official then under indictment for perjury in connection with Department documents acquired by Russian agents. Declaring emphatically that his "friendship is not easily given, and it is not easily withdrawn," he said that Alger Hiss had been and still was his friend and that he would not disavow a friend who had a right to be regarded innocent until he had been proved guilty.

As a diplomatist, Acheson was aware of "human limitations" in resolving the great conflicts in world affairs. In this important respect he had little in common with most of his twentieth-century predecessors. Although he had once imbibed the liberal doctrines of Woodrow Wilson, he was by instinct a conservative. The son of an Episcopalian bishop, he attended Groton and then Yale, from which he was graduated in 1915. He received his LL.B. from Harvard. After a year in the Navy, he served two years as law clerk to Supreme Court Justice Louis D. Brandeis and then joined the celebrated Washington law firm of Covington and Burling, with which he is still associated. In 1933 he accepted an appointment as Under Secretary of the Treasury from President Franklin D. Roosevelt, but he resigned within a year because he regarded Roosevelt's monetary policies as unsound. During the late thirties he served as chairman of the Attorney General's Committee on Administrative Procedure. In February, 1941, he became Assistant Secretary of State, handling economic matters for the Department. In December, 1944, Stettinius assigned him the task of representing the Department before Congress. Having served as Marshall's Under Secretary until July, 1947, he loomed as a natural successor when illness forced Marshall to resign his office late in 1948.

Acheson's concept of America's proper role in world affairs reflected his historic conservatism. He rejected Wilsonism as the principal foundation of national behavior. He did not share Wilson's confidence in international organization as a substitute for power politics, for he disputed the assumption that faith alone could achieve the Wilsonian goal of peace under law. "I do not believe that the purpose of American policy is to carry out a 'crusade' or 'mission' to bring about equal justice or to vindicate international law," he once wrote. "Its purpose is to protect and further the deepest and most vital interests of the United States and those states which are working toward the same end of safeguarding our Common Civilization."

As Secretary of State, Acheson warned that appeals to abstract principles of right and wrong often excluded a sense of responsibility in the exercise of power. In November, 1950, he informed a Washington audience:

> Instead of wholeness, we get fragmentation, if those who have a keen sense of our moral obligations do not also think responsibly—that is, if they do not confront themselves with the actual conditions with which we must deal in the world, if they do not begin with the actual, available alternatives from which choices must be made. Moral guidance is not effective if it directs itself to ideal, but unavailable, solutions. Morality, if it is not to be divorced from the practical world of action, must inform itself and relate itself to things as they are. The exercise of responsibility involves making real choices in a real world, which rarely affords the luxury of ideal conditions.

To bring morality and power into the same plane of action was, to Acheson, the central problem of achieving wholeness in foreign relations. Nothing less would permit a nation to bear its responsibilities maturely. For him the only genuine morality in international life was that which dictated restraint in national conduct under the realization that a country cannot act without affecting the well-being of others.

In Acheson's view, foreign policy rested on the fulcrum of power.

There was little room for sentiment in his scheme of things. Relations among nations, he believed, could not be controlled by any consensus of world opinion. Even if nations agreed on certain principles in the abstract, their ability to uphold such principles was always commensurate with their willingness to employ actual power. Principles, whatever their validity, were never self-enforcing. If the actions of individuals within one society could be judged and restrained by the society itself, the actions of nations, Acheson saw, could be limited only by the balance of power and the threat of war. For that reason, stable settlements were possible only when matters of power had been resolved in advance. Acheson attributed the failure at Versailles in 1919 to the fact that there was no relationship between the hopes of Wilson and the state of affairs in the political world. And if Acheson felt that there was no possibility of a Wilsonian settlement in 1919, he was equally certain that there was none in 1949.

II

For a nation troubled by the specter of Soviet power, Acheson's qualifications for the Secretaryship appeared to meet the specific requirements of his time. The *Washington Post*, speculating on Marshall's successor, noted simply: "A man's stature is measurable by the time he has had the Soviet's aggressive number. . . ." Judged by such a criterion, Acheson was a reassuring choice, for he had long been in the vanguard of those Americans who regarded the Soviet Union with profound distrust. As early as February, 1947, he had termed Kremlin policy "aggressive and expanding," and he had been a creative participant in the development of both the Truman Doctrine and the Marshall Plan. To the Senate Committee on Foreign Relations, nothing else seemed to matter; its inquiry never went beyond Acheson's views toward Russia. Even Republican leaders agreed that his subsequent confirmation by an overwhelming Senate vote was propitious. "I believe him to be a brilliant man," observed Bourke Hickenlooper of Iowa. "He . . . brings to the office personal integrity, high ability, and unusual experience. . . . I am convinced that he is completely devoted to and is fully aware of the necessity of unswerving advancement to the principles by which our Government lives, and that he will defend these principles for us and for the world."

Acheson's first task as Secretary of State was that of completing the containment policies inaugurated under Marshall. What mattered to him essentially was the power and unity of the Atlantic community. If the Kremlin ever succeeded in breaking up the Western coalition, it would secure a free hand in dealing with not only the nations of Europe but also the new states of Asia and Africa. By 1949 the Economic Cooperation

Administration was already achieving astonishing results in Europe under its director, Paul G. Hoffman. What remained was the even greater task of creating a viable military structure in the West to offset Soviet power. It was essential that American leadership be devoted primarily—almost singly—to its establishment, for the United States was the keystone of Western defense. This project, the Secretary felt, required coalition diplomacy at its best—the recognition of common interests and the determination to defend them through common action and mutual sacrifice. "Our active foreign policy," Acheson declared in April, 1949,

> has given rise in Europe to a great momentum of recovery and a great increase in the will to resist. The hope for peace lies in maintaining this momentum. The free countries of Western Europe must be encouraged to continue their efforts toward recovery. Their will to resist and their ability mutually to defend themselves must be strengthened. They must be encouraged and assisted to build up their defense forces, through self-help and mutual aid, to a point where aggression cannot take place through internal disorders growing from the seeds sown by a potential aggressor, or under the guise of border incidents. In short, they must regain, individually and collectively, their ability to maintain their independence and national security.

In April, 1949, Acheson appeared before the Senate Foreign Relations Committee to defend the newly formed North Atlantic Treaty Organization. NATO, he said, was a defensive alliance—an agency designed primarily to carry out the purposes of the United Nations Charter. But he refused to dodge the issue of involvement. "If you ratify the Pact," he told the Senators, "it cannot be said that there is no obligation to help, but the extent, the manner, and the timing is up to the honest judgment of the parties." The Secretary's vigor and frankness in defending the Atlantic Pact led the *Washington Post* to observe: "Secretary Acheson is showing himself capable of translating the stature of the United States into effective action and leadership in behalf of his policy." Acheson secured not only the passage of the treaty through the Senate but also the adoption by NATO of a standing committee, comprising the United States, Britain, and France, empowered to make the initial decisions for the defense of the Atlantic community. Eventually he gained congressional approval for the largest peacetime military program in the nation's history.

With the outbreak of the Korean conflict in June, 1950, the new American defense program assumed even greater urgency. The administration interpreted the North Korean aggression as the beginning of a general Communist assault on the free world. "The attack upon the Republic of Korea," the President warned the nation, "makes it plain beyond all doubt that the international Communist movement is prepared to use armed invasion to conquer independent nations." Official statements everywhere during the summer of 1950 pointed to a clear Soviet challenge. If aggression succeeded in Korea, it would be repeated elsewhere, until it rendered a third world war inescapable. To prevent attacks in Southeast Asia, the President increased American military assistance to the Philippines and Indochina and ordered the Seventh Fleet to defend Formosa.

The fear engendered by the Korean conflict enabled the administration to win congressional authorization for defense measures that Acheson had urged repeatedly during his previous months in office. In June the Secretary had asked Congress for 1 billion dollars to strengthen the defenses of Western Europe. In August the administration added almost 4 billion to its request. This Congress approved quickly, with only one opposing vote in the House and none in the Senate. Despite its importance in the Secretary's thought, the Korean conflict did not alter his Europe-first orientation. He saw that the chief deterrent to Communist expansion everywhere rested in the collective forces of the North Atlantic community.

For Acheson it was essential that West Germany be incorporated into the Western defense structure. By the London agreement of June, 1948, the Western zones of Germany were authorized to establish a provisional government, democratic and federal in character. The Western powers accepted the fact of a divided Germany and held out to their zones the hope of membership in the community of free nations. With the arrival of American aid, the West German economy began to recover rapidly. After the Paris meeting of the Council of Foreign Ministers in June, 1949, Acheson concluded that the impasse on German unification was profound. That month the West Germans established the Federal German Republic at Bonn. In October the Soviets created the German Democratic Republic in the Eastern zone. Acheson denounced the new Russian move, terming the Communist-controlled election a fraud and extending the sympathy of the United States government to the East German people for the "contemptuous and humiliating" treatment accorded them by the Kremlin.

Acheson, convinced that Germany was less a military than a political problem, secured both the transfer of West German administration from the War to the State Department and the extension of greater freedom to the West Germans in the management of their internal affairs. He sought a policy that would permit Germans of internationalist bent to gain control of their country, so that the Bonn government would become a source of stability in European politics. As early as February, 1950, he urged that West Germany be accepted as a constructive partner in the North Atlantic community, ready to employ its skills and energies in association with the free world. By making Germany a part of Western Europe, Acheson believed, the West could better limit the growth of German nationalism.

After the shock of Korea, Acheson recommended the final step in the reconstruction of West Germany. He declared before a Senate subcommittee that the long-range effectiveness of American defense policy required the rearming of West Germany as well as France. In September, 1950, the Foreign Ministers of the United States, Britain, and France agreed that the re-creation of a German national army would serve the best interests of both Germany and Western Europe and authorized the Federal German government to establish its own foreign office and enter into diplomatic relations with foreign countries.

Mainland China's entry into the Korean conflict in November, 1950, tended to substantiate the administration's assumption that the Communist threat of aggression was world-wide. If the new assault should prove successful in Korea, ran a White House press release in December, "we can expect it to spread through Asia and Europe to this hemisphere. We are fighting in Korea for our own national security and survival." Because the danger was world-wide, it was more necessary than ever before to increase the combined military strength of the free nations. Much remained to be done in building a NATO defense force. The increasing urgency of the administration was apparent in Acheson's New York speech of October 8. "The period of gathering and organizing strength is a period of great peril," he said. "The job has to be done despite the danger. The alternative is not merely greater danger; it is certain disaster." In December, the NATO Council unanimously asked the President of the United States to select a Supreme Commander. Mr. Truman responded by naming General Dwight D. Eisenhower, then president of Columbia University, to the task of translating military plans into actual armed forces. Acheson's deep conviction that the West required "situations of strength" both to prevent a general war and to permit realistic negotiations with the Soviet Union had been written into national policy.

Beyond the containment of Soviet expansion, Acheson expected little of American policy. Nowhere did he anticipate a world of this nation's own choosing. "Good and evil," he admitted, "can and do exist concurrently in the whole realm of human life. They exist within every individual, within every nation and within every human group." He made it clear that American purpose did not encompass the destruction of the Soviet system or Soviet independence. He promised no easy or total solutions. "Once we understand that we have a long period of work before us," he declared in May, 1949, "then we can see that the object of our efforts is not to remove these problems. They are not removable. The object of our work is to reduce these problems to manageable proportions." But the Secretary counseled against despair. His address before the General Assembly of the United Nations in September, 1949, carried a note of optimism. "It is true," he cautioned, "that the problems are serious, that they are bitter, and that they are not susceptible of any sudden and dramatic solutions. But it has not been proven that they will not eventually yield to the effects of time and patience and hard work."

Acheson expected little of negotiation at mid-century. He was convinced, after the Council of Foreign Ministers meeting of 1949, that the U.S.S.R. was not prepared to relax its grip on the area behind the Iron Curtain, including East Germany, or to concede its purpose of eliminating the United States from the defense of Western Europe. At Berkeley, California, in March, 1950, the Secretary outlined the steps by which the Kremlin might re-establish good faith in international relations. First, the Soviets could fulfill their Tehran pledge to support the self-determination of peoples. In Germany, the Soviet leaders could accept the principle of unification under a government chosen by free elections. In Austria, they could stop sabotaging all efforts at treaty making. In the critical region of Eastern Europe, the Soviets, Acheson declared,

> could withdraw their military and police force and refrain from using the shadow of that force to keep in power persons or regimes which do not command the confidence of the respective peoples, freely expressed through orderly representative processes. In other words, they could elect to observe, in practice, the declaration to which they set their signatures at Yalta concerning liberated Europe.... Nothing could so alter the international climate as the holding of elections in the satellite states in which the true will of the people could be expressed.

Acheson was equally adamant in demanding that the Kremlin leaders, if they sought international confidence in their policies, alter their conduct toward nations outside their sphere. They could, for example, stop their obstructionism in the United Nations and their defiance of the concept of majority decisions by engaging in walkouts and boycotts. They could refrain, added the Secretary, "from using the Communist apparatus ... to attempt to overthrow, by subversive means, established governments with which the Soviet Government stands in an outward state of friendship and respect." It was essential that the Soviets eventually give some assurance that they were not bent on further aggression. Despite his varied conditions for serious diplomacy in the cold war, Acheson insisted only that he sought the evidence of good faith, not a settlement in conformity with American principles. His stipulations, he said, did not

> go to the depths of the moral conflict. They are not things that promise the Kingdom of Heaven. They have been formulated by us, not as moralists but as servants of government, anxious to get on with the practical problems that lie before us and to get on with them in a manner consistent with mankind's deep longing for a respite from fear and uncertainty.

III

Granted the times and the problems, Acheson's record was excellent, his stature considerable. His performance at the Council of Foreign Ministers meeting at Paris, for example, was refreshing and impressive. Unlike his predecessor, Marshall, who usually said nothing or read a prepared speech, Acheson spoke extemporaneously from a carefully constructed brief. This gave his arguments a flexibility and persistence which caused Soviet Minister Vishinsky unprecedented difficulty. When the Russian spokesman argued over the matter of the order in which questions would be introduced into the conference, Acheson commented:

> I can see how the discussion here is going to revert to that favorite proverb which has been used by all of us with such inconclusive results in the last few days about the cart and the horse, so I suggest instead of saying which is the cart and which is the horse that we try a new method of propulsion and try to have the cart and the horse go along side by side.

In reply to a completely unacceptable Soviet proposal regarding the mutual withdrawal of troops from Germany, he remarked: "Now, I say in all conscience, that sort of argument is not a worthy one; it is not worthy of the Council of Foreign Ministers and it is just as full of propaganda as a dog is full of fleas. In fact, I say it is all fleas and no dog!"

Acheson acknowledged no successes for the Paris conference, for he was always scrupulously careful not to overclaim in his dealings with the Soviet officials. Yet there were gains in Europe for American policy during 1949 which, if not attributable to his leadership, at least reflect his sensitive handling of foreign affairs. In Yugoslavia, Tito broke from the Kremlin. If this decision was that of the Yugoslav leader, the moderation of Acheson in revealing neither too much hostility nor too much cordiality toward the Tito regime helped the break to take place. In Greece, the normal functioning of the Truman Doctrine removed that nation from the danger of a Communist take-over. Third, the ambitious Western airlift into Berlin broke, at last, the Soviet blockade.

Managing the State Department and directing and exploiting its considerable talent in the creation of policy had become, by mid-century, an almost impossible assignment. During the preceding decade the Department had grown from a small and intimate organization to one of vast complexity, with resulting inertia, inflexibility, and loss of efficiency in the utilization of personnel. But whatever the cumbersomeness of the policy-making process, individual policies, to bear the stamp of genuine statesmanship, must ultimately reflect individual rather than collective judgment. Advisers can refine and enrich decisions; they cannot make policy. Merely to permit a staff to arrive at a consensus reduces policy to the least common denominator—to a collection of platitudes usually inferior to any of the individual concepts available.

Acheson's relations with this huge structure were aided immeasurably by his own eloquence, clarity, and knowledge, as well as by his ten years of work in the Department. His own detailed preparation for Departmental conferences permitted him to preside at the head of the table mentally as well as physically. His personal standards were conveyed to his officers, so that they also came to meetings prepared. Unlike Marshall, he did not wait for his staff to settle on policies and then present them to him for rejection or approval. Rather, he preferred to tackle the important questions earlier and influence the entire policy-making procedure.

Acheson encouraged the officers of the State Department to develop new concepts and ideas. "Men capable of having them," he wrote later, "were welcomed, respected, and both stimulated and supported. In Washington and in the field, a group, without regard to party affiliation, from inside and outside the permanent service, brought together uncommon ability, experience, and alertness. The result was a renaissance of thought and inventiveness which was unexcelled—and it is not too much to say, unequaled—in any chancellery in the world." Among his top advisers were Counselor George F. Kennan, replaced in 1950 by Charles E. Bohlen, another professional student of Soviet affairs; Paul Nitze, head of the Policy Planning Staff; Philip C. Jessup, Ambassador at Large; and such noted Republicans as John Foster Dulles and John Sherman Cooper. Unlike many of his predecessors, Acheson viewed himself more as the conductor of an orchestra than as its soloist. He seldom left the capital, preferring to remain at his desk close to his official staff. He was even more reluctant to see the President leave Washington to conduct actual negotiations with other nations.

Acheson's relations with the President reflected mutual affection and esteem. Their friendship defied amazing differences in background, education, taste, and personality. But both men were in agreement on the necessity of building a strong Western coalition, and together they took pleasure in the administration's record of standing firm against possible Soviet encroachments. The Secretary was Truman's chief adviser on foreign affairs in every sense of the word. He had conferences with the President at the White House almost daily and dispatched telegrams to the President several times a week when the Secretary was absent from Washington. Seldom did the President ignore Acheson's advice.

By 1951 the Truman-Acheson leadership had created a coalition of free nations as the surest reliance for living through the present troubled times without war. For the Secretary of State this was a remarkable achievement. Referring to the evolution of United States cold-war policy between 1947 and 1950, he wrote:

> The sweep, coherence, and energy of all that was done is hard to grasp from a mere catalogue of measures, or even to convey at all. The financial effort was immense. So were the production and military efforts. But these do not go to the heart of the real achievement. It lies, I think, in the boldness, the imaginativeness, the creativeness of the thinking, and perhaps most of all in the will which those in charge maintained and communicated to the country. This stemmed straight from President Truman himself. The sustained leadership and effort put forth by the government and people of the United States in these years represented a revolution in American foreign policy and the assumption of burdens and responsibilities wholly new to us.

Despite his considerable successes, Acheson was not without critics within his own political and official family. At issue for many conservatives was not the correctness of his concept of containment but his conditions for serious negotiations. Obviously the Secretary anticipated something less than the dissolution of the Soviet empire and the elimination of the Soviet offensive against the West. But what he demanded as evidence of Soviet dependability appeared only narrowly removed from a total Russian capitulation to American principles. For some Americans, there was sufficient compatibility between the essential security interests of the Soviet Union and those of the Western nations to permit greater accommodation in the American position. Without some search for a settlement based on interest, not principle, American foreign policy seemed to comprise nothing but the accumulation of military power. The almost total rejection of the postwar Soviet position as the basis of negotiation assured little but a divided world, for it was doubtful that the United States could ever secure those initial concessions which alone would demonstrate that the Kremlin was prepared for serious diplomacy. American leadership seemed more devoted to creating conditions for successful settlements than to arriving at the settlements themselves.

Acheson's definition of national objectives vis-à-vis the Soviet Union largely in terms of self-determination led some American writers, often friends of the administration, to accuse the Secretary of that very moralism which he specifically condemned. Without some American willingness to accept the Russian gains of World War II, there seemed to remain only the prospect of eventual war. One *Washington Post* editorial declared: "If it is assumed that every proposal coming from the other side is made in bad faith, then obviously no negotiation is possible. But negotiation is the essential business of diplomacy." Arthur M. Schlesinger, Jr., attacked what he regarded as a fundamental moralism in American foreign policy in the *Foreign Policy Bulletin* of February 23, 1951:

The policy of abstract moralism is an honorable and high-minded policy; but it is so concerned with being right in the abstract that it forgets to be effective.... The function of foreign policy is not to provide an outlet for moral indignation, however warranted that indignation may be. The function of foreign policy is to produce desired results.

European spokesmen, concerned with their region's security, lauded Acheson's vigorous leadership in building the Western defense structure. But to Winston Churchill and British students of the U.S.S.R. it made considerable difference whether Western capacity was being designed to negotiate a suitable division of interests in Europe or to secure the unconditional surrender of the Soviet Union. If successful negotiation was its purpose, then delay might be futile. Western power vis-à-vis Russia appeared as strong in 1950 as it was likely to become. Churchill argued for a negotiated settlement in January, 1948, in an address before the House of Commons:

> I will only venture to say that there seems to me to be very real danger in going on drifting too long. I believe that the best chance of preventing a war is to bring matters to a head and come to a settlement with the Soviet Government before it is too late. This would imply that the Western democracies ... would take the initiative in asking the Soviet for a settlement.

Two years later, Churchill put his case before the House of Commons with even greater urgency. The Western position, he warned, was becoming weaker. "Therefore," he concluded, "while I believe there is time for further effort for a lasting and peaceful settlement, I cannot feel that it is necessarily a long time, or that its passage will progressively improve our own security. Above all things, we must not fritter it away."

But to Acheson the territorial *status quo* at mid-century seemed to provide neither the Soviet Union nor the United States with a suitable basis for negotiation. The lines of demarcation in Europe, he knew, were sufficiently well established that any effort to alter them by military action would endanger the peace and bring no gain commensurate with the risk. But the situation was still too fluid to permit a permanent or semi-permanent settlement. For the Soviets still anticipated the disintegration of Western unity, which would permit the strengthening of the Soviet position in Europe. American leadership still harbored the countering conviction that the Soviet hegemony behind the Iron Curtain would eventually disintegrate. There could be no serious negotiation over the future of Europe, the Secretary was convinced, as long as neither side believed that the other had achieved a stable position.

Acheson was assured, after the Foreign Ministers Conference of 1949, that the U.S.S.R. would negotiate realistically only when a particular issue had become stabilized. He noted in February, 1950, that the Kremlin had repeatedly adjusted to established facts. "We have seen . . . ," he said, "that agreements reached with the Soviet Government are useful when those agreements register facts or a situation which exists, and that they are not useful when they are merely agreements which do not register the existing facts." The secret diplomacy which led to the settlement of the Berlin issue in 1949 proved to him that the Soviets would come to terms when faced with stark reality, but not before. When the ultimate occasion for negotiation had been reached, settlements would come quite automatically. "We want peace," Acheson said in March, 1950, "but not at any price. We are ready to negotiate, but not at the expense of rousing false hopes which would be dashed by new failures." What mattered even more to him was the conviction that the West should engage in no diplomacy which might weaken its unity or its determination to resist the blandishments of the Soviet Union.

IV

Eventually Acheson could not prevent a serious partisan onslaught on his leadership and policies. Nowhere had he promised victory over the Soviet Union or an end to the financial burden entailed in the maintenance of the Western military establishment. To many Americans, accustomed to living in a world of absolute security at relatively little cost, the postwar position of the United States was both intolerable and inexcusable.

Late in 1950, former President Herbert Hoover and Senator Robert A. Taft of Ohio launched their attack on the Truman-Acheson defense of Europe. In a radio address of December 20, Hoover demanded that the United States place less reliance on the European Allies and more on the defense of the Western Hemisphere. "The foundations of our national policies," he said, "must be to preserve for the world this Western Hemisphere Gibraltar of Western civilization." Doubting that Europe possessed the will to defend itself, he opposed the commitment of American ground forces to the Continent. Like the isolationists of the thirties, he preferred to rest this nation's security on naval and air superiority.

Taft was concerned primarily with the financial burden imposed by American policies. This, he said, threatened both individual initiative and individual freedom. "Just as our nation can be destroyed by war," he declared, "it can also be destroyed by a political and economic policy at home which destroys liberty and breaks down the financial and economic structure of the United States." Neither of these critics denied the importance of the North Atlantic alliance to the preservation of free Europe; they preferred simply to whittle down the American economic and military commitment to Europe. They did not have their way. Supported by the impact of the Korean conflict, Acheson carried his European policies before Congress and the nation.

The immediate and far more pervading threat to Acheson's leadership and stature lay in Asia. In December, 1949, Chiang Kai-shek, the Nationalist leader of China, had taken refuge on the island of Formosa, the victim of the rising tide of Communist power on the China mainland. For many Americans Chiang's new isolation was a bitter reality. This was true particularly for those thousands of American missionaries, businessmen, students, and travelers who had developed a deep affection and sense of paternalism toward China during the decades prior to World War II. Now they dreaded the total destruction of the China they admired under the new regime of Mao Tse-tung. This sudden transfer of power in China accentuated, rather than diffused, the powerful emotional allegiance which many influential Americans felt for the exiled Chinese leader. Refusing to accept the finality of the revolution that deposed the Kuomintang, they were determined to bind future American policy to Chiang's return to the mainland. Since his enemies were avowed Marxists, this purpose had the advantageous claim of patriotism.

Because the China issue was so fraught with emotion, the administration viewed it as far more dangerous politically than the problem of containing the Soviet Union. When Chiang's collapse appeared imminent in February, 1949, the President called Acheson, Senator Arthur H. Vandenberg, and Vice President Alben Barkley to the White House to formulate a policy that would forestall congressional criticism. Vandenberg opposed desertion of the Nationalists for fear that the United States would "never be able to shake the charge that we [were] the ones who gave poor China the final push into disaster." He urged the administration to wait until the fall of Chiang was "settled *by China* and *in China* and not by the *American government in Washington.*" Vandenberg never evinced any hope for preventing the immediate Communist conquest of China, but he wanted the United States to avoid the responsibility "for the *last push* which makes it possible." Unable to formulate a long-range policy for China, the administration continued to give the Nationalists a moderate amount of economic aid but in every other respect maintained a free hand.

Chiang's final collapse loomed so large on the immediate diplomatic and political horizon that the administration felt compelled to explain it to the American people. In August, 1949, it published the famous China White Paper, a bulky document which attempted to show that the upheaval in China was the result of massive internal changes over which the United States had no control. The Secretary summarized the administration's defense of its policies in one terse statement: "Nothing that this

country did or could have done within the reasonable limits of its capabilities would have changed the result, nothing that was left undone by
this country has contributed to it." Before the National Press Club in
January, 1950, Acheson again summarized his concept of the upheaval
within China: "The Communists did not create this condition. They did
not create this revolutionary spirit. They did not create a great force
which moved out from under Chiang Kai-shek. But they were shrewd
and cunning to mount it, and to ride this thing into victory and into
power."

Acheson accepted Marshall's estimate of the situation in China—that
the Nationalists had lost all effective support among the Chinese people
and could be returned to power only through the direct military involvement of the United States. To Acheson, the Chinese upheaval emanated
from indigenous conditions in China, and for that reason he felt that any
attempt to suppress it lay beyond the bounds of prudent and legitimate
action. He wanted the American people to have access to all information
coming out of China, including the Wedemeyer Report, for without broad
national agreement on the situation in China, a firm policy could not be
built. But his evaluation of the forces operating within China ruled out
any decision to extend the Truman Doctrine to that country. His stand
on this issue revealed his basic pragmatism:

> The United States, in my judgment, acts in regard to a foreign nation
> strictly in regard to American interests. ... And if it is to American in-
> terest or those wider interests which affect it, to do one thing in one
> country and another thing in another country, then *that* is the con-
> sistency upon which I propose to advise the President, and I am not in
> the slightest bit worried because somebody can say: "Well, you said
> so and so about Greece, why isn't all of this true about China?" I will
> be polite. I will be patient, and I will try to explain why Greece is not
> China, but my heart will not be in that battle.

Many Americans who knew something of events in China found Acheson's analysis reassuring. They hoped that he could convince Congress of
its validity. The object of American policy in the Orient, ran a *Washington Post* editorial of January 10, "should be to drive a wedge between
authentic nationalism and aggressive communism. This is a job that is
essentially diplomatic, requiring the pooling of American wisdom and
effort, for Asia is going to be the problem of the century." What pleased
the British was the apparent American decision to recognize the new Chinese government and thus extricate the United States from its involvement
in that nation's internal affairs. The Secretary had declared in September,
1949: "We maintain diplomatic relations with other countries primarily
because we are all on the same planet and must do business with each
other. We do not establish an Embassy in a foreign country to show

approval of its Government." British officials assumed that the United States would follow their lead and shortly recognize Peiping.

Early in 1950, the Nationalist China bloc in the Senate moved to force its program on the nation. On January 2, Senator William F. Knowland of California released a letter from Herbert Hoover which declared that the United States should support the Kuomintang on Formosa and develop a policy to return China to the road of freedom. If necessary, wrote Hoover, this nation should extend its naval protection to Formosa and the Pescadores. Three days later, President Truman countered with the statement that the United States had no intention of becoming involved further in China's civil war by establishing bases on Formosa or by utilizing American Armed Forces to protect the Nationalist government. Economic aid would continue, but no "military aid or advice." Acheson was convinced that those who demanded continued support for Chiang were motivated less by the belief that the Nationalists could be saved than by the political advantage to be gained from the charge that the Truman administration was responsible for the loss of China. The Secretary warned the nation that the persistent effort to tie United States policy to Chiang would not only isolate this nation diplomatically but "mobilize the whole of Asia's millions solidly against the United States and destroy the possibility in our time of a friendly power, and friendly peoples, in Asia."

Senator Joseph McCarthy of Wisconsin quickly submerged the China question even deeper into the mire of partisanship. In February, 1950, without presenting any evidence, he captured the headlines with the charge that the State Department was "thoroughly infested" with Communists. "How can we account for our present situation," he said, "unless we believe that men high in the government are concerting to deliver us to disaster? This must be the product of a great conspiracy on a scale so immense as to dwarf any previous venture in the history of man." The Senator's sensational accusations at Wheeling, West Virginia, supplied the rationale which tied the unlimited expectations of a counterrevolution in China to the concept of limited expenditures. By unloading the responsibility for Chiang's failure on American leadership, he found the argument which would permit a show of aggressiveness in Asia without the corresponding assumption of any expensive military commitment. If the United States had failed to control the revolution in China, it did not mean that Asia had unleashed new energy. It meant simply that the State Department was full of Communists. With their removal, the nation could anticipate the return of the Kuomintang to power.

Immediately, much of the Republican party moved into line behind the Wisconsin Senator, for he had discovered an effective means of attacking the Democratic past and at the same time a formula which assured a doubting nation that it could still have its way whatever the power of its antagonists. With such expectations of success, Americans need ask nothing less than the total elimination of the Peiping regime. Backed by this rationale, the supporters of Chiang Kai-shek suddenly found themselves in an unshakable position to control United States China policy.

V

The illusion that perfect security was still obtainable in the postwar world exposed the State Department and the Foreign Service to unlimited attack. For such extremism created a gap between what was held to be possible and what actually was possible. Here was an area in which the national performance was of necessity inadequate but one in which the resulting discrepancy between unrealistic expectations and actual achievements produced a field of doubt and suspicion for partisan exploitation.

Gradually the attack on the State Department simmered down to a persistent flaying of Acheson. For those who wanted to reduce the public estimate of the Truman administration, he was the most vulnerable target in sight. His personality, his genteel New England background, his faultless grooming (one congressman habitually referred to him as "that goddam floorwalker"), his air of aristocratic detachment, and his intellectual superiority all contributed to his vincibility. As Lester Markel observed early in the fray, "You soon discover in the Secretary his quick intelligence. You suspect this gets him into trouble, because though he may not mean to condescend, he seems often to be condescending." At times the Secretary's words of rebuttal cut too cleanly. Congressmen who might expect to be mauled occasionally in a long, clumsy exchange resented being deflated with a few well-selected phrases.

After the opening rounds of the China debate, Acheson's continued insistence that the problem of Asia stemmed, not from American foreign policy, but from vast revolutionary changes blanketing the Orient kept him in the direct line of fire. Eventually he was forced to carry the chief burden for the collapse of the Nationalist government of China. To men who believed China more essential to American security than England, and Chiang's cooperation more important than that of Clement Attlee or Winston Churchill, the Europe-first orientation of Acheson's policies appeared weak and un-American.

Singling out the Secretary of State to bear the attack revealed a certain irrationality in his assailants. In his astonishingly successful handling of the containment policy in Europe, Acheson had done more to check the Russian advance than had any other public official. These achievements, noted the London *Economist*, caused him to be "regarded in the outside world not merely as a good Secretary of State, but as the best the United

States has had in modern times." The *Manchester Guardian*, noting that Acheson was receiving no support from Democrats in Congress, suggested that Churchill deliver a broadside in defense of the American Secretary. "But between now and the summer," ran its editorial of March 23, "we shall know whether he is able to hold his office by the native ability he brings to it, or lose it because the American system is not yet ready for a career man of the highest type who is not an old trusted lieutenant of the party."

In the United States, Acheson merely became symbolic of that official-dom whose culpability had to be established to prove the soundness of the rationale that American leadership, not power revolutions abroad, was responsible for the decline of this nation's security. Consequently the assault on him reached an unprecedented virulence. To the British, whose interpretation of the great changes transforming the world coincided with his own, the charges were unbelievable. John Duncan Miller of the London *Times* interpreted the attack as essentially "a revolt of the primi-tives against intelligence." In December, 1950, a Republican caucus in the House adopted a resolution declaring that the Secretary of State had "lost the confidence of the Congress and the American people." The Senate Republicans demanded a replacement "for the good of our country." Senator Pat McCarran, the Nevada Democrat, chimed in, "Whether what has been said about him is either proper or correct doesn't matter now." Acheson had been made a public liability and had to go.

So powerful were the expectations that flowed from the charges of dis-loyalty that millions of well-meaning Americans were led to assume that all national losses in Asia could be recouped by placing wiser and more trustworthy men in charge of United States policy. Once it was assured, through the misreading of history, that the nation might have had its way in China and that Chiang Kai-shek was the victim of foul play, any American officer who appeared responsible had to be pursued. Whether a huge conspiracy actually existed was not material. The charges had to be made and repeated to substantiate a specific body of dogma relative to the collapse of the Kuomintang in China. In a letter to the *New York Times* in March, 1950, former Secretary of State Henry L. Stimson warned that the assault on Acheson had a significance beyond that of the rise and fall of an individual. "Every Secretary of State," he wrote, "second only to the President, and alone among appointive officers of the Government, stands before the world as the representative of the United States of America.... The man who seeks to gain political advantage from per-sonal attack on a Secretary of State is a man who seeks political advantage from damage to his country."

After the Chinese entered the Korean conflict in November, 1950, many Americans again found a scapegoat for their frustration in Acheson. During its initial phases the Korean conflict had been popular in the United States and claimed vigorous bipartisan support. It was Acheson who sponsored the "Uniting for Peace" proposal in September, 1950, which authorized the General Assembly of the United Nations to act against aggression without the approval of the Security Council, where the Soviet Union enjoyed the veto power. But when the mainland Chinese sent the war into a long, dreary military stalemate, critics of the administration found arguments which rendered the war the unnecessary consequence of past decisions. The United States, they charged, had invited the aggression in Korea by failing to create an army in South Korea capable of matching the power of the Communist-led forces of North Korea. Also, the critics recalled, the Secretary of State, in January, 1950, had excluded specifically both Korea and Formosa from the perimeter which the United States would defend against military attack. The North Koreans, charged Senator Taft, merely took the Secretary at his word. "They knew that we had permitted the taking over of China by the Communists," he added, "and saw no reason why we should seriously object to the taking over of Korea. The Korean War and the problems which arise from it are the final result of the continuous sympathy toward communism which inspired American policy."

Under the pressure of events in Asia and domestic attacks on past decisions in China, the American posture toward Peiping began to harden into one of extreme antagonism. In February, 1951, the United States managed to push a resolution through the United Nations—by a vote of 44 to 7, with 9 abstentions—that branded the mainland Chinese aggressors in Korea. To the British, the continued drift in United States China policy was deeply disturbing. They deplored the American obsession with Formosa and the half million Nationalists based there. They could discern no realistic alternative to the recognition of the Peiping regime and assumed, as late as January, 1951, that the two nations were in general agreement on long-range policy for China. It was for this reason that they were disturbed at the American resolution in the United Nations. The British press concluded that Acheson had been pursued by his opponents to the point where he had to prove, in some dramatic fashion, that he was as devotedly anti-Communist as they were.

Republicans increased the intensity of their attack in April, 1951, when President Truman, partially on Acheson's advice, recalled General Douglas MacArthur from his Pacific command. Immediately, House Republicans proposed an amendment to the State Department's appropriation which would have removed the Secretary from the Federal payroll. The measure was defeated, largely because of its bill-of-attainder aspects, by a vote of 171 to 81. During July, Representative George H. Bender of Ohio blamed Acheson for "all the casualties in Korea," and Representative

Charles J. Kersten of Wisconsin even managed to find the Secretary responsible for "setting up the police state of Poland."

During the congressional hearings that followed MacArthur's return to the United States, Acheson assured the senators that he was not about to recognize the Peiping regime or permit the United Nations to do so. This promise followed, ironically, the Secretary's long and brilliant defense of past United States action in China, which no one challenged. But at that precise moment, with a war raging in Korea, the recognition of mainland China could not have been under consideration. Acheson never intended that the policy of nonrecognition should continue indefinitely beyond the termination of that war.

What eventually moderated the extreme partisan attacks on the Secretary of State was his skillful and unruffled performance as presiding officer at the San Francisco Conference which ratified the Japanese Treaty in September, 1951. His firm disposal of Soviet obstructiveness, viewed by millions on television, gave an extraordinary boost to his prestige and won the open plaudits of many of his political opponents.

VI

Acheson's relationship to the essentially democratic elements in American society—Congress, the press, and the public—was characterized by a strange ambivalence. During those months that he was carrying his European program through Congress with little opposition, he was engaged in a bitter feud with many of its members. At times his response to questions before congressional committees varied from open ridicule to profound contempt—responses quite understandable considering the nature of the charges being directed at him elsewhere by members of those committees on matters of China and Korea. But despite the high level of mutual animosity, Acheson never failed to defend administration policy with vigor and success. In fact, he did not regard Congress as a barrier to the development of his basic foreign policies.

Good press relations, by mid-century, had become almost as essential to the proper functioning of the American government as cooperation between executive and Congress. The press conference permitted a Secretary of State to explain important policies and to keep public attention riveted to them. Through the Washington reporters he might speak effectively to foreign governments as well. So powerful had the Washington press become, Patrick O'Donovan of the London *Observer* noted, that it performed "an almost constitutional function."

Acheson recognized the need of popular support for government policies. He once said that his chief problem was deciding, not what to do, but how to get consent for doing what he believed should be done. Admittedly, it would have been difficult for him to command the attention of reporters, yearning for the big headline, in competition with congressmen accusing the administration of harboring Communists. Congress, not the executive, had become the chief source of news and opinion. But Acheson did not even make an appreciable effort to strike back at his tormentors through the press. Certainly he had the talent to use the Washington reporters as skillfully as any other public official; yet his relations with them became increasingly strained. The *Washington Post* attributed Acheson's disinclination to utilize the press to his impatience with public processes and his conviction that it was not the duty of a Secretary of State to tickle "the ears of the groundlings."

James Reston, Washington correspondent of the *New York Times*, visited Acheson on his last day in office to inquire of him bluntly why they had not managed a better working relationship. There was in Reston's question the inescapable accusation that the Secretary had permitted the publicity of previous years to run against him by default—that the erosion of his position before the American people had resulted from a failure of communication. Acheson's answer was equally blunt, for he was dedicated to the traditional methods of privacy. It was the duty of a Secretary of State, he said, to inaugurate new policies and to bring them to maturity free from public scrutiny and pressure. It was the Secretary's task to shield evolving concepts from the public; it was the reporter's purpose to get the news, whatever the effect on policy. Reston would not deny the latter role of the press, but he believed that Acheson had failed to employ a powerful democratic agency in defense of his actions in both Europe and Asia. At any rate, Acheson neither informed the public adequately himself nor created any information service in the State Department. He resisted the whole trend toward governmental public relations, preferring to have the record speak for itself.

The enormous dichotomy between Acheson's performance as Secretary of State and his eventual loss of stature in the public image is a simple measure of the persistence and vituperation of the accusations leveled at him. No Secretary of State in living memory had commanded such respect abroad; none had been so thoroughly discredited at home. To the Russians he had become the most feared diplomat in the Western world; to millions of Americans he was the official most suspect of playing the Russian game. Among European leaders many of the events in Washington were totally beyond comprehension. During those critical years in which the United States had soared, in the words of Churchill, to the summit of the earth, it had a Secretary of State fit to represent it. The *Washington Post* added: "Mr. Acheson leaves his high office not unruffled by his cruel exposure, but fully on top of his job; and he has whatever satisfaction there is in the knowledge that he has made a remarkable dent on his times. . . ."

Acheson had sought to give the nation a sense of direction, but the incessant charges of his opponents weakened or destroyed many of the assumptions upon which his policies had been based. For in the continuing promise that more could be achieved at less cost lay the seeds of vacillation, confusion, and sheer irrelevance in the American response to world affairs. What was tragic in the radical right's attack on Acheson was its total disregard of feasible alternatives. In creating the devil myth about the American role in China, the extremists dealt almost mortal blows at any rational American posture in Asian affairs. In arranging for the national repudiation of the Korean conflict to carry their party to victory in 1952, they denied to themselves and the nation the only concept upon which a reasonable foreign policy could be built—the employment of limited means for limited objectives. It was not clear by 1952 how the nation thereafter could marshal its strength or employ it effectively. And those conservatives who encouraged the attack in the hope of reaping political rewards and those liberals who sat mutely in the hope of making Acheson the scapegoat for Democratic policies must share responsibility for the resulting chaos.

15

John Foster Dulles

1953-1959

BY HANS J. MORGENTHAU
University of Chicago

A contemporary American Secretary of State must perform two basic and difficult tasks: he must defend and promote the interests of the United States abroad, and he must establish and defend his position at home. Whereas the former task is inherent in the office, the latter is a result of five interconnected constitutional and political factors inherent in the American system of government. The position of the Secretary of State must be secured, first of all, against competition from four quarters: the President, Congress, other agencies of the executive branch, and other members of the Department of State. The fifth factor is public opinion, and it, of course, affects the Secretary's relation to the other four.

The President bears, according to the constitutional scheme, the chief responsibility for the conduct of foreign policy. This he is supposed to discharge with the help of the Secretary of State as his principal adviser and administrative officer. Yet, in actuality, the distribution of responsibility between the President and the Secretary of State has run the gamut from Presidential predominance—the President determining foreign policy without the advice and administrative support of the Secretary of State—to the predominance of the Secretary of State—the latter determining and administering foreign policy and the President merely ratifying his decisions.

The competition between the executive branch and Congress for control of American foreign policy began in Washington's administration and is the result of a constitutional distribution of functions which, in the words of Professor Corwin, "is an invitation to struggle for the privilege of directing American foreign policy." It is also the result of the dynamics of the American political system, which deprives the Secretary of State of most of the political weapons of rewards and reprisals with which the President and other members of the Cabinet can stave off congressional opposition and secure congressional support.

The need for the Secretary of State to maintain the prerogatives of his office against competition from other executive departments arises from the dispersal of responsibility for the conduct of American foreign policy among a multitude of executive departments. In 1949, the Hoover Commission, which investigated the organization of the executive branch, found that about forty-five executive agencies, aside from the Department of State, were dealing with one or another phase of foreign policy. The Secretary of State must maintain, against the parochial interests of all these agencies, the over-all direction of foreign policy.

The Secretary of State must also establish and maintain his authority within his own Department. He must keep in check the members of his staff who owe their position to political influence or who otherwise enjoy political support for independent policies.

Finally, the accomplishment of these four competitive tasks depends in great measure upon the ability of the Secretary of State to marshal public opinion at large to the support of his person and his policies. Without the support of public opinion, the Secretary of State is bound to be utterly vulnerable to competition from any of the quarters mentioned, especially, however, from Congress, which in most circumstances is likely to enjoy the public support that the Secretary of State is lacking. On the other hand, with that support secured, the Secretary of State is in a strong position vis-à-vis his competitors, especially those who, like himself, draw much of their strength from public opinion.

Thus the American Secretary of State must perform a domestic political task of great complexity and delicacy as a precondition for the performance of his primary task in the field of foreign policy. Nor are these two tasks separate in execution. Quite to the contrary, each impinges upon the other. The kind of foreign policy the Secretary of State pursues exerts an influence, favorable or unfavorable, upon his domestic position. The kind of domestic position he is able to make for himself predetermines in good measure the limits within which he is able to move on the international stage. The attempt to reconcile the demands of foreign policy and those of domestic politics, without sacrificing the indispensable substance of either, involves more complications and calls for greater finesse than any of the tasks previously mentioned. It is here that the Secretary of State faces the supreme test of his ability to do justice to the requirements of his office.

II

How has John Foster Dulles performed those tasks which impose themselves with existential force upon whoever occupies the office? What conception of the office did he bring to these tasks, and in what concrete terms did he execute them? The answers to these questions must be sought in three factors that exerted a fundamental influence on Dulles: his sense of mission, the state of mind of the Republican party, and the example of his predecessor, Dean Acheson.

Dulles's appointment to the position of Secretary of State must appear to the observer as the natural culmination of a development foreshadowed by his family background and prepared for step by step by his diplomatic career. Both his maternal grandfather, John W. Foster, after whom he had been named, and his uncle, Robert Lansing, had been Secretaries of State. Dulles had started his diplomatic career virtually at the earliest possible moment: in 1907, when he was nineteen and a junior in college, he acted as his grandfather's secretary at the Second Peace Conference at The Hague. He served in 1917 as a member of the Second Pan-American Scientific Congress and as a special agent of the Department of State in Central America. In 1918–1919 he was counsel to the American Commission to Negotiate Peace, and in 1919 he became a member of the Reparation Commission and of the Supreme Economic Council. He was a member of the American delegation to the San Francisco Conference of 1945 and to the United Nations General Assembly in 1946, 1947, 1948, and 1950. He served as adviser to the Secretary of State at meetings of the Council of Foreign Ministers in 1945, 1947, and 1949 and as consultant to the Secretary of State in 1950. In 1950–1951, as special representative of the President with the rank of ambassador, he negotiated the peace treaty with Japan and the security treaties with Australia, New Zealand, the Philippines, and Japan. When Thomas E. Dewey ran for the Presidency in 1944 and 1948, Dulles was generally regarded as his choice for Secretary of State.

To Dulles himself, this record seemed to reveal a providential design which had singled him out to be Secretary of State, which had endowed him with the qualities required for that position, and which would not let him fail. In a speech to the staff of the Department of State on the assumption of his office, Dulles pointed to the fact that his grandfather had been Secretary of State, that his uncle had been Secretary of State, and that he was now Secretary of State. His conviction that there was something virtually inevitable and foreordained in his holding this exalted position accounts at least in part for Dulles's confidence in his ability to shoulder alone the momentous responsibilities of his office and to face alone the dreadful uncertainties of foreign policy. The self-confidence which all statesmen need, faced as they are with these responsibilities and uncertainties, and which others have found in superstitions, such as astrology or other forms of soothsaying, exhaustive information and advice, or a simple faith in divine guidance, Dulles found in his sense of predestination, derived from his family background and his career and supported by a strong, self-reliant personality.

Dulles was destined to become Secretary of State as a member of a party whose support for an active but restrained foreign policy—moving somewhere between isolationism and imperialism—was still precarious at the beginning of the fifties. The Republican party had entered World War II committed to isolationism and had emerged from it with a split personality. Senator Vandenberg, strongly influenced and supported by Dulles and a minority of his party, initiated bipartisanship in foreign policy. Thus one wing of the Republican party came to approve the fundamental changes by which American foreign policy was transformed in the forties, whereas another wing, more vociferous and more influential with public opinion at large and represented by men like Senators William E. Jenner and Joseph McCarthy, remained in uncompromising opposition. Between these two groups stood a vacillating center which hankered back to isolationism but would almost, though not quite, admit that isolationism was beyond the reach of a rational foreign policy. Senator Taft was the most eminent spokesman of this group.

Dulles had to come to terms with the problem of gaining the support of his own party for his person and policies. Two roads were open to him. He could attempt to impress the internationalist wing and the wavering center with the rationality and even the inevitability of the foreign policy to which he was committed, letting the intransigent right wing wither on the vine, or else he could try to gain the support of the right wing by giving the appearance of being really one of them and of actually pursuing their policies. Dulles chose the latter course, primarily under the impact of what had happened to his predecessor.

The third fundamental experience which molded Dulles's conception of his office, and the policies realizing it, was the opportunity of witnessing, and contributing to, the fate that befell Dean Acheson. Here was a Secretary of State who was intellectually at least as well equipped for the office as any of his predecessors since John Quincy Adams, whose dedication to the common good was exemplary, and whose achievements in fashioning a new foreign policy for the United States commensurate with its interests were outstanding. In short, in terms of the requirements of foreign policy, here was one of the best Secretaries of State the United States had ever had. Yet here was also, in terms of the requirements of domestic politics, one of the least successful Secretaries of State. For large sectors of American public opinion Acheson's State Department became synonymous with softness toward communism—if not toleration of, or even connivance in, treason. When Acheson's loyalty was attacked and his resignation asked for in Congress, not a member dared to come to his defense. Only the President's support kept him in office.

Witnessing the terrifying spectacle of a good and able man—as great a Secretary of State in terms of foreign policy as Dulles could ever hope to be—being haunted as a threat to the Republic and shunned as an outcast, Dulles resolved that what happened to Acheson would not happen to him. In consequence, to secure his domestic position became his overriding concern. To that end, he set out to achieve three objectives: to create for the American public the image of himself as a stanch and dynamic fighter against communism and thus as a Secretary of State without any of the faults attributed to his predecessor; to prevent at all costs the development of an opposition in Congress to his person and policies; and to establish and maintain a relationship with the President which would assure his control of foreign policy.

III

The creation of the image of a foreign policy radically different from that for which the preceding administration had been responsible proceeded essentially through six spectacular pronouncements: "liberation," the unleashing of Chiang Kai-shek, "agonizing reappraisal," the "new look," intervention in Indochina, and "brinkmanship."

During the election campaign of 1952 and during the first months of his tenure of office, Dulles and other spokesmen for the new administration announced that the old policy of containment, which Dulles had called in the Republican platform of 1952 "negative, futile and immoral," was to be replaced by a policy of liberation. Yet, as the London *Economist* put it as early as August 30, 1952, "Unhappily 'liberation' applied to Eastern Europe—and Asia—means either the risk of war or it means nothing. . . . 'Liberation' entails no risk of war only when it means nothing." The Eisenhower administration, however, shied away from the risk of war at least as much as had its predecessor. And when the East German revolt of June, 1953, and the Hungarian revolution of October, 1956, put the policy of liberation to the test of actual performance, it became obvious that liberation was indistinguishable from containment.

In his State of the Union message of February 2, 1953, following Dulles's public and private advice, President Eisenhower declared: "In June, 1950, following the aggressive attack on the Republic of Korea, the United States Seventh Fleet was instructed both to prevent attack upon Formosa and also to insure that Formosa should not be used as a base of operations against the Chinese Communist mainland." In view of the Chinese intervention in the Korean conflict, the President declared that he was "issuing instructions that the Seventh Fleet no longer be employed to shield Communist China." This announcement implied a fundamental change in the Far Eastern policies of the United States from the preservation of the *status quo* to the active attempt to restore Chiang Kai-shek's rule on the Asiatic mainland. In actuality, no such change occurred. Quite to the contrary, the Eisenhower administration seems to have been at least as anxious as its predecessor to limit the military activities of Chiang Kai-shek to strictly defensive measures. By making this limitation part of the agreements negotiated with Chiang Kai-shek at the end of 1954, the Eisenhower administration went even beyond the unilateral declaration of policy contained in President Truman's instruction to the Seventh Fleet of June, 1950.

On December 14, 1953, Dulles declared at the meeting of the North Atlantic Council: "If, however, the European Defense Community should not become effective, if France and Germany remain apart, so that they would again be potential enemies, then indeed there would be grave doubt whether Continental Europe could be made a place of safety. That would compel an agonizing reappraisal of the basic United States policy." This statement implied that in certain contingencies the United States might lose its interest in the military defense of Europe and leave it to its fate. This threat called forth much comment but little anxiety in Europe and elsewhere. As an incentive for France to ratify the European Defense Community, it was ineffective. For in order to take this threat seriously, one would have had to assume that the United States had committed itself to the defense of Western Europe, not because it deemed its own security dependent upon it, but because it happened to approve of the policies of certain European nations. Few observers, and no responsible statesmen, were willing to make such an assumption.

The most far-reaching and most widely commented-upon announcement of this kind, however, was Dulles's speech of January 12, 1954, proclaiming a "new look" in American foreign policy as the result of "some basic policy decisions" which the President and the National Security Council had taken. This new policy was anchored to the concept of "massive retaliation." Lester Pearson, then Canadian Secretary of State for External Affairs, thought as late as March 15, 1954, that this speech "may turn out to be one of the most important of our times." The present writer, on March 29, 1954, published an article in the *New Republic* interpreting and evaluating this speech as if it meant what it said. Yet Walter Lippmann could say on March 18 that "the official explanations of the new look have become so voluminous that it is almost a career in itself to keep up with them." Characterizing Dulles's speech as "a case of excessive salesmanship," Lippmann concluded: "There is no doubt that the words of the text convey the impression that something momentous and novel has been decided. But everything that has been said since then by the Chiefs of Staff, notably by Admiral Carney, and no less so by Mr. Dulles himself, make it plain that there has been no radical change in our strategic policy."

On the same day, the *Manchester Guardian* summed it all up by saying: "The 'new look' in American military strategy is mainly old merchandise in a new package. There is really nothing new in relying on 'massive mobile retaliatory power' as the principal safeguard of peace—nothing new, that is, except the sales campaign by which the Administration is trying to persuade the American people that some small changes make the strategy of 1954 fundamentally sounder than the strategy of 1953." On March 19, the Senate Committee on Foreign Relations was the scene of the following dialogue between Senator Mike Mansfield and Dulles, who for all practical purposes buried the "new look" under the cover of military secrecy:

> Senator Mansfield: Do you consider this new policy a new policy?
> Secretary Dulles: It certainly has new aspects.
> Senator Mansfield: What are they?
> Secretary Dulles: Well, I am sorry I cannot go into that here. All I can say to you, and you will have to take it on faith, is that a series of new decisions have been taken by the National Security Council and many have been involved, close, and difficult decisions, but there is today on the record a series of decisions which are largely derived from this basic philosophy which were not there a year and a half ago.

Although the "new look" was the most sweeping of these announcements, the official declarations concerning the Indochina War were politically and militarily the most serious; for they dealt, not with general principles of United States policy, but with a concrete situation which required action here and now. On March 25, 1954, the President declared at his news conference that the defense of Indochina was of "transcendent importance." On March 29, the Secretary of State announced: "Under the conditions of today, the imposition on Southeast Asia of the political system of Communist Russia and its Chinese Communist ally, by whatever means, would be a grave threat to the whole free community. The United States feels that that possibility should not be passively accepted, but should be met by united action. This might have serious risks, but these risks are far less than would face us a few years from now if we dare not be resolute today." The President and the Secretary of State referred to Indochina as the cork in the bottle of Southeast Asia and as the first in a row of dominoes whose fall would necessarily cause the downfall of the others. Yet no action of any kind reflected even faintly the conception of policy which these words seemed to convey. It was, in the words of the *Economist* of August 21, 1954, this "spectacle of vociferous inaction" which led to the "worst diplomatic disaster in recent American history."

The most sensational and also the most patently implausible of these pronouncements concerned "brinkmanship." In an article in *Life* magazine of January 16, 1956, Dulles was reported as having declared, in the course of an interview, that his policy of firmness and daring, fully supported by the President, saved the peace and protected the interests of the United States on three occasions: in Korea, Indochina, and the Formosa Straits. "Of course," Dulles was quoted as having said, "we were brought to the verge of war. The ability to get to the verge without getting into the war is the necessary art. If you cannot master it, you inevitably get into war. . . . We walked to the brink and we looked it in the face. We took strong action." The article praises this technique as "the greatest display of personal diplomacy since the great days of the Franklin-Adams-Jefferson triumvirate in the Europe of the 1780's."

Although this is obviously not the place to test these claims in detail against the available historic evidence, it must be pointed out that, in regard to Indochina, Dulles was prevented from going to war by the unwillingness of the President and of Great Britain to do so. Whether the government of the United States had really resolved to use atomic weapons against Manchuria in June, 1953, if the Communists renewed the war in Korea and whether the Communists were deterred by that knowledge are at present matters of speculation. It is also a moot question whether the congressional resolution of January, 1955, authorizing the President to defend the offshore islands in the Formosa Straits under certain conditions was interpreted by both the administration and the Chinese government as a threat implying the certainty of atomic war. Yet what in actuality was either speculative or simply untrue was presented, in the *Life* article, as a set of historic facts supporting a most favorable evaluation of Dulles's policies.

Dulles's six major pronouncements served the purpose of creating the image of a new, forceful, aggressive foreign policy in order to gain the support of public opinion for both the person of the Secretary of State and the foreign policies he pursued, policies which were not essentially different from those of his predecessor and were certainly not different in the respects in which they were claimed to be. These endeavors culminated in the first Cabinet meeting ever televised, in which Dulles reported on the London Conference which met from September 28 to October 3, 1954. Arthur Krock recalled in the *New York Times* of May 6, 1960, that "the television show . . . was billed as a 'Cabinet meeting' . . . and turned out to be more of a sham performance than any rigged quiz program."

In the *Manchester Guardian Weekly* of October 23, 1954, Alistair Cooke gave a striking account of that performance:

> The whole show had a relaxed, closed-door air, almost like a Cabinet meeting. In the lead part ... Mr. Dulles gave a naturalistic performance of great ease and articulateness. Mr. Henry Cabot Lodge made the most of a single-sentence tribute to the President for his peaceful atomic energy proposals. Cast as the unsleeping watchdog of the people's purse, Mr. Secretary of the Treasury Humphrey expressed with moving verisimilitude his concern that the Paris Agreement should not cost the American taxpayer one extra nickel. Mrs. Hobby conveyed an intelligent anxiety over the Saar.
>
> Only Secretary of Agriculture Ezra Benson, an artless man from the West, had to be prodded into his line by Mr. Dulles, who suggested after an anxious pause that some of them might now be wondering "how the Soviet Union is taking this." Mr. Benson was indeed wondering just that, and made an alert retrieve. It was the only missed cue in an otherwise flawless performance, surely an enviable record for any amateur dramatic company.

IV

The position of the Secretary of State vis-à-vis Congress was secured by two basic tactics. Dulles disarmed the potential congressional opposition, consisting of the right wing of the Republican party, by pursuing its policies and by allowing it to exert a governing influence, at least temporarily, over certain personal and substantive matters which remained but nominally under the control of the Secretary of State.

Dulles's execution of the personnel policies of the congressional right wing was predicated on the assumption, with which the Republican party had attacked the preceding administration, that the Department of State at the very least was not a reliable guardian of the interests of the United States vis-à-vis other nations and, more particularly, Communist ones. In carrying out these policies, Dulles proceeded in two stages: the first was a purge and the second the application of stringent security regulations. By the end of 1953, most members of the Foreign Service who had held high positions in the Department of State had been dismissed, had voluntarily resigned, or had been transferred to politically nonsensitive positions.

Executive Order No. 10450 of April 27, 1953, as applied to the Department of State, in effect institutionalized the purge by establishing extremely stringent security regulations for employment, promotion, and surveillance. The case of John Paton Davies, Jr., a prominent member of the Foreign Service, who underwent nine security investigations before he was dismissed, is but an extreme example of what was then a fairly typical situation. His case is typical also in that it reveals clearly the political purpose of the purges which, in so far as the Secretary of State was concerned, were undertaken primarily in order to satisfy the potential opposition in Congress. Davies, who had been stationed in China after World War II and who afterward joined the Policy Planning Staff, was a favorite target of that opposition. There can be no doubt, even though the documentary evidence to prove it is not yet available, that Davies was deliberately sacrificed, regardless of the merits of his case, and was subjected to as many security investigations as were necessary to prove him a security risk. It is revealing in this connection that, after the last investigating board had rendered the desired unfavorable verdict and Davies had been dismissed, he received a telephone call from the Secretary of State congratulating him upon his attitude before the board and authorizing him to use Dulles's name as a reference in his search for a new position.

Executive Order No. 10450, which provided the legal basis for these proceedings, was a general order, issued under the authority of the President for all executive departments. Yet since this order left wide discretion to the heads of the departments, the Secretary of State was responsible for the way it was implemented in his own Department. Not only did he establish, and suffer to be established, a rigid system of security regulations, but he also added to this system measures of his own. Department Circular No. 95 of April 15, 1954, for instance, imposed upon all officials of the Department of State the duty to be informers:

> I am aware that no agency of the government can improve, or even maintain its level of effectiveness unless it is receiving a stream of new ideas and constructive criticisms. I hope that the inspection operation will be the focal reception point of that stream. I have told Mr. McLeod that in his capacity as administrator of the inspection operation he should be available at any time to receive personally from any of our people the benefit of their thinking on improving operations and procedures or on other problems, official and personal.
>
> In brief, I regard the internal inspection operation of the Department as one of its most important concerns. Its success will depend upon the cooperation and aid received generally from employees of the Department.

Dulles's efforts to disarm the potential opposition by pursuing its policies were assured success by the ability of that opposition to place its representatives in key positions within the Department of State. The right-wing bloc thus came to dominate the Bureau of Security, whose leading officials controlled, directly or indirectly, security, consular affairs, personnel, and inspection of United States missions abroad. The bureau adopted the political philosophy and the policies of the congressmen to whom its principal members owed both their positions and their primary loyalties.

It reported to them and executed their orders. To an extent which changed with the ebbs and tides of political fortune, it was these congressmen, and not the President or the Secretary of State, who determined the operations of the Department of State and its affiliated agencies.

The most spectacular instance of this extraconstitutional influence that has come to light is provided by the International Information Administration. The report published by Martin Merson, the chief consultant to the Director of that agency, leaves no doubt that, at least from February through July, 1953, Senator McCarthy and his friends in Congress had taken over the functions which, according to the Constitution, the President and the Secretary of State are supposed to perform. These members of Congress determined, in large measure, both the substantive and the personnel policies of the International Information Administration. It was to them that the top officials of the agency reported, it was their approval which they had to seek, and it was their orders which they were supposed to execute. And when they finally incurred the displeasure of their congressional masters, they had to resign.

In the *New York Times* of January 17, 1954, five of the most distinguished older diplomats of the United States, four of whom have been Ambassadors and an equal number Under or Assistant Secretaries of State, summarized the "sinister results" of these policies:

> The conclusion has become inescapable, for instance, that a Foreign Service officer who reports on persons and events to the very best of his ability and who makes recommendations which at the time he conscientiously believes to be in the interest of the United States may subsequently find his loyalty and integrity challenged and may even be forced out of the service and discredited forever as a private citizen. A premium therefore has been put upon reporting and upon recommendations which are ambiguously stated or so cautiously set forth as to be deceiving.
>
> When any such tendency begins its insidious work it is not long before accuracy and initiative have been sacrificed to acceptability and conformity. The ultimate result is a threat to national security. In this connection the history of the Nazi and Fascist foreign services before the Second World War is pertinent.
>
> The forces which are working for conformity from the outside are being reinforced by the present administrative set-up within the Department of State which subordinates normal personnel administration to considerations of security.
>
> It is obvious, of course, that candidates for the Foreign Service should be carefully investigated before appointment and that their work should at all times be under the exacting scrutiny of their professional superiors. But when initial investigation attaches undue importance to such factors as even a temporary departure from conservative political and

economic views, casual association with persons holding views not cur-
rently in fashion or subscription to a periodical labeled as "liberal";
when subsequent investigation is carried to the point of delaying a
promotion list for a year and routine transfers from one post to another;
when investigations of individual officers must be kept up-to-date to
within ninety days; when an easy path has been opened to even the
anonymous informer; and when the results of these investigations are
evaluated not by persons experienced in the Foreign Service or even
acquainted at firsthand with conditions abroad, but by persons of
quite different experience, it is relevant to inquire whether we are not
laying the foundations of a Foreign Service competent to serve a totali-
tarian government rather than the government of the United States as
we have heretofore known it.

Fear is playing an important part in American life at the present
time. As a result the self-confidence, the confidence in others, the sense
of fair play and the instinct to protect the rights of the non-conformist
are—temporarily, it is to be hoped—in abeyance. But it would be
tragic if this fear, expressing itself in an exaggerated emphasis on security, should lead us to cripple the Foreign Service, our first line of
national defense, at the very time when its effectiveness is essential to
our filling the place which history has assigned to us.

As far as personnel policy in the State Department and Foreign Service
was concerned, the potential opposition was conciliated simply by the dual
device of pursuing its policies and handing over to it in good measure the
control of those policies. With regard to substantive policies, three different devices were used to propitiate the opposition. First, the great pronouncements, which, as we have seen, were intended to impress public
opinion at large with the novelty, dynamism, and aggressiveness of Dulles's
foreign policy, served the same purpose for congressional opinion. Although the foreign policies which had been established by the preceding
administration and which had proved their worth by their success were
essentially continued, the Secretary's pronouncements created the impression of a succession of drastic innovations. Second, the Department
shunned actual initiative and innovation where they were called for by
new conditions, for a new departure in foreign policy might antagonize
the potential opposition and was bound to create the domestic political
complications that Dulles was resolved to forestall. Thus the twofold
need of giving the appearance of innovation and avoiding it in practice
resulted in a consistent contrast between what American foreign policy
was declared to be and what it actually was.

In regard to the Far East, however, Dulles did permit a certain degree
of innovation. His third major conciliatory tactic was to adjust the substance of foreign policy to the preferences of the potential opposition for
the cause of Chiang Kai-shek, both by identifying himself, at least to some

extent, with those preferences and by handing over the control of foreign policy in that area to men committed to pursue those preferences vigorously. There can be no doubt that the majority of the leading officials who advised Eisenhower on foreign affairs during his first years in office were opposed to his policies in the Far East. That majority was composed of two groups: by far the larger of these groups wanted to advance toward a more aggressive position, even at the risk of a limited war with Communist China; the smaller group would have liked to retreat into less exposed positions. The actual policy of the United States was to maintain an intermediate position between those two extremes, which followed the line of least resistance by trying neither to advance nor to retreat but to maintain the *status quo*.

Yet a rational examination of the forces opposing each other in the Far East and their probable dynamics could only lead to the conclusion that a commitment to the *status quo* was not likely to be tenable in the long run. Both the United States and Communist China would have to go forward or backward; they were not likely to remain indefinitely where they were. Why, then, was the policy of the United States based upon an assumption that could not be supported by rational argument? The answer is to be found in the surrender to the concepts, if not the policies, of an opposition whose reasoning, contradictory in itself, could not provide the basis for a rational policy but whose voice, by default of the executive branch, was powerful enough to mold public opinion.

Public opinion with regard to Communist China was dominated by two strong contradictory desires: to make good somehow the defeat which the United States had suffered through the defection of China to the Communist camp and to do so without getting involved in a major war on the continent of Asia. The opposition presented a program designed to meet these two emotional demands. It promised the overthrow of the Communist regime of China and the restoration of Chiang Kai-shek's rule through aerial bombardment and a naval blockade, using Formosa as a springboard. Yet a careful reading of the minutes of the joint congressional committee investigating, in 1951, the dismissal of General MacArthur can leave no doubt in the mind of the unbiased reader about the military and political emptiness of this program. For the opposition could not devise any policy, short of all-out war, that would assure the destruction of the Communist regime of China. In short, the program of the opposition served as an effective instrument to achieve an illusory reconciliation of policy with popular demands, but since the two could not be reconciled in practice, it offered no basis for a rational policy.

Nevertheless, the Eisenhower administration, frightened like its predecessor by the specter of public opinion, at least appeared to have accepted the objectives and expectations of the opposition and thus allowed its own policies to be judged by the standards of the opposition. By these standards, its policies could not help being found wanting. For, on the one hand, the administration was responsible enough not to embark upon military adventures; on the other, it committed itself at least to the defense of Formosa, whose indispensability for the defense of the United States was accepted as a dogma by government and opposition alike. In consequence, the executive branch found itself continuously on the defensive, apologizing, as it were, for not living up to its own standards and feeling compelled from time to time to substitute for policy a momentous announcement or a grandiose gesture suggesting the imminence of forceful action. The executive branch had thus become the prisoner of the opposition. Too responsible to do what the opposition wanted it to do but prevented by its fear of public opinion from devising and executing a positive policy of its own, the President and Secretary were reduced to having no policy at all, while trying to make it appear as though they were following, however cautiously, in the footsteps of the opposition.

V

Dulles's task of making his position and policies secure with public opinion and Congress was greatly complicated by his uncertainty about the extent to which public opinion and Congress were willing to endorse him as Secretary of State and to support his policies. It was this uncertainty, amounting in Dulles's mind to extreme doubt, which resulted not only in his opening the gates of the State Department to the potential opposition and allowing it to influence substantive policies but also in his making pronouncements on foreign policy that contrasted with the policies he actually pursued.

Dulles's task of making his position and policies secure with the President encountered no such complications and hence necessitated no such complex measures for its achievement. President Eisenhower very soon trusted Dulles so completely and admired his ability as Secretary of State so unreservedly that he gave him, for all practical purposes, a free hand to conduct the foreign policy of the United States as he saw fit. Although Dulles was continuously and deeply concerned with the support he could expect from Congress and public opinion, he did not need to worry about the President's support.

Echoing Thomas E. Dewey's statement that Dulles was "no ordinary mortal" in his ability to understand and conduct foreign policy, President Eisenhower paid frequent tribute to Dulles as the greatest Secretary of State he had known. On the occasion of Dulles's fiftieth anniversary as a diplomat, on June 15, 1957, President Eisenhower wrote him a personal letter, saying: "Your accomplishments will establish you as one of the greatest of our Secretaries of State." And when Dulles's tenure as Secretary of State was at an end, President Eisenhower said in his press conference of April 18, 1959: "I personally believe he has filled his office with greater distinction than any other man our country has known—a man of tremendous character and courage, intelligence and wisdom." The President acted in accordance with his estimate of Dulles's ability, for he almost always followed his Secretary's advice in things great and small. The only important instance on record of Dulles's having been overruled by Eisenhower occurred in 1954 when the President refused to accept Dulles's advice to intervene with military means in the Indochina War.

Although Dulles did not need to exert much effort to create his extraordinary relationship with the President, he was from the very outset careful lest it be disturbed by third parties. And, as in his relations with public opinion and Congress, it was his knowledge of what had happened to other Secretaries of State in this respect that determined his attitude. According to a report by James Reston in the *New York Times* of February 2, 1958, Dulles remarked privately at the beginning of his tenure of office "that he would oppose any system of divided authority between the White House staff and the State Department for the conduct of foreign policy." He called attention to the examples of his own uncle, Robert Lansing, who had been hampered by the influence Colonel House had exerted upon Woodrow Wilson, and of Edward R. Stettinius, Jr., many of whose Secretarial functions had been performed by Franklin D. Roosevelt's assistant, Harry Hopkins. Dulles concluded, therefore, that "he could not take lightly any attempt to establish in the White House a competing center of foreign policy information and negotiation."

Thus Dulles opposed successfully a plan, devised by the White House staff, to reorganize the office of the President by creating three Vice Presidents, one of whom would have been in charge of foreign policy. He did not oppose, in 1956, the appointment of General Bedell Smith, who had served as his Under Secretary, as special adviser to the President in the field of foreign policy; this appointment fell afoul of the opposition of Herbert Hoover, Jr., then Under Secretary of State. But the men who were actually appointed to similar positions, however limited in scope— C. D. Jackson, Nelson A. Rockefeller, William Jackson, and Harold Stassen—met with Dulles's opposition and sooner or later had to yield to it by resigning. Of these conflicts, the most dramatic was the controversy with Stassen, the President's adviser for disarmament. Stassen, who had strong ideas of his own on the conduct of disarmament negotiations, challenged openly the authority of the Secretary of State, and the latter did not hesitate to take up the challenge. To this conflict over policy was added a clash of personalities. The result was a complete triumph for Dulles. In February, 1958, Stassen was forced to resign, the possibility of his further employment by the Eisenhower administration having come to an abrupt end.

VI

The position of Dulles vis-à-vis other executive departments and the Department of State itself was made secure both by his unique relationship to the President and by his extraordinary forensic ability and force of personality. When Dulles spoke in the councils of the government, he spoke not only as the President's principal adviser on foreign affairs, as would any Secretary of State, but also and patently as the President's alter ego. When Dulles spoke, it was for all practical purposes the President of the United States who spoke. The voice of so trusted and admired a servant was not challenged lightly. This relationship between the President and his Secretary of State made it impossible from the outset for any executive department to bypass the Secretary of State by gaining the ear of the President and to pursue a foreign policy of its own in competition with that of the Secretary of State. Yet that same relationship allowed the Secretary of State to bypass other executive departments, either singly or assembled in the National Security Council, and to obtain without bureaucratic complications the President's approval for what he had decided.

The voice of the Secretary of State, however, carried an authority derived not only from his identification with the President but also from the qualities of Dulles's personality and mind. In force of personality, only the Secretary of the Treasury, George Humphrey, was his equal in the councils of government; in knowledge of foreign affairs and skill of argumentation, Dulles was clearly superior to all the President's other advisers. Thus, in the National Security Council, the Cabinet, and the informal discussions on foreign policy, Dulles generally carried the day. He was in uncontested control of American foreign policy. In its conduct he had no rival above him, that is, in the President; beside him, that is, in other executive departments; or below him, that is, in the Department of State itself.

Rivalry from within the Department was precluded by two facets of Dulles's *modus operandi*. It has been frequently asserted that Dulles carried American foreign policy under his hat. Although this is an exaggeration, it contains an element of truth. It is true that Dulles used to confer with a small number of aides and that these conferences, especially during President Eisenhower's first term, were frequently characterized by a vigorous give-and-take. But they apparently served less to provide the Secretary with information and advice than to give him an opportunity of trying his ideas out in informal debate. The Department of State at large was not affected by these debates in its day-by-day operations and was hardly aware of them. Nor was the Secretary of State, in either his thinking or his decisions, much affected by what the Department of State knew and did. Dulles devised the foreign policies of the United States by drawing upon his own knowledge, experience, and insight, and the Department of State merely implemented these policies.

Dulles assumed personal responsibility, not only for formulating American foreign policy, but also, in good measure, for carrying it out, at least on the higher levels of execution. The public image of Dulles as a constant traveler comes indeed close to reality. During his tenure of office, he traveled 559,988 miles, of which 479,286 were outside the United States. He visited 47 nations—France, 19 times; Great Britain, 11 times; Italy, 4 times; and West Germany, 6 times. By personally performing many of the major political functions which had traditionally been performed by high-ranking diplomats, Dulles greatly reduced opportunities for the latter to take political initiative of any kind. By divorcing his operations to a considerable degree from those of the Department of State and at the same time taking over the higher political functions of the Foreign Service, Dulles for all practical purposes disarmed the Department of State as a rival in the management of foreign affairs. It must also be kept in mind that the purge of 1953 and the regime of surveillance accompanying and following it had made it inadvisable for a member of the Department of State to develop a foreign policy of his own.

Thus the *Life* article quoted above had a point when it commented:

> Dulles ... altered drastically the basic concept of the job of Secretary of State. . . .
> President Truman's Secretaries of State worked essentially in the pattern of the administrative executive. They counted time away from Washington as serious neglect of the Department. Dulles took the opposite view. He regarded too much time spent in Washington as neglect of the U.S. task of free world leadership.
> Reverting to an older tradition, he undertook personal direction of the country's foreign affairs, assigning himself the role of No. 1 diplomat of the U.S. The day-to-day routine of departmental administration he has delegated to his undersecretaries. . . .

However, operational efficiency was bound to suffer from Dulles's methods of securing his position from the rivalry of subordinates and of other executive departments. The price of his success was lack of political coordination for all concerned. In some cases the Secretary made decisions without regard to political and military information available in the Department of State and other executive agencies; in other cases he neglected to prepare the Department of State and the related agencies for the policies to be adopted. For instance, the concept of massive retaliation, taken at its face value, was obsolete from the military point of view when Dulles presented it as the "new look" of American foreign policy in 1954. On the other hand, the decision to intervene in Lebanon in 1958 took many high officials of the State Department by the same surprise that it did the general public.

VII

Comparing Dulles's conception of the office of Secretary of State with the results of his administration of the office, one cannot doubt that he was eminently successful. Everywhere he seemed to achieve his purposes. When he took office, he resolved that what had happened to Dean Acheson would not happen to him; that he would make himself master of American foreign policy, without competition from any of the quarters from which such competition had traditionally come; that he would give the appearance of being the initiator of new, dynamic, and successful foreign policies. Dulles accomplished what he had set out to do. Yet it is characteristic of the dilemma which of necessity faces a modern Secretary of State that Dulles had to pay a price for his triumph in making his position and policies secure on the domestic political scene, just as Acheson had to pay a price for shielding his foreign policies from the intrusion of domestic politics. Although what happened to Acheson did not happen to Dulles, something else did. The price Dulles had to pay for his domestic success consisted in the stagnation of American foreign policy and the diminution in prestige that both his person and his office suffered abroad.

Although Dulles consistently strove to make it appear that his foreign policies were different from, and superior to, the foreign policies of his predecessors, it is a historic fact that he essentially continued those very policies. Refusal to recognize the legitimacy of the *status quo* in Europe and defense of the *status quo* in Europe and elsewhere through containment, as well as foreign aid, were the cornerstones both of his and his predecessors' foreign policies. Dulles introduced only two major variations: he endeavored to extend the policy of military containment, originally applied to Europe, systematically to the Middle East and Asia through a network of alliances, and he postulated the inadmissibility of violence as an instrument of national policy, putting that principle into effect by opposing the 1956 invasion of Egypt by France, Great Britain, and Israel.

Regardless of the intrinsic merits of these policies, it is hardly open to doubt that they were not sufficient to meet the new issues arising from the growing military, economic, and political power of the Soviet Union, the emergence of Africa from colonial rule, the unrest in Latin America, and the endemic crisis of the Atlantic alliance. A case can of course be made in support of the thesis that Dulles, acting essentially as the resourceful advocate of his client, the United States, was contitutionally incapable of transcending his responsibility to defend the position in which he found his client, that is, the *status quo*, and of creating new situations by virtue of new policies more in tune with the interests of the United States in a new environment. However, even if Dulles had had the attributes of the creative statesman, he would have been greatly handicapped in his creative task by his overriding concern with his domestic position. To stand as still as possible while appearing to move was the safest course to take in view of this concern, and so was the limitation of any actual movement to the military sphere. A fresh political initiative, a really creative political effort, would in all likelihood have raised a domestic political issue, dividing Congress and public opinion at large into supporters and opponents, and it was such a division which Dulles was resolved to forestall.

The support which Dulles enjoyed at home was not matched by a similar response from abroad. Neither his person nor his policies were popular with foreign statesmen and foreign peoples. To a degree, unpopularity is the price that powerful nations and forceful personalities pay for their power and force, and to that extent it cannot be helped. In Dulles's case, however, the negative foreign reaction was in good measure the direct result of the preoccupation with domestic support that dictated both the conception and the administration of his office. Foreign public opinion and foreign statesmen were more sharply aware than American public opinion could be of the contrast between what American foreign policy was declared to be and what it actually was. Once this contrast had developed into a consistent pattern, Dulles's public and private pronouncements were bound to be carefully scrutinized abroad for their real meaning. Since foreign statesmen could not be sure that Dulles's policies would conform to his pronouncements, they lost confidence in his person and his policies.

Dulles's *modus operandi* also contributed to the distrust he ultimately encountered abroad. By concentrating not only the direction but, to a large extent, also the implementation of foreign policy in his own hands, he escaped the handicap of involvement with the bureaucracy of the State Department, but he thus created another hazard. By taking over the functions ambassadors have traditionally performed, Dulles deprived himself of that protection with which ambassadors are intended to shield their chiefs from too frequent contacts with their opposite numbers. Such contacts breed not only familiarity but also distrust; for it is in the nature of diplomacy to try, sometimes by devious means, to use other statesmen for its own purposes. The statesman who has been so used for some length of time is likely to get tired of, and lose confidence in, the man who has so used him, and then it is time to replace that man. For that reason ambassadors frequently become expendable after a few years of service in a particular capital and are transferred elsewhere. The foreign minister who assumes the task of his ambassadors simultaneously in many capitals cannot easily be replaced when, for the same reason, his usefulness has been impaired. Thus he carries on with his prestige damaged and his trustworthiness compromised.

Dulles compounded the liability inherent in his *modus operandi* by his use of the advocate's technique. The advocate, trying to advance his client's case as far as possible, can afford to disregard the interests and reactions of other parties who have advocates of their own, both relying upon the judge to sift the truth from ex parte statements, hyperbole, and deception. What the advocate can afford, the foreign minister cannot. For the foreign minister is not only the advocate of his nation, but, in a manner of speaking, also the advocate of the other side and the judge who recognizes and respects the interests of the other side and at least tentatively decides how the two interests ought to be reconciled. The foreign minister who limits himself to being the advocate of his nation will be acclaimed at home as the stanch defender of the national interest, but he will be handicapped in his conduct of foreign policy because he will be distrusted personally and will be incapable of performing the supreme task of diplomacy: to create out of disparate and contradictory national interests a higher harmony.*

Such was the price in terms of substantive foreign policy that Dulles had to pay for his domestic triumph. Did it have to be paid? The answer to that question depends upon one's judgment of the strength of the potential domestic opposition and of the need for different foreign policies. This writer is convinced that the price was unnecessarily high by far; for Dulles, fully supported by President Eisenhower's unprecedented prestige, could have pursued whatever foreign policies he chose without fear of a domestic opposition. But, then, would different foreign policies have been desirable, and would Dulles have wanted to pursue them had he not feared that opposition? Future historians will debate these questions, and perhaps history will one day answer them.

* A close associate of Dulles has graphically described in private conversation one facet of Dulles's technique and its results. He compared Dulles dealing with two foreign ministers with a man who had to explain the same landscape to two associates. Knowing that foreign minister A was interested in mountains, he would tell him only about the mountains. Knowing that foreign minister B was interested in valleys, he would tell him only about the valleys. When the two foreign ministers later compared notes, they both felt that they had been deceived.

Bibliography

1. The Year of Transition

There are no general studies which attempt to define the essential nature of United States diplomacy in the nineteenth century. The available analyses of American thought and action in the realm of foreign affairs prior to 1900 are limited either to textbook surveys or to monographic works which deal with precise episodes and the men who at such moments were responsible for national action. In the first category are such well-known and useful volumes as SAMUEL F. BEMIS, *A Diplomatic History of the United States* (4th ed., New York, 1955); THOMAS A. BAILEY, *A Diplomatic History of the American People* (6th ed., New York, 1955); and JULIUS W. PRATT, *A History of United States Foreign Policy* (New York, 1955).

Several general studies analyze well the evolution of the State Department and the institutional framework in which American foreign policy has been created since the days of Washington's Presidency. GRAHAM H. STUART has written two standard works on institutional development: *The Department of State: A History of Its Organization, Procedure and Personnel* (New York, 1949) and *American Diplomatic and Consular Practice* (2d ed., New York, 1952). Older, but still useful, volumes are GAILLARD HUNT, *The Department of State of the United States: Its History and Functions* (New Haven, Conn., 1914) and EUGENE SCHUYLER, *American Diplomacy and the Furtherance of Commerce* (New York, 1895). A more recent general text covering all phases of the policy-making process is ELMER PLISCHKE, *Conduct of American Diplomacy* (New York, 1950).

Each broad theme of American diplomatic experience in the nineteenth century, with the exception of this nation's relationship to the European balance of power, has received its share of attention from American scholars. Much of excellence has been written on the diplomacy which gave the United States command of its continental domain. The following monographs analyze this nation's success in removing the Spanish, French, and English barriers from the Mississippi Valley: A. B. DARLING, *Our Rising Empire, 1763–1803* (New Haven, 1940); two volumes by S. F. BEMIS: *Jay's Treaty* (New York, 1923) and *Pinck-*

ney's Treaty (Baltimore, 1926); two works by A. P. WHITAKER: *The Spanish-American Frontier: 1783–1795* (Boston, 1927) and *The Mississippi Question, 1795–1803* (New York, 1934); and A. L. BURT, *The United States, Great Britain, and British North America* (New Haven, Conn., 1940). A superb treatment of the acquisition of the Floridas and the negotiation of the transcontinental boundary line of 1819 can be found in S. F. BEMIS, *John Quincy Adams and the Foundations of American Foreign Policy* (New York, 1949) and in P. C. BROOKS, *Diplomacy and the Borderlands: The Adams-Onís Treaty of 1819* (Berkeley, Calif., 1939). Among the useful books on the acquisition of Texas are JUSTIN H. SMITH, *The Annexation of Texas* (New York, 1911) and E. D. ADAMS, *British Interests and Activities in Texas, 1838–1846* (Baltimore, 1910). On American expansion to the Pacific are NORMAN A. GRAEBNER, *Empire on the Pacific* (New York, 1955) and JUSTIN H. SMITH, *The War with Mexico* (2 vols., New York, 1919). The standard work on the Gadsden Purchase is P. N. GARBER, *The Gadsden Treaty* (Philadelphia, 1923).

Three volumes by DEXTER PERKINS dominate the literature on the evolution of the Monroe Doctrine in the nineteenth century: *The Monroe Doctrine, 1823–1826* (Cambridge, Mass., 1927), *The Monroe Doctrine, 1826–1867* (Baltimore, 1933), and *The Monroe Doctrine, 1867–1907* (Baltimore, 1937). These volumes have been summarized in *A History of the Monroe Doctrine* (Boston, 1955).

United States relations with Europe during the late decades of the nineteenth century were both less spectacular and less productive of tangible results than those with Asia. Consequently the latter have attracted the greater attention of American scholars. Two valuable volumes by FOSTER RHEA DULLES on the expansion of American interests in the Eastern Hemisphere are *The Imperial Years* (New York, 1956) and *Americans in the Pacific* (Boston, 1932). On the precise questions of Samoa and Hawaii are G. H. RYDEN, *The Foreign Policy of the United States in Relation to Samoa* (New Haven, Conn., 1933); HAROLD W. BRADLEY, *The American Frontier in Hawaii: The Pioneers, 1789–1843* (Stanford, Calif., 1942); and G. R. DULEBOHN, *Principles of Foreign Policy under the Cleveland Administrations* (Philadelphia, 1941). Three useful volumes on the coming of the Spanish-American War are J. W. PRATT, *Expansionists of 1898* (Baltimore, 1936); A. L. P. DENNIS, *Adventures in American Diplomacy, 1896–1906* (New York, 1928); and J. E. WISAN, *The Cuban Crisis as Reflected in the New York Press, 1895–1898* (New York, 1934).

No historian as yet has attempted a synthesis of the important conflict between idealism and realism in American foreign-policy thought and action before 1900. That realism invariably triumphed, however, is clear from a number of monographic studies that analyze the American reaction to recurrent European liberal movements. The Hamilton-Jefferson debate over this nation's proper relationship to the French Revolution has been discussed briefly, but well, by HANS J. MORGENTHAU in his *In Defense of the National Interest* (New York, 1951). M. A. CLINE, *American Attitude toward the Greek War of Independence, 1821–1828* (Atlanta, Ga., 1930) and E. H. TATUM, JR., *The United States and Europe, 1815–1823* (Berkeley, Calif., 1936) reveal clearly the nature of the American reaction to the Greek revolt of the early 1820s. On American thought and the Revolutions of 1848 are such excellent studies as MERLE E. CURTI, *Austria and the United States, 1848–1852* (Smith College Studies in History, no. 11, 1926); J. G. GAZLEY, *American Opinion of German Unification, 1848–1871* (New York, 1926); and A. J. MAY, *Contemporary American Opinion of the Mid-century Revolutions in Central Europe* (Philadelphia, 1927).

Not all the nineteenth-century Secretaries of State have received, nor do many of them merit, extensive study. In an age when the United States was still far removed from a troubled Europe and Asia, the American Secretary of State was not always involved in important events abroad. Even when diplomacy achieved great, if temporary, significance, as it did during the incumbency of James Buchanan in the 1840s, foreign policy was often dominated by the President. But an excellent survey of Secretarial activity can be found in S. F. BEMIS (ed.), *The American Secretaries of State and Their Diplomacy* (10 vols., New York, 1927–1929). For analyses of several successful practitioners as Secretaries of State in the nineteenth century, see the volume on John Quincy Adams by S. F. BEMIS, cited above; the essay on William H. Seward by NORMAN A. GRAEBNER: "Northern Diplomacy and European Neutrality," in DAVID DONALD (ed.), *Why the North Won the Civil War* (Baton Rouge, La., 1960); ALLAN NEVINS, *Hamilton Fish* (New York, 1936); C. C. TANSILL, *The Foreign Policy of Thomas F. Bayard, 1885–1897* (New York, 1940); and ALICE F. TYLER, *The Foreign Policy of James G. Blaine* (Minneapolis, 1927).

For a survey of the historical literature on American foreign relations at the turn of the century, see the following bibliographical essay on the Secretaryship of John Hay.

2. *John Hay*

The John Hay papers in the Library of Congress, together with those of a number of his contemporaries, most notably Theodore Roosevelt, provide a first source for Hay's career as Secretary of State. They are supplemented by the extensive material in the Department of State archives; the annual volumes of the *Papers Relating to the Foreign Relations of the United States*, published by the Department of State; and a number of special Senate documents and other official reports. There are also the *Letters of John Hay and Extracts from Diary* (3 vols., Washington, 1908) and the further selections from his correspondence included in WILLIAM ROSCOE THAYER, *The Life and Letters of John Hay* (2 vols., Boston, 1915). Other significant primary material may be found in E. E. MORISON (ed.), *The Letters of Theodore Roosevelt* (8 vols., Cambridge, 1951–1954) and HENRY ADAMS, *The Education of Henry Adams* (New York, 1931).

The outstanding biography is TYLER DENNETT, *John Hay: From Poetry to Politics* (New York, 1934). Every student of John Hay owes an immense debt to this excellent book, but it is more favorable to its subject than recent scholarship would appear to justify. The sketch of Hay's diplomatic career by A. L. P. DENNIS in S. F. BEMIS (ed.), *The American Secretaries of State and Their Diplomacy* (vol. IX, New York, 1929) is also very helpful.

A very considerable number of books dealing with the various phases of American foreign policy at the turn of the century further illumine Hay's role.

On the Open Door, there are A. WHITNEY GRISWOLD, *The Far Eastern Policy of the United States* (New York, 1938); PAUL A. VARG, *Open Door Diplomat: The Life of W. W. Rockhill* (Urbana, Ill., 1952); and CHARLES S. CAMPBELL, JR., *Special Business Interests and the Open Door* (New Haven, Conn., 1951). Also pertinent, although the Open Door policy itself is very briefly treated, is GEORGE F. KENNAN, *American Diplomacy, 1900–1950* (Chicago, 1951).

On Latin-American policy during this period a basic treatment may be found in the general study SAMUEL F. BEMIS, *The Latin American Policy of the United States* (New York, 1943). Among the many other books that provide valuable material are WILFRED H. CALCOTT, *The Caribbean Policy of the United States, 1890–1920* (Baltimore, 1942) and DWIGHT C. MINER, *The Fight for the Panama Route* (New York, 1940).

The relations between the United States and Great Britain are interestingly discussed in LIONEL M. GELBER, *The Rise of Anglo-American Friendship: A Study in World Politics, 1898–1906* (New York, 1938) and the more recent and even more pertinent CHARLES S. CAMPBELL, JR., *Anglo-American Understanding, 1898–1903* (Baltimore, 1957).

The important question of the relationship between Hay and Theodore Roosevelt is touched upon in HENRY PRINGLE, *Theodore Roosevelt* (New York, 1931), an excellent biography of the President, but the Roosevelt foreign policy is most comprehensively treated in HOWARD K. BEALE, *Theodore Roosevelt and the Rise of America to World Power* (Baltimore, 1956).

There is as yet no definitive study of McKinley's foreign policy. CHARLES S. OLCOTT, *The Life of William McKinley* (2 vols., Boston, 1916) is still perhaps the best available. Three valuable biographies of other Hay contemporaries are ALLAN NEVINS, *Henry White* (New York, 1930); PHILIP JESSUP, *Elihu Root* (2 vols., New York, 1938); and JOHN A. GARRATY, *Henry Cabot Lodge* (New York, 1953).

Reference should also be made to such special studies as A. L. P. DENNIS, *Adventures in American Diplomacy, 1896–1906* (New York, 1928); J. H. FERGUSON, *American Diplomacy and the Boer War* (Philadelphia, 1939); and G. H. RYDEN, *The Foreign Policy of the United States in Relation to Samoa* (New Haven, Conn., 1933).

3. *Elihu Root*

To date, the standard biography of Root is still PHILIP C. JESSUP, *Elihu Root* (2 vols., New York, 1938). Based on official and personal sources, including interviews, this work presents a considerable amount of valuable detail on all phases of Secretary Root's activities. A more recent and generally sympathetic study is RICHARD W. LEOPOLD, *Elihu Root and the Conservative Tradition* (Boston, 1954), which attempts to place Root within the social milieu of his time. Though interesting and readable, it is rather uncritical in its treatment of Far Eastern affairs during the Roosevelt administration. JAMES B. SCOTT's essay on Root in volume IX of S. F. BEMIS (ed.), *The American Secretaries of State and Their Diplomacy* (New York, 1929) is a briefer survey of Root's manifold activities by a devoted contemporary.

Essential to any study of Elihu Root are numerous papers found in the Library of Congress, the New York Public Library, and the archives of the State and Defense Departments. Elihu Root spoke frequently before public and private groups, and many of his addresses are included in the eight-volume work edited by ROBERT BACON and JAMES B. SCOTT and published between 1916 and 1925 by Harvard University Press. The most important volumes for a study of Root as Secretary of State are *The Military and Colonial Policy of the United States* (Cambridge, Mass., 1916), *Addresses on International Subjects* (Cambridge, Mass., 1917), *Latin America and the United States* (Cambridge, Mass., 1917), and *Miscellaneous Addresses* (Cambridge, Mass., 1917). Numerous articles by Elihu Root are to be found in the World Peace Foundation Pamphlet Series and in the issues of *International Conciliation* and the *American-Journal of International Law*. It might be noted here that there is a chronological list of Root's important public speeches and papers in the second volume of the study by PHILIP C. JESSUP, cited above.

Indispensable to any study of the period of Root's Secretaryship are the rewarding chapters in FOSTER RHEA DULLES, *America's Rise to World Power* (New York, 1955); the stimulating volume by HOWARD K. BEALE: *Theodore Roosevelt and the Rise of America to World Power* (Baltimore, 1956); and GEORGE E. MOWRY, *The Era of Theodore Roosevelt, 1900–1912* (New York, 1958). The Roosevelt papers in the Library of Congress are basic for any study of this period, and an invaluable aid is ELTING E. MORISON (ed.), *The Letters of Theodore Roosevelt* (8 vols., Cambridge, 1951–1954). Valuable materials are also to be found in the Harvard College Library and the New York Historical Society.

In regard to the specific issues with which Elihu Root was concerned, there are a number of important studies. In connection with the Algeciras Conference, EUGENE N. ANDERSON, *The First Moroccan Crisis* (Chicago, 1930) is still valuable, as is A. L. P. DENNIS, *Adventures in American Diplomacy, 1896–1906* (New York, 1928). The latter work is important also for its introductory material on the subject of arbitration and the Hague Conferences. Basic to an understanding of American efforts at The Hague are the contributions of JAMES B. SCOTT: *The Work of the Second Hague Conference* (New York, 1908) and *The Hague Conferences of 1899 and 1907* (Baltimore, 1909).

For an excellent background to American relations with the Far East, see A. WHITNEY GRISWOLD, *The Far Eastern Policy of the United States* (New York, 1938), together with the valuable chapters in FOSTER RHEA DULLES, *China and America* (Princeton, N.J., 1946). *Forty Years of American-Japanese Relations* (New York, 1937), by the same author, is also very helpful toward understanding this aspect of foreign policy. THOMAS A. BAILEY, *Theodore Roosevelt and the Japanese-American Crises* (Stanford, Calif., 1934) offers an excellent account of the anxious months of 1907–1908, and the same author's "The Root-Takahira Agreement of 1908," *Pacific Historical Review*, vol. IX (1940) is a good critical evaluation of the Root-Takahira Agreement. Another helpful study for this period is ELEANOR TUPPER and G. E. McREYNOLDS, *Japan in American Public Opinion* (New York, 1937).

There are a considerable number of good texts covering foreign policy and

diplomatic relations with Latin America, among the most noteworthy being
SAMUEL F. BEMIS, *The Latin American Policy of the United States* (New York,
1943) and GRAHAM H. STUART, *Latin America and the United States* (New York,
1943). JACK DAVIS, *The Latin American Policy of Elihu Root* (Urbana, Ill.,
1956) is a competent doctoral study, available on microfilm (Ann Arbor, Mich.,
1956). Also valuable for this period is WILFRED H. CALCOTT, *The Caribbean
Policy of the United States, 1890–1920* (Baltimore, 1942). Important source
material is also to be found in *The International Conferences of American States,
1888–1928* (New York, 1928), published by the Carnegie Endowment for International Peace. The speeches of Elihu Root during his South American tour are
found in ROBERT BROWN and JAMES B. SCOTT (eds.), *Latin America and the
United States,* cited above.

4. Philander C. Knox

The William H. Taft and Philander C. Knox papers at the Library of
Congress, as well as the Department of State files at the National Archives for
the years 1909 to 1913, are essential to any study of American foreign relations
during the Taft administration. Also of importance are the papers of Elihu Root,
Theodore Roosevelt, Leonard Wood, Andrew Carnegie, and Whitelaw Reid at
the Library of Congress. The Huntington Wilson papers at Ursinus College and
the Lord Bryce papers at the Bodleian Library, Oxford, England, are helpful.

The volumes in the *Papers Relating to the Foreign Relations of the United
States, 1909–1913,* are indispensable. General works containing useful material
are GEORGE E. MOWRY, *The Era of Theodore Roosevelt, 1900–1912* (New York,
1958); GRAHAM H. STUART, *The Department of State: A History of Its Organization, Procedure and Personnel* (New York, 1949); and ARCHIE BUTT, *Taft and
Roosevelt: The Intimate Letters of Archie Butt* (New York, 1930).

The following biographies and autobiographies give insights on Knox and the
Department of State: H. F. PRINGLE, *The Life and Times of William Howard
Taft* (2 vols., New York, 1939); O. S. STRAUS, *Under Four Administrations*
(Boston, 1922); H. CROLY, *Willard Straight* (New York, 1924); H. HAGEDORN,
Leonard Wood (2 vols., New York, 1931); F. M. HUNTINGTON WILSON, *Memoirs
of an Ex-diplomat* (Boston, 1945); and P. A. VARG, *Open Door Diplomat: The
Life of W. W. Rockhill* (Urbana, Ill., 1952). Among the helpful area studies are
E. H. ZABRISKIE, *American-Russian Rivalry in the Far East . . . 1895–1914* (Phila-
delphia, 1946); J. G. REID, *The Manchu Abdication and the Powers, 1908–1912*
(Berkeley, Calif., 1935); CHARLES VEVIER, *The United States and China, 1906–
1913* (New Brunswick, N.J., 1955); WILFRED H. CALCOTT, *The Caribbean Policy
of the United States, 1890–1920* (Baltimore, 1942); J. F. RIPPY, *The Caribbean
Danger Zone* (New York, 1940); and SAMUEL F. BEMIS, *The Latin American
Policy of the United States* (New York, 1943).

Articles of importance are S. W. LIVERMORE, "Battleship Diplomacy in South
America, 1905–1925," *Journal of Modern History,* vol. XVI (1944) and
D. G. MUNRO, "Dollar Diplomacy in Nicaragua, 1909–1913," *Hispanic American
Historical Review,* vol. XXXVIII (1958).

5. *William Jennings Bryan*

The dearth of material on Bryan's career in the Department of State makes it necessary for the student to consult his papers in the Library of Congress and, in addition, to rely upon the far more extensive published materials about Woodrow Wilson and American participation in World War I. The most useful study of Bryan's foreign policy remains MERLE E. CURTI, *Bryan and World Peace* (Smith College Studies in History, no. 16, 1931). Useful, but noncritical are such biographies as PAXTON HIBBEN, *The Peerless Leader* (New York, 1929); WAYNE C. WILLIAMS, *William Jennings Bryan* (New York, 1936); and J. C. LONG, *Bryan: The Great Commoner* (New York, 1928). *The Memoirs of William Jennings Bryan* (Philadelphia, 1925) are incomplete and, on many important issues, merely reproduce isolated memoranda or scattered entries from his wife's diary.

There are two short accounts, both of value, of Bryan's work in the Department of State: JOSEPH V. FULLER, "William Jennings Bryan," in S. F. BEMIS (ed.), *The American Secretaries of State and Their Diplomacy* (vol. X, New York, 1929) and GRAHAM H. STUART, *The Department of State: A History of Its Organization, Procedure and Personnel* (New York, 1949).

In the many biographies of Woodrow Wilson, by far the most important discussions of Bryan's work are to be found in ARTHUR S. LINK, *Wilson: The New Freedom* (Princeton, N.J., 1956) and ARTHUR WALWORTH, *Woodrow Wilson* (2 vols., New York, 1958). Also useful are JOHN MORTON BLUM, *Woodrow Wilson and the Politics of Morality* (Boston, 1956) and EDWARD H. BUEHRIG, *Woodrow Wilson and the Balance of Power* (Bloomington, Ind., 1955). Any student of Bryan must consult the two standard sources for the Wilsonian period: RAY STANNARD BAKER, *Woodrow Wilson: Life and Letters* (8 vols., Garden City, N.Y., 1927–1939) and CHARLES SEYMOUR (ed.), *The Intimate Papers of Colonel House* (4 vols., Boston, 1926–1928).

DANIEL M. SMITH, *Robert Lansing and American Neutrality, 1914–1917* (Berkeley, Calif., 1958) is a useful study, although it emphasizes the role of Lansing. *The War Memoirs of Robert Lansing* (New York, 1935) is helpful on certain points.

For Latin-American policy during the period of Bryan's Secretaryship, the essential account is still SELIG ADLER, "Bryan and Wilsonian Caribbean Penetration," *Hispanic American Historical Review*, vol. XX (1940), but see also SAMUEL F. BEMIS, *The Latin American Policy of the United States* (New York, 1943) and DEXTER PERKINS, *A History of the Monroe Doctrine* (New York, 1955). For Bryan's Far Eastern policies the most helpful studies are ROY W. CURRY, *Woodrow Wilson and Far Eastern Policy* (New York, 1957) and TIENYI LI, *Woodrow Wilson's China Policy* (New York, 1952).

Among the published memoirs, letters, and diaries of the Wilson period, the most useful for a study of Bryan are ANNE W. LANE and LOUISE WALL (eds.), *The Letters of Franklin K. Lane* (Boston, 1922); DAVID HOUSTON, *Eight Years with Wilson's Cabinet* (2 vols., Garden City, N.Y., 1926); JOSEPHUS DANIELS,

The Wilson Era: Years of Peace, 1910–1917 (Chapel Hill, N.C., 1944); WILLIAM PHILLIPS, *Ventures in Diplomacy* (Boston, 1953); and, of course, BURTON J. HENDRICK, *The Life and Letters of Walter Hines Page* (3 vols., Garden City, N.Y., 1924–1926).

6. Robert Lansing

Unpublished materials for a study of Secretary Lansing are abundant. The private papers of Robert Lansing, 1911–1928, are housed in the Manuscripts Division of the Library of Congress. These comprise sixty-two volumes of correspondence; daily desk diaries, or appointment books; and private memoranda books, containing policy observations. The Library of Congress also has the papers of Woodrow Wilson, as well as those of other figures in the Wilson administration. The indispensable papers of Colonel E. M. House are in the Yale University Library.

Official diplomatic correspondence and departmental memoranda are available in the Foreign Affairs section of the National Archives. The State Department has published a selection in the annual volumes for 1914 to 1920 in the *Papers Relating to the Foreign Relations of the United States*. Special supplements in this series include the thirteen-volume *Paris Peace Conference, 1919* and the two-volume *The Lansing Papers, 1914–1920;* the latter is a selection of papers taken from Lansing's personal files after his death in 1928.

Lansing wrote and published extensively after his resignation in 1920. Two works deal with the Paris Peace Conference: *The Big Four and Others of the Peace Conference* (Boston, 1921) is a series of often penetrating sketches of Allied statesmen; *The Peace Negotiations: A Personal Narrative* (Boston, 1921) is a sharp, acute criticism of Wilson and a defense of Lansing's own course at the conference. A series of articles were published posthumously: "Drama of the Virgin Islands Purchase," *The New York Times Magazine*, July 19, 1931; "The Difficulties of Neutrality," "When Wilson Failed as Peacemaker," and "War Days in the White House," *The Saturday Evening Post*, April 18, June 20, and August 8, 1931. *The War Memoirs of Robert Lansing* (New York, 1935), incomplete because of Lansing's untimely death, covers the years 1915 to 1917 and are based on his private memoranda notes and official papers.

A full-length biography of Lansing has yet to be written. A brief sketch of his life, by JULIUS W. PRATT, appears in *The Dictionary of American Biography*, edited by Dumas Malone (vol. x, 1933). The same author's "Robert Lansing" in S. F. Bemis (ed.), *The American Secretaries of State and Their Diplomacy* (vol. X, New York, 1929) is still useful, although based on limited access to the materials. Recent studies utilizing official and private collections are DANIEL M. SMITH, *Robert Lansing and American Neutrality, 1914–1917* (Berkeley, Calif., 1958); the same author's "Robert Lansing and the Formulation of American Neutrality Policies, 1914–1915," *Mississippi Valley Historical Review*, vol. XLIII (1956) and "Robert Lansing and the Wilson Interregnum, 1919–1920," *The Historian*, vol. XXI (1959); and BURTON F. BEER's provocative "Robert Lansing's Proposed Bargain with Japan," *Pacific Historical Review*, vol. XXVI (1957). LOUIS G. KAHLE, "Robert Lansing and the Recognition of Venustiano Carranza,"

Hispanic American Historical Review, vol. XXXVIII (1958) analyzes Lansing's Mexican policy in 1915.

The voluminous and still-growing literature on America and the World War I period bears on Lansing to some degree. For a recent guide, see OSCAR HANDLIN et al. (eds.), *Harvard Guide to American History* (Cambridge, Mass., 1954). Among the most important later works are three volumes by ARTHUR S. LINK: *Woodrow Wilson and the Progressive Era, 1910–1917* (New York, 1954), *Wilson: The New Freedom* (Princeton, N.J., 1956), and *Wilson the Diplomatist* (Baltimore, 1957). These studies attribute a large role to Lansing in influencing neutrality and Latin-American policies. A. L. GEORGE and J. L. GEORGE, *Woodrow Wilson and Colonel House* (New York, 1956) points out that House and Lansing adjusted their advice to Wilson's susceptibilities. An excellent and broad study of the neutrality period is ERNEST R. MAY's *The World War and American Isolation, 1914–1917* (Cambridge, Mass., 1959). EDWARD H. BUEHRIG, *Woodrow Wilson and the Balance of Power* (Bloomington, Ind., 1955) credits Lansing with aiding Wilson's transition from neutrality to belligerency. Far Eastern developments are treated in ROY WATSON CURRY, *Woodrow Wilson and Far Eastern Policy, 1913–1921* (New York, 1957). GEORGE F. KENNAN, *Soviet-American Relations, 1917–1920* (2 vols., Princeton, N.J., 1956–1958) emphasizes Lansing's role in shaping the Siberian intervention and the nonrecognition policy toward the Soviet regime. Lansing's course in favoring independence of the Austrian-Hungarian subject nationalities is detailed in VICTOR S. MAMATEY, *The United States and East Central Europe, 1914–1918* (Princeton, N.J., 1956). In LOUIS A. R. YATES, *United States and French Security, 1917–1921* (New York, 1957), Lansing is portrayed, questionably, as an isolationist opposed to the French Security Treaty.

7. *Charles Evans Hughes*

The most important source of information on Charles Evans Hughes as Secretary of State is the very extensive collection of his papers in the Library of Congress. Hughes had commissioned his secretary, Henry C. Beerits, to prepare an official, documented account of thirty or forty pages for each of his major undertakings as Secretary of State. In addition there are memoranda of his conversations with the officials of the important foreign governments and a precisely arranged file of correspondence. Even more revealing of the man are the biographical notes, an extensive series of interviews with Merlo J. Pusey, covering Hughes's entire career. The Secretary's selection of topics and his approach to major issues of his public service often are more informative than the accounts themselves. These sources can be supplemented by the full record given in the volumes for 1921 to 1925 of the *Papers Relating to the Foreign Relations of the United States,* published by the Department of State. Also of interest are the collections of Hughes's speeches relating to foreign policy: *The Pathway of Peace* (New York, 1925), *Our Relations to the Nations of the Western Hemisphere* (Princeton, N.J., 1928), and *Pan-American Peace Plans* (New Haven, Conn., 1929).

The standard biography of Hughes is MERLO J. PUSEY, *Charles Evans Hughes*

(2 vols., New York, 1951). This excellent work is of necessity somewhat limited in dealing with Hughes's work as Secretary. The author at times reflects Hughes's own opinion that, as Secretary of State, Hughes did the best that could be done at the time and in the circumstances. Some stimulating views on Hughes's policies are given by DEXTER PERKINS in "The Department of State and American Public Opinion," in GORDON A. CRAIG and FELIX GILBERT (eds.), *The Diplomats: 1919–1939* (Princeton, N.J., 1953). CHARLES CHENEY HYDE, who was associated with Hughes in the State Department, gives a valuable contemporary account in "Charles Evans Hughes," in S. F. BEMIS (ed.), *The American Secretaries of State and Their Diplomacy* (vol. X, New York, 1929). Hughes's work at the Washington Conference is treated in J. CHAL VINSON, *The Parchment Peace: The United States Senate and the Washington Conference, 1921–1922* (Athens, Ga., 1955).

A very interesting commentary on Hughes's policies is given in DAVID D. BURKS, "The United States and the Geneva Protocol of 1924: 'A New Holy Alliance'?" *American Historical Review*, vol. LXIV (1959). Among the other articles on Hughes as Secretary are three essays by J. CHAL VINSON: "The Drafting of the Four-Power Treaty of the Washington Conference," *The Journal of Modern History*, vol. XXV (1953); "Hughes, Borah and the Far East: Congressional vs. Executive Leadership," *World Affairs Quarterly*, vol. XXVII (1956); and "The Annulment of the Lansing-Ishii Agreement," *Pacific Historical Review*, vol. XXVII (1958).

8. *Frank B. Kellogg*

The manuscripts housed in the Department of State files in the National Archives constitute the prime source for any study of Kellogg. Selections from these are published in *Papers Relating to the Foreign Relations of the United States* for the years 1925 through 1929, but the manuscripts themselves must be consulted for the complete story. Kellogg's papers, including copies of some material found in the National Archives, many letters not included in the Departmental files, and voluminous scrapbooks of newspaper clippings, are in the Library of the Minnesota State Historical Society at St. Paul; they throw a good deal of additional light on Kellogg's contacts and mental processes. The Diary of William R. Castle, still in the hands of its author, is extremely useful, as are the Joseph C. Grew papers in the Houghton Library of Harvard University. Some of Grew's papers have been published in WALTER JOHNSON (ed.), *Turbulent Era: A Diplomatic Record of Forty Years, 1904–1945* (2 vols., Boston, 1952), but much of the important material remains in manuscript. The Henry L. Stimson papers in the Yale University Library contain material on the Nicaragua and Tacna-Arica episodes. The papers of Chandler P. Anderson, William E. Borah, Calvin Coolidge, Leland Harrison, Charles Evans Hughes, and Nelson T. Johnson—all housed in the Manuscripts Division of the Library of Congress—also contain much essential information.

The authorized biography, written with considerable assistance from Kellogg, is DAVID BRYN-JONES, *Frank B. Kellogg: A Biography* (New York, 1937). The author of this work has drawn heavily upon his own unpublished study of the four-year period of Kellogg's Secretaryship and upon his article "Dwight Morrow and the Church-State Controversy in Mexico," *Hispanic American Historical Review,* vol. XXXVIII (1958). The following list of special studies bearing on the period is by no means complete, but it will introduce the interested reader to the pertinent literature: DOROTHY BORG, *American Policy and the Chinese Revolution, 1925–1928* (New York, 1947); JAMES MORTON CALLAHAN, *American Foreign Policy in Mexican Relations* (New York, 1932); ISAAC JOSLIN COX, *Nicaragua and the United States* (Boston, 1927); W. J. DENNIS, *Tacna and Arica: An Account of the Chile-Peru Boundary Dispute and of the Arbitrations by the United States* (New Haven, Conn., 1931); ROBERT H. FERRELL, *Peace in Their Time: The Origins of the Kellogg-Briand Pact* (New Haven, Conn., 1952); WESLEY R. FISHEL, *The End of Extraterritoriality in China* (Los Angeles, 1952); PHILIP C. JESSUP, *Elihu Root* (2 vols., New York, 1938); HAROLD NICOLSON, *Dwight Morrow* (New York, 1935); MERLO J. PUSEY, *Charles Evans Hughes* (2 vols., New York, 1951); HENRY L. STIMSON, *American Policy in Nicaragua* (New York, 1927); MERZE TATE, *The United States and Disarmament* (Cambridge, Mass., 1948); and BENJAMIN H. WILLIAMS, *The United States and Disarmament* (New York, 1931).

9. *Henry L. Stimson*

HENRY L. STIMSON and McGEORGE BUNDY's *On Active Service: In Peace and War* (New York, 1948) is a kind of collaborative memoir. It is described by Stimson as a "pilot biography" intended to "forestall possible biographies written without the careful aid of my papers or myself." Though written in the third person, it has, as Bundy explains, "no other purpose than to present the record of Mr. Stimson's public life as he himself sees it." In this purpose, the book succeeds admirably. HERBERT HOOVER presents the record as *he* sees it in *The Memoirs of Herbert Hoover,* volume 2, *The Cabinet and the Presidency* (New York, 1952).

The most recent and comprehensive scholarly account is ROBERT H. FERRELL, *American Diplomacy in the Great Depression: Hoover-Stimson Foreign Policy, 1929–1933* (New Haven, Conn., 1957). Ferrell contends that "in reality" Stimson and Hoover "agreed far more than they disagreed." The disagreements are set forth in RICHARD N. CURRENT, *Secretary Stimson: A Study in Statecraft* (New Brunswick, N.J., 1954), a rather critical appraisal. See also the same author's "The Stimson Doctrine and the Hoover Doctrine," in the *American Historical Review,* vol. LIX (1954). DREW PEARSON and CONSTANTINE BROWN, *The American Diplomatic Game* (New York, 1935) is a journalistic account, but it reveals information that the authors could only have got from confidential sources in the State Department. GEORGE F. KENNAN, *American Diplomacy, 1900–1950* (Chicago, 1951) evaluates the policies of Stimson along with those of other twentieth-century policy makers.

Book-length monographs dealing with particular phases of Hoover-Stimson diplomacy are comparatively few. ALEXANDER DeCONDE presents a concise and clear study in his *Herbert Hoover's Latin American Policy* (Stanford, Calif., 1951). A. WHITNEY GRISWOLD gives considerable attention to Stimson, whom he criticizes for antagonizing Japan, in a work of extensive scope: *The Far Eastern Policy of the United States* (New York, 1938). SARA R. SMITH, in *The Manchurian Crisis, 1931–1932: A Tragedy in International Relations* (New York, 1948), suggests that Stimson did not go far enough in the direction in which Griswold thinks he went too far. The acceptance and application, after 1933, of some of Stimson's ideas may be traced in ROBERT LANGER, *Seizure of Territory: The Stimson Doctrine and Related Principles in Legal Theory and Diplomatic Practice* (Princeton, N.J., 1947).

10. *Cordell Hull*

The manuscript sources relevant to Hull's career as Secretary of State offer tremendous bulk and great variety. The official record may be traced in the files of the Department of State, and the chief unofficial collections are Hull's personal papers, in the Library of Congress, and the Franklin D. Roosevelt papers, in the Roosevelt Memorial Library, Hyde Park, New York. Also housed at the Roosevelt Library are the papers of Harry L. Hopkins and of Henry Morgenthau, Jr. Most useful of the published documentary collections is the voluminous and discursive *Pearl Harbor Attack: Hearings before the Joint Committee on the Investigation of the Pearl Harbor Attack* (39 parts, Washington, 1946), which contains much fascinating information on the entire range of American foreign policy in the period from 1937 to 1941. Many aspects of the nation's Far Eastern diplomacy can be examined in *Papers Relating to the Foreign Relations of the United States: Japan, 1931–1941.*

For Hull's own detailed and sincere, if somewhat pedestrian, story, see *The Memoirs of Cordell Hull* (2 vols., New York, 1948). Three highly personal accounts by SUMNER WELLES—*The Time for Decision* (New York, 1944), *Where Are We Heading?* (New York, 1946), and *Seven Decisions That Shaped History* (New York, 1950)—cover much of the same ground from a different point of view and clarify the essential incompatibility that burdened relations between the Under Secretary and his superior. Among other published memoirs by persons associated with Hull, the following deserve special mention: WILLIAM PHILLIPS, *Ventures in Diplomacy* (Boston, 1953); NANCY H. HOOKER (ed.), *The Moffat Papers: Selections from the Diplomatic Journals of Jay Pierrepont Moffat* (Cambridge, Mass., 1956); JOSEPH C. GREW, *Ten Years in Japan* (New York, 1944); HENRY L. STIMSON and McGEORGE BUNDY, *On Active Service: In Peace and War* (New York, 1948); and ARTHUR H. VANDENBERG, JR., and JOE ALEX MORRIS (eds.), *The Private Papers of Senator Vandenberg* (Boston, 1952). Though none of these sources deals extensively with Hull, they offer numerous side lights on his methods and mannerisms and help define his place in the Roosevelt administration. ROBERT E. SHERWOOD, *Roosevelt and Hopkins: An Intimate History* (New York, 1948), which is based directly upon the Hopkins papers, answers the same purpose.

A sympathetic account of Hull's early career is provided in HAROLD B. HINTON, *Cordell Hull: A Biography* (Garden City, N.Y., 1942). For an interesting prewar analysis of reciprocal trade in the Western Hemisphere, see RAYMOND LESLIE BUELL, *The Hull Trade Program and the American System* (New York,

1938). E. O. GUERRANT, *Roosevelt's Good Neighbor Policy* (Albuquerque, N.M., 1950) is a later, livelier, and more inclusive treatment of inter-American affairs during the Roosevelt era. The monumental volumes by WILLIAM L. LANGER and S. EVERETT GLEASON, *The Challenge to Isolation, 1937–1940* (New York, 1952) and *The Undeclared War, 1940–1941* (New York, 1953), are indispensable for the period of Hull's most active involvement in power politics; DONALD F. DRUMMOND, *The Passing of American Neutrality, 1937–1941* (Ann Arbor, Mich., 1955) is a shorter study of those crucial years. WILLIAM L. LANGER, *Our Vichy Gamble* (New York, 1947) and HERBERT FEIS, *The Road to Pearl Harbor* (Princeton, N.J., 1950) provide excellent coverage of policy phases closely associated with Hull. For an introduction to the "revisionist" historiography of the period, see HARRY ELMER BARNES (ed.), *Perpetual War for Perpetual Peace* (Caldwell, Idaho, 1953).

The standard work on the organization and history of the Department of State is GRAHAM H. STUART, *The Department of State: A History of Its Organization, Procedure and Personnel* (New York, 1949). JAMES MACGREGOR BURNS, *Roosevelt: The Lion and the Fox* (New York, 1956) offers a number of extremely shrewd comments regarding the internal structure of the Roosevelt administration.

11. *Edward R. Stettinius, Jr.*

Of primary importance in any study of Edward R. Stettinius, Jr., are his diaries, deposited at the Alderman Library of the University of Virginia. The Stettinius collection here also includes copies of unpublished State Department material and a significant unpublished, incomplete manuscript, which STETTINIUS wrote with the aid of WALTER JOHNSON, covering the period from his becoming Under Secretary of State through the Yalta Conference. STETTINIUS's account of the conference itself, also prepared with the assistance of WALTER JOHNSON, was published as *Roosevelt and the Russians: The Yalta Conference* (New York, 1949).

HARLEY NOTTER, *Postwar Foreign Policy Preparation, 1939–1945* (Washington, 1949) is the official account of the Department's postwar planning activities. RUTH B. RUSSELL, assisted by JEANNETTE E. MUTHER, *A History of the United Nations Charter: The Role of the United States, 1940–1945* (Washington, 1948) is a careful, important study. ROBERT E. SHERWOOD, *Roosevelt and Hopkins: An Intimate History* (New York, 1948) contains useful material on Roosevelt's view of the Department, and JOSEPH M. JONES, *A Modern Foreign Policy for the United States* (New York, 1944) reflects the type of criticism to which the Department was subjected at the time. HARRY S. TRUMAN, *Years of Decision* (New York, 1955) and ARTHUR H. VANDENBERG, JR., and JOE ALEX MORRIS (eds.), *The Private Papers of Senator Vandenberg* (Boston, 1952) reveal the attitudes of these prominent men toward Stettinius.

JOHN L. SNELL, FORREST C. POGUE, CHARLES F. DELZELL, and GEORGE A. LENSEN, *The Meaning of Yalta: Big Three Diplomacy and the New Balance of Power* (Baton Rouge, La., 1956) is the best scholarly discussion of foreign affairs during Stettinius's Secretaryship. *Foreign Relations, Diplomatic Papers, The*

Conferences at Malta and Yalta, 1945 (Washington, 1955), published by the Department of State, is an important source. WALTER H. C. LAVES and FRANCIS O. WILCOX, "The Reorganization of the Department of State" and "The State Department Continues Its Reorganization," *American Political Science Review*, vols. XXXVIII and XXXIX (1944, 1945) are well-done accounts. GRAHAM H. STUART, *The Department of State: A History of Its Organization, Procedure and Personnel* (New York, 1949) provides a useful summary of the changes under Stettinius but underestimates Stettinius as Secretary.

12. *James F. Byrnes*

Memoirs, diaries, and official papers are now becoming available on the period immediately following World War II, but relatively little historical analysis has yet been attempted. Most of the works dealing with the origins of the cold war devote only a few pages to the crucial years of 1945 and 1946. For these reasons there are few good secondary accounts of Byrnes's Secretaryship.

BYRNES's autobiography, *All in One Lifetime* (New York, 1958), provides an interesting and intimate review of the Secretary's distinguished public career. The value of BYRNES's *Speaking Frankly* (New York, 1947) lies in the fact that it was written immediately after his departure from the State Department. WALTER MILLIS (ed.), *The Forrestal Diaries* (New York, 1951) and A. H. VANDENBERG, JR., and JOE ALEX MORRIS (eds.), *The Private Papers of Senator Vandenberg* (Boston, 1952) deal with many of the high-ranking personalities who were active in determining foreign policy, in addition to presenting the views of these two important officials. President HARRY S. TRUMAN's *Memoirs* (2 vols., Garden City, N.Y., 1955–1956) and Senator TOM CONNALLY's hard-hitting autobiography, prepared with the help of ALFRED STEINBERG, *My Name is Tom Connally* (New York, 1954), though of less historical merit than the foregoing two volumes, do provide additional insights into Byrnes's relationships with the President and the Senate.

Perhaps the single most valuable book on this period is *The United States in World Affairs, 1945–1947*, edited by JOHN C. CAMPBELL for the Council on Foreign Relations (New York, 1947). Whereas it suffers from a lack of documentation, it contains a bibliography of immense value and a helpful chronology of events. A fine collection of government documents can be found in the State Department's *Postwar Foreign Policy Preparation, 1939–1945* (Washington, 1949), prepared by HARLEY NOTTER. The last volume of WINSTON CHURCHILL's series on World War II, *Triumph and Tragedy* (Boston, 1953), contains valuable letters and memoranda for the period from Yalta to Potsdam. Admiral WILLIAM D. LEAHY's *I Was There* (New York, 1950) and PHILIP E. MOSELY's *Face to Face with Russia* (Foreign Policy Association Headline Series, no. 70, 1948) provide accounts of the Potsdam Conferences. Far more detailed is HERBERT FEIS, *Between War and Peace* (Princeton, N.J., 1960). For reference to the London Conference of 1945, see JOHN FOSTER DULLES, *War or Peace* (New York, 1950). *Negotiating with the Russians*, edited by RAYMOND DENNET and JOSEPH E. JOHNSON (Boston, 1951), contains three valuable essays on this period: GEORGE H. BLAKESLEE's "Negotiating to Establish the Far Eastern Commission," MARK

ETHRIDGE and C. E. BLACK's "Negotiating on the Balkans, 1945-1947," and FREDRICK OSBORN's "Negotiating on Atomic Energy, 1946-1947." Additional information concerning international conferences during this period can be found in the State Department Conference Series. Particularly helpful is *Participation of the United States in International Conferences, July 1, 1945 to June 30, 1946* (Conference Series, no. 95). For a discussion of the impact of domestic politics on foreign policy, see H. BRADFORD WESTERFIELD's <u>*Foreign Policy and Party Politics: Pearl Harbor to Korea*</u> (New Haven, Conn., 1955).

Byrnes's foreign-policy views are discussed in T. CATLEGE, "Secretary Byrnes: Portrait of a Realist," *The New York Times Magazine*, July 8, 1945; "Conversion of Our Three Peace Bargainers to Tough Attitudes," *United States News*, May 3, 1946; and "James Byrnes: Hardening of a Bargainer," *United States News*, September 13, 1946. Also see "Byrnes and Vandenberg," *America*, March 10, 1946.

HERBERT FEIS summarizes the story of Ambassador Hurley's resignation in his <u>*The China Tangle*</u> (Princeton, N.J., 1953). Primary source material on the Hurley resignation can be found in the *Hearings of the Senate Foreign Relations Committee: Investigation of Far Eastern Policy* (mimeographed, December, 1945) and in Hurley's testimony at the MacArthur dismissal in *Hearings of the Senate Armed Services and Foreign Relations Committees: Military Situation in the Far East* (June, 1951). The State Department's *United States Relations with China* (Washington, 1949) contains information on the Marshall mission to China as well as on the Hurley resignation.

Many contemporary magazine articles discussed foreign-policy questions. Some, like the following, were trying to fathom Soviet policy aims: MILES BOULTON, "Behind Soviet Foreign Policy," *American Mercury*, November, 1946; EARL BROWDER, "Report on Russia," *New Republic*, August 5, 1956; JOHN F. DULLES, "Thoughts on Soviet Foreign Policy," *Life*, June 3 and 10, 1946; MAX EASTMAN, "Behind Soviet Foreign Policy," *American Mercury*, September, 1946; ANTHONY EDEN, "No War with Russia," *Collier's*, August 24, 1946; and REINHOLD NIEBUHR, "Europe, Russia, and the U.S.A.," *Nation*, September 14, 1946.

13. *George Catlett Marshall*

George Marshall was one of the few leaders of World War II and the immediate postwar years who refused to write his memoirs or to allow anyone else to present his story from his own papers and recollections. As Secretary of State, apparently, he never set forth his views on the office in letters, memoranda, or diaries. The principal sources for a study of his Secretaryship, therefore, are the limited public records left by Marshall, the records of his associates, his published statements, official documents, newspaper records, articles, and printed biographical materials. In addition, there are pertinent materials in the State Department archives and in the Harry S. Truman Library in Independence, Missouri, but at the time of writing, these collections were not yet open to researchers.

Dr. Forest C. Pogue, Director, and Mrs. Arlene Pratt of the George C.

Marshall Research Center at Lexington, Virginia, not only examined the manuscript and saved the author from a number of errors but Mrs. Pratt also kindly searched the Center's holdings and certain State Department files for pertinent material on Marshall as Secretary of State. Dr. E. Taylor Parks and Mary C. Chapman of the Historical Division of the Department of State kindly read the essay and offered useful criticism, but all interpretations and remaining errors are the author's own.

The only biography of Marshall, ROBERT PAYNE, *The Marshall Story: A Biography of General George C. Marshall* (New York, 1951), is weak on the period of Marshall's Secretaryship. For Marshall's career from 1880 to 1945, see the more accurate study, WILLIAM FRYE, *Marshall: Citizen Soldier* (Indianapolis, 1947), and the account by the General's wife, KATHERINE TUPPER MARSHALL, *Together: Annals of an Army Wife* (New York, 1946). For a brief evaluation of Marshall as Secretary of State written by a man who worked closely with him in the Department, see GEORGE F. KENNAN, "Tribute to Gen. Marshall," *The New York Times Magazine*, October 18, 1959. An invaluable source, based on papers not yet open to the researcher, is HARRY S. TRUMAN, *Memoirs* (2 vols., Garden City, N.Y., 1955–1956). Illuminating material on the relations between Truman and Marshall is included in JONATHAN DANIELS, *The Man of Independence* (Philadelphia, 1950). The best source on the origins of the Truman Doctrine and the Marshall Plan and the work of Marshall's State Department staff, which tends to emphasize the work of Under Secretary Dean G. Acheson, is JOSEPH M. JONES, *The Fifteen Weeks: February 21–June 5, 1947* (New York, 1955). HARRY B. PRICE, *The Marshall Plan and Its Meaning* (Ithaca, N.Y., 1955) also contains valuable material on the origins of the Marshall Plan and is based upon personal interviews with Marshall. For Under Secretary William Clayton's contribution to the plan, see ELLEN CLAYTON GARWOOD, *Will Clayton: A Short Biography* (Austin, Tex., 1958). For accounts of diplomacy and other pertinent material, see the 1947 and 1948 volumes of the *U.S. Department of State Bulletin* and of *The United States in World Affairs*, edited by JOHN C. CAMPBELL (New York, 1948–1949). JOSEPH R. MCCARTHY, *America's Retreat from Victory: The Story of George Catlett Marshall* (New York, 1951), is a condensed version of a speech McCarthy delivered in the Senate in June, 1951, bitterly attacking Marshall's public career.

Among numerous magazine articles, memoirs, and special studies, the following are particularly useful: ROBERT S. ALLEN and WILLIAM V. SHANNON, *The Truman Merry-go-round* (New York, 1950); DENNIS W. BROGAN, "The Two Secretaries," *The Spectator*, January 14, 1949; JAMES F. BYRNES, *Speaking Frankly* (New York, 1947) and *All in One Lifetime* (New York, 1958); TRIS COFFIN, *Missouri Compromise* (Boston, 1947); TOM CONNALLY, as told to ALFRED STEINBERG, *My Name is Tom Connally* (New York, 1954); CECIL V. CRABB, *Bipartisan Foreign Policy: Myth or Reality?* (Evanston, Ill., 1957); W. PHILLIPS DAVISON, *The Berlin Blockade: A Study in Cold War Politics* (Princeton, N.J., 1956); JOHN FOSTER DULLES, *War or Peace* (New York, 1950); ROBERT T. ELSON, "New Strategy in Foreign Policy: A General and a Banker Bring Order and Method to the U.S. State Department," *Fortune*, December, 1947; CYRIL FALLS, "A Window on the World: General George Marshall,"

Illustrated London News, January 22, 1949; RICHARD F. FENNO, JR., *The President's Cabinet: An Analysis from Wilson to Eisenhower* (Cambridge, Mass., 1958); ERIC F. GOLDMAN, *The Crucial Decade* (New York, 1956); JOHN HERSEY, "Mr. Secretary Marshall," *Collier's*, March 29, April 5, April 12, 1947; SAMUEL P. HUNTINGTON, *The Soldier and the State: The Theory and Politics of Civil-Military Relations* (Cambridge, Mass., 1957); WILLIAM D. LEAHY, *I Was There* (New York, 1950); WALTER MILLIS (ed.), *The Forrestal Diaries* (New York, 1951); "A Regrettable Appointment," *The Christian Century*, January 22, 1947; DONALD ROBINSON, "Secretary of State Marshall," *American Mercury*, July, 1948; WALTER BEDELL SMITH, *My Three Years in Moscow* (Philadelphia, 1950); JOHN LEIGHTON STUART, *Fifty Years in China* (New York, 1954); WALTER TROHAN, "The Tragedy of George Marshall," *American Mercury*, March, 1951; REXFORD GUY TUGWELL, *A Chronicle of Jeopardy, 1945-55* (Chicago, 1955); U.S. Department of State, *United States Relations with China* (Washington, 1949); ARTHUR H. VANDENBERG, JR., and JOE ALEX MORRIS (eds.), *The Private Papers of Senator Vandenberg* (Boston, 1952); JAMES P. WARBURG, *Put Yourself in Marshall's Place* (New York, 1948); ALBERT C. WEDEMEYER, *Wedemeyer Reports!* (New York, 1958), a bitterly critical account of Marshall's China policy; BRADFORD WESTERFIELD, *Foreign Policy and Party Politics: Pearl Harbor to Korea* (New Haven, Conn., 1955); and WILLIAM S. WHITE, "Again for Marshall, It Is Duty," *The New York Times Magazine*, September 24, 1950. Two useful articles written shortly after Marshall's death in October, 1959, are JOHN P. SUTHERLAND, "The Story General Marshall Told Me," *U.S. News & World Report*, November 2, 1951, and DEAN G. ACHESON, "Homage to General Marshall," *The Reporter*, November 26, 1959.

14. Dean G. Acheson

Although historians must still view the Secretaryship of Dean G. Acheson without the benefit of the official records of the State Department, few Secretaries of State in the nation's history have expressed themselves so fully on the crucial international events of their time. McGEORGE BUNDY, in *The Pattern of Responsibility* (Boston, 1952), which includes excerpts and paraphrases of Acheson's many speeches during his Secretarial years, is the best single source of information on his actions as Secretary. A useful compilation of his early speeches as Secretary has been prepared by the Department of State: *Strengthening the Forces of Freedom: Selected Speeches and Statements of Secretary of State Acheson, February 1949-April 1950* (Washington, 1950). Also replete with observations on Acheson's leadership are the 1949 to 1953 volumes of *The United States in World Affairs* (New York, 1950-1954), prepared by RICHARD P. STEBBINS for the Council on Foreign Relations. The excellent survey of postwar American diplomacy, WILLIAM REITZEL et al., *United States Foreign Policy, 1945-1955* (Washington, 1956), is also useful.

Acheson's own voluminous writings on American foreign policy reveal a remarkable consistency. He has written three books, all of which contain much on the subject of foreign affairs: *A Democrat Looks at His Party* (New York, 1955), *A Citizen Looks at Congress* (New York, 1957), and *Power and Diplo-*

macy (Cambridge, Mass., 1958). His articles have appeared from time to time in *The New York Times Magazine*, generally for the purpose of introducing his usually pungent views into some continuing debate. To indicate what the American people might expect of their foreign policies, he wrote "What Is the Present? What of the Future?" August 5, 1951; his reply to the concept of massive retaliation can be found in " 'Instant Retaliation': The Debate Continued," March 28, 1954; on the requirements of successful negotiations with the Russians, he wrote such articles as "To Meet the Shifting Soviet Offensive," April 15, 1956, "The Bases of a Foreign Program," January 6, 1957, and "On Dealing with Russia: An Inside View," April 12, 1959; and his views on the problems of public administration are revealed in "Thoughts about Thought in High Places," October 11, 1959. In response to George F. Kennan's doctrine of disengagement, Acheson wrote "The Illusion of Disengagement," *Foreign Affairs*, vol. XXXVI (1958). Two articles in which he condemned moralism in foreign policy are "Foreign Policy and Presidential Moralism," *The Reporter*, May 2, 1957, and "Morality, Moralism, and Diplomacy," *Yale Review*, vol. XLVII (1958).

Many of the memoirs cited in the two preceding bibliographical essays apply equally to the Acheson years, especially those of Truman, Vandenberg, and Connally. A good early evaluation of Acheson's policies is CHARLES SHAW, "Mr. Acheson's Foreign Relations," *Plain Talk*, vol. IV (1950). On Acheson's relationship to the decision-making process under Truman, see ANTHONY LEVIERO, "How the President Makes Decisions," *The New York Times Magazine*, October 8, 1950. Defending Acheson against his detractors in Congress are ELMER DAVIS, "The Crusade against Acheson," *Harper's*, March, 1951; GEORGE F. KENNAN, "Let Peace Not Die of Neglect," *The New York Times Magazine*, February 25, 1951; LESTER MARKEL, "The Great Need: An Informed Opinion," *The New York Times Magazine*, April 9, 1950; and JOHN FISCHER, *Master Plan U.S.A.* (New York, 1951). Three excellent and generally friendly character studies of Acheson are JAMES RESTON, "Secretary Acheson: A First-year Audit," *The New York Times Magazine*, January 22, 1950; WILLIAM S. WHITE, "The Misunderstood Conservative," *Harper's*, September, 1958; and CABELL PHILLIPS, "Dean Acheson Ten Years Later," *The New York Times Magazine*, January 18, 1959.

15. *John Foster Dulles*

Probably no other American Secretary of State, during his term of office, has had his actions, techniques, and thoughts subjected to such thorough analysis as did Dulles. The unprecedented publicity which Dulles received as Secretary resulted partly from the uniqueness and vigor of his own views, which could hardly be ignored either by those who upheld them or by those who opposed them. It also emanated in part from his own emphasis on public relations. Lastly, the unorthodoxy of his methods—his disregard of the State Department and his many plane trips about the world—set him apart from tradition sufficiently to subject his actions to endless comment. Only the publication of State Department documents at some future date may reveal the nature of many of his private arrangements and determine his motivation in specific episodes with some precision, but to a large extent Dulles's career as Secretary of State, despite its recency, is already an open book.

The most detailed source of information on Dulles's Secretaryship are the 1953 to 1959 volumes of *The United States in World Affairs* (New York, 1954–1960), written for the Council on Foreign Relations. RICHARD P. STEBBINS prepared all these volumes except the one for 1955, which was done by HOLLIS W. BARBER. Dulles's many public addresses can be found in the *U.S. Department of State Bulletin* for the years of his Secretaryship. In addition, he wrote many articles. Two which reveal much of his basic thought are "A Policy of Boldness," *Life*, May 19, 1952, and "Policy for Security and Peace," *Foreign Affairs*, vol. XXXII (1954). The Secretary's concept of brinkmanship is developed in JAMES SHEPLEY, "How Dulles Averted War," *Life*, January 16, 1956.

Dulles's views regarding this nation's proper role in world affairs, especially toward mainland China and the Soviet satellites of Eastern and Central Europe, raised the issue of moralism in American foreign affairs more forcefully than did those of any other leader in the nation's history. It is no wonder that his words produced almost limitless devotion in those who agreed with his fundamental purpose of liberation. Among the volumes that have presented interpretations of recent American policy favorable to Dulles's general method of operation are THOMAS I. COOK and MALCOLM MOOS, *Power through Purpose: The Realism of Idealism as a Basis for Foreign Policy* (Baltimore, 1954); JOHN ROBINSON BEAL, *John Foster Dulles: A Biography* (New York, 1957); MERLO J. PUSEY, *Eisenhower the President* (New York, 1956); ROBERT STRAUSZ-HUPÉ et al., *Protracted Conflict* (New York, 1959); and ROBERT J. DONOVAN, *Eisenhower: The Inside Story* (New York, 1956).

On the other hand, both Dulles's views and his methods have been subjected to extensive criticism. On his actions prior to his appointment, see RICHARD H. ROVERE, *Affairs of State: The Eisenhower Years* (New York, 1956). Among the general criticisms of his leadership as Secretary are JOSEPH C. HARSCH, "John Foster Dulles: A Very Complicated Man," *Harper's*, September, 1956; WILLIAM HARLAN HALE, "The Loneliest Man in Washington," *The Reporter*, October 18, 1956; WILLIAM LEE MILLER, "The 'Moral Force' behind Dulles's Diplomacy," *The Reporter*, August 9, 1956; MAX ASCOLI, "The Ordeal of Mr. Dulles," *The Reporter*, March 5, 1959; and C. L. SULZBERGER, *What's Wrong with U.S. Foreign Policy* (New York, 1959). Pointing to Dulles's concern with domestic political pressures is NORMAN A. GRAEBNER, *The New Isolationism* (New York, 1956). Critical of Dulles's concepts of the Soviet threat are GEORGE F. KENNAN, *Russia, the Atom, and the West* (New York, 1958) and ISAAC DEUTSCHER, *The Great Contest: Russia and the West* (New York, 1960). HANS J. MORGENTHAU had criticized specific aspects of Dulles's leadership more fully in a series of articles which appeared in *The New Republic*: "Is 'Instant Retaliation' the Answer?" March 29, 1954; "Military Illusions," March 19, 1956; "Ideological Windmills," March 12, 1956; and "The Danger of Doing Too Much," April 16, 1956.

Index

ABC powers, 92, 112
Acheson, Dean G.: as Assistant Secretary of State, 212, 215, 221; as Under Secretary of State, 249–251, 253, 255, 256, 264; becomes Secretary of State, 267, 269; characterization, 267–268, 283–284, 287–288, 292–293, 306; background, 268–270; conservative views on world affairs, 269–270, 273–274; and Russian threat, 270, 273–274; views on North Atlantic community, 270–272; secures military program, 271–273; policies toward Germany, 272–273; states conditions for peace at Berkeley, California, 274; at Paris Conference of Foreign Ministers of 1949, 275; as administrator of the State Department, 275–276; relations with Truman, 276–277; criticised for neglect of diplomacy, 277–278; argument against cold war settlement, 278–279; faces attack on European policies, 279–280; and problem of China, 280–283, 285–286; attacked for events in China, 283–285; presides at San Francisco Conference of 1951, 286; and Congress, 283–284, 286; and the press, 286–287; unpopularity in United States, 287–288; experience of, and Dulles, 292–293
Act of Havana, 198
Adams, Brooks, 5
Adams, Charles Francis, 13
Adams, Henry, 24, 26, 37, 38
Adams, John Quincy, 7, 8, 13, 44, 292
Adee, Alvey A., 26
Advisory Committee on Postwar Problems, 191, 206–208

Africa, 270, 306
"Agonizing reappraisal," 294
Alaska boundary controversy, 35–37
Algeciras Conference, 43–45
Alien land laws, 115, 142
Allen, Robert S., 175
Allied blockade (World War I), 108
Allied Control Council for Japan, 240
Alsop Claim, 66
Alverstone, Lord Chief Justice, 36
American Bar Association, 144, 150
American Historical Association addressed by Hughes, 144
Ancona sinking, 107
Anglo-French Arbitration Treaty of 1903, 55
Anglo-Japanese Alliance, 138, 140
Arabic sinking, 106
Arabs, 256
Arbitration principle, 54, 121, 163
Arbitration treaties, United States, 35, 56, 75–76
Argentina, 65–66, 199
Armistice (1918), 121
Army War College, 41
Article X of League Covenant, 133–135
Article 51 of United Nations Charter, 261
Asia, 5–6, 270, 280–281 (*See also* China; Far East; Japan; Southeast Asia)
Atlantic alliance (*see* North Atlantic alliance)
Atlantic Charter, 197, 205, 228–229, 234, 238, 244
Atlantic community (*see* North Atlantic community)
Atlantic Conference (1941), 246